Broken

Made

Beautiful

Daily Devotions of Hope and Encouragement
for the Healing Journey

Allyson Long

DEDICATION

For you, fellow traveler, as we journey together on this adventure called Life, seeking His hope and healing.

With thanksgiving to the Father, the One who redeems us, restores us, and transforms our brokenness into blessing.

And with gratitude to my "mat carriers," whose intercession on my behalf knows no bounds and leaves me with no words except these: I love you and thank God every day for weaving each one of you into the tapestry of my life.

INTRODUCTION

I used to really struggle with the New Year's transition. I felt saddened to let the old year go, fearing what lay ahead. The old year had brought its share of pain, but at least I knew what the pain *was*. The new year stretched out vast and blank before me, stark and unnerving. It's often the same with our pain. Although the old may be painful, we dread the uncertainty of the new, of the unknown. Yet as we clutch our old and familiar pain to our chests, our hands remain too encumbered to receive the blessings our Father longs to place within them.

God can create beauty from our areas of brokenness—if we choose to surrender the pieces to Him. The last few years, the New Year's transition has gotten easier for me. Although we go in blindly, my friend, we never go in alone. The same God who walked faithfully with us through the preceding year, the One who carried our bruised and battered hearts and spoke peace to our churning minds, is the same One who journeys forth with us into this new year now. Whether you're starting this book in January or in June, this is your new beginning.

Whatever is causing you pain—be it a giant-sized weight or an assortment of daily struggles—it is my heartfelt prayer that this devotional will provide hope and encouragement to you each day through God's Word. It took me a long time to realize that it isn't our willpower, our determination, our best efforts, or our intellect that heals us. It is our *God* who heals us, and He does this through the power of His Word. As we spend time with Him each day—reading His Word, pondering His heart, meditating on His truths and promises—we will begin to experience healing in our hurting places and transformation of our brokenness into a beauty that glorifies Him.

So welcome to the journey, my friend. I cannot wait to see what this new year holds for us as we seek God's healing and wholeness together. I'm honored to have your company. May we live each day for His glory.

Allyson

Broken

Made

Beautiful

JANUARY 1

But we ought always to thank God for you, brothers and sisters loved by the Lord, because God chose you as firstfruits to be saved through the sanctifying work of the Spirit and through belief in the truth. 2 Thessalonians 2:13

I wonder if you can relate to that dreaded time of recess as a child when two athletes would name themselves "team captains" and choose up sides for a game of soccer, kickball, or basketball. Did you linger near the back of the crowd, hoping and praying you would not be the last one picked? Did you ever feel as though one of the team captains finally, begrudgingly agreed to choose you, but solely out of obligation or pity?

Guess what, my friend: You are loved and chosen by God. First in line. Valued, sought after, and known by name. He has your picture in a frame on His dresser. He knows you completely and loves you infinitely. He equips each and every one of us in unique and special ways and wants each one of us on His "team." We are His game-changers on this playing field of Life, and there are no substitutions and no benchwarmers! Each one of us is called to play the whole game, for as long as it lasts—to go where He sends us, to defend the ground He gives us, to win other souls to Christ as He cheers us on.

Know, today, that you are CHOSEN. Wanted. Intimately known and dearly loved. Child of the Most High God, Creator of the Universe. You weren't a last-round draft pick that God reluctantly agreed to take. No, Beloved: *from the very beginning*, God chose you. He chose you "before the creation of the world [...] in accordance with His pleasure and will" (Eph. 1:4-5). He has always wanted you on His team, and did you catch that last part? It *pleased Him* to choose you!

Father, thank You for choosing me and equipping me for the challenges I will face in this game called Life. Keep my focus on You as I await Your directions and instructions for me today. In Jesus' name, Amen.

JANUARY 2

Moreover, our eyes failed, looking in vain for help; from our towers we watched for a nation that could not save us. Lamentations 4:17

My teenage years and most of my twenties were tumultuous. Perhaps you can relate. Many people experience varying degrees of tumult during those difficult years; mine were marked by an outer façade of achievement, competency, and happiness that masked the deep, underlying pain within—the depression, the constant feelings of unworthiness, and the brutal, unrelenting self-condemnation. I spent many years searching for someone who could save me from my pain and from myself. Every time I thought I had found that person, I was proved wrong; I searched and searched for help that never came.

It took me years to realize that I had been looking in vain for help because I had been looking outward, not upward. I had grown up with head knowledge of Jesus, but lacked heart knowledge of Him. I knew He loved me but wasn't sure He really loved *all* of me. When I invited Him into the deepest vaults of pain that I carried, acknowledging that apart from Him I truly had no hope of ever being well or whole, I embarked upon a deeply personal journey with Him that has been the greatest blessing of my life.

I wonder where this verse meets you today. In what people or habits are you looking for help that will never come? In what things of this world have you placed your hope? Dear Friend, I long to tell you today that there is only One who can save you. Place your hope in Jesus, who loves you with an unfailing love (Ps. 130:7). The intimate journey you make with Him will be more meaningful than any other in your life.

Heavenly Father, I confess to You my human tendency to look to other things and people for help that can only come from You. Draw my gaze upward onto You today, and pour Your perfect and abiding love into every part of my being. In Jesus' name, Amen.

JANUARY 3

Commit to the Lord whatever you do, and He will establish your plans. Proverbs 16:3

Is God capable of fulfilling our wildest dreams? Absolutely! Yet we must be deeply aware of how we are approaching the throne of our Almighty God when we make our requests. He is not a genie who grants wishes without regard to the soundness of mind or heart behind the wish. He is the Alpha and the Omega (Rev. 1:8), infinitely wise and fully aware of how our choices and plans will affect not only ourselves, but others as well—from beginning to end. And He carefully looks at and weighs the motives of our hearts (1 Cor. 4:5).

My husband Kevin is a civil engineer, and one of the main parts of his job is reviewing plans that have been submitted to his office. Others create and submit the plans, and it's Kevin's job to be aware of all the rules, ordinances, and logistics involved so that when something in the plans will not work well or would cause problems, he can make suggestions to improve it. We are the architects and engineers of our lives; we draw up plans and have a vision in our minds of how we want things to look in the future. However, the next crucial step is that we submit those plans to God for careful review. If we attempt to carry out plans that have not been meticulously checked by the Head Engineer of Creation, guess what—our human-made plans will inevitably lead us into snags, delays, danger, and dead-ends.

God reviews all of the plans we submit to Him, and our relationship with Him is deepened when we consult with Him each day. When we say to Him, "This is where my heart is, Lord. Please direct my path"—He is able to take His finger, make some notations on our plans, and bring forth astonishing blueprints that will guide us with precision and perfection. "For I know the plans I have for you," He says (Jer. 29:11). Will you allow your plans to intertwine with His today, my friend? Amen!

JANUARY 4

Do you not know that your bodies are temples of the Holy Spirit, who is in you, whom you have received from God? You are not your own; you were bought at a price. Therefore honor God with your bodies. 1 Corinthians 6:19-20

These two verses were the catalyst for one of the biggest turning points in my life. Never before had I considered that God cared about how I chose to treat myself. Never before had I realized that He saw me as His holy temple here on earth. A deep root of self-hatred had spawned several unhealthy behaviors that harmed my temple both outwardly and inwardly. I kept telling myself that as long as I wasn't hurting any-one else, it was okay for me to make those choices.

It was not okay, Beloved, because these verses suddenly made it very clear to me that God cared very much about my choices. I was honestly dumbstruck when I realized this. I read the words "You are not your own; you were bought at a price," and realized afresh that Jesus had paid an exorbitant price for me—and that I, in turn, was called to treat my holy vessel as sacred, using it to honor God. I had to learn to walk in a brand new way, changing my long-held beliefs and attitudes about myself and my body, replacing my misconceptions with the truth of God's Word. It's been the most challenging battle I've fought to date, simply because the warfare is continuous and the casualty is my own will. However, God is faithful to bless our efforts!

Did you know that God sees you as His holy temple, the dwelling place of His Spirit here on earth? Have you considered the fact that He cares deeply about how you treat yourself? We can harm our temples in many ways. If you've been making choices that hurt, rather than honor, your temple, I pray these verses will be a turning point for you, too.

Father, thank You for this truth from Your Word! Enable me to live in ways that honor Your temple here on earth and bring glory to Your name. Amen.

JANUARY 5

Come to Me, all you who are weary and burdened, and I will give you rest. Matthew 11:28

How I long for the Father's rest. In our frantic, frenzied, fast-paced society, "well-rested" is not a way we typically choose to describe ourselves. "Oh, I'm so busy!" we say. "I'm exhausted!" Listen, my friend—the Lord did not come to give us lives of exhaustion. He came to give us lives of abundance and fullness through Him (John 10:10).

What is the key to obtaining Jesus' perfect peace and rest? "Come to Me," He says. "Come." Note that we have to intentionally pursue this rest. We have to agree to lay down whatever load we're staggering around with, and come to Jesus. He will not force us; He will not corner us. (Have you ever tried to "force" a small child to rest? It doesn't work, does it?) Notice, too, that Jesus says, "I will give you rest." He will *give* it. We cannot earn it. We cannot create it. It is a *gift*. This also means we can choose to ignore it, return it, or exchange it for the busyness we enjoy ever so much more.

One day at the thrift store I came upon an old and faded brown shirt. Emblazoned across the chest was a picture of an airport "Baggage Claim" sign, with letters and arrows pointing the way to concourses, dining options, restrooms, and so forth. I loved it! And then I noticed that in tiny print right under the words "Baggage Claim" (and an arrow pointing straight up), there were these words: "Matthew 11:28." As it dawned on me what the correlation was, I started grinning from ear to ear. How awesome is our God?! He longs to give us *rest*! *He* will manage our bags for us; He will help us carry the load. He is infinitely more able than we!

Will you choose to come to Him today, Beloved? Will you choose to accept the gift of His rest, to allow Him to work out all things for you, rather than continuing to strive on your own? Let Him have those bags, my friend! Just come to Him and rest. Amen.

JANUARY 6

The Lord your God is with you, the Mighty Warrior who saves.
He will take great delight in you; in His love He will no longer
rebuke you, but will rejoice over you with singing. Zephaniah 3:17

I'm wondering what particular portion of our verse for today means the most to you in your present circumstances. If you are in the midst of a season of suffering, trial, and testing, I pray that the knowledge that God Himself is with you brings encouragement and hope. If you are battling longstanding addictions and habits that no amount of effort or willpower seems able to break, I pray that the knowledge that God is mighty to save brings comfort and endurance to you in your struggle. If you are feeling overlooked, unnoticed, or just plain invisible, I pray that the knowledge that the Creator of all the universe takes great delight in you will bring joy and a sense of renewed purpose to your precious heart today. If you are walking through the valley of grief, I pray that the knowledge that the God of all comfort (2 Cor. 1:3) will quiet you with His love will bring peace and consolation to your hurting places within.

And to all of God's children, no matter the season, I pray that the knowledge that the Lord of all creation rejoices over you with singing— not for anything you are or have done, Beloved, but simply because you are His child—brings warmth, joy, gratitude, and blessing to your soul. Can you imagine what it will be like to hear God sing? And He sings, Beloved, over you. He does not love us from afar, my friend. He is with us in every moment: helping us, rescuing us, restoring us, comforting us, saving us, delighting in us, and singing over us. He loves fully and demonstratively, holding not one thing back from His precious children.

Father, I thank You for Your incomprehensible, lavish love for me. Help me to rely on You for all of my needs in every moment today. In Jesus' name, Amen.

JANUARY 7

"Martha, Martha," the Lord answered, "you are worried and upset about many things, but few things are needed—or indeed only one. Mary has chosen what is better, and it will not be taken away from her." Luke 10:41-42

As a "Martha" through and through, I can get a little prickly with these verses. I am a do-er; I feel the need to be working and striving and persevering in my task at hand. These verses probably nettle me because I see my own shortcomings in them: "You are worried and upset about many things, but few things are needed." Actually, only One is needed. When my focus slides away from Him, onto all of the other "things" that I think may help me achieve whatever it is I think I need to be achieving, I miss out on the blessings He could pour out on me if I would only take the time to sit at His feet, listen to Him, and be still. The time we spend with Jesus, whether in prayer or in the pages of God's Word, is an investment that can *never* be taken away from us.

This is not to say that being a "Martha" is wrong or bad. After all, Martha was the one who invited Jesus into her home, and Martha was the one who prepared something for Him to eat. Acts of service in God's kingdom are also needed and appreciated by the Lord! It becomes an issue of balance in our lives. Pencil in a time to sit and talk with the Lord, to read and study His Word. And then stick to it! Better yet, keep up a running dialogue with Him as you go about your day. When we find the balance of Mary and Martha moments in our lives, we become more complete, well-rounded individuals, filled with the goodness and power of Christ's indwelling Spirit—so that we in turn are able to effectively go out and minister to a hurting world.

Father, thank You for the parts of me that seek You and the parts of me that serve You. Help me to strengthen both today. Amen.

JANUARY 8

Esau said to his father, "Do you have only one blessing, my father? Bless me too, my father!" Then Esau wept aloud. Genesis 27:38

My heart breaks for Esau here, who has just been cheated by his brother Jacob (at the direction of his own mother, Rebekah) and so misses out on his father Isaac's one and only blessing. The family blessing, once pronounced, could not be revoked or redone, which meant that Jacob had successfully "stolen" Esau's blessing—and there was nothing more that could be done about it.

As children of the Most High God, our Father is *never* lacking in blessings for all of us. Never will we come to Him, grief-stricken, after finding that someone else has already received His one and only blessing. Never will we discover that someone else has received the one blessing we so hoped to receive ourselves. He is infinitely able—and willing—to bless each of us as though we were the only one.

Where does this meet you in your journey today, my friend? Do you feel as though someone else has come along and stolen the blessing you had so been counting on, or hoping for, for yourself? Are you encouraged to know that God has more than one blessing? In what areas are you most seeking God's blessing in your life right now? Are you encouraged to know that God is able to infinitely bless *all* of His children, without limit? And does that knowledge challenge you to be more daring in your asking? However this truth strikes you today, my friend, I pray that it brings you renewed hope.

Almighty Father, I thank You that Your love and blessings are without limit. I thank You that no one can steal Your blessings away from me, and that I need not fear when another Child is blessed by You. I know full well that there are still many more blessings in store for me—and for all of us, Your beloved children. In Jesus' name, Amen.

JANUARY 9

I am the Lord your God, who brought you out of Egypt so that you would no longer be slaves to the Egyptians; I broke the bars of your yoke and enabled you to walk with heads held high.
Leviticus 26:13

God brought you out of your Egypt (we all have different Egypts, but we all *have* an Egypt!) so that you would no longer be a slave to that bondage. Are you, like the Israelites, tempted to return to that land of captivity? Does it seem like that life was easier, more familiar, or at least something predictable that you felt as though you "knew," even if it also happened to be painful? Please know that God brought you out of your Egypt *so that* you could live free in Him! Galatians 5:1 says, "It is for freedom that Christ has set us free. Stand firm, then, and do not let yourselves be burdened again by a yoke of slavery."

If God has led you to freedom through Christ but you are still living with the mindset of a slave, I understand. I spent many years in my own dungeon of pain, despair, and self-loathing, sitting there with the key in my hand, because I did not think I deserved to come out. Praise God that He does not wait until we deserve it before He decides to do it! "While we were still sinners, Christ died for us" (Rom. 5:8b)!

God broke the bars of your yoke and enabled you to walk with your head held high, but are you doing it? Are you walking as a freed child of God, unfettered by those past chains of your Egypt? If not, I ask you today: What is causing your head to remain bowed low, Beloved? Is it shame? Guilt? A sense of unworthiness or deficiency? Paul writes that there is no condemnation for those who are in Christ Jesus (Rom. 8:1). Why? Because if you have accepted Christ as your Savior, your debt has been cancelled, your ransom has been paid, and your chains to that former life have been broken! We are called, Dear Friend, to live free!

Father, thank You for the freedom You graciously offer me through Your Son. Enable me to experience it afresh as I walk with You today. Amen.

JANUARY 10

"Even now," declares the Lord, "return to Me with all your heart, with fasting and weeping and mourning." Rend your heart and not your garments. Return to the Lord your God, for He is gracious and compassionate, slow to anger and abounding in love, and He relents from sending calamity. Joel 2:12-13

In Old Testament times, people tore their clothes as a visible display of sorrow and pain. I find God's call here curious: Don't just tear your clothes to show your sorrow... rend your *heart* as well. *Feel it.* He calls us to more than just an outward expression of repentance; He wants to see some inward evidence as well—the rending of our hearts.

"Even now," God says, "return to Me." How far along are you in your "even now"? My "even now" was a painful place of feeling much too far gone for God to redeem the mess I'd made of things. Praise God that He is undeterred by how far gone we think or believe or know we are! With the Lord, it is never too late; there is always an "even now." He will never give up on you; you are His dearly beloved child!

What in your heart needs rending today? What areas of darkness, sin, or resentment are being harbored that the Lord is calling you to bring forth into His glorious and healing light? He desires every piece of your heart, Beloved. Every shard, every fragment, every splintered, fractured remnant. In His mighty, healing hands, He can make your heart whole again. Are you willing?

Almighty Father, enable me today to commit to a lasting inner change with You. Soften my heart, that it would be open to Your will, Your leading, and Your plan for my life. I know that You are able and willing to repair and restore my heart, if I will dare to hand over all the pieces. Give me the courage and faith to trust You fully. Thank You for Your unending love and faithfulness. In Jesus' name, Amen.

JANUARY 11

There is no fear in love. But perfect love drives out fear, because fear has to do with punishment. The one who fears is not made perfect in love. 1 John 4:18

Lately I've been struggling with the fear of both potential and inevitable loss in my life. As I recently sat and wrestled with my thoughts, searching for what I felt God was trying to tell me, this verse from 1 John is what lodged in my mind—specifically, "There is no fear in love." The antidote to fear is *faith*. When I trust God's plan and purposes for my life, I need not live my life in fear. Many of our fears are rooted in a place of dreading the experience of future pain. The problem is that we're missing out on the blessings of *today*, of this very moment, because our minds are running ahead to an as yet non-existent future in which someone or something we love is conspicuously and painfully absent. God calls us to trust Him and to be present with Him in the here and now of *today*.

I've also realized that fear is an opportunity to build my faith. Our trials can serve as stumbling blocks or as a step up to the next level of trust and fellowship with God. The ones I've had recently have sent me sprawling face-first onto asphalt. I certainly have not been "stepping up." It takes effort to step up, my friend—to engage our muscles, challenge our strength and balance, and rise to the next level. It's okay if we sprawl sometimes! The important thing is that we get back up and try again, this time focusing not on the circumstances clustered around our feet tripping us up, but upon the One who is before all things and is fully able to deliver us from any and all harm. If I find myself slipping back into fear, I gently remind myself that I'm stumbling, not stepping.

Father, You are with me in every moment—and for that reason, I need not ever be afraid. When Fear comes knocking, help me to reaffirm my commitment to trust in You and in Your saving power, regardless of my circumstances. In Jesus' name, Amen.

JANUARY 12

The sea was getting rougher and rougher. So [the sailors] asked [Jonah], "What should we do to you to make the sea calm down for us?" "Pick me up and throw me into the sea," he replied, "and it will become calm. I know that it is my fault that this great storm has come upon you." Instead, the men did their best to row back to land. But they could not, for the sea grew even wilder than before. Jonah 1:11-13

I find this incredibly touching. Here you have Jonah, who worships the living God, amongst these pagans. They realize that Jonah's God is sending this storm, and want to know what they have to do in order to avoid destruction. Jonah has an answer at the ready, and one would think that the pagans would readily accept it and immediately toss him overboard. But instead, *they did their best to row back to land.* Amid this furious squall, these poor sailors were valiantly trying to spare the life of the man who had *caused* the calamity in the first place, because they valued his life. And why was Jonah on that boat? Because he *didn't* want the lives of 120,000 Ninevites to be spared.

So the sailors try to row back to shore, "but they could not, for the sea grew even wilder than before." God was in a spot here. His message was for Jonah, the disobedient prophet, yet because of Jonah's disobedience, the lives of others also hung in the balance. Although the sailors were trying hard to do the right thing, if God had blessed their efforts to get safely back to shore then Jonah would have missed the biggest lesson of his life. Instead, God had to thwart the compassionate efforts of the sailors in order to teach Jonah *his* lesson. I wonder how often God has to choose not to accept what we feel are selfless acts of compassion towards another because of the fact that if He allowed them, that person would miss the lesson.

Father, thank You for Your sovereign plan. Equip me to serve You obediently, even when things don't seem to make sense. Amen.

JANUARY 13

Put all things to the test: keep what is good and avoid every kind of evil. 1 Thessalonians 5:21-22 GNT

There's a lot of gray out there in our world today. Oftentimes there's no clear-cut answer for questions that arise, and we're left to discern for ourselves what the best option may be for us and for our families. Hebrews 5:14 says that mature believers "by constant use have trained themselves to distinguish good from evil." And Paul writes that a spiritually minded person "makes judgments about all things" (1 Cor. 2:15a). Obviously spiritual discernment is something we have to practice and work at—continually! How do we know that we are making a right judgment and holding on to what is good? The key is in Paul's next statement: "But we have the mind of Christ" (1 Cor. 2:16b). Is this not staggering? When we invite Christ into our hearts through our confession and belief in Him, His Spirit comes and dwells within us. That is how we have the very mind of Christ! And Friend, I daresay we are expected to *use it*!

How did Christ deal with temptation, betrayal, and questions meant to entrap Him? He used the Sword of the Spirit—the Word of God (Eph. 6:17). Solomon wrote, "Surely you need guidance to wage war, and victory is won through many advisers." (Prov. 24:6). He also noted, "Whoever walks with the wise becomes wise" (Prov. 13:20 ESV). Who, then, are our advisers? Who are the wise ones with whom we should walk? They are also known by these names: the Prophets, the Gospel writers, the Historians and Letter writers; the Revelator, the recorders of the Law, the Psalmists and Poets. God gave us exam notes, my friend. He has prepared us for the test. When gray areas confront us and we need clarity and discernment, we follow two steps: We remind ourselves that we have the mind of Christ, and we seek God's truth from His Holy Word. In that way, Beloved, we are equipped to test everything and hold on to the good. Amen.

JANUARY 14

Therefore, there is now no condemnation for those who are in Christ Jesus, because through Christ Jesus the law of the Spirit who gives life has set you free from the law of sin and death.
Romans 8:1-2

These verses in Romans are heavily marked in my Bible. I battled the stronghold of self-condemnation for decades, with only the briefest moments of relief and little progress on the whole. It was a difficult time in my life, living each day in defeat and pain, feeling "less than" in every way. Even though I knew the Lord and loved Him, I still wrestled with the pervasive feelings of failure and not being good enough.

There is a vast difference between conviction and condemnation, and I want us to talk about that today. Conviction is the job of the Holy Spirit, which dwells within us. The Holy Spirit convicts us of sin in our lives with the goal of cultivating awareness, regret, and repentance, which ultimately results in our reconciliation with God. Condemnation, on the other hand, is from the enemy. Condemnation accuses, shames, and belittles, and the goal is to push us further into our dungeons of self-loathing, further away from God.

When the Holy Spirit convicts us of an area of sin or bondage, it will be in love. We will not feel judged or condemned. We will experience the conviction as an awareness of a need for change. And, it will be an awareness of a specific behavior or habit. Condemnation, on the other hand, feels like someone has dumped a bucket of slimy, stinking garbage over your head. It's humiliating. You feel a general sense of failure as a human being, as though your entire existence is meaningless or a waste of space. My friend, that kind of demeaning, discouraging message is *never* from God! If you're experiencing any of those kinds of feelings today, go to God. He longs to hear from you, and He loves you so much! It is never His desire for His beloved children to walk in defeat or condemnation. Christ died so we could be set free! Amen.

JANUARY 15

The Lord said, "I have indeed seen the misery of My people in Egypt. I have heard them crying out because of their slave drivers, and I am concerned about their suffering." Exodus 3:7

It gives me such comfort to know that God is never busy with other things and unaware of our needs. He doesn't become intently focused on one thing and then realize later on that He neglected half of His children and now they are all in dire need. No, He is aware. He sees, He hears, and He is concerned about our suffering.

Do you need to hear and know this truth today, my friend, that God is concerned about your suffering? Not just aware of your suffering. Not just casually interested in your suffering. And certainly not ambivalent about your suffering. Child, no. Your Father is *concerned* about your suffering! I don't know where that meets you today. You might be thinking, "Praise Him, yes He is!" You might be thinking, "He *is*?!" And you may even be thinking, "Apparently He has forgotten I exist; there is no way He's even aware of my suffering." If you are in that last camp today, I want you to know I have also been there. When we endure a seemingly endless season of trial and suffering, it becomes all too tempting to believe that God must surely have forsaken us or forgotten about us. Please hear me: He has done neither!

In our human condition, we often equate trials with punishment. God's Word does not support this reasoning! Jesus Himself warned His disciples in John 16:33, "In this world you will have trouble. But take heart! I have overcome the world." We can train ourselves to focus our minds upon this truth whenever the going gets tough. Yes, we will have troubles, and we will have difficult seasons in life. Yet we can take heart, Beloved, because Jesus has already overcome the world—He has already won the victory for us—and He *cares about our suffering.*

Father, thank You for Your concern for every detail of my life. Help me remember that You are with me in every moment of my day. Amen.

JANUARY 16

They marched across the breadth of the earth and surrounded the camp of God's people, the city He loves. But fire came down from heaven and devoured them. Revelation 20:9

Most of us, myself included, probably don't often turn to the book of Revelation when we are in need of some peaceful, calming, soothing words from the Lord via His Word. We tend to shy away from this particular book, perhaps because we feel inept to understand it well, or perhaps because we prefer not to really dwell upon end time events and the ensuing death, destruction, chaos, and depravity. I can't fault you there. However, I bring good news today, and that is the fact that the book of Revelation is not solely limited to heart-pounding destruction and allegory! In fact, there are some wonderfully uplifting gems in this book, and this is one of them. Take a moment to read our verse for today again, if you will.

The *"They"* in this verse refers to the army, "in number [...] like the sand on the seashore" (20:8) that Satan has marshalled together to go out in battle against the Lord's people. They have "marched across the breadth of the earth and surrounded the camp of God's people, the city He loves" (v. 9). So often in our lives, we feel the desperation of this situation acutely. Everywhere we look, it appears that we are surrounded. We can feel the walls closing in; death and destruction seem imminent. But just at that moment when things are looking bleakest for us, our God can save us.

What I love most about this verse is how God chooses to act. His people were surrounded; on every side the enemy had gained a foothold. We so often look around at the demands and trials pressing in on us on every side, and we feel suffocated and entrapped. We fail to look *up*. God is there! And He can send fire down from heaven and save us. His deliverance from our trials is so typically in ways we never could have imagined or expected! And I love Him all the more for that. Amen!

JANUARY 17

A man with leprosy came and knelt before Him and said, "Lord, if You are willing, You can make me clean." Jesus reached out His hand and touched the man. "I am willing," He said. "Be clean!"
Matthew 8:2-3a

Something about this exchange makes me want to cry every time I read it. Maybe it's the fact that Jesus never drew back in disgust from those who were afflicted, tormented, or needy. Maybe it's the hope in the voice of the man asking, "Lord, are You willing?"—knowing that his future and his very life hung on the answer Jesus would give.

Maybe it's the fact that Jesus typically healed others by touching them, even when speaking a word would do it. He chose to touch them, He chose that personal interaction. Or maybe it's the absolute beauty of His answer to the man's question: *"I am willing."* Not just to heal a man of a debilitating disease. Not just to restore sight or cast out a demon. He was also willing to die a terrible death on the cross *for us*. So that we can be clean. So that we can receive sanctification through His precious blood. So that we can have eternal life with the Holy Trinity in heaven.

Would you let our Savior's words fall afresh on you today, Beloved? What pain are you in today? What concerns are weighing on your heart, and on your mind? From what area of grief, confusion, brokenness, or sin in your life are you so earnestly seeking His healing? Are you wondering if He's still willing to help you? If He's still aware of your troubles and your pain? Have you lost all hope that He would ever be willing to meet you or your loved one in "that place" or in "that state" and bring healing? Hear Him today, Dear Friend: *"I am willing."*

Lord Jesus, I know that You are willing and able to heal! Help me to place my trust in You and to seek Your healing in my life. Amen.

JANUARY 18

However, I consider my life worth nothing to me; my only aim is to finish the race and complete the task the Lord Jesus has given me—the task of testifying to the good news of God's grace.
Acts 20:24

When my son Blake was a little over a year old and still suffering from early evening cranky spells, I took up running. Being cooped up in the house with a wailing toddler was exhausting, and I just needed to get *out*. Although I was athletic, I had never thought of myself as a runner. It seemed nonsensical to me to just *run*, but since I needed the fresh air I thought I might as well give it a try. To my surprise, it has become one of my primary means of stress relief, and one of my most focused times of prayer. However, I did have a few things to learn.

I quickly discovered that you can't run effectively while looking side-ways. Or backward. Or down at your feet. You have to keep your head up and eyes focused ahead, so your pace will be steady and your pos-ture will be sure. So often in life we find ourselves craning our necks to look backward at the past (the "glory days" when all was right with our world), or sideways at others as they jog past (their stride seems so much better, and their path so much easier than ours—right?), or down at our own feet in shame. Beloved, God intends for our focus to remain on *Him*. It's imperative that we keep our attention on our own race. If we try too hard to match our race to someone else's, we'll be thrown off course. We must focus on our end goal, commit ourselves to achiev-ing it, and then be committed to finding blessings in the journey.

Paul knew about running a good race. His end goal was the work God had given him of testifying to the Gospel, and he allowed nothing to distract him from the task! When we, like Paul, run our races (live our lives) with our eyes fixed on Jesus, what everyone else is doing won't matter so much. You can be certain, my friend, that He will make sure you get to the finish line and receive the crown of life! Amen.

JANUARY 19

He tends His flock like a shepherd: He gathers the lambs in His arms and carries them close to His heart. Isaiah 40:11a

If you are a parent, you know all about carrying. I remember when my younger daughter Stella first learned how to say "Up!" When she did, we'd bend down and lift her up, holding her close. She would smile and laugh, pleased to have communicated her wishes. Nowadays, though, it often doesn't go as smoothly as it did in those first days. Sometimes we pick her up when she has not requested it—times when she's running towards the street or getting into her siblings' stuff; times when it isn't a safe place for her to walk. Sometimes it's easy to carry her, and sometimes it's really hard. Sometimes she's compliant and happy; sometimes she's flailing about in her temper or running in the other direction. And make no mistake, once they've graduated from toddlerhood, we still carry them, don't we? We carry them forever in our hearts, sharing their joys and sorrows, shouldering their burdens. That's what it means to be a parent—we are "carriers" for life!

What do you often find yourself carrying? Have you noticed that carrying something generally places it close to your heart? We carry a lot of junk around sometimes, stuff that gets in the way and encumbers our walk. God carries precious things. As our Father, He carries *us* close to His heart. Sometimes we simply raise our arms and say, "Up!" Sometimes we run in the opposite direction. Sometimes we're mad and give in to a tantrum. No matter how much we struggle, even if we flail about and cry, He scoops us up and holds us close—protecting us with His mighty arms, with His calming presence, with His unfailing love. He is our Shepherd, and He knows when we need to be carried—even if we feel otherwise. He will carry us through the ups and downs of this life, and beyond.

Father, thank You for holding me close and loving me so much! In Jesus' name, Amen.

JANUARY 20

...a time to tear down and a time to build. Ecclesiastes 3:3b

Rebuilding work is hard. The process of healing from whatever has wounded us in life is ongoing, demanding, and intense. It requires a two-fold process of tearing down the things that hinder and harm, and rebuilding what remains into a structure that is strong and whole. When I feel fatigued by the ongoing work, it's usually because I've been trying to build in my own strength rather than relying on God. Psalm 127:1a cautions us: "Unless the Lord builds the house, the builders labor in vain." God's rebuilding is the kind of work that lasts, and we are invited to cooperate with Him in the process.

Paul writes in Ephesians 4:22-24, "You were taught, with regard to your former way of life, to put off your old self [...]; to be made new in the attitude of your minds; and to put on the new self, created to be like God in true righteousness and holiness." What parts of your "old self" need tearing down today, Beloved? What parts of your mind are in need of His fresh renewal? What thoughts have been plaguing you that need to be shown the door? We are in charge of our own "mind maintenance." God certainly helps us with this task upon our invitation, but we are responsible for the thoughts that we allow to come into our minds and the ones we allow to dwell within. Our minds require daily sweeping to make sure they are free of cobwebs, dirt, and grit. Whenever I find myself slumping back into a negative pattern of thinking, I can be certain that I've neglected my daily thought-sweeping duties. The surest cleaning agent to banish the dirt and grime is the clear, purifying truth provided to us in God's Holy Word. Let's let our minds soak in His truth today—for the "tearing down" does no good unless we replace the old with the new.

Father, thank You for Jesus, the firm foundation for my life that will not fail. May I abide in Him as You rebuild my smoldering ruins into a beautiful vessel that bears Your name. In Jesus' name, Amen.

JANUARY 21

Show me Your ways, Lord, teach me Your paths. Guide me in Your truth and teach me, for You are God my Savior, and my hope is in You all day long. Psalm 25:4-5

Where are you putting your hope today, Beloved? David wrote, "my hope is in You all day long." I feel convicted about this today, realizing that my hope is often in other people or in myself.

When we place our hope in others, we inevitably find ourselves disappointed, disillusioned, and let down. When we place our hope in ourselves—in our own ability to do enough or be enough, to provide enough or give enough—then we will find ourselves exhausted, insufficient, and resentful. Only God has infinite stores of love, grace, patience, and truth. Only God has infinite wisdom for every circumstance and accurate judgment for every situation. Only God can work all through the day and all through the night and never lose His focus, His energy, His skill, or His mind! Only God can strengthen us and encourage us without depleting His own stores in the process. Our hope must be in God, our Savior!

David also asked God for His teaching, guidance, and direction. Having a teachable spirit and a willingness to learn makes our hearts and minds fertile soil in which God is able to sow the seeds of His wisdom, insight, and revelation. When we earnestly seek His guidance and direction, He is always faithful to provide it.

Father, thank You for Your truth and Your teaching. Help me to put my hope in You today, resting in the certainty that You are well aware of all my needs and that You are faithful to provide for them (Phil. 4:19). Direct my footsteps along Your path for me today. In Jesus' name, Amen.

JANUARY 22

This is what the Lord says: "What fault did your ancestors find in Me, that they strayed so far from Me? They followed worthless idols and became worthless themselves." Jeremiah 2:5

When Blake was two years old, he called any round object a ball. This was not a problem for most items, and in fact it was a rather endearing generalization—until the day when he mistook a cantaloupe for a "ball" at the grocery store. He then proceeded to have a meltdown of epic proportions at the indignity of the fact that I would not allow him to touch or play with the "ball" that was *just* out of reach—yet still within his sight—in the cart. As the parent, I knew good and well that that melon was not a ball, and I also knew what would invariably happen if I allowed him to play with it (to the tune of "Smashing Melons in Aisle Five"). He, however, was incensed.

The Lord sees and knows when we have set up counterfeit gods in our lives. We call them "hobbies," "harmless habits," "occasional indulgences," "something that just helps me unwind." And it becomes a bit tricky to navigate this sometimes, because the idols in our lives can even be *good things*, such as work, family, exercise, organizations we support, or close relationships in our lives. And yet, *anything* that takes first place in your heart and your thought life, above the Lord, is an idol! God loves us enough to discipline us in whatever ways necessary in order to bring us back to Him. Jeremiah 10:10a says, "But the Lord is the true God; He is the living God, the eternal King." He is not willing, as our Perfect and Loving Parent, to watch us settle for a false knock-off of the real thing.

What habits, hobbies, people, positions, or tangible possessions have become idols in your life—or are dangerously close to taking that position? Don't mistake your cantaloupe for a ball. We want our allegiance to be to the One, True, Living God. Amen!

JANUARY 23

Let us hold unswervingly to the hope we profess, for He who promised is faithful. Hebrews 10:23

For some reason, this verse reminds me of riding a horse. (Stay with me here.) If the horse is walking or cantering, you can sit upright and let the reins be a bit slack in your hands. But if that horse starts galloping, you'd better flatten down, dig in with your knees, and hold on for dear life. When Life starts galloping away with us, we are called to hold on to our reins of hope with all we've got. And yet, holding on to hope "unswervingly" is really a challenge for me.

What makes me "swerve"? Doubt, fear, insecurity, anxiety, discouragement, unbelief—basically all of the "default" patterns I turn to when I am living in my flesh rather than in God's power. These are all things I can call out and rebuke through Christ, and over time, as I make this a habit, I'll "swerve" much less. The Hope we profess is Jesus, the One who gives us the assurance of His salvation in our lives if we have accepted Him as our personal Savior. We are called to hold on to Him rather than the "things of swerve."

What things cause you to "swerve" in your daily walk with the Lord? Take some time to really search for the answer. Would you be willing to bring these "swerve-inducing" things before God today and recommit yourself to holding fast to Him, our Hope Eternal? Even when my mind is at "full swerve," I find myself calmed and strengthened by the truth from our verse today that "He who promised is faithful." God never makes a promise that He fails to keep! Even when we cannot understand His reasons, we know that we can trust His heart and place our hope in His unfailing Word.

Thank You, Father, that You are always faithful. May I hold fast to You today, remembering that You are the rock of my stability amidst the daily swirling (or galloping) chaos of life. In Jesus' name, Amen!

JANUARY 24

Instead, speaking the truth in love, we will grow to become in every respect the mature body of Him who is the Head, that is, Christ. Ephesians 4:15

If we are called to speak the truth in love to others, then shouldn't we also be speaking the truth to ourselves? One of the most difficult and long-standing battles I've wrestled with in my life is that of negative, condemning self-talk. The unkind and critical words I spoke to myself wounded me deeply, and yet it seemed to be a continuous cycle that I could not manage to break. I felt ashamed of myself for being so unable to just *stop it already*, which then only added more fuel to the fire of my perceived inadequacies, shortcomings, and lack. I wonder how many of us tend to treat ourselves with aggravation, impatience, and irritation that we'd never dream of directing towards another living soul.

Awareness and accountability are both good qualities—there is a lot to be said for being able to recognize and take ownership of one's mistakes and shortcomings. But I was not doing this. I did not speak "the truth in love," but rather the condemnation in hate. We can wound ourselves by telling ourselves hurtful things that are lies: we are worthless, stupid, unloved. On the flip side, we can deceive ourselves by avoiding truths that need to be let in: God loves and cherishes us, Jesus gave up His life on the cross for us, the Holy Spirit of God dwells within us. If this is an area of struggle for you, I have good news: God, in His infinite faithfulness and mercy, is graciously helping me out of this pit. He can do the same for you. The key is learning to recognize the lies we tell ourselves and then replacing them with God's truth. What is God's truth? It's His Word (John 17:17). When we speak His truth to ourselves and others in love, we grow to become more like Him. When we speak lies in hate, we wither.

Father, teach me Your truths, that I might speak them to myself and others in love, bringing glory and honor to You. In Jesus' name, Amen.

JANUARY 25

For everything God created is good. 1 Timothy 4:4a

When I was eight years old my parents divorced, and my mom and I moved to another state. As an only child, I was left to navigate all of the transitions between two parents, two houses, two cities, and two lives—alone. Just when I had become acclimated to my new environment, it was time to switch again. Perhaps for this reason, I dislike change and am not a fan of traveling. I don't like to be away from home. I have also been reluctant to let my children spend the night away from home. A while back, however, circumstances arose in which it was going to be necessary for my older daughter Tessa to spend the night at a friend's house.

I worried that she'd be anxious or upset, but the truth is, *I* was the one who was anxious. I confided my worries to my husband Kevin, who calmly said: "Allyson, the only baggage Tessa's taking with her is what's in her little blue suitcase." I nearly wilted in limp relief. I had been bringing my own baggage into the situation and had tried to cram it into Tessa's suitcase—whereas she was completely unencumbered and was so looking forward to this wonderful new experience! Of course it all went beautifully, no problems whatsoever.

Sometimes our past experiences can cause us to over-complicate the simple, my friend. I have no doubt that God is able to use our past pain and struggles to benefit others, but wisdom is called for in the process. We have to make sure that we are not tossing our own burdens into the suitcases of others, creating a potential crisis where none exists. Our awareness may be heightened—we may "see" things in a situation that others don't or can't, simply because of our past experience. Again, wisdom. When we seek to use our past experiences "for the good," God will be faithful to help us distinguish between the two (or blessedly send us someone who can offer fresh perspective, in case we are already too far gone).

Father, thank You for all of the good in Your creation. Amen!

JANUARY 26

And my God will meet all your needs according to the riches of His glory in Christ Jesus. Philippians 4:19

Please note: God will (WILL) meet all your needs! He may not meet all of your *wants*, Beloved, but He will meet every need that you have! Jesus Himself—His person, His love—meets all of our needs. In Him, we already have everything we need—we just have to tap into His wonderful and perfect provision, learning to trust it and rest in it.

Where are you feeling needy today, Dear One? What area of your life is in need of reassurance, healing, direction, or transformation? Take a moment to find a scrap piece of paper and a pen, and write it down—or note it in the margin here. Maybe it's a health condition that is debilitating or exhausting. Maybe it's a relationship that causes chronic stress, pain, or conflict. Maybe it's parenting. Maybe it's caring for an aging parent or a special needs child. Maybe it's a difficult relationship at your place of work—or maybe it's a lack of work. Maybe it's an area of ongoing conflict with your spouse. Maybe it's a financial strain your family is facing. Maybe it's a loss in your life that is bringing pain and despair. Maybe it's a habit or an addiction that now controls you, rather than you controlling it. Whatever it is, Beloved, please take a moment to write it down.

Now, over the top of that concern, please write our verse for today, and make it personal: *My God will meet ALL of my needs according to the riches of His glory in Christ Jesus!* I invite you to feel the empowerment and the victory that declaration gives you today! May you feel the truth of God's power and might, coupled with the knowledge of His unending, abundant love for you and His concern for each and every one of your cares—and may this bring you much peace today as you face whatever lies ahead. I am praying for you today! He will meet your every need. In the mighty name of Jesus, Amen!

JANUARY 27

One who was there had been an invalid for thirty-eight years. When Jesus saw him lying there and learned that he had been in this condition for a long time, He asked him, "Do you want to get well?" "Sir," the invalid replied, "I have no one to help me into the pool when the water is stirred. While I am trying to get in, someone else goes down ahead of me." John 5:5-7

I used to dread this chapter of John because I knew this story was lurking there. I hated being confronted with this question from Jesus in my own life: "Child, do you *want* to get well?" To be honest, for a long time, I just didn't. I was ashamed of my lack of healing and wholeness, but at the same time I was angry and felt I deserved to live in the brokenness. I was also deeply afraid of trying to get better and failing. I eventually found myself in a state of hopeless complacency that I would never really experience life any differently, so why even try?

It was at this point that I felt the firm weight of conviction settle on me, and I spent a lot of time wrestling with God about my attitudes and beliefs—specifically, how they were *not* lining up with the Truth of His Word. I finally realized that I could not be fully used by God in the purpose for which He had made me if I continued to allow myself to be so wrapped up in my infirmities that I missed out on (or worse, rejected) His healing.

What about you? How long have you been an invalid? What excuses have you made for your lack of healing, lack of wholeness, lack of wellness? Do you feel you "deserve" the pain you are in? Have you lost hope? Are you afraid of trying and failing? It is my joy to meet you here today and let you know that there is *nothing* beyond the healing, transforming power of our God! So I ask you, today, Beloved: *Do you want to get well*? Talk it over with the Lord today. Seek His counsel. Contemplate what would happen if you answered, today, with a *"Yes."* Amen.

JANUARY 28

They have greatly oppressed me from my youth, but they have not gained the victory over me. Plowmen have plowed my back and made their furrows long. But the Lord is righteous; He has cut me free from the cords of the wicked. Psalm 129:2-4

Being oppressed is not the same thing as being overcome. Though my childhood and teenage struggles were difficult and resulted in many years of oppression and bondage, the enemy has not gained the victory over me. This is not due in any part to my own goodness or worthiness or valiant efforts. It is due to God alone, who has watched over my life and shielded me with His mighty wings (Ps. 61:4). He will continue to deliver me and work in me as I continue on my journey with Him. And I take great comfort in the certainty that although "plowmen have plowed my back and made their furrows long," God can come behind them and plant wonderful things in that freshly turned soil. He will not let those furrows be made for nothing.

Can you relate today, my friend? In what ways have you suffered oppression and bondage? Have you had furrows plowed into your back? What good seeds can you imagine God planting there? One thing God plants in us is His Word (Jas. 1:21). And because He sows good seed (Matt. 13:37), the result of His planting is always fruitfulness (see Eze. 36:8-12). When the good seed falls on good soil—which refers to those who "hear the Word, accept it, and produce a crop" (Mark 4:20)—we begin to bear fruit. It is to our Father's glory that we "bear much fruit" (John 15:8), and He longs to make us fruitful! Part of bearing fruit is bearing up under the seasons of plowing so that what is unfruitful can be turned under, and God's good seed can take root and begin to grow.

Father, plant good seed in me, that my brokenness may become a blessing, bringing glory to Your name. Amen.

JANUARY 29

I am the Lord your God, who teaches you what is best for you, who directs you in the way you should go. Isaiah 48:17b

Back before I became a stay-at-home mom to my three children, I taught high school French. In my French II class, I gave directions in French as much as possible. One day I was standing at the front of the classroom taking roll while the kids worked, and I noted that Pierre, a quiet boy who sat in the back by the door, was chewing gum. (French is hard enough to speak when your mouth is unencumbered—much less when it's full of a wad of gum.) So as they worked, I quietly said, *"Pierre, jette la gomme dans la corbeille, s'il te plaît."* He looked up at me like a deer caught in the headlights. He stared at me for a moment, thinking. Finally his neighbor leaned over a bit and whispered, "She said—" "I know what she said!" he huffed back. I smiled. He got up, walked over to the door, closed it, and sat back down. I got so tickled. He looked at me, and I pointed to my mouth and whispered: *"La gomme, Pierre! Pas la porte!!"* It dawned on him what I had "really" been asking, and his cheeks turned pink as he said, "Oh." He got back up, put the gum in the trash can, and sat back down again. I gave him the thumbs up and he grinned.

Oh, Beloved. Some days God's instructions to us just don't quite come through clearly, do they? I can be seeking His wisdom and guidance and praying for clarity, and in turn it feels like I'm receiving the directions back in Swahili—if at all. This is just one of the many reasons why we really do need each other! If you are seeking God's direction in an area of your life, He is absolutely able—and quite likely!—to use other people to help validate and confirm the instructions you feel you might be receiving from Him. Don't discount a neighbor's help at interpretation when it's needed!

Father, thank You for sending others to help guide me as I seek Your directions for my life. In Jesus' name, Amen.

JANUARY 30

Gold and silver are tested in a red-hot furnace, but we are tested by praise. Proverbs 27:21 CEV

We know what it's like to be tested by a time of trial, don't we? It can be frightening, disorienting, and painful. Yet have you ever considered that we can also be tested by *praise*? This is so intriguing! And yet, if we stop and think about it, it is so true, isn't it? When we find ourselves on top of the world, surrounded by the shimmering lights of fame and the adoring gazes of others—*that*, my friend, is a test! For at the height of success and personal glory, what will we do? What will we say? Will we find ourselves traipsing down the path of self-congratulation for our talent, gifts, and charisma? Or will we instead deflect the attention away from our own ability and instead give the credit and glory to God?

The Bible is filled with men and women who gave credit to God for their success. Joseph and Daniel both told the supreme rulers of Egypt and Babylon that God alone was to receive credit for enabling them to interpret the rulers' dreams (see Gen. 41:16; Dan. 2:27-28). In the New Testament we see John the Baptist, and later Peter and John, also pointing the finger away from themselves and to the glory and power of Christ (see John 3:26-30; Acts 3:12, 16).

How about you, my friend? Are you enjoying a time of success right now? Are you receiving acclaim and affirmation? To whom are you giving the glory? When you receive praise, do you immediately point back to Jesus as the One who is greater, who has equipped you for all things? Or do you begin to allow pride to infiltrate your heart and perceived self-sufficiency to creep into your mind? There is no time at which we are more vulnerable. No wonder praise is likened to a red-hot furnace, something designed to test our mettle and see what we're truly made of. My friend, may we be especially conscious today of the test of praise in our lives. May we each come forth as gold, giving Him the glory! In Jesus' name, Amen.

JANUARY 31

...the Lord turns my darkness into light. 2 Samuel 22:29b

Between our second and third child, we suffered a miscarriage. The morning of the day it began, I had been reading back through some notes I had made in my prayer journal. The Bible verse I had just read was Job 29:3b, "by His light I walked through darkness!" The notes I had jotted down in my prayer journal said this: "When we are in the midst of our darkness, we must remember that God *is* light. When we are blinded by pain, grief, circumstance, or our own limitations, we can trust Him to lead us through our darkness and into His light. Every time." When I began bleeding and realized what was happening, I got down on the floor, on my face, and cried out to the Lord: "We want this child! Whatever its needs are, we are committed to providing all the care it requires. If it is Your will, Lord, please save this child!" Then I got up and re-read those words I had written, now facing the potential agony of loss in my life. I put my hand on the last two words as tears streamed down my face. And I whispered, "Every time. *Every time.*"

This, then, was the test: Do I really believe what I say I believe? Will I really praise God and believe God and trust God, even as I face the loss of this precious baby we had so wanted? I did believe it. I did trust Him, even though it didn't turn out the way I had wanted. The miscarriage completed itself about ten days later, leaving me emotionally shattered. I was so angry at myself, and with my body, for refusing to keep this child. I felt like I had failed. Although I realized that my body had done exactly what God created it to do, it still deeply wounded my heart. Yet He carried me through that experience in the most powerful, gentle, amazing ways that I cannot even begin to put into words. He provided exactly what I needed, throughout that time, in order for me to be okay.

He does turn our darkness into light, Beloved. *Every time.* And no one but our mighty God can do that. May He transform any darkness threatening you today into His glorious light. In Jesus' name, Amen.

FEBRUARY 1

My dear brothers and sisters, take note of this: Everyone should be quick to listen, slow to speak and slow to become angry, because human anger does not produce the righteousness that God desires. James 1:19-20

I am reminded afresh today that the Lord blessed each of us with two ears and one mouth and expects us to use them accordingly! James gives us three exhortations: First, be quick to listen. Seek the other person's viewpoint before charging ahead to make your own known. Second, be slow to speak. And when you do speak, season it, weigh it, carefully consider it. Whatever comes forth cannot be taken back, so speak carefully, speak thoughtfully, speak lovingly. Third, be slow to anger. This one gave me pause. How do you become angry *slowly*? Typically anger is a reactive emotion and comes upon us quickly and in power. Perhaps we must approach this more as, "Let your irritation threshold be high." Learn to tolerate petty annoyances and infractions. Save the anger for the really big and important things. This is so difficult, especially with certain behaviors that are your own personal pet peeves, or with certain people in your life who cannot seem to be in your presence without tap dancing on every last nerve you have!

Today I challenge you to identify one specific behavior or habit in others that drives you batty—and then make a conscious choice to stretch your "irritation threshold" for that one specific behavior just a centimeter today. And then try another centimeter tomorrow. I am trying this, too! Maybe by the end of this week we will note some genuine improvement in our ability to allow the things of lesser importance to loosen their grip on our anger tripwires. In turn, we can become more focused on really listening to the thoughts of others and speaking God's love over each person we encounter.

Father, You have gifted me with the ability to listen and the ability to speak. Help me to use each one in proper proportion today. Amen.

FEBRUARY 2

He will wipe every tear from their eyes. There will be no more death or mourning or crying or pain, for the old order of things has passed away. Revelation 21:4

In my mind I imagine God greeting each one of us in heaven with love and tenderness as He holds our faces in His hands, looks into our eyes, and wipes away our tears with His fingers. Somehow I think we will understand the why of everything when we are finally in the presence of the One who calls all things into being. In the meantime, things down here on earth can get pretty heavy, can't they? Burdens arise from many sources, threatening to crush our mortal frames into the ground. Today I want to talk about grief.

We grieve to the extent that we loved—and for that reason, we cannot deny the existence of our grief or repress it within. We must work through the grief out onto the other side of it. Yet, what happens when we get mired in the grief, stuck there, as years stretch behind us and we still cannot let that loved one go? Paul writes, "Brothers and sisters, we do not want you to [...] grieve like the rest of mankind, who have no hope" (1 Thess. 4:13). God does not ask us to deny our grief or pain. However, He does ask that we work through those feelings with Him, and that we lay them to rest and seek peace—in other words, we do not continue to grieve as though we have no hope. Our hope is in the fact that Jesus Christ has destroyed death (2 Tim. 1:10), which means that loss is never the end of the story. God crafted our hearts and enabled us to have the feelings that dwell within. We are not meant, however, to dwell in one feeling for all time.

Father, help me to see the hope beyond the hurt and the life You have for me beyond the loss. Enable me to release my loved one into Your eternal care, knowing that in doing so I am demonstrating my love for them and my desire to honor them by living well—until we see one another again. In Jesus' name, Amen.

FEBRUARY 3

But [King David] replied to Araunah, "No, I insist on paying you for it. I will not sacrifice to the Lord my God burnt offerings that cost me nothing." So David bought the threshing floor and the oxen and paid fifty shekels of silver for them. 2 Samuel 24:24

What are you sacrificing to the Lord today? There are several sacrifices we make in the name of obedience to God. We sacrifice the desires of the flesh. We sacrifice a portion of our income. We sacrifice the habit that we know is not in alignment with God's will for our lives, the one that is drawing too much of our attention away from Him. We sacrifice our right to listen to certain kinds of music, watch certain kinds of television shows, or read certain kinds of books. We sacrifice the right to say whatever pops into our minds, knowing that we are called to hold on to our tongues. We sacrifice Sunday mornings and Wednesday nights, forgoing birthday parties and sporting events in order to observe God's command to not forsake the gathering together of believers, that we might encourage one another in the faith (Heb. 10:25). John writes that we show our love to God by obeying His commands (1 John 5:3a). Sometimes obedience is a sacrifice. To not do that which I want to do—that can be tough. But, like David, I also do not want to offer a sacrifice to the Lord that costs me nothing. That's lip service, not sacrifice.

I am reminded of Jesus' ultimate sacrifice for me, for you, for each one of us in the body of Christ—an excruciating death on a cross so that we might *live*—a sacrifice that literally cost Him everything. When I keep my focus on Jesus and what it means to yield my will to the ultimate will of the Father, I am encouraged and empowered in my daily attempts to sacrifice, to lay down all of the false substitutes and things that entangle me, to follow God with my whole heart. What will you lay down for the Lord today, my friend?

Father, empower me to commit to my sacrifice and follow through. In Jesus' name, Amen.

FEBRUARY 4

Guard your heart above all else, for it determines the course of your life. Proverbs 4:23 NLT

Initially when I think of "guard your heart," I think about self-protection. I think about making sure that others cannot get in to hurt me and break my fragile heart. I imagine this comes from several past experiences of having my heart broken, which left me considerably suspicious and gun-shy. I could easily misapply this verse to mean that I am to keep my distance, not allow others to get too close, and keep that strong wall of protection up around my fragile heart.

And yet, I don't think that's what this verse is talking about at all as I consider it. Like Jesus' teachings to the Pharisees about what is clean versus unclean, this verse speaks to whether our hearts are more attuned to good or to evil, and how that consequently affects our lives. Jesus said that "the mouth speaks what the heart is full of" (Luke 6:45b). When our hearts are carefully guarded against intruders such as envy, bitterness, resentment, and prejudice, our souls will have a healthy spring of water from which to draw strength, and that spring of water will pour forth words of love, affirmation, encouragement, and hope whenever we speak.

What about you? Do you tend to have a guarded and distrustful heart, or does your heart feel open, receptive, and free? Do you experience success in the work of guarding your heart from bitterness, envy, and resentment, or is this an area of intense or ongoing struggle for you? There is no right or wrong answer! God sees our hearts exactly as they are, and you can be certain that His greatest desire is for us each to have a heart like His.

Father, enable me to entrust my heart to You today. Bring Your light into its darkened places, bring Your hope into its hollow places, and infuse its broken places with Your healing love. In Jesus' name, Amen.

FEBRUARY 5

Do not conform to the pattern of this world, but be transformed by the renewing of your mind. Then you will be able to test and approve what God's will is—His good, pleasing and perfect will.
Romans 12:2

I don't mind confessing to you that this was once one of my least favorite verses in the Bible, ranking right up there with the chapters on mildew in Leviticus, the endless chronicling of land acquisition for the twelve tribes in Joshua, and the somewhat tedious allegories in Ezekiel that confused me to no end. The reason Romans 12:2 was not in contention for my list of "Top One Hundred Favorite Bible Verses Ever" was because I disliked the truth it continually confronted me with, a truth that I was not at all interested in embracing or pursuing.

After many long, tedious years of struggling with my diseased thought life and pervasive stores of self-condemnation, I finally came face to face with this realization: I am not getting any younger. And I am limiting my effectiveness in reaching others and sharing the love of Christ with them because I am so narrowly focused on myself, my shortcomings, and all the ways in which I need to improve. I hated myself, but the sad truth was that I was still focusing all of my energy *on myself.* Finally my mind began to accept and own this truth: Until I choose to rewrite those thoughts, to retrain my brain, to feed myself God's truths instead of my own warped lies, I will handicap myself and limit my effectiveness in His kingdom. He's called me to more than that. And He's called you to more than that. If this is an area of struggle for you, too, let's take our burden to God together today.

Father, I confess my distorted thinking patterns to You, and I commit myself to the renewal of my mind and my thought life with the truths of Your Word. Empower me to make this change in my life, that I might live fully for You and fulfill the purposes for which You created me. In Jesus' mighty name, Amen.

FEBRUARY 6

Who of you by worrying can add a single hour to your life?
Luke 12:25

I recently found myself tied up in knots over an issue with Blake. He had an appointment that we had been anticipating for months, and it kept getting rescheduled due to things like stomach viruses and ice storms. I was so ready for him just to be able to get this appointment over with so we could move on and have it behind us, and as the waiting period lengthened I became more and more anxious.

I've noticed that oftentimes I have no trouble interceding for a friend who is having an area of worry or anxiety, because I can clearly see that it will not last forever and I am convinced that God will work in those circumstances! And yet, with my own concern, I became increasingly uneasy and agitated. We can fret our lives away like this! Or, we can refocus our gaze and our thoughts onto the One who never fails us, the One who knows all things and therefore holds us together in all things.

I sought God's peace in the matter, and finally it came to me as I heard Him saying to my heart, "Allyson. Do you trust Me with your son?" This stopped me in my tracks. Of course I do. Of course I trust God with my son! "Yes, Lord," I said back. And then I sensed His response: "Okay, then." And I let it go. Whatever worry it is that has you in a chokehold today, my friend, hear the Father asking you: "Beloved. Do you trust Me with _____?" Let Him have that concern. It takes all the weight off of us, and places it back into the hands of the One who can carry it effortlessly.

Father, thank You for Your care and provision in every area of my life. I entrust my concerns to You today, confident that You are indeed working in every circumstance. In Jesus' name, Amen.

FEBRUARY 7

Those killed by the sword are better off than those who die of famine; racked with hunger, they waste away for lack of food from the field. Lamentations 4:9

I'm wondering if you can relate to Jeremiah's illustration above. Is there an area of your life where you are slowly starving to death? Perhaps it's a dead-end job or crushing debt. Maybe it's a loveless marriage or an ongoing family conflict. I'm wondering if you would have preferred a sword in that situation rather than a famine, a clean break instead of a shattered fracture. Sometimes an abrupt and final ending seems far less painful than an agonizing, incremental death.

This verse makes me think of my dad. We are estranged, and have been for more than twenty years. Over the years I've thought on occasion that it would have almost been "better" (for want of a better way to express it) had he just died, rather than circumstances unfolding as they did. Instead of a sword, I got a famine. Not knowing if your own parent would recognize you if you passed each other on the street is a strange and sad feeling.

Is there a relationship in your life that has unfolded in this way? Maybe it's with a parent, a sibling, a child, or a friend. These kinds of "famine" losses can continue to ooze and throb over time because there is no sense of closure. Sometimes we are called to reconciliation, and sometimes we are called to make peace with the loss through the process of grieving it and completing it. Only careful discernment from the Lord can enable you to know which path is best for your situation.

God has been faithful to provide nourishment and strength for me during my time of famine. He is able to fill us with good things that more than make up for the lack. Commit your area of famine to Him today, Dear One, trusting in His unfailing provision for you—His precious and beloved Child. Amen.

FEBRUARY 8

I pray for them. I am not praying for the world, but for those You have given Me, for they are Yours. [...] My prayer is not that You take them out of the world but that You protect them from the evil one. John 17:9, 15

The knowledge that Jesus prays for us astounds me continually—and yet God's Word has several places in which we are assured of this fact! Take, for example, Hebrews 7:25: "Therefore He is able to save completely those who come to God through Him, because He always lives to intercede for them." Or 1 John 2:1b: "But if anybody does sin, we have an advocate with the Father—Jesus Christ, the Righteous One." Is this not amazing?

In the verses for today, Jesus is praying for His disciples. I find His specific prayer fascinating. Knowing what His chosen ones would face in the world—all the hardship, all the pain, all the struggle—He specifically told the Father, "My prayer is not that You take them out of the world but that You protect them from the evil one." His prayer applies to us as well. If we are not in the world, how can we spread His light to those in darkness? If we are not in the world, how can we bear fruit that evidences His glory? It is imperative that we be here; even when life is painful, it is purposeful. Jesus prays for our protection from the evil one. If the prayer of a righteous person is powerful and effective (Jas. 5:16), how much more will the Father answer the prayers of His perfect Son?

Does it bring you great encouragement to know that Jesus intercedes for you in heaven? In what areas of your life are you especially in need of His prayers for you? Let Him know of those areas today, thanking Him in advance for His love for you and His intercession on your behalf.

Father, thank You for Your Son, who intercedes on my behalf! In His name I pray, Amen.

FEBRUARY 9

...the Lord has anointed me [...] to comfort all who mourn, and provide for those who grieve in Zion—to bestow on them a crown of beauty instead of ashes.... Isaiah 61:1b, 2b-3a

I have ashes on my mind today. In Isaiah's time (as well as long before), putting ashes on one's head or lying in ashes was a sign of deep sorrow, mourning, and lament. The earliest recording in Scripture of a person wearing ashes to signify grief is the account of Tamar in 2 Samuel 13 after she suffers the rape of her half-brother Amnon. (Other early accounts can be found in Esther [4:1; 4:3] and Job [2:8; 42:6].) I'm wondering today what your ashes are, Beloved. What has burned in your life? What has caused you the deepest sorrow and the rawest anguish? I bring good news to you today.

Chapter 61 of the book of Isaiah is a beautiful foretelling of how the Lord will restore the fortunes of Israel, the ways in which He will build them up and reestablish them as His holy nation, exchanging their pain for His promise. I chose this portion of the chapter specifically because my ashes became so much a part of me that I forgot that they need not be permanent. Jesus longs to trade our ashes for His beauty. He is willing to exchange our deepest pain and grief for His glorious healing and restoration. Our ashes are a part of who we are, but we need not wear them and lie down in them forever.

I picture God's dearly beloved daughter Tamar, who lived out her days "a desolate woman" (2 Sam. 13:20), being met by our Savior, Jesus. I imagine Him gently placing His own nail-scarred hand under her chin, lifting up her bowed head, wiping the ashes from her hair, and setting a beautiful crown of jewels upon her head—as is fitting for a daughter of the King. He meets us in our ashes today as well. He lifts our downcast heads, searches our tear-stained faces, and smiles as He says to us, "Child, it is finished. 'Go in peace and be freed from your suffering'" (Mark 5:34b). Amen.

FEBRUARY 10

...what I want is not your possessions but you. 2 Corinthians 12:14b

Paul's words here to the believers at Corinth strike a chord within me every time I read them. I imagine this is how God feels towards us, His children, as well. He does not want our possessions—He has no need of them! He does not want our scattered attention as we rush through our daily Bible reading so we can check it off the list. He does not want a "good deed each day keeps the devil away" kind of approach, either. Yes—tithing is important, Bible study is important, kindness and love and compassion are important. But God does not want the things you *do*, Beloved. He wants YOU. Your undivided heart, your willing mind, your worshipful and teachable spirit, given and yielded fully to Him.

The first commandment is the one that so often trips us up: We are to have no other gods before Him (Ex. 20:3). He must come first, Dear One, and He does not want our leftovers! Please understand that I say that in the fullest humility because I struggle with this as well! Sometimes it feels like my prayer time and Bible study are just two more things on my to-do list, which is already far too long. When we get to that point of relegating God to the back seat, rather than allowing Him the position of our navigator in life, things spiral out of control. We feel harried, frantic, put-upon, and grouchy. There's not enough time, there's not enough *us*, there's too much to get done and not enough time to complete it. And this, my friend, is how we know we've gotten off track.

The good news is that we can choose to stop the madness at any time and turn things around. The next time you are rushing from one activity to the next, I pray God's voice will whisper this truth into your soul: "Child, what I want is not your possessions, but *you*." May His truth recalibrate our focus, so that we can find our stability and our rest in Him. In Jesus' name, Amen.

FEBRUARY 11

[God] called you out of darkness into His wonderful light.
1 Peter 2:9b

What areas of your life are causing some darkness for you today, my friend? What is that one circumstance that is a wearying, ongoing source of anxiety, struggle, and fear in your life?

You may have the intellectual knowledge that God is able to manage that problem for you; you may logically understand that He wants wholeness and healing for you in your life; and yet you may still find yourself wrestling with the same tired thoughts, emotions, and feelings. I have been there. I still go there sometimes. And, when I do, it is hard for me to understand why I am still determined to sit in the darkness rather than allow myself to come out into His light. I realize the insanity of this, but some days I just can't seem to get myself together and do any better. I do realize that He *calls* me to come out of the darkness. He does not *drag* me out of the darkness. He allows me the freedom to choose. Some days I wish He wouldn't. Some days I wish He'd just yank me out of my dank, dark pit in a huff. Somehow I don't think that's going to happen either, do you? Our God is long-suffering in His patience with us!

So, my friend, what this comes down to is an issue of obedience. When we find ourselves in the darkness, when we find ourselves sliding down towards hopelessness, a firm mental shake is in order. We must remind ourselves of what God has done for us in the past, and we must remember that He has the power to overcome every obstacle that sets itself up against us—even death itself. He is mighty to save, and You are His precious child, intimately known and dearly loved. Can you hear Him calling you to come forth today, Beloved? Let's trade our heavy darkness for His wonderful and freeing light. Amen!

FEBRUARY 12

For we do not have a high priest who is unable to empathize with our weaknesses, but we have One who has been tempted in every way, just as we are—yet He did not sin. Let us then approach God's throne of grace with confidence, so that we may receive mercy and find grace to help us in our time of need. Hebrews 4:15-16

Today I want us to reflect upon the fact that as we are being tested, the members of the Holy Trinity are not simply sitting up in heaven with feigned concern or lackadaisical care. We *matter* to them; our sufferings matter to them. They feel pain and sorrow just as we do, and I think sometimes we lose sight of that.

Genesis 6:6 says that as God surveyed the wickedness of men's hearts upon the earth, He regretted creating mankind and His heart was filled with pain. Hebrews 2:18 states that Christ suffered when He was tempted. Sometimes I think we miss the fact that Jesus agreed to lay down His own will, taking on human flesh and all of the infirmities that come along with it, so that He might truly be able to empathize with us in our struggles. Isaiah 63:10 and Ephesians 4:30 both indicate that our actions and choices can grieve the Holy Spirit, which means the third member of the Trinity can also experience pain.

Our Father does not cut Himself off emotionally from us, a fact that nearly boggles my mind every time I try to think about it. One of the most challenging parts of parenting for me is witnessing and experiencing my children's pain—and I've only got three kids! Imagine the utterly incomprehensible heart of God, so wide and vast that He intimately knows and cares for each of His children's concerns, hurts, hopes, and fears. Jesus and the Holy Spirit are also in tandem with us, with hearts open to feel the same things we are feeling. You are never alone, Beloved. May that assurance fill your heart with comfort, peace, and thanksgiving today. In Jesus' name, Amen.

FEBRUARY 13

Do two walk together unless they have agreed to do so? Amos 3:3

When my older daughter Tessa started kindergarten, her school was less than a mile from our house. So every day, rain or shine, I walked her to school in the morning and went back over to walk her home in the afternoon. Starting each day being out in God's creation was a wonderful blessing to me. I don't believe my daughter always felt likewise. If you don't happen to know this already from personal experience, please allow me to share it with you: It can be a real pain to try to walk with someone who doesn't want to walk with you.

This verse would constantly come to mind as I tried to walk with Tessa to school. Most days she either ran ahead of me or lagged behind. Sometimes it was because she was excited and happy and joyfully running ahead, but most of the time she was miffed about something and was refusing to walk with me as a means of making her displeasure known. On many occasions my muscles began to atrophy as I stood and waited for her to snail-crawl her way to me. It could be really irritating—which, of course, was the point. I finally solved the problem of "useless waiting" by adopting the personal mantra, "You poke; I pray." There is no telling how many concerns were lifted up to the Lord throughout the course of that school year!

I think of the Lord, *our* Father, and how much He desires to walk with us, His children, on each step of our journey. I think of how often we run ahead, thinking we know exactly what's coming and what we need to do—or how often we drag behind, sulking, because He hasn't done things our way. The bottom line is that we cannot walk daily with the Lord *at our side* unless we *agree to do so.* As for Him, He is always willing. He allows us the freedom of that choice.

Dear Father, I choose to walk with You today! Amen.

FEBRUARY 14

Keep yourselves in God's love as you wait for the mercy of our Lord Jesus Christ to bring you to eternal life. Jude 21

I am so intrigued by Jude's wording here: "Keep yourselves in God's love." Since God's love is always around us and in us, this seems to indicate that we must sometimes *choose* to remain in and accept the love He is there offering to us. Sometimes we feel as though He's not there or that He doesn't love us if "this" is happening to us. Not so. It is especially in those times that we must *keep ourselves* in God's constant and abiding love, refusing to heed the siren song of our false comforts.

What is in your heart today, Dear One? To those of you who love this day of love, I celebrate with you and honor your efforts to show love, give love, receive love, express love, speak love, and BE loved! But why stop at just today? Every day should be a day when we are challenged to go out of our way to lavish God's love onto others. Do it!

For others of you, today is arguably one of the most difficult days of the year to endure. On a day when our calendar tells us to feel love and celebrate love and give love and express love, for some of us this is not cause for celebration but rather something that inspires us to withdraw, hide, and even grieve. To those who are single and despairing of God ever providing a mate; to those who have gone through divorce and are left with the shattered remnants of a once-full heart; to those who have lost loved ones and cannot yet feel anything but numb; to those feeling ignored, unnoticed, unloved, or forsaken by your family, your friends, your church, or even God today, I want to say this to you: God sees you, Beloved. He loves you beyond all human understanding. He treasures you, He knows your heart, and He honors whatever pain you are feeling.

May God keep you in His perfect love today, Dear Friend, and may you choose to remain there. In Jesus' mighty name I pray, Amen.

FEBRUARY 15

Cast your burden on the Lord [releasing the weight of it] and He will sustain you. Psalm 55:22a AMPC

I like the Amplified Bible, Classic Edition version of this verse because it specifies that it isn't just our "cares" we are to cast on the Lord, but our "burdens." To me, a burden weighs a lot more than a care. Then there is the further directive that we are to "release the weight of it." We aren't to cast it and then reel it back in; we aren't to throw it and then run and catch it! We are to release it *into His care*. Then note His response to our casting: He will sustain us. He isn't distracted by whatever your burden was, my friend. His focus is on *you*. Our burdens are weightless to Him, which is why it takes so much effort for us to heave them over to Him and so little effort for Him to receive them. Once we let go of the burden (or the care), He will see to it that we are "sustained"—that we can rest in His comfort, trusting that He is in control and is able to manage whatever "cares" we have cast on Him.

Now let's see what this looks like in action: Grab a sheet of paper and a pen. On the paper, write down your burden. (Remember that God is already aware of the burden, so now is not the time for verbosity. A name will suffice. Or a one-word summation of a habit, struggle, or addiction. Or the place of struggle: work, school, home, etc.) Next, crumple up that piece of paper into a tight little ball. Then, I want you to say aloud to God, "Lord, I am casting this burden over to You. I am entrusting it into Your care, and I am letting go of it. Thank You for sustaining me in all areas of my life!" And then, Dear One, cast it, throw it, or hurl it straight into the wastebasket. (Remember, you can't pick it back up!) Rest assured that once you cast it over to Him, He is taking care of it. I am praying today that you will feel and experience the weight of that burden falling off of your shoulders, right into the mighty and capable hands of Your God—who loves you, cherishes you, and longs to be your Sustainer. In Jesus' name, Amen!

FEBRUARY 16

Finally, be strong in the Lord and in His mighty power. [...] Take the helmet of salvation and the sword of the Spirit, which is the Word of God. Ephesians 6:10, 17

You may remember the song *Kyrie Eleison* that was released by the band Mr. Mister in late 1985. As a child listening to the lyrics on the radio, I always thought they were saying, "Carry a laser down the road that I must travel / Carry a laser through the darkness of the night...." Obviously I was a little off there, and it was many years later before I realized they were singing *"Kyrie eleison."* I finally put two and two together and realized this song was not about wielding weapons at all; rather, it was in essence a prayer—*Kyrie eleison* literally meaning, "Lord, have mercy" in Greek.

Here's how this relates to Paul's exhortation in the book of Ephesians today: We are called to be strong *in the Lord* and in *His* mighty power. Ephesians 6 outlines the "Armor of God" that we are to clothe ourselves with daily. Amongst the battle armor we wear (belt, breastplate, shoes, helmet), we are given just one offensive weapon—the sword of the Spirit, otherwise known as the *Word of God*. Here's the thing: In order for us to actually be able to *use* the sword God has given us, we have to be *in* the Word of God and have it dwelling within us. Soldiers don't arrive on the battlefield with instruction manuals in hand, ready to read about how to use their weapons while the enemy is staring them down. No! We must read, study, memorize, and personalize the Word of God so that we will be equipped in every battle situation we face in order to stand firm in the power of our God. No lasers necessary.

Dear Father, thank You for equipping me through Your Word with the truths I need to take my stand against the enemy. Help me to fight as a soldier of Christ—armor on, sword in hand. Amen.

FEBRUARY 17

For He wounds, but He also binds up; He injures, but His hands also heal. Job 5:18

I struggled with this verse for a long time; it was always difficult for me to understand the idea of God wounding us and injuring us. Then it occurred to me that this is all about the pruning that He, as the Master Gardener, has to perform so that we can bear much fruit (John 15:1, 5). Pruning hurts. Even if a branch *looks* dead, there's always a chance that there is still some life in it, and there's always a chance that if a clean cut isn't made, part of the living plant could be injured in the removal of the dead part. Yet pruning is essential, or else we grow wild, running off in every direction, and we cannot abide faithfully in the Vine.

This verse also makes me think about what is required to graft a tree. Living parts of branches have to be cut, and notches have to be made in the host in order to receive the branch being grafted in. Once the cut part of the branch is carefully fitted into the notch prepared for it, the Gardener must bind it up tightly and securely so that when the branch heals, it will have become part of the larger tree.

We as Gentile believers have been grafted in; Christ bears on His hands, feet, and side the notches carved into Him so that we could be bound to Him, reconciled to the Father through Him, and come to bear much fruit. The process of pruning and grafting is a wounding, an injury, a process that involves pain for all involved. Yet Jesus believed that we were worth it! That truth moves my heart afresh today.

Father, help me to accept Your pruning in my life as evidence of Your desire for me to grow, thrive, and bear much fruit. Redirect my gaze from my temporary struggles here on earth onto the eternal glory of the kingdom of heaven that awaits me as Your beloved Child. In Jesus' name, Amen.

FEBRUARY 18

Hear me, you heavens! Listen, earth! For the Lord has spoken: "I reared children and brought them up, but they have rebelled against Me." Isaiah 1:2

This verse often comes to mind when I'm having a particularly challenging day with my children. I find it exceedingly comforting to know that our Almighty Father, the one and only Perfect Parent, had children who were stubborn and rebellious and who refused to listen to Him.

It started out with Adam and Eve, who decided their Dad was trying to keep something from them in which they rightly deserved a share, and thus sin entered into God's perfect creation. And it didn't stop there. Not just one or two children went haywire, mind you, but entire *nations* of people turned their backs on God, accused Him of not really loving them, worshipped idols, engaged in pagan rituals, and treated the Lord of all creation with open contempt or appalling indifference. And He loved them and pursued them all the same. Still does today.

Have you experienced a season of being a wayward child of God? What prompted your rebellion? Sometimes we get angry with God because we think He's not listening to us. We then tell ourselves that means He doesn't care about us. I've noted of late that when my children accuse me of not listening to them, the reality is usually this: I've heard their requests clearly, I've weighed them in my mind, and I've given this answer: "No."

Whether we're two or ninety-two, we just do not like to be told *No!* As the parent, I can see a bigger piece of the picture than my children can. And I have my own good reasons for my answer, which I may or may not feel inclined to share with them at length. So it is with God, my friend. He sees the *whole* picture, and if we get a "No," we can be certain there's something there that we cannot yet see. He's always listening. He's always loving us. His actions through the millennia prove it. Amen.

FEBRUARY 19

[Hagar] gave this name to the Lord who spoke to her: "You are the God who sees me," for she said, "I have now seen the One who sees me." Genesis 16:13

Hagar knew about living a painful life. The Egyptian maidservant of Abram's wife, Sarai, Hagar was "given" by Sarai to Abram in the hopes that she would become pregnant and provide an heir for Abram and Sarai. The son she would bear would technically "belong" to Sarai, in accordance with the customs of that day. When Hagar discovered she was pregnant, Sarai resented her and mistreated her to the extent that Hagar fled.

When the angel of the Lord comes to Hagar in the desert he asks, "Hagar, slave of Sarai, where have you come from, and where are you going?" She answers: "I'm running away from my mistress Sarai" (v. 8). "Go back," the angel tells her, "and submit to her. I will increase your descendants so much that they will be too numerous to count. You are now pregnant and you will give birth to a son. You shall name him Ishmael, for the Lord has heard of your misery" (vv. 9-11).

What desert are you in today, Beloved? From what or whom are you running? Do you hear God's voice and sense His presence, even in your desert wandering? What is He calling you to do? God is not simply aware of your presence on planet earth—He *sees* you. He sees each hurt you are carrying and any pain in your heart. He does not miss a single tear you have shed. He knows your frustrations and fears. He is the God who sees you. It is safe to rest in Him.

Father, thank You for the gift of knowing that You miss nothing and see every hurt that I experience. Meet me today in my desert space; reassure me of Your love and care. Please bring hope anew, for my hope is in You. In Jesus' name, Amen.

FEBRUARY 20

Bear with each other and forgive one another if any of you has a grievance against someone. Forgive as the Lord forgave you. And over all these virtues put on love, which binds them all together in perfect unity. Colossians 3:13-14

I don't know about you, but as I get older I'm realizing more and more often that time is so fleeting. I don't want to waste a moment of my tenure here on earth steeped in bitterness, anger, indignation, fear, resentment, anxiety, or self-loathing. I so desperately want to *love*!

Verse 14 says that we are to "put on love," which seems to indicate that we have to intentionally clothe ourselves with it. In our natural fallen state, we default to all interests of Self rather than Other. I long to wear love, to be a channel of God's love into this confused, lost, and hurting world. So many people desperately need a fresh word of hope and encouragement that we serve a *living* God who is very much present in our lives and especially in the midst of our most difficult circumstances!

The call to forgiveness is also timely. I am prompted today to do a personal inventory of any areas of unforgiveness that may be lurking within my heart, and I am committing myself to bringing those out into the light, before the Lord, to ask for His help in choosing to release any lingering feelings of bitterness, resentment, hurt feelings, or offense. Will you join me?

Father, thank You for the forgiveness You have so freely offered me each time I have come to You confessing my sin with a repentant heart. Empower me through Your indwelling Spirit to offer that same measure of pardon to others who may have wronged me. Above all, Father, I choose to wrap myself in Your love today so that I can share it abundantly with others. In Jesus' name, Amen.

FEBRUARY 21

Then the nations around you that remain will know that I the Lord have rebuilt what was destroyed and have replanted what was desolate. I the Lord have spoken, and I will do it. Ezekiel 36:36

What are the ongoing areas of struggle in your life today, Dear One? What has the enemy destroyed in your life; what places seem most desolate? Are you dealing with outward repercussions such as estrangement, exhaustion, conflict, or imprisonment? Or are you harboring inner repercussions like shame, guilt, despair, or anger? Is your pain being controlled and deadened by addictions, harmful habits, or mind-numbing distractions? Have you fully thrown yourself into an eighty-hour work week, or joined every committee and organization that you possibly can, just to distract yourself from the pain?

Sometimes our current life circumstances or past personal tragedies leave us with ruins far beyond our ability to rebuild and wastelands far beyond our ability to replant. When those times come, my friend, instead of distracting ourselves from our pain in unhealthy ways, we can lay the devastation at the feet of our God. Ezekiel's words bring us such good news today. We need not live in an ongoing state of resignation, hopelessness, or defeat. Our God is not limited to just regeneration or rehabilitation. Our God works to bring about restoration. He is able to rebuild the unbuildable and replant the unplantable. And please note the words and tone of His promise: "I the Lord have spoken, and I will do it." Not "I could," or "I might," or "We'll see," Beloved—but "*I will.*" I want to hold fast to that promise, to keep it as my anchor when the storms of life toss my little vessel around on the waves. He is *faithful.* If He says He will do it, Dear One, *He will.* Hold on for the blessing.

Father, I thank You and praise You for Your faithful care. As you rebuild and restore my broken places, may I give all the praise and glory to You. In Jesus' name, Amen.

FEBRUARY 22

For we are God's handiwork, created in Christ Jesus to do good works, which God prepared in advance for us to do. Ephesians 2:10

My garlic press recently broke, right in the middle of my dinner preparations. I was at a loss. The specific tool I needed for my task lay in two pieces in my hands. As I took out a knife and cutting board and set out to complete my task "the old-fashioned way," I began to contemplate my arsenal of kitchen gadgetry and what happens when we try to use the wrong tool for the task. Imagine, for instance, trying to open a can of soup with a potato masher. Or trying to turn your pancakes with a soup ladle. Or snipping fresh herbs with a pair of tongs. Or trying to grate fresh Parmesan with a spatula. (Obviously I could go on!) What occurred to me as I chopped my garlic was that on occasion, we can settle for a substitute and "make do." But for most tasks in life we have a specific tool that has been designed to meet a specific purpose.

God has a tool box as well, filled with millions of pieces—each with a different and specific purpose. When one is absent or missing, there aren't any substitutes. I'm sure you've caught on by now that *we* are the tools in God's tool box! Each one of us is uniquely crafted and specifically designed with certain strengths, experiences, and traits that enable us to be *the* tool for certain tasks that God has prepared *in advance* for us to do! Each tool is valuable. Each tool is needed. Each tool is handcrafted by the Master and is skillfully employed by our Lord Jesus—who was, you may remember, a carpenter by trade (Mark 6:3). Our Lord *knows* how to use His tools well, Beloved!

Father, thank You for creating me so uniquely. Thank You for the good works that You have prepared in advance for me to do. I entrust myself into Your capable hands. Put me to work in Your kingdom today, that I might bring honor and glory to Your name. Amen.

FEBRUARY 23

Blessed are those whose strength is in You, whose hearts are set on pilgrimage. As they pass through the Valley of Baka, they make it a place of springs; the autumn rains also cover it with pools. They go from strength to strength, till each appears before God in Zion. Psalm 84:5-7

What does it mean to set your heart on pilgrimage? Perhaps it refers to the choice to focus on the broader concept of one's journey with God through the day-to-day ups and downs of life. In other words, the choice not to become caught up in the moment and overwhelmed by the present circumstance, but instead choosing to view all of life's seasons as resting points along the journey.

The Psalmist states that as the pilgrims passed through the Valley of Baka, they made it a place of springs. It may interest you to know that "Baka" means "weeping, lamentation, or tears." Thus, when these people traveled through the Valley of Tears, they *transformed it* into a place of springs. Are you allowing your difficult circumstances to transform you, or are you transforming your circumstances?

These pilgrims also went "from strength to strength." This makes me think of swinging across the monkey bars as a child: hanging on to the bar with one hand while propelling myself over the chasm to reach out for the next one ahead. When we go "from strength to strength" in our lives, we have awareness of how God's strength carried us over and through that last chasm and trial, and we trust that His strength will continue to carry us through the subsequent one on into our next victory in Him. With each chasm crossed, we grow stronger in the Lord, deeper in our faith, and closer to our final resting place with Him.

Father, help me to set my heart on my pilgrimage with You today, embracing my journey with peace. May I continue to go from strength to strength in Your perfect love. In Jesus' name, Amen.

FEBRUARY 24

Yes, and I will continue to rejoice, for I know that through your prayers and God's provision of the Spirit of Jesus Christ what has happened to me will turn out for my deliverance. Philippians 1:18b-19

Paul knew quite a bit about suffering. He had been beaten several times, stoned and left for dead, falsely imprisoned on many occasions, and shipwrecked three times. In addition to the physical brutality he suffered, he had also been hungry, thirsty, cold, exhausted, and naked; and he carried the burden of concern for all of the churches on a daily basis as well (see 2 Cor. 11:16-33). Though Paul is honest about his sufferings and struggles, one thing we don't witness him doing is going through an endless and repetitive cycle of questioning the Lord about why he had to endure such atrocities. In fact, his general attitude is that of humility in being seen as worthy of suffering for the cause of Christ.

It isn't always easy to take that viewpoint, is it? I suffered sexual abuse as a child, and for a long time I struggled with trying to understand why it had happened to me. Although I no longer wrestle with that specific question, I do still struggle with some of the repercussions that remain. It can be discouraging and frustrating. Yet, I also realize that those struggles are what have deepened my relationship with the Lord. The curious thing about our trials, Dear Friend, is that they are precisely what drive us headlong into the mighty arms of Jesus. Without trials, we plunge into the dangerous waters of self-sufficiency, the perceived power to manage our lives all on our own. As God reminded Paul in 2 Corinthians 12:9, His power is made perfect in our weakness. It is when we are weak, my friend, that He can show Himself strong on our behalf.

Where do Paul's words meet you in your journey today? In what places of suffering in your own life are you struggling to see His provision and deliverance? May the Spirit of Christ help you and bring peace to your heart and mind as you entrust each area to the Father. Amen.

FEBRUARY 25

So Naaman went with his horses and chariots and stopped at the door of Elisha's house. Elisha sent a messenger to say to him, "Go, wash yourself seven times in the Jordan, and your flesh will be restored and you will be cleansed." But Naaman went away angry and said, "I thought that he would surely come out to me and stand and call on the name of the Lord his God, wave his hand over the spot and cure me of my leprosy. Are not Abana and Pharpar, the rivers of Damascus, better than all the waters of Israel? Couldn't I wash in them and be cleansed?" So he turned and went off in a rage. 2 Kings 5:9-12

I have learned some valuable lessons from Naaman. First, as the commander of the army, he tended to put his trust in things of might: his horses, his chariots, his victories, his plunder. He was used to giving orders, not taking them. Being an important man, he was terribly offended to travel all the way to see the prophet of God, only to be greeted by a servant. Then, once he received the word Elisha had sent via the servant, he became angry again because it seemed ludicrous and far too simple. Perhaps the most telling part of all is found in these words: *"I thought surely...."* We get into all kinds of problems and predicaments when we try to conjure up solutions for God.

Not only was Naaman enraged about the solution itself, he also grumbled about the instructions pertaining to *where* he was to do this. When we're used to being our own bosses, we have a hard time taking direction from others, even the Lord. This is to our detriment. Oftentimes God will use others to deliver His message and His directions. If we scorn the message because it is not coming from the messenger we think it ought to come from, we are simply revealing our sins of pride and arrogance. He speaks. Our job is to listen.

Father, give me ears to hear You and a heart that trusts in Your ways. May I walk in obedience to Your call. Amen.

FEBRUARY 26

I urge you, brothers and sisters, by our Lord Jesus Christ and by the love of the Spirit, to join me in my struggle by praying to God for me. Romans 15:30

Intercessory prayer, my friend, is the act of joining someone in their struggle. It's jumping into the ring and being willing to take a few hits from the enemy. It's love in action. It's mat carrying and boulder shouldering. It's taking up your sword—the Word of God (Eph. 6:17)—and using it to fight against the enemy on someone else's behalf. We must *never* discount the power and importance of our prayers.

We are meant to be soldiers of Christ—not gladiators (see 2 Tim. 2:3). Gladiators stand alone, while soldiers fight against the enemy *together*. The more people who walk out onto the battlefield, the better chance of victory for all. Today, Paul models the wisdom of asking for help.

Have you ever before considered that when someone asks you to pray for them, they are asking you to join them in their struggle? This is not to be taken lightly. They are entrusting you to guard their back as they aim to move forward in the Lord's strength. We cannot be lazy and lukewarm in offering protection with our prayers! This gives me fresh perspective and renewed resolve to wield my weapon of prayer today with precision, joining those who are fighting for the children of God. I long to give the battle-weary a fresh draught of resolve, strength, and hope as they see other soldiers come running to fight alongside them!

What if we're afraid? It's a legitimate question. The invitation to join someone in their battle with cancer, in their profound grief following a loss, or in their ongoing struggle in an area of immense pain is not for the faint of heart. Praise God that He gives us the strength to accept: "But we do not belong to those who shrink back and are destroyed, but to those who have faith and are saved" (Heb. 10:39). Let's strap on our armor and head out onto the field, my friend. We have a battle to wage for those we love. May God's strength give us the victory! Amen.

FEBRUARY 27

For God hath not given us the spirit of fear; but of power, and of love, and of a sound mind. 2 Timothy 1:7 KJV

I like the NIV translation best as a whole, but for this verse it's got to be the King James Version every time. As much as I long to have self-discipline (which is how the NIV translates the last part of the Greek), having a sound mind is what I want and need above all else. I'm wondering if you can relate with me today.

So much of our struggle is waged on the battlefield of our own minds—our thought life, our self-talk—and what we choose to tell ourselves affects how we perceive the world! This is my primary area of struggle. For the better part of my life, I truly believed that something was just inherently wrong with me—that I was irreparably broken in some way. God finally brought it to my attention that if I chose to tell myself that I was irreparably broken, that meant I could also choose to tell myself that I was not! I can't begin to describe what a staggering and blessed revelation that was for me.

For the longest time, I repeatedly wished that I could take my brain out, rinse it under some warm water, get it squeaky clean and sparkly, and replace it in my cranium—where it would then behave appropriately and think the thoughts it should be thinking. The change I was seeking began to occur once I realized that cleaning the outside of my brain was not going to make the inside of it do things any differently (to para-phrase Matthew 23:26). I had to begin the task of replacing my mis-guided, condemning self-talk with the truths God had laid out for me in the pages of His Word. No one else could be in charge of my thoughts but me. I can honestly tell you, my friend, that the work has not been easy. But I am certain that it will be worth it.

Father, I commit myself fully to the task of cultivating a sound mind through the truths of Your Word. Please help and guide me in my work, enabling me to fill my mind with Your love, light, and truth. Amen.

FEBRUARY 28

For God is not a God of disorder but of peace. 1 Corinthians 14:33a

I frequently call this verse to mind when I feel as though I am teetering on the brink of total chaos. The cause could be the physical exhaustion that leaves me feeling completely sapped after a long day. It could be the emotional sensation of feeling utterly overwhelmed and alarmingly close to having a meltdown. It could be the mental fatigue of carrying multiple to-do lists around in my mind. It could be the upsetting sense of things being out of balance in my spiritual life. Or it could just be a mixture of all of the above! Whatever it is, I call this verse to mind to remind myself that God is not a God of disorder, but of peace.

God routinely brings order from chaos. Genesis 1:2a says, "Now the earth was formless and empty, darkness was over the surface of the deep." And where was God? "The Spirit of God was hovering over the waters" (1:2b), waiting to speak the words that would set our world in motion. God brings light from darkness, beauty from brokenness, healing from hurts, purpose from pain. Even when we are in the middle of a maelstrom, Jesus can step out onto the water and walk to us in the storm, calling the winds and waves to cease.

What circumstances or decisions are you facing today that are leaving you with a decided sense of disorder? Maybe you're having anxieties about whether to keep working or retire. Perhaps you're worried about how you can make ends meet when an unforeseen expense (or three) has come up for you this month. Perhaps you have four kids, two hands, and one car and it always seems like they all need to be different places at the same moment in time. Maybe you're embroiled in a family conflict that has no clear-cut answer or end in sight. Perhaps there's an ongoing issue or rift at your workplace. Whatever the "disorderliness" in your life is today, Beloved, take it to God. Remind Him of this truth from His Word, and expect that He will answer!

Father, I claim Your peace in my life today. In Jesus' name, Amen.

FEBRUARY 29

But for you who fear My name, the sun of righteousness shall rise with healing in its wings. You shall go out leaping like calves from the stall. Malachi 4:2 ESV

I'm wondering if you need to look out your window and picture the sun rising with healing in its wings for you today. I would imagine that each and every one of us has at least one area of ongoing struggle, weariness, or brokenness in our lives right now that could use a special touch from the Lord, a renewed hope in His healing, a fresh wind of assurance in His almighty power and grace blowing through our lives like a mighty gale. It is my joy to bring you this verse from Malachi today, words from the last chapter of the last book of the Old Testament.

According to our verse for today, healing comes to those who fear the Lord. "Fearing" the Lord means many things. Do you revere the Lord's name, honoring Him as holy? Have you placed all your trust and hope in Him? Are your current behaviors, choices, and attitudes in alignment with His will and His Word? If so, rejoice in Him today, knowing that He is merciful, good, trustworthy, and true. He will never forget us nor forsake us! We matter to Him. If you find today that you have veered off the path, take heart—we can go to the Lord at any time and confess our areas of sin, and He is faithful to bring restoration (see 1 John 1:9).

I pray that today you will sense His healing reaching into those areas of struggle, weariness, and brokenness within as you bask in the light of the Son. As long as the sun rises, my friend, He is still working. As He continues to direct our paths, we can trust in His faithfulness. Being fully assured of this, I invite you to go out and leap like calves released from the stall. Though our calendar says this only happens once every four years, with our Almighty God every day can be "Leap Day."

Father, I rejoice in Your vast and unending love for me and in Your assurance that healing will surely come. In Jesus' name, Amen.

MARCH 1

I remember my affliction and my wandering, the bitterness and the gall. I well remember them, and my soul is downcast within me. Yet this I call to mind and therefore I have hope: Because of the Lord's great love we are not consumed, for His compassions never fail. They are new every morning; great is Your faithfulness. I say to myself, "The Lord is my portion; therefore I will wait for Him." Lamentations 3:19-24

These are some of my favorite verses in the Bible. They contain the one spark of hope in Jeremiah's book of lament, a beautiful ray of light piercing through the darkness of all the pain and sorrow he is experiencing. I have been here so many times. I wonder if you have, too: remembering the pain, remembering it *well*... with your soul feeling broken and shattered. Or maybe, dear friend, you're still living it. But then, the light: "Yet this I call to mind and therefore I have hope." I love that we have to call it to mind! We have to *choose* to seek the light. Even in the midst of the darkness and pain, we can blindly grasp for the Truth that we know can illuminate our darkness: "Because of the Lord's great love, we are not consumed... His compassions never fail... they are new every morning." Like manna to wandering Israelites, like ravens bringing food to a terrified prophet (see 1 Kings 17:2-6), God bends down to place in front of us exactly what we need each day.

At the end of these verses we see that the pain and darkness have not magically vanished. The circumstances are as dire as they ever were; the destruction just as devastating. What *has* changed, though, is Jeremiah's focus—from the circumstances themselves to the One who can change them, from the limitations of mortals to the omnipotence of the Immortal. Therefore, my friend, *we wait for Him* with hope.

Father, thank You for Your love and compassion, which greet me anew every morning. In You I place my hope and trust. Give me strength and courage to endure my time of waiting. In Jesus' name, Amen.

MARCH 2

Do not be misled: "Bad company corrupts good character."
1 Corinthians 15:33

Confession time: I actually like the smell of skunks. And I'm not talking about their fur, mind you—I'm talking about the *eau de skunk* you inhale when one gets frightened and sprays that signature scent into the air. It doesn't faze me a bit, and I'll tell you why. When I was about seven and taking piano lessons, my teacher would let me choose a special sticker to affix to the front of my music folder if I had done well during our lesson that day and practiced well the week before. One week she offered me a sheet of adorable skunk stickers to choose from. I was thrilled. I loved animals, and skunks were no exception.

It was only later, my friend, that I discovered that the stickers were scratch-and-sniff. And don't be fooled into thinking they smelled like flower perfume. Oh, no. They smelled *exactly* like *skunk* perfume. By that time I had amassed at least three different skunk stickers across the front of that green folder, and let me tell you—every day as I practiced, every week at my lesson, I inhaled the smell of skunk. At first it was nauseating—powerfully overwhelming, and potently disgusting. You can guess, though, what happened: Over time, I became used to the stench. Comfortable with the smell. And after a while, I almost didn't even notice it anymore. It was no longer offensive.

The company we keep can influence our character in exactly the same way. At first, the behaviors and attitudes we witness may seem shocking. Yet we continue to tolerate them, telling ourselves all manner of falsities in order to maintain that relationship. After a while, we become so accustomed to the habits and beliefs of our skunk friends that we begin to seamlessly assimilate them ourselves. And then, my friend, *we* are the ones that others find smelling like skunk.

Father, open my eyes to any habits or relationships in my life that are not in alignment with Your truth. I long to honor You above all. Amen.

MARCH 3

In an attempt to escape from the ship, the sailors let the lifeboat down into the sea, pretending they were going to lower some anchors from the bow. Then Paul said to the centurion and the soldiers, "Unless these men stay with the ship, you cannot be saved." So the soldiers cut the ropes that held the lifeboat and let it drift away. Acts 27:30-32

It would be hard to be in the place of any of the people in this story. The sailors were professionals, realizing better than the others on board how likely it was that the ship would smash into the rocks ahead. One can certainly understand their deceptive actions as they tried to ensure their own safety. Yet the centurion and soldiers were also in a tight spot, since Paul plainly told them: "Unless these men stay with the ship, you cannot be saved." It may seem unfair to us that the actions of the sailors would have affected the safety of the soldiers and the centurion, but such is life. Our choices affect one another.

The soldiers responded by cutting the ropes of the lifeboat and letting it go. Certainly this, too, was an act of faith, for what individual on a boat, fearing a shipwreck, would wish to cut the ropes of the *life*boat? At times we find ourselves in a similar situation, one in which the "lifeboat" we feel certain is our only means of escape to safety only proves to be the stumbling block to someone else's well-being. This story reminds us how important it is that we trust God instead of relying on our own understanding (Prov. 3:5). Unlike us, God always sees the whole and complete picture.

Almighty Father, help me to trust in You, realizing that the solutions that seem obvious to me may in fact be a detriment to someone else. Open my eyes to my own "lifeboats" in which I have falsely placed my hope and trust. Draw my heart and my focus back onto You, Giver and Sustainer of all life. In Jesus' name I pray, Amen.

MARCH 4

But you are to hold fast to the Lord your God, as you have until now. ...yield your hearts to the Lord. Joshua 23:8; 24:23b

This is part of Joshua's final farewell to the Israelite assembly before his death. I find his wording in both of these verses so interesting. First, the directive to *hold fast* to the Lord. When I try to conjure up a mental picture of "holding fast," I picture myself clinging to something for dear life, with my arms and legs wrapped around it as chaos erupts around me. Wouldn't it be remarkable indeed if we could train ourselves to "hold fast" to God? To figuratively wrap our minds, our hearts, our spirits, our bodies around nothing but Him, trusting Him to carry us through the storm? Guess what—*we can*. We will always "hold fast" to something in life, whether it be false gods or the One true God. We can train ourselves to seek Him first in every situation and circumstance.

And then another interesting choice of words—*yield your hearts* to the Lord. Yielding means holding back your own will in favor of someone else's. Accepting that someone greater than yourself has the right-of-way. Yielding requires conscious awareness in order to carry out. You will never yield by accident. It is our default mode to plow full steam ahead, looking neither to the right nor to the left, convinced that our way is the best way and that therefore we have the right-of-way. Since His ways are higher than our ways (Isa. 55:9), this is not so!

Father, make me aware of areas in my life where I need to "hold fast" to You, trusting You in the midst of the swirling storm. Draw my eyes away from other substitutes on which I have been falsely relying for strength. My strength comes from You alone! I also ask today Father that You would enlighten me in any areas in which I need to yield myself to You. In each moment of my day, help me to pause and seek Your leading, before plowing ahead in my own will and strength. I know that You will never lead me astray. In Jesus' name, Amen.

MARCH 5

And God is able to bless you abundantly, so that in all things at all times, having all that you need, you will abound in every good work. 2 Corinthians 9:8

I burned a pot of spaghetti today. Friend, I did not even think that feat was possible, but I now know otherwise (and so do you). Here's what led up to that fateful moment: I was busy. Trying to do ten different things at once. I was making a casserole ahead of time, early in the day, so it would be ready to put into the oven when I got home that evening after a trip I planned to make to help a friend with a task we had started, and my entire family was coming over for dinner. At the same time, I was also trying to mediate a dispute between my two older children (and if you're thinking, "Let them work it out themselves!"—please understand, there was a near-concussion on the driveway that had happened due to some over-enthusiastic "dancing"), and my youngest was repeatedly flushing the toilet, which is apparently a fascinating pastime. You get the picture. So I took the chicken out of the pot, put the spaghetti in, stirred it, and thought, *That doesn't look like enough water. Maybe I should add some more.* Guess what. I didn't. Four minutes later, as I passed by the kitchen en route to the bathroom to stop the mad flushing, I smelled the acrid aroma of burning pasta. I rushed to the stove and stared down into my pot of spaghetti, the bottom layer now browned and crisp.

I know what the lesson is. You know what the lesson is. Do one thing at a time. Entrust your day to the Lord, and He will magnify your efforts and supply sufficiency to meet *all needs*! I *know* this! And still, so often, I fall into the frenzied, harried pattern of flitting from one thing to ten others, and end up doing none of them well—and *burning a pot of pasta* too, for crying out loud! Then I have to start from the beginning and do it all again. God desires our hearts and minds to rest in His peace and rely on His sufficiency. Let's not allow the demands of life to run away with us. May we rely on His perfect strength each day. Amen!

MARCH 6

Then Saul dressed David in his own tunic. He put a coat of armor on him and a bronze helmet on his head. David fastened on his sword over the tunic and tried walking around, because he was not used to them. "I cannot go in these," he said to Saul, "because I am not used to them." So he took them off. Then he took his staff in his hand, chose five smooth stones from the stream, put them in the pouch of his shepherd's bag and, with his sling in his hand, approached the Philistine. 1 Samuel 17:38-40

It's tempting to look to others for inspiration when it comes time to fight our battles. The problem is that when we try to use the same tactics as others, our efforts are clumsy and futile. We are never quite comfortable with their weapons or their armor. David was wise enough to know that if he attempted to fight the Philistine wearing armor that was too big and too heavy, wielding a sword that he could barely hoist, he would not be likely to have the victory. He chose to go with what he knew: his staff, his sling, and his stones. And also, most importantly, his God. We all have strengths that are uniquely ours, and God will help us utilize them in our battles to gain the victory through Him.

What strengths has God gifted you with, Beloved? Perhaps you possess a resilience of spirit, or a powerful mind you've trained to focus on the positive. Perhaps you have enduring physical strength that carries you through days of labor that would be crushing to others. Maybe you are a prayer warrior, interceding for others in their times of trial. Maybe you have the gift of expressing emotions through art, music, drama, or song. There is not a soul God breathes life into that does not also house mighty gifts that He has given to the bearer. When your Goliath-sized obstacle rears its ugly head, ask God to open your eyes to the weapons you have on hand, that you already know how to use. Then go slay that giant, my friend. In His mighty and powerful name, Amen!

MARCH 7

In their hearts humans plan their course, but the Lord establishes their steps. Proverbs 16:9

Recovery work, whether physical or emotional, is tedious and taxing. We know what we want the end result to be, but instead of the quick and precise linear route we intended to take to get there, the Lord often has us trekking all over creation in order to get us to where *He* wants us to be. In my own healing journey, I've gotten into things I didn't even know needed getting into! It has often been frustrating and heart wrenching and well beyond my capacity for understanding. But I trust Him and I trust His leading. He will get me there in His own time and in His own way—just as He will for you.

What about you today, my friend? In what part of your life journey are you experiencing some unnerving delays, confusing wanderings, or a general sense of despair of ever really *arriving* where you'd like to be? I bring good news today: God will be as thrilled as we are when we at last reach our final destination—but Dear One, we'll also be dead. So instead of focusing so much energy and intention on *arriving*, let's choose to see this as a *journey*. It's our walk with God along the unique path He has set out before us to explore. We have a say in the direction we go, but the Lord gets to determine our steps.

On our journeys, we may experience times of mystifying wandering or a lack of direction that causes us to question if we're even on the right path. There is more good news: God has promised us that "Whether you turn to the right or to the left, your ears will hear a voice behind you, saying, 'This is the way; walk in it'" (Isa. 30:21). Guess Whose voice that would be. He will be with us every moment of our individual journeys, Beloved, until He calls us home.

Father, guide my steps that I may walk in the path that You have set for me. In Jesus' name, Amen!

MARCH 8

Do not be quickly provoked in your spirit, for anger resides in the lap of fools. Ecclesiastes 7:9

As all three of my children pirouetted around me this morning as I tried to finish up my workout—before fixing breakfast and getting everyone ready for school—I felt anger spark and flare within me. I struggle with irritability and flexibility; when my routine gets interrupted, I feel out of sorts and ornery. I don't like myself when I act this way, and I imagine others don't enjoy me much, either.

As I was stretching after my workout (with one child still draped lovingly over my back), I recalled that for the first twenty-some-odd years of my life, I couldn't touch my toes. My hamstrings were so tight, despite my being athletic, that I just could not do it. It wasn't a more strenuous workout routine that enabled me to finally be able to reach my toes; it was a daily regimen of gently stretching those muscles and ligaments, encouraging them to relax and increase their flexibility. My leg muscles are now not as tight as they once were, but it took *years* just to make that tiny little bit of progress!

So it is with our lives as well. We have to keep being stretched in order to increase our flexibility and tolerance. I was reminded of my resolution to try to raise my "irritation threshold" (based on James 1:19), which is exactly what I was dealing with this morning. If I'm going to be provoked to anger every time someone does something I don't like (or does it differently than I think it ought to be done!), I'm going to find myself grouchy and unpleasant to be around. I'd prefer to do it a better way. How can you relate in your own life today?

Father, help me to continue working on my flexibility, allowing You to gently stretch me in areas where I need to grow. Help me yield to Your gentle pressure, gaining the strength and balance I need in my life. In Jesus' name, Amen.

MARCH 9

After all, no one ever hated their own body, but they feed and care for their body, just as Christ does the church—for we are members of His body. Ephesians 5:29-30

For a while now I have wrestled with Paul's apparent assumption here that no one would ever be foolish enough to sabotage one's own earthly vessel. For those of us who have struggled—and are struggling—mightily with this area of sin, it can invite a sense of shame if we are not careful. If you are wrestling today with an area of sin that is harming your body—alcoholism, anorexia, bulimia, drug addiction, excessive exercise, overeating, promiscuity, self-injury—I want you to know that I understand. Even now, if I am not careful, I can slide back into a desire to "punish" my body for areas of sin or struggle. God does not want or need for us to punish ourselves, Beloved. He created our earthly bodies to be His temple here on earth (1 Cor. 6:19) and He takes all harm to His vessels very seriously—whether others harm us or we harm ourselves.

We need to tend to our bodies with the same care and concern that Christ has as He tends to us, the Church. It is only in seeing these two concepts linked together in this way that I am able to grasp what Paul is trying to say. He is not scoffing at us for being confused enough to harm ourselves. He is encouraging us to focus on how Christ lovingly cares for each of us, as we are all parts of His body, and he's saying that this is also how we ought to treat ourselves. When we mess up, Christ does not rush to condemn us or punish us, inflicting pain and berating us with shame. No, Dear One. He treats each of us with love, forgiveness, and mercy. We are to care for ourselves in the same way.

Father, when I am tempted to neglect, mistreat, or harm my body, I ask You to remind me of Your desire for me to care for my body as Christ cares for the Church—with nurturing and acceptance. Help me to follow His compassionate example. Amen.

MARCH 10

And we know that in all things God works for the good of those
who love Him, who have been called according to His purpose.
Romans 8:28

I want us to examine this oft-quoted verse from Romans today and carefully consider its implications. Sometimes we tend to fall into the errant belief that because we belong to God, because we love Him and serve Him and seek to please Him, only "good things" should come into our lives. Paul's words say nothing of the sort; rather, he makes it clear that *in all things*—whether good or bad—God works *for the good* of those who love Him. Not all things that come to us are good, Beloved. And we need not call loss, pain, heartbreak, and suffering "good." The good comes from walking through that time with the Lord, gaining a closer and deeper relationship with Him. *That* is the good that He is able to work in and through all things.

Consider God's words in Jeremiah 19:5: "They have built the high places of Baal to burn their children in the fire as offerings to Baal—something I did not command or mention, nor did it enter My mind." God is light, love, goodness, and peace. Of course the notion of burning one's children in a fire as an offering would not have entered His mind. This passage helps comfort me in the knowledge that the evil, wicked, abhorrent atrocities that man comes up with and carries out do not originate from our God, but from the sinful nature brought into this world by evil and the powers of darkness (Eph. 6:12). Hear me clearly: God is *never* the author of sin, abuse, or harm. Because He is omnipotent, He can *use* those painful things; He can turn the curse into a blessing because He loves us (Deut. 23:5)—but He does not ever deliberately inflict atrocities upon His children.

Father, thank You for Your pure and loving heart that always seeks to transform the fiery darts of the enemy into a mighty flame within me that longs to share Your amazing power and glory with others. Amen.

MARCH 11

Then Isaiah son of Amoz sent a message to Hezekiah: "This is what the Lord, the God of Israel, says: Because you have prayed to Me concerning Sennacherib king of Assyria, this is the word the Lord has spoken against him...." Isaiah 37:21-22a

This fascinates me. In Isaiah's account of this event, he specifies that the Lord's message to Hezekiah contains these words: "Because you have prayed to Me concerning Sennacherib...." Yet in the book of 2 Kings, this same account says: "Then Isaiah son of Amoz sent a message to Hezekiah: 'This is what the Lord, the God of Israel, says: I have heard your prayer concerning Sennacherib king of Assyria'" (19:20). Now, I realize it's almost splitting hairs here to focus on the difference between "Because you have prayed to Me about this" and "I have heard your prayer concerning this," but I still think the difference is striking.

The first leads us to believe that had Hezekiah *not* prayed about this, the results may have been catastrophically different; it seems to indicate that God's actions of deliverance hinged upon the condition of Hezekiah's humbling himself and asking for help. The second has more of an "I knew you would do that and now I will do this" sort of feel. There are probably events and circumstances in our lives that follow both of these patterns. Sometimes maybe God acts *because* we prayed about something, and sometimes maybe God acts *when* we have prayed about something. Either way, both of these verses make it abundantly clear that it is important for us to pray!

Almighty Father, I am struck yet again today by the awesome wonder of the fact that You hear me when I pray, and that my prayers can affect Your answer! Thank You for hearing my petitions, thank You for Your faithfulness to respond, and thank You for the gift of prayer—the means by which I can come and talk to You about anything on my heart. In Jesus' name, Amen.

MARCH 12

Then he said, "Take the arrows," and the king took them. Elisha told him, "Strike the ground." He struck it three times and stopped. The man of God was angry with him and said, "You should have struck the ground five or six times; then you would have defeated Aram and completely destroyed it. But now you will defeat it only three times." 2 Kings 13:18-19

This is one of those passages that I find bothersome, probably because I can so easily see myself "failing the test" as well. Elisha tells Jehoash, the king, to shoot his arrows into the ground. He does—three times— and then stops. Elisha becomes angry with him and says, "You should have struck the ground five or six times!"

The issue here, as it so often is with the Lord, is not of semantics and particulars but of a general attitude of obedience. We don't know why Jehoash struck the ground three times and stopped. He may have been waiting for further instruction. He may have thought Elisha's command made no sense (as Naaman did). He may have balked at the idea of shooting his arrows, the weapons of his time, into the ground— rendering them useless. We don't know.

The application for us is to ask ourselves some questions: *Where am I only shooting three of my arrows? Where is my effort only lukewarm, only fifty percent? Where am I afraid to give too much, for fear I won't have enough left? Where am I operating out of a mindset of scarcity and lack rather than abundance in Christ?*

When we face uncertain circumstances in life, our instinct is to clutch what we have even more tightly to our chests. Yet here I am reminded of God's command in Malachi 3:10 for the people to bring "the whole tithe into the storehouse." We are not called to fear and stinginess but to trust and generosity. This is difficult. Praise God that He equips us with enough arrows in our quivers to meet all of our needs. Let's shoot our arrows wisely today, my friend. Amen.

MARCH 13

Therefore, although in Christ I could be bold and order you to do what you ought to do, yet I prefer to appeal to you on the basis of love. Philemon 8-9a

The tiny New Testament book of Philemon is a personal letter that Paul wrote from a Roman prison to his friend Philemon. It's interesting to consider, as we read the New Testament letters, that we are actually reading other people's mail! So why are they included in the Bible? Because "all Scripture is God-breathed and is useful for teaching, rebuking, correcting and training in righteousness, so that the servant of God may be thoroughly equipped for every good work" (2 Tim. 3:16-17). Let's see what we can learn.

The book of Philemon houses many beautiful encouragements and exhortations from Paul in its single chapter containing just twenty-five verses. Our verses for today begin the section of the letter in which Paul is setting forth his request to Philemon to accept Onesimus, a runaway slave who had become a Christian, back into fellowship. Paul reminds Philemon that he (Paul) could certainly "pull rank" and order him to take Onesimus back; however, he is choosing instead to write his request as an appeal.

This is how God approaches us as well—He could certainly force us to do what is right or what He wants for us to do, but He doesn't. Instead, He gently *appeals* to us on the basis of His love, encouraging us to walk in the way that leads to life. In spite of our mistakes, defiance, and negligence, He still allows us free will. Perhaps this is one of the clearest evidences of selfless love: that we allow one another the freedom of choice. Paul knew his friend, and he knew Philemon's heart. He was confident that Philemon would do not only what he had asked, but that he would do "even more" (v. 21).

Father, when You appeal to me to act, empower me to do "even more" than You ask, bringing glory to Your name. In Jesus' name, Amen.

MARCH 14

For though we live in the world, we do not wage war as the world does. The weapons we fight with are not the weapons of the world. On the contrary, they have divine power to demolish strongholds. 2 Corinthians 10:3-4

With what are you doing battle today, Beloved? Is it a brand-new challenge, or an age-old foe? Are you waging war in your own strength, or are you relying on the Lord for direction and provision?

What strongholds are currently affecting your life? In what areas are you finding it difficult to lay aside your own desires and walk in the ways of the Lord? It could be a long-held habit, perhaps the "need" to soothe yourself with a shopping trip or a certain food or a television program. It could be the desire to "zone out" by spending hours playing that video or computer game. Or maybe it takes on the innocuous guise of "managing your family," which may veer precipitously on the edge of "controlling" what seems to be the one thing left you are able to control. Are you hoarding things in fear, or spending too freely? Are you harming yourself with addictive behaviors or hurting someone else in anger? Whatever that stronghold is, Beloved, whatever it looks like, know this for certain: God's eyes can see it. You may successfully hide it from others, and you may even fool yourself. You will not fool the Almighty.

These verses indicate that as soldiers of Christ, we are *expected* to wage war against the strongholds that set themselves up against us. We have no power in and of ourselves, but God equips us with divine weapons that will ensure our victory—namely the Sword of the Spirit, which is the Word of God (Eph. 6:17). No matter what your area of struggle, God's Word speaks to it and provides the Truth that you need to demolish that stronghold in your life! Come to Him and confess it today, Beloved. He longs to meet your needs and empower you as a mighty warrior who gains the victory through Him. Amen!

MARCH 15

A strong wind was blowing and the waters grew rough. When they had rowed about three or four miles, they saw Jesus approaching the boat, walking on the water; and they were frightened. But He said to them, "It is I; don't be afraid." Then they were willing to take Him into the boat, and immediately the boat reached the shore where they were heading. John 6:18-21

How often do we find ourselves in the same "boat" as the disciples here? We're exhausted in every way, we've fought and struggled and are losing the battle, and we're afraid. Then Jesus calls out to us: "I am here. Don't be afraid." Do we trust Him? Or do we just keep rowing? Here's the key point: "They were willing to take Him into the boat." Once they did so, the boat "immediately" reached the shore of the place they'd been struggling so desperately to reach.

What is the lesson here for us? Well, we can row three or four miles against the wind, in a storm, in the dead of night, exhausting ourselves and still despairing of ever getting where we need to be—OR—we can be willing to take Jesus into the boat with us and cease striving on our own. The "arrival" at our intended destination is not as much in terms of full resolution to the problem we may have been facing, but rather the fact that in taking Jesus into the boat with us, the journey itself will undoubtedly become easier.

Sometimes we find that we're not journeying quickly enough for our liking through our sea of pain or discomfort, so we decide to toss Jesus overboard and do things our own way. That's a guaranteed recipe for disaster in our lives, my friend. Let's recommit ourselves today to seeking Jesus' presence in our lives, in our "boat," through *all* circumstances we face—whether it be a placid lake or a mighty squall. When we take Him into our boat, He can calm every storm and bring us safely to our destination. In His mighty and saving name, Amen!

MARCH 16

Yet You, Lord, are our Father. We are the clay, You are the Potter; we are all the work of Your hand. Isaiah 64:8

When I was in college, I took a pottery class as an elective one semester. On my first day, as I stared at the lump of clay that I was supposed to make into a wondrous creation, I felt a decided sense of bewilderment and inadequacy. See, it's the potter's job to figure out what that lump of clay will actually become. The clay has a different job: to submit to the potter's hands.

Looking at that lump (and many subsequent lumps) of clay, I gradually became more adept at figuring out what I wanted. Two lumps became vases, one became a square plate; several became bowls, one was made into a cup, and one turned out as something I'm still not sure what to call, but my grandmother loved it and it sits on her side table holding pens and pencils.

Experienced potters make "throwing pots" look easy. It's not. The clay can be a real challenge. To get it to "stay put" on the wheel, you have to slam it down on there so it will stick. Then, as you start spinning the wheel and working to shape the clay, all kinds of things can happen. If the clay is too hard, it will not submit to molding like you want it to. If the clay is too soft, it folds in on itself and cannot hold its shape. Once I watched a neighbor's little lump of clay just go flying off the wheel, mid-spin. Clay can be temperamental.

Once the clay is finally molded into the shape that you want (or at least resembles something acceptably close to what you had in mind), the process is far from done. You take a long piece of wire and run it underneath the object to detach it from the wheel. Then it has to sit and dry, and then be painted with glaze. The glaze is what thoroughly perplexed me. The jars would say things like "deep cerulean" and "jade green" and "fiery copper," and to tell you the truth the liquid in each one of them looked about like what I'd call "brown." You had to trust that what you were painting onto your creation would turn out the way it was advertised.

After glazing the pottery, it then goes into the kiln, the big oven that bakes it until it is strong and hard and the color sets. This was the most fascinating step of all. First, because the clay has to submit to the incredible heat of the kiln in order to truly become the vessel for which it was intended; and second, because when the pots and bowls and plates and vases come out of that kiln, the glaze has become exactly the rich color that was promised. All "brown" has suddenly come forth as auburn, chrysolite, sapphire, ruby, jade, topaz, and amethyst—beautiful jewel tones that, looking at those pieces sitting on a table awaiting their journey into the kiln, you never would have thought possible.

So it is with our Potter. He knows from the beginning what shape we will take. Some of us are a bit too hard; some of us a bit too soft. He doesn't give up on us. He just keeps shaping us. Then, we receive the glaze and await our time in the kiln. Some of us would prefer to remain our safe brownish shade and just avoid the fires of the kiln entirely. But the Potter knows how much beauty still lies within, if only we will agree to submit to the heat. In we go, and then, to the amazement of all—except the Potter who knew all along—we emerge as beautiful, exquisite vessels, each one crafted by the hands of the Potter, each one unique, each one with purpose, each one the stunning work of His hands. You have been crafted by His hands, Beloved. And you are dearly and fiercely loved by your Creator.

Dear Father, thank You for sculpting me into a beautiful vessel that can be used by You. Help me be willing to submit to Your careful shaping, the timeframe of Your work, and the fires of Your kiln, that I may come forth as a vessel that can be used in Your kingdom to bring honor and glory to Your name. Amen.

MARCH 17

When [Peter, James, and John] heard this, they fell facedown to the ground, terrified. But Jesus came and touched them. "Get up," He said. "Don't be afraid." When they looked up, they saw no one except Jesus. Matthew 17:6-8

When we're looking forward into the future, anxiously fretting about what may or may not happen; when we're looking backward into the past, full of regret, grief, or unforgiveness; when we're looking all around in our present circumstances, worried about all of the situations and people and burdens that are pressing against us and threatening to overtake us, it is no wonder we feel terrified. Yet, if we can remember to direct our gaze *upward* instead of forward, backward, or around us, we will see what truly matters: no one except Jesus.

To what is your gaze drawn today, my friend? Is it an ongoing battle with the demons of your past? Take heart: Your God is healer and restorer of all broken places (Isa. 61:4). Is it an anxious worry for things in the future? Take heart: Your God goes before you to give you the victory (Deut. 9:3), and nothing can separate you from His love (Rom. 8:39). Is it a circumstance that is burdensome in your current daily life? Take heart: When you cast that burden onto His almighty shoulders, He can carry it far better than you could, and He will sustain you in the days to come (Ps. 55:22).

Look upward, my friend. Focus your gaze on our God, seated on His throne. See His Son, Jesus, seated at His right hand. Imagine the angels, worshipping the Holy Trinity. Envision the "great cloud of witnesses" (Heb. 12:1) that have gone on before you, cheering you on. Hear the resounding voices of the heavenlies declaring the wonderful, incomprehensible, never-ending power and might of our God. *Your* God. Look up, my friend. Trust Him. May He speak His love and peace over your heart and mind today. Amen.

MARCH 18

He is before all things, and in Him all things hold together.
Colossians 1:17

I find great comfort in knowing that Christ is *before all things.* He is already in my next breath, in my next hour, in my next day. During the hardest trials of life, sometimes just making it *to* the next minute is an accomplishment that will take immeasurable effort. In those kinds of seasons, my friend, He faithfully meets us in each one of those minutes as we make our way through the day. In Him *all things hold together,* even our fragile selves. Knowing that Christ is "before all things" gives us great hope and dispels fear. Knowing that whatever is to come, He is already in that moment, ready to equip us and to carry us through, gives us a sense of peace, security, and confidence, knowing that we will never be alone, abandoned, or forsaken.

You may remember the *Choose Your Own Adventure* books that featured harrowing exploits that you, the reader, were allowed to control. You would read a page of text and then be given two options: "If the treasure hunter should enter the dungeon, go to page 76! If the treasure hunter should retreat and meet up with a guide for help, go to page 142!" Our lives are like a *Choose Your Own Adventure* book. We get to make these choices for ourselves. The wonderful news, Beloved, is that Christ is there to meet us on every single page.

Almighty Father, thank You for being in every moment of my adventure here on earth. Thank You for Your indwelling Holy Spirit that guides me into Your truth, counsels me, and leads me. Thank You for Your Son, Jesus, who intercedes on my behalf and serves as my Advocate. Thank You for Your lavish love for me, blazing a pathway ahead into all of my tomorrows. And thank You, Father, for Your presence in my life today. In Jesus' name, Amen.

MARCH 19

The Israelites are stubborn, like a stubborn heifer. How then can the Lord pasture them like lambs in a meadow? Hosea 4:16

Not that I really care to draw parallels between myself and those of a bovine nature, but I have to own it when it's obvious: I can be so stubborn about my beliefs, behaviors, and truths! I can almost imagine God having this thought go through His mind: "Allyson is so stubborn, like a stubborn heifer! How then can I pasture her like a lamb in a meadow?" Please don't leave me hanging here... can you envision the Father substituting your name in this as well?

This verse makes me realize that when we behave as sheep, listening to the Shepherd's call, we will be gently tended to and cared for, protected and watched over. When we behave as stubborn cattle, we instead invite the Lord's discipline—which, when we are actively resisting it, may very well prove painful for us.

I also find it interesting that the comparison is between a "stubborn heifer" and "lambs." A heifer is a female cow that has not yet calved. If you have children, I think you would probably agree that parenting softens us a bit. We are brought face to face with our glaring lack and inefficiency to manage these other people entrusted to our care without the constant help and guidance of the Father. This passage specifies a cow that has not yet borne a calf. She'd rather go out and party with her friends and carouse in other pastures than heed the direction of the farmer. But the lambs, now... that's a different story. These are the babies, those fully dependent on the Shepherd for care and safety. They have innate trust in the Shepherd, that His will for them is good, and that even His gentle discipline is for their well-being.

Are you feeling heiferish today, my friend? Let's work on being lambs, open to the Father's leading. He is faithful to bring us into safe pasture. In Jesus' name, Amen.

MARCH 20

See! The winter is past; the rains are over and gone. Flowers appear on the earth; the season of singing has come. Song of Songs 2:11-12a

As we prepare to greet the arrival of spring, I am wondering how many of us still bear the vestiges of winter in our hearts. In winter there is a lot of watching and waiting; there is also a lot of hoping that when spring comes, there will be new growth rather than continued barrenness. But as yet that growth has not come forth, and we find ourselves battling wearying days of ice, snow, sleet, and bitter cold. Winter can sometimes feel unending. And then, just when we least expect it, the days become milder and the crocuses, daffodils, and tulips hear and awaken to the call of the Creator to come forth, to reach upwards to the sun, to bless us all with their beauty. And we are filled with the renewed hope that we, too, can emerge from frozen, barren ground into something beautiful.

In what season of life do you find yourself right now, Dear One? What season are you in, chronologically? What season are you in, internally? We are blessed not to be forced for those two to coincide, although they may. I am in the season of summer in my life, and spring in my soul. For many, many years, I lived in winter. Like the land of Narnia under the spell of the White Witch, I felt as though my life were in a perpetual state of frozen, icy barrenness. There was a lot of waiting and hoping that spring would eventually come—that I would be able to break free of the icy grasp of the condemnation and brokenness and ongoing defeat that enshrouded me. You know what finally brought spring into my life, Friend? I got tired of living in winter. God made seasons for a reason, Beloved, and we are not meant to live in just one of them for all time. Be challenged to grow, be challenged to change, be challenged to hope.

Almighty Father, bring me into new life today in You. Amen.

MARCH 21

...the wise heart will know the proper time and procedure. For there is a proper time and procedure for every matter, though a person may be weighed down by misery. Ecclesiastes 8:5b-6

Being aware of the proper time and procedure for something is not an easy task—particularly when we are feeling "weighed down by misery." In those times especially, we want the fastest track to relief possible. Whatever will numb, dull, or alleviate the pain. This also means that in our haste to find relief, we will most likely not choose the best option. We will opt for a topical anesthetic rather than a bone-deep cure. Having the patience and resilience to wait for the proper time *and procedure* in a circumstance is a trait that only develops through an ongoing and deeply personal relationship with the Lord. Even then, it can be hard.

In what area of your life are you seeking the "proper time and procedure" today? In what area is your misery weighing heavily upon you? Perhaps you are facing a decision that seems to have no clear-cut answer. Perhaps you are struggling with an ongoing issue with your sixth-grade son... or your forty-year-old daughter. Perhaps an unforeseen expense has put a terrible strain on your finances. Perhaps you have received a diagnosis that requires you to make some tough decisions about treatment options. Perhaps you have been putting off a difficult conversation with a friend or relative, dreading the sparks that might fly. Perhaps you are torn between two job offers or two colleges or two investments, and no clear answer seems to be forthcoming. Whatever it is, Beloved, know that God is fully aware of your situation! Continue to seek His will and His wisdom in your difficult circumstance. He will lead you safely forward, even when you cannot see.

Father, thank You for providing guidance and wisdom in my life. I recommit my circumstance to You today, Lord, seeking Your direction. In Jesus' name, Amen.

MARCH 22

I am the Lord your God, who brought you up out of Egypt. Open wide your mouth and I will fill it. Psalm 81:10

Last spring a mother robin built her nest under an overhang above our back patio, and every time I went into the back bedroom I could look out the window and just barely see the heads of the baby robins appearing over the top of the nest. It was fascinating to watch them. There were four babies in the nest, and they would remain still and quiet until their parent arrived to feed them—at which point they would all pop up and open their mouths, swaying gently back and forth, waiting for their food. It was the strangest sight! For the first several days they were blind, and fully dependent on their parents to feed them. The parents' job was no small task either; they took turns flying back and forth constantly in order to keep their little ones fed.

I realized that we, too, are often in a state of blindness. The crucial choice that we have in those moments (or seasons) is how we respond to our blindness. We can either grope around for other things that will temporarily satisfy or distract us, or we can be still, open ourselves, and wait for God to fill us with what we need. The latter will always be the better choice, although there is no doubt that it is often harder. It's okay if we struggle with it. Our Father sees us and knows us intimately. He is aware of our limitations, our areas of blindness, and our areas of weakness. When we are desperate for His constant care, He will provide it. As we gain strength in Him and grow sturdier and more resilient, He also knows the appropriate time to encourage us to stretch our wings and accept increasing responsibility for ourselves. It's a process that takes about two weeks for a baby robin. Fortunately, God is willing to wait a bit longer for His precious children.

Thank You, Father, for Your faithful care and provision in my life. Help me to look to You, rather than the momentary comforts of this world, when I am in need of filling. In Jesus' name, Amen.

MARCH 23

Day after day men came to help David, until he had a great army, like the army of God. 1 Chronicles 12:22

As a child, David was able to kill bears and lions that threatened his father's sheep (1 Sam. 17:34-36), and he managed to slay Goliath with a slingshot and five stones (1 Sam. 17:48-50). Yet as an adult, he was no longer able to defend his "sheep" alone.

It is amazing how resourceful and resilient children are. They can survive devastating, life-altering situations and develop skilled coping methods to aid them in their survival. Yet we tend to have problems as adults when we revert to those same coping skills to help us navigate through a new set of challenges. The methods that worked for us as children tend to hinder us as adults. We have to re-learn how to do battle with the things that threaten us, and oftentimes we'll find ourselves in need of an army.

Can you relate to this today? I can. As a child, I survived some difficult and painful situations, and managed to thrive in spite of them. I'm sure you did, too. It seldom occurs to children to do anything else. Yet as an adult, I have realized time and time again that I can no longer do this by myself. I need help. I love the way this verse states that men just kept coming to David, day after day, willing to help him, until he had a great army. He didn't even have to seek them out! God has graciously placed person after person in my life—the friends and family who have become my "army," the ones I rely on for accountablllty, encouragement, and perspective. Like David, I realize that true victory will only come with full reliance on the Lord for guidance and deliverance—but I do believe God fully intends for us to have some fellow human beings here on earth to aid us in our battles as well.

Thank You, Father, for being the Commander of my army and for sending help when I need it. May I serve others in turn when You direct me to go. In Jesus' name, Amen.

MARCH 24

His disciples asked Him, "Rabbi, who sinned, this man or his parents, that he was born blind?" "Neither this man nor his parents sinned," said Jesus, "but this happened so that the works of God might be displayed in him." John 9:2-3

The disciples' misguided thinking in this verse is a trap we often fall into ourselves if we're not careful. In our finite human minds, we equate God's love with God's blessing. Our faulty math looks something like this: I'm a good person + I do good things = God blesses me with a pain-free life. There is nothing in the Word of God to substantiate this. Here I am reminded of ninth grade geometry class, and the tedious work of doing "proofs." Our beliefs about God need to be tested and proved against His Word. We cannot assume.

These verses from John make this "proof" absolutely clear: Adversity is not God's punishment for our mistakes or missteps. He allows *nothing* to happen in our lives that He cannot redeem. Anything that causes us to struggle can be used to strengthen us. Anything that challenges us can change us for the better. Anything that breaks our heart open allows spaces for His light and healing to infuse the chasm. Anything that causes devastation can also be used for His glory.

We see only our present moment. He sees the rest of our lives, and He already knows how our story ends: We win, Dear One. *We WIN.* Because we are the children of God, redeemed through His Son into everlasting life!

Loving Father, sometimes circumstances happen in my life that knock me to my knees or flatten me to my face. In these times, Lord, I struggle to see You, and I wrestle with questions about Your will and Your character. Help me, Lord, to run straight into Your arms, seeking Your comfort. Help me to turn to Your Word, seeking Your wisdom. Enable my heart to trust and rest in You. In Jesus' name, Amen.

MARCH 25

I Myself will tend My sheep and have them lie down, declares the Sovereign Lord. I will search for the lost and bring back the strays. I will bind up the injured and strengthen the weak, but the sleek and the strong I will destroy. I will shepherd the flock with justice. Ezekiel 34:15-16

Do you have trouble resting? Just sitting down and resting? Letting your mind shift into neutral, being aware of thoughts as they come and go, but not feeling a need to get up and act on them—to go and do and produce and fulfill? How about lying down? Do you ever take time to lie down and rest? It isn't something we do very well, is it? Yet look at the first part of our verses for today: "I will tend My sheep and have them lie down," declares the Lord. The Lord created the whole concept of Sabbath rest because He knew that we would need it. He also realized He would have to *command* His people to observe a day of rest, because otherwise we'd never slow down enough to do so. Sabbath rest is becoming a lost art in our culture, which is to our detriment. He calls us, repeatedly, to come and rest in Him.

God mentions six categories of sheep in the verses above: the lost, the strays, the injured, the weak, the sleek, and the strong. I don't know about you, but I've certainly been in each one of these groups throughout the course of my life. No matter what my condition or infirmity, He has been there—shepherding and guiding. Sometimes parts of me become "the sleek and the strong"—when I become overly preoccupied with my appearance, or with how others perceive me, or when I think myself "strong" in my own power. Those self-enamored parts of ourselves God will seek out and destroy, because they are stumbling blocks in our relationship with Him—cataracts that blind us from seeing His glory, His strength, and His will clearly.

Thank You, Father, for being my Shepherd and for tending to all parts of me so faithfully. In Jesus' name, Amen.

MARCH 26

"I have loved you," says the Lord. "But you ask, 'How have You loved us?'" Malachi 1:2a

This makes me wince. How often do we not take the Lord at His word? How often do we question truths and promises as fundamental as His love for us? Especially for New Testament believers, I have to wonder: When has the cross not been evidence enough of His love for us? The Bible itself is essentially the love story of God and His people. He created us because He wanted to have relationship with us. He did not choose to create puppets, robots, or androids. No, He chose to create living, breathing human beings, gifting them with hearts that could feel and minds that could think—knowing fully in advance that those same hearts and minds could, and would, also turn against Him and begin to doubt, accuse, rebel, betray, and reject. How that must grieve the heart of our Father! And yet, He loves us enough to pursue us.

The Old Testament is the story of God's lost, wandering, rebellious children and His faithful covenant to redeem them and save them. The New Testament opens with the fulfillment of God's promise—the gift of His Son, Jesus, the Word made flesh, dwelling among us. Was the Son welcomed and loved, cherished and adored? No. He encountered the same stubborn hearts and the same betrayals that His Father had experienced with the Israelites. And then we crucified Him. You may be thinking, "*I* didn't crucify Him!" Yes, we did. It was not the nails that held our Savior to that cross, Beloved. It was His love for us, and His willingness to submit to death so that we might be free from the penalty of sin. The next time life gets hard, and you are tempted to ask God how He has loved you, recall the cross, my friend. Maybe you're thinking, "I wasn't worth it." I thought that for a long time too. I finally realized that I wasn't the One who had the final say. Accept and rest in His unfathomable love for you, dear friend. He believes you were worth it.

Thank You, Jesus, for Your ultimate act of love for me. Amen.

MARCH 27

This is what the Lord says: "Cursed is the one who trusts in man, who draws strength from mere flesh and whose heart turns away from the Lord. That person will be like a bush in the wastelands; they will not see prosperity when it comes. They will dwell in the parched places of the desert, in a salt land where no one lives."
Jeremiah 17:5-6

I firmly believe that God created us for community; I believe He fully intends for us to be a brotherhood of believers who encourage and support one another. The problem for us comes when we begin to trust in one another with the kind of trust that belongs only to God. When we begin to trust in other human beings for deliverance, restoration, and fullness, things begin to unravel—and we end up living in a dry and desolate desert, lacking the Living Water that quenches our souls.

As human beings, we will inevitably fall short, make mistakes, and fail one another. If we have erroneously placed our deepest trust and hope in another human being, we will be devastated when that person eventually, unavoidably, lets us down. This happened to me over and over again in my life. For a long time I distrusted the idea of God as Father, since I was estranged from my own—so I put my trust and my hope in other people, thinking they could fill that void. It never happened. And it never will. It took me a long time to learn that lesson, but I am so thankful that I did. I have a deeper and sweeter relationship with the Lord now because of the complete reliance I have placed in Him alone to meet my needs.

Yes, we must love one another, building one another up and seeking true fellowship as the body of believers, rooted in Christ. But our trust for salvation and deliverance must be in God alone, and our hearts must continually seek Him above all else. Do you need to adjust your trust today, Beloved? I'm asking myself the same thing. Let's make sure that we are looking to God to fulfill all of our needs. In Jesus' name, Amen.

MARCH 28

But blessed is the one who trusts in the Lord, whose confidence is in Him. They will be like a tree planted by the water that sends out its roots by the stream. It does not fear when heat comes; its leaves are always green. It has no worries in a year of drought and never fails to bear fruit. Jeremiah 17:7-8

Yesterday we examined the dry, dusty, desolate place in which we will find ourselves if we choose to place our trust in other people to meet our needs and "deliver" us from our trials and tribulations. Today we receive the blessing of seeing how different our lives will become when we choose to place our trust fully in the Lord.

I love trees. I deeply, deeply love trees. Growing up, we had some woods behind our house—and I frequently sought refuge in them, whiling away my time amongst the saplings and the giants. I felt safe and protected in my woods, and even now the woods are my "safe place." When life is spinning out of control, I know I need to find some trees. When we place our trust and confidence in the Lord, we are like trees, planted by the water. Our roots drink deeply of Christ's Living Water; our parched souls find satiety and satisfaction. We are not afraid when (not *if!*) heat and drought come, because His water keeps us fortified and fruitful even amidst the dry and barren seasons of life. And Beloved, we never fail to bear fruit. When we abide in the Lord, when we abide in the Vine, we are fruitful. Not because of our own efforts, but because He is able to produce His good fruit in us—things like love, joy, peace, patience, kindness, goodness, faithfulness, gentleness, and self-control (Gal. 5:22-23).

Perhaps what touches my heart most about this notion of us as trees is found in Ezekiel 47:12b—"Their fruit will serve for food and their leaves for healing." *Healing*, Beloved. When we are rooted in Christ, trusting in the Lord, we bear good fruit that serves for food and healing. I want that in my life. How about you? In Jesus' name, Amen.

MARCH 29

...God disciplines us for our good, in order that we may share in His holiness. No discipline seems pleasant at the time, but pain-ful. Later on, however, it produces a harvest of righteousness and peace for those who have been trained by it. Hebrews 12:10b-11

When was the last time you found yourself in a season of discipline? Were you obedient to the Lord's training in your life, or did you choose to respond in classic Jonah fashion instead? I've done both. Sometimes we lose sight of the fact that God disciplines us *because He loves us* (Prov. 3:12) and because He cares about how we are choosing to live our lives. Paul wrote, "For God did not call us to be impure, but to live a holy life. Therefore, anyone who rejects this instruction does not reject a human being but God" (1 Thess. 4:7-8a). I don't know about you, but I find that thought pretty sobering.

Sometimes we persist in sin because we choose not to see the truth about it in God's Word. Or perhaps God sends us a "Nathan" (see 2 Sam. 12:1-14) to confront us with our sin, and our response is to make excuses for ourselves. Whether the word of conviction comes from Scripture or from a human vessel used by God, if we choose to reject that word, it is not a matter of rejecting *that word*. We are rejecting God. His commands are for *our* benefit. When we lose sight of that, we've lost sight of Him. The result of that distance, left unchecked, can be devastating—to which many books of the Old Testament can attest.

Enter, then, the season of discipline. God intervenes in an effort to draw our attention, our focus, back to Him. He wants us to live lives that honor Him because *He* honors *us*. Sometimes we perceive God's discipline as a "lack of love," when it's really a "lack of enabling." He cares more about our character than our comfort, Beloved. When we agree to be trained by His discipline, we gain "righteousness and peace." I could use both of those in my life today. How about you? Let's accept instruction and walk in obedience to the Lord. Amen.

MARCH 30

How long must I wrestle with my thoughts and day after day have sorrow in my heart? How long will my enemy triumph over me? [...] But I trust in Your unfailing love; my heart rejoices in Your salvation. I will sing the Lord's praise, for He has been good to me. Psalm 13:2, 5-6

At any given point on any given day in the last twenty years, if you had set these three verses in front of me and asked me which one I related to best, I would have said "Verse 2" in a heartbeat.

Not today. Today I am able to fully embrace the truths of verses 5 and 6, knowing, relying upon, and trusting in God's unfailing love to bring me out of my darkness and into His light. I still have periods of darkness, but it is no longer as suffocating. I am no longer sitting in my self-made dungeon of failure and condemnation. I finally realized that I was the one holding the key to get out of that cell. God loves me passionately, but He is not going to force me to do things His way or to live my life in joy and obedience and abundance. He allows me, and you, to make those choices for ourselves. Can we still share the love of Christ with others, even while we battle our own secret shame and wrestle with our own private pain? Yes. But we can do it ever so much more effectively, my friend, when we have allowed God's healing and restoration to begin (and continue) a mighty work in our lives.

Are you still in the dungeon of Verse 2 today? If so, I more than understand. I can remember reading encouraging and truthful words from others who had walked out of their cells, words that should have encouraged me to do the same. They didn't. The pain was too overwhelming, the self-hatred too suffocating, and the thought of ever doing things any differently just seemed impossible. Here's the thing, Dear One: In our own strength, it *is* impossible. But with God, *all things are possible* (Matt. 19:26). Choosing to believe that He can work in and through us without being limited by our limitations is the turning point to a new beginning. May we trust in His love today. Amen.

MARCH 31

Dismiss all anxiety from your minds. Present your needs to God in every form of prayer and in petitions full of gratitude. Then God's own peace, which is beyond all understanding, will stand guard over your hearts and minds in Christ Jesus. Philippians 4:6-7 NAB

This is a verse that's essential to have in your mental Rolodex, memorized and ready for retrieval at a moment's notice. Most translations begin verse 6 with "Do not be anxious" or "Do not worry" or "Have no anxiety." I came upon this translation from the New American Bible in the most bizarre of ways—which confirmed my suspicion that God had placed it directly in front of me because He knew I dearly needed the directives set forth therein. As a logical, methodical rule-follower, sometimes it was difficult for me to tell myself, "Do not be anxious," because I still *felt* anxious. This version gives me the *step-by-step procedure*! Walk through it with me:

1. Dismiss all anxiety from your mind. There is an *action* to which we are called: *Dismiss it!* Tell it to *go!* Order it right on out of there! 2. Present your needs to God through prayer and petitions full of gratitude. Tell God what it is that you most desperately need right now. 3. Then follow it right up with your earnest thanksgiving for all He has already done for you, and assert the faith and belief you have now rekindled in your heart and mind that He *will* come through for you again— and then *expect* that He will!

That's your part. Have you done it? Now look what happens: God's *own peace* will *stand guard* over your heart and mind in Christ Jesus! Can you feel Him there? Can you just picture it? The Lord of all creation is standing guard over your thoughts and your heart! To Him be the glory!

Father, thank You for Your amazing grace and unfailing mercy in my life each day. In Jesus' name, Amen.

APRIL 1

Fools find no pleasure in understanding but delight in airing their own opinions. Proverbs 18:2

Have you ever tried to have a conversation with someone who wasn't listening? No matter how patient your demeanor, no matter how valid your viewpoint, no matter how wise your counsel, this person kept coming back at you with the strangest, most nonsensical arguments imaginable, to the point where you found yourself thinking, *Do they honestly believe this?!* I've been there. And, I might as well confess, I feel certain that sometimes I *am* the one acting foolish and refusing to listen to good reason! At times I get so caught up in needing to be "right" that I hang on to my side of an argument long after I've realized that the other person's side is making some good sense! That, my friend, is just plain foolishness.

To be clear: Sometimes we need to be open to a change of view, and sometimes our solid stance on a belief is non-negotiable. The Spirit provides us with the wisdom needed to distinguish between the two. Today's verse, however, focuses specifically on those who habitually prefer to hear themselves talk rather than take the time to listen to others or learn from them.

Let's not be April fools today, my friend. As you journey through your day, pay close attention to your conversations. Are you seasoning your speech with wisdom and grace? Are you seeking to truly understand what other people are saying, or are you simply preparing your rebuttal as they speak? Are you rushing through conversations with a palpable air of impatience or superiority, or are you taking the time to truly hear the heart and thoughts of another? Let's remember that there is always something more for us to learn, and anyone with whom we come in contact could be a wonderful teacher.

Father, enable me to have a teachable spirit! Amen.

APRIL 2

This day I call the heavens and the earth as witnesses against you that I have set before you life and death, blessings and curses. Now choose life, so that you and your children may live and that you may love the Lord your God, listen to His voice, and hold fast to Him. For the Lord is your life. Deuteronomy 30:19-20a

We can condense this down into one statement: "Now choose life, for the Lord *is* your life." In other words, in everything, choose the Lord. Choose His will, choose His love, choose His heart. Choosing life means submitting to God and His plans for us; choosing death means succumbing to the flesh (also known as self-gratification). Perhaps that is why our fleshly desires and pursuits are so often at complete odds with God's will for us—because the temporal things of this world often draw us down the path toward destruction, whereas God is always calling us back to Himself, into the paths of peace. When we choose "death" (indulging our flesh), we will never be full or satisfied; we'll always be left hungering for more. God promises us that when we choose Him, we will be "filled to the measure of all the fullness of God" (Eph. 3:19)—with the Bread of Life and Living Water that will never leave us hungry or thirsty again.

Choosing life also means choosing obedience. In John 14:21 Jesus says, "Whoever has My commands and keeps them [...] loves Me." Love equals obedience, even when obedience equals sacrifice. Many examples of this can be found in the Bible, but the one that comes to my mind first is of Abraham's willingness to sacrifice Isaac, his only son, to the Lord. God didn't need Isaac's life; He needed Abraham's obedience. And He blessed it beyond all bounds. In what area are you struggling with obedience today, Beloved? In what area are you struggling to choose life, to choose God, over choosing death—the desires of your own flesh? Hold fast to the Lord, my friend, even in the face of trials and temptation. He blesses your obedience, and is always "working in you to make you willing and able to obey Him" (Phil. 2:13 CEV). Amen.

APRIL 3

Saul the son of Kish was taken by lot. But when they sought him, he could not be found. So they inquired again of the Lord, "Is there a man still to come?" and the Lord said, "Behold, he has hidden himself among the baggage." 1 Samuel 10:21b-22 ESV

I know Saul got pretty crazy towards the end and could be given over to violent outbursts and homicidal fits of rage and paranoia (see 1 Sam. 19:9-10; 20:30-34), but this portrait of him at the beginning, before things went downhill, just warms my heart towards him. I know all about being lost and suffocated amongst the baggage of my own life, and I am moved by the fact that Saul willingly sought out the baggage as a refuge. That can be fairly tempting to do when we are feeling over-whelmed and underqualified in a new situation—or in any situation! I think what makes me smile the most about this passage, though, is that when the people inquire of the Lord as to Saul's whereabouts, God doesn't miss a beat: "Oh yes, he's over there... check amongst all the baggage." Even when we are hiding amongst our baggage, God knows *exactly* where we are. I hope this knowledge lightens your heart today, Beloved, as it does mine.

I had a college suitemate who was flawlessly knowledgeable about eve-rything concerning makeup, hair, fashion, etc. This fact mutually dis-mayed us and simultaneously entertained us, since I was woefully defi-cient in knowledge in *any* of those areas. She made no pretense about my total ineptitude when it came to the art of cosmetics, and I will nev-er forget her once looking me over quite dismissively and saying, "Ally-son, you ain't got bags under your eyes; you got a three piece set of luggage." I still laugh when I think about it. I certainly did—and in more ways than one! You may feel like you've got enough baggage to fill a train car, and I can so relate. But take heart today, Dear One—even if you've taken refuge in it, God still sees you and He meets you there to help you carry it. Glory and praise to His almighty name. Amen!

APRIL 4

I have no greater joy than to hear that my children are walking in the truth. 3 John 4

I know how much I resonate with this verse as a parent; how much more so it must resonate with God as He watches His beloved children trying their best to walk in His truth. It also applies to our relationships within the body of Christ: We are all encouraged and edified when we see brothers and sisters walking in the truth, sharing the message of Christ with others through their daily lives, and bringing glory to our amazing God.

Sometimes it may seem as though someone else's achievement in one area translates as our lack. This is not so! God has gifted all of us uniquely and specifically, and each one of us has a purpose that only we can fulfill. Your walk will not look like anyone else's walk, because God specifically designed your walk for *you*! If you've been tempted to walk someone else's path, it's time to get back on track. Not only are you crowding them; you're leaving your own path vacant!

On another note, "walking in the truth" does not mean "never stumbling or falling." All children who are learning to walk spend a lot of time stumbling, wavering, and falling down. Then they get back up and try again, and we continually cheer them on! As adults, we sometimes take one figurative spill, and then refuse to get back up and try again. (We also take literal spills, which should routinely remind us that just because we've mastered a skill doesn't mean we will never falter!) Our faith is like that, too. It requires practice, training, exercise, and testing in order to remain vibrant rather than stagnant. As you continue to walk in God's truth, picture Him smiling and cheering you on: "Keep going, Child! You're doing a great job! I'm so proud of you!"

Thank You, Father, for walking with me each day. Help me to remain in Your love and walk in Your truth. In Jesus' name, Amen.

APRIL 5

My soul is in deep anguish. How long, Lord, how long? Psalm 6:3

We all have our "how long" moments. Usually the "how long" moment comes after a season in which the battle has raged fierce, and we are flagging from exhaustion. Our family experienced this when my husband Kevin, a civil engineer, endured a period of unemployment that lasted for twenty months—and I am a stay-at-home mom. That was a "how long" season for us, especially when every job lead fell through, and the weeks continued to tick by.

I will never forget what it felt like to be so uncertain about things. I didn't know whether we should purchase the small yearbook for my daughter's elementary school, because it cost twenty dollars. I would shower, dress, and eat in the dark because I didn't want to waste electricity by having the light on. I was thrilled to receive nothing but socks for Christmas, because every sock I owned had at least one hole in it. Paying for our children's field trips at school caused me anxiety. And each week I wrote out the check to put in the offering plate at church, wondering how much longer it would be until we had any numbers to enter into the "deposit" column again. When people asked us how we managed, all we could say was that it was clearly God. We were fortunate to have savings that He had blessed us with, and like the loaves and the fish, He just multiplied what we had until it was somehow always enough. It was still a scary time for us, but we knew that the Lord would bring us through it. And He did.

Where are you in your "how long"? Has it just begun, or are you bone-weary from the waiting and exhaustion? I want to encourage you today, my friend. He is watching; He knows the weight of that burden on your shoulders. When the time is right, He will not tarry in removing it.

Father, reassure me of Your presence and faithfulness in my life and strengthen me to withstand the "how long," knowing that You are with me in the waiting. In Jesus' name, Amen.

APRIL 6

He is not here; He has risen, just as He said. Matthew 28:6a

I was born on Easter Sunday. My mom's regular obstetrician was on vacation, and the doctor who attended her at the hospital did not endear himself to her in the least when he insisted on placing a fetal monitor in my scalp. It ended up saving my life, alerting the staff that I was in distress. They used forceps to pull me out of a womb I had evidently not wished to vacate, leaving my cheeks bruised and head smushed. The umbilical cord was wrapped around my neck three times, and I was a ghastly blue color. The nurses whisked me away to try to untangle the cord and pump oxygen into my paralyzed lungs. After several agonizing moments, my mom heard my first sound. I didn't cry. I sneezed—as though to say, "Whew! Just thankful to be here, people! Let me clear this stuff out of my nose and let's get on with life, shall we?" My mom wrote that doctor a thank you note.

I love Easter Sunday, and not because it has anything to do with my birthday. In fact, Easter hasn't fallen on my birthday since, and won't again until 2042. I love Easter because it is the culmination of Christ's purpose, His sacrifice, His triumph, and the fruition of God's amazing plan to bring salvation to His children. We are Easter people, my friend. The joy of Easter should sing within our souls every single day. No matter what circumstances we face here on earth, God has already given us the final verdict: "You win, Child! You will overcome in Christ!"

What area of your life needs a fresh breath of Easter renewal today? In what area of struggle do you need a reminder of Jesus' power to conquer anything that sets itself up against you? As you contemplate the circumstances that feel like a grave to you today, remember that your victory is assured: *He has risen*. He is in heaven, interceding for you, entreating God to work all things for your good.

Father, thank You for the joy of Easter! Amen.

APRIL 7

Now Jesus loved Martha and her sister and Lazarus. So when He heard that Lazarus was sick, He stayed where He was two more days. John 11:5-6

Today we'll explore this story from Jesus' perspective; tomorrow we'll look at it from the sisters' point of view. When Jesus receives word that Lazarus is sick, this is His response: "This sickness will not end in death. No, it is for God's glory so that God's Son may be glorified through it" (v. 4). However, then comes the puzzling part: Jesus pronounces these positive words of encouragement to His disciples, and then stays where He is for two more days. Why?

It isn't because He did not take the news of Lazarus's illness seriously, nor is it due to a mismanagement of time. *He is fully aware that Lazarus will die.* Please hear me on this: The pain we suffer is *never* because Jesus is unaware. Why, then, does He wait? The answer can be found in verse 15, in which Jesus tells the disciples, "for your sake I am glad I was not there, so that you may believe." And not only did the disciples believe after seeing Jesus raise Lazarus from the dead; all of the Jews who had come out to comfort Mary and Martha also witnessed this miracle and believed (v. 45). Sometimes Jesus' tarrying has nothing at all to do with us, and everything to do with a lesson that others need to learn, so that *they* might "see and believe."

One last thing: Even though Jesus knew ahead of time that Lazarus would be raised to life, it did not stop Him from experiencing His own grief when He witnessed the depth of pain that Mary and Martha felt. Our Savior *shares* in our sufferings. Fully aware of how we will overcome in the end, He is still present with us *in* our suffering, grieving right alongside us. To me, that is astounding.

Father, I know that I must choose to set my mind on trusting Your heart, even when I cannot understand Your timing. Enable me to do this through the power of Your Holy Spirit dwelling within me. Amen.

APRIL 8

"Lord," Martha said to Jesus, "if You had been here, my brother would not have died." [...] When Mary reached the place where Jesus was and saw Him, she fell at His feet and said, "Lord, if You had been here, my brother would not have died." John 11:21, 32

Have you experienced a "Where were You, Lord?" moment in your life yet? Have you experienced times in your life in which you searched for the Lord and could not seem to find Him? Times when He seemed aloof, distant, and unwilling to come to your aid? This is the place in which Martha and Mary find themselves in John chapter 11.

Yesterday we saw that when Jesus received the sisters' message, He provided immediate reassurance (v. 4). The only problem was that Mary and Martha weren't there to hear it. Their side of the experience went like this: "We sent for Jesus, knowing and believing that if He came quickly, Lazarus would be saved. Jesus did not come. Lazarus has died, he's been in the tomb for four days, and Jesus has finally shown up. We are disappointed, confused, and grief-stricken. Why did He not just come when we called Him? All of this could have been prevented in the first place!" Yes, that's true. However, could *this* have happened if Jesus had intervened sooner?: "Therefore many of the Jews who had come to visit Mary, and had seen what Jesus did [in the raising of Lazarus from the dead], believed in Him" (v. 45).

This is a hard lesson to accept sometimes, but I do believe that on occasion our seasons of suffering have a lot more to do with how other people are affected in witnessing our experience rather than how it affects us personally. God knows we will be victorious in the end. And He grieves right along with us as we struggle. He may not step in and intervene right when we want Him to, but He is always on time.

Father, when I am in a difficult season, strengthen me and enable me to endure. I know that You are with me! In Jesus' name, Amen.

APRIL 9

Therefore encourage one another and build each other up, just as in fact you are doing. 1 Thessalonians 5:11

A few weeks ago I ran in a 5K race. There were many other runners, and I was mindful of the fact that I needed to focus on running my own race and not allowing myself to be distracted or discouraged by others running past me or around me. I had my earbuds in and music going as I completed the first mile and moved into mile 2. Then, over the music, I heard the voice of a guy on my right, talking to a little girl who was running on his other side: "Way to go; you're doing great! You ran that first mile in seven and a half minutes!" I smiled, and my heart lifted.

We continued on, and as we got through the second mile, we began to encounter some of the 10K runners who were joining us for a short distance before veering off on their own again. The guy started high fiving the 10K runners and saying, "Way to go, guys! Nice job, ladies! Keep it up; you can do it!" Now *this* is the kind of guy you want on your team and by your side! I was blessed just being in his presence.

Running a race is challenging. You're breathing hard, you're focused on the finish line, and you're trying to pace yourself so you don't end up exhausted or nauseated (or both). I'm still learning. But this guy, who was clipping along at a respectable pace, was teaching me a lesson I won't soon forget. He was making the extra effort to encourage others in *their* race, rather than just focusing on his own. He paced himself not so that *he* could finish strong, but so that he had enough breath to speak words of affirmation to other runners!

I thought later on about how we are all "running a race" in life, and many times I'm so focused on my goals that I forget to look around and encourage others along my race route for the day. Will you join me in being mindful of this today, and seeking out opportunities to cheer others on? I guarantee you that it will be worth it. Amen.

APRIL 10

Do not neglect your gift. 1 Timothy 4:14a

Every spring we have a woodpecker that returns to our yard. Or maybe it's a family line that just has an affinity for our home. Either way, this woodpecker arrives every spring—and we are always apprised of his presence by the unmistakable and horrifically loud sound of bird beak boring into metal gutter (or at least trying). And did I mention that this imposition always occurs before 7 a.m.? On a weekend, naturally?

It's as though our bird friend feels compelled to announce his arrival in the grandest fashion possible, thinking we must have dearly missed him during his absence. We have not. Being awakened to the sound of a woodpecker hammering into our tulip poplar would be one thing, but the fact that he tries to drill into our gutters—repeatedly—is beyond vexing. The only way to get rid of him is for me to go outside and startle him into flight by my presence. I am normally a lover of all animals, even the creepy crawly friends that find their way into our home by accident. I gently escort them back outside, wishing them well. However—with this bird, I draw the line.

Is there a vexing woodpecker in your life, my friend? Someone whose presence you find ingratiating and bothersome, mainly because they seem to be so misguided in what they've taken on? I recently realized that my woodpecker friend has a God-given gift in that powerful beak that can bore through wood. The purpose of the gift is to help the bird feed itself. When properly channeled, the gift yields benefits—but when misused, leaves the host under-nourished and with a pounding headache.

What about your own woodpecker friend? If you are able to look past that initial 7 a.m. hammering annoyance, can you see a gift in them that, if properly channeled, could bring about real blessing? I invite you to search for that gift in that person, and call their attention to it. Perhaps they can be encouraged to use the gift accordingly! Amen.

APRIL 11

When Esther's words were reported to Mordecai, he sent back this answer: "Do not think that because you are in the king's house you alone of all the Jews will escape. For if you remain silent at this time, relief and deliverance for the Jews will arise from another place, but you and your father's family will perish. And who knows but that you have come to your royal position for such a time as this?" Esther 4:12-14

Esther, the queen, is in a tight spot indeed. The decree has been issued to annihilate the Jews, and she is the only one with the king's ear. However, the law states that anyone who approaches the king without being summoned must be put to death—the only exception being if the king himself extends the golden scepter to him and spares his life (v. 11). And to heap even more fear upon Esther's heart, she confesses to Mordecai: "But thirty days have passed since I was called to go to the king" (v. 11). Had she lost favor in Xerxes' eyes? Did he no longer find her attractive or desire her company? Would he be so angered by her audacity to appear without his summons that he would allow her to be put to death? Mordecai, her cousin, is not without sympathy for her plight; however, he also makes the valid point that if she *doesn't* go, her death (as well as his) is certain. If she *does* go, perhaps she will succeed, for maybe she has come to her precise position "for such a time as this."

What is your "for such a time as this," Beloved? In what situation do you currently find yourself that could only be explained as the perfect positioning of God? Whose ear do you have? What call is God giving you? Are you afraid to act? Esther was afraid, and yet she took courage in the words of her cousin, the man who had been faithful and steadfast to her, taking her in when she was an orphan. She knew that he would never lead her astray and would remain true to her in any circumstance. Can you think of anyone in your life who plays that role? I can. His name is Jesus. And when He sends us, Beloved, let us go. Amen.

APRIL 12

I am forced to restore what I did not steal. Psalm 69:4b

I'm wondering if you can relate to David's words today. Have you ever been forced to restore something that you did not steal? To make restitution for a loss that was not your fault? To rebuild something you hadn't broken?

This verse sobers me anew every time I come upon it. What comes to mind for me is the sexual abuse I suffered as a child, and how I have been left to restore what was lost through that experience. I know that some of you can relate to this specific struggle. Any kind of abuse or misuse of our person forces us to restore things that we did not steal. We are rebuilding, my friends. We are reconstructing and reconsecrating our earthly temples (1 Cor. 6:19). We didn't do the stealing—of the innocence, the trust, or the security that we deserved—but as adults, we're the ones left to restore what was lost or taken from us. It hurts. It's difficult. It's challenging. Praise God that He works alongside us and *inside* us throughout the process!

As I consider that, I am reminded of these beautiful words from the book of Isaiah: "They will rebuild the ancient ruins and restore the places long devastated" (61:4a). This becomes even more poignant when you consider that the "they" to which the verse is referring are the captives that God sets free. Know anything about ancient ruins? Or places *long devastated*? I sure do. We, the captives set free, get to do the work of restoration. But praise God, we never have to do the work alone! He is always with us.

I know the work is tough, Beloved. I also know you're tougher. And you've got the God of all creation on your side. "I am the Lord, the God of all mankind," He says; "Is anything too hard for Me?" (Jer. 32:27). No, Father, it is not! I believe in the unparalleled power of Your name and in the mighty, saving, limitless strength of Your hands. Amen!

APRIL 13

[Epaphras] is always wrestling in prayer for you, that you may stand firm in all the will of God, mature and fully assured. Colossians 4:12b

When was the last time you found yourself "wrestling in prayer"? For me it was just this morning. I felt like a sumo wrestler, slowly circling a massive opponent that I was trying to pin down to the mat. Usually my "opponent" is a mixture of the deep concern I feel for the person for whom I am praying, the issue itself for which I am praying, and my mind's effort to sort out and cover all of the different components of the request that I need to make sure I address. Prayer is no small task, and it can be exhausting. Yet we are warriors, my friend, and our prayers *matter*—especially those intercessory ones. Revelation 5:8 says that our prayers go up to God as fragrant incense, and sit in golden bowls before Him. Please don't miss this, dear friend: *Not one second we spend in prayer will ever be wasted.*

Paul exhorted the believers to "pray without ceasing" (1 Thess. 5:17 KJV), which simply means that we are to be in constant, running dialogue with God throughout the course of our day. If a thought is big enough to occupy your mental space, it's a big enough concern to lift up to the Lord in prayer. Prayer is our privilege as followers of Christ and, what is even more astounding, prayer *affects* God. He responds to it. Job 22:27a says, "You will pray to Him, and He will hear you." Is anyone but me just overcome today by the thought that the Most High God, the Creator of all the Universe, *hears us*? Not one person or thing on this earth can ever keep you from praying, Beloved—except you.

We may wrestle with it, we may wonder if the answer will ever come, we may feel as though we've said the same thing a thousand times, but God's Word assures us that He hears us, and that if we ask anything according to His will—we know that we will have what we asked of Him (1 John 5:14-15). Amen and amen.

APRIL 14

But now, O Jacob, listen to the Lord who created you. O Israel, the One who formed you says, "Do not be afraid, for I have ransomed you. I have called you by name; you are Mine. When you go through deep waters, I will be with you. When you go through rivers of difficulty, you will not drown. When you walk through the fire of oppression, you will not be burned up; the flames will not consume you. For I am the Lord, your God, the Holy One of Israel, your Savior." Isaiah 43:1-3a NLT

I prefer the New Living Translation's wording of these verses because it specifies that we will go through "deep waters," "rivers of difficulty," and "fires of oppression." Most other versions just have "waters, rivers, and fires." Either way, the message from the Lord is clear: It's not a question of *if* we have to pass through these difficult circumstances in life, but rather of *when*. And whenever that may be, He promises us that though we walk through difficulty, it will not consume or destroy us because He is with us.

I also love the possessiveness with which He stakes His claim over us from the enemy: "I have called you by name; you are Mine." We can rest assured in the deliverance of the One to whom we belong—He is mighty to save (Zeph. 3:17)! In what deep waters, rivers of difficulty, or fires of oppression are you currently finding yourself? Take heart today in the knowledge that the God who saved Jonah and Moses from the waters and the three Hebrew children from the fiery furnace (Dan. 3:16-18, 26-27) is the same God who has pledged His deliverance for you!

Almighty Father, thank You for being my Savior. Thank You for being with me through every trial. I take comfort in the knowledge that You have called me by name as Your very own, and that You will never leave me or forsake me (Deut. 31:8). In Jesus' name, Amen.

APRIL 15

In Him we were also chosen, having been predestined according to the plan of Him who works out everything in conformity with the purpose of His will, in order that we, who were the first to put our hope in Christ, might be for the praise of His glory. And you also were included in Christ when you heard the message of truth, the gospel of your salvation. Ephesians 1:11-13a

My grandfather had a Rubik's Cube that sat on a bookshelf in the den next to his recliner. I was mesmerized by it. As much as I worked at it, twisting and turning, moving and maneuvering, I don't think I ever got all of the colors to line up perfectly on their respective sides. Just when I got one side lined up, I'd turn it over and lo and behold four others would be in disarray. On a much larger scale, it's as though we are God's "Rubik's Cube" of people, and He is continually working to move us, mold us, twist us, and turn us so that we will be equipped to carry out the distinct purposes that He has for us at any given time.

Sometimes, however, we are not feeling inclined to move. We kind of like where we are, right there next to the Green Team, and we become sullen and miffed if God's hands suddenly place us over by the Red Team. The Blue Team is used to being next to the White Team, and isn't at all sure about those folks on the Yellow and Orange Teams. Sure, the cube looks neat and tidy when all of the colors are in their respective groups, but that's not how God meant for us to be. In His eyes, we are most beautiful when all of the colors are intermingling together, sharing their unique gifts and blessings with one another, collectively edifying the Body of Christ.

God is always working out His purposes in each one of us. Perhaps we are simply called to submit to His skillful hands and enjoy the twists, turns, and unexpected blessings of life. Amen!

APRIL 16

Let my teaching fall like rain and my words descend like dew,
like showers on new grass, like abundant rain on tender plants.
Deuteronomy 32:2

We have a longstanding joke in our family that stems from an Easter card my mom got for me one year. It says something like, "Daughter, with you it's like springtime all the time." Of course, the message was meant to be encouraging and uplifting; however, we have had many a laugh over the fact that spring is also accompanied by (and known for) its fair share of sudden cloudbursts, untimely frosts, allergens galore, and tornadic activity. Suddenly the card seemed more fitting than ever! All the more reason for me to take this verse from Deuteronomy to heart—and to pray it over myself as I parent my three children.

Nothing in my life has ever challenged me more than parenthood. As parents it's our job to teach, but sometimes we let teaching fall by the wayside as we give way to demanding, threatening, nagging, bargaining, or punishing. These are all things I try hard to avoid, but as an imperfect parent I certainly have my moments. I need to be aware of not just *what* I teach my children, but *how* I teach it. Am I speaking love but in a frostbitten tone? Am I doling out dinner in a tornadic rush of irritation or fury? Am I asking how their day was and rushing off before hearing their answer? Our children pick up on all of our nonverbal cues and silent messages better than we could ever imagine, a realization that sobers my heart every day.

When I picture a light rainfall, or the dew descending, that has a much different feel to me than a cloudburst or a hurricane. It's so important that we see our children as the new grass and tender plants that are entrusted to our care. Without tenderness and careful attention, we can trample them with our harshness or impatience.

Father, I long to be a good parent to the children You have entrusted to me. Guide me today to lead them in the paths of Your love. Amen.

APRIL 17

The only thing that counts is faith expressing itself through love.
Galatians 5:6b

Lately I've been pondering just how crucial and critical it is that we love one another—openly, abundantly, and freely, holding not one thing back in fear, selfishness, or pettiness of heart. If we do not love, Beloved, Christ came for nothing. If we do not love God, we have no desire to obey Him. We feel no call to love our neighbor. Society falls into chaos. It is only through love that we can be made complete in Christ. As Jesus said to the Pharisees in Matthew 22, "Love the Lord... love your neighbor... all the Law and the Prophets hang on these two commandments" (vv. 37a, 39b-40). Why is love the key? Because "whoever does not love does not know God, because God is love" (1 John 4:8).

The Pharisees were so fixated on keeping the letter of the Law that they completely missed out on the loving! Jesus told them, "You study the Scriptures diligently [...] yet you refuse to come to Me to have life" (John 5:39a, 40). When we have hearts that know God and love God and wish to obey His will for our lives, the keeping of His commandments is not burdensome to us—we naturally align ourselves with God's call and purpose in our lives. Our hearts intuitively focus on the needs and desires and feelings of others, and we long to show them that each of their needs can be fully met in the presence, power, and personhood of Jesus Christ (Phil. 4:19).

In what area of your life are you most in need of God's love today, Beloved? In what specific area are you in need of His touch, His reassurance, His healing, and His grace? What part of you needs to feel and experience His streams of Living Water and His endless mercies flowing into it today? Spend some time just sitting with Him, letting your heart speak to Him, and waiting for His answer in return. He is so delighted by you. Amen.

APRIL 18

But Moses said, "Here I am among six hundred thousand men on foot, and You say, 'I will give them meat to eat for a whole month!' Would they have enough if flocks and herds were slaughtered for them? Would they have enough if all the fish in the sea were caught for them?" The Lord answered Moses, "Is the Lord's arm too short?" Numbers 11:21-23a

I love this exchange between a harried and grouchy Moses and the ever-patient Almighty. I can almost picture Moses railing at the Lord, red-faced, hands waving wildly about. What makes the whole situation almost laughable is that Moses, of all people, should have known from the miracles he had personally seen God perform that providing meat in a desert would be nothing for Him!

However, Moses was fed up and grouchy, tired and spent, and had forgotten the infinite ability and provision of the Lord he served. We are all too quick to do the very same thing ourselves. We come face to face with a time of trial, and instead of remembering what God has done for us in the past and rehearsing the qualities we know to be true of Him, we instead default into harassed, indignant rants about how difficult life is and how ill-equipped we are to manage it.

My favorite part of this exchange is the Lord's response to Moses: *Is My arm too short?* I remind myself of this over and over again when things seem bleak: The Lord's arm is *never* too short to save! Every single time, He backs me up on this. What circumstances in your life seem "out of reach" today? I invite you to rest in the knowledge that your trials are never beyond the reach of God's love, faithfulness, and care.

Almighty Father, I thank You anew today that Your mighty arm is never too short to provide for my needs. In times of stress and frustration, bring these verses to my mind and enable me to trust fully in You and in Your perfect and unfailing provision in all circumstances. In Jesus' name, Amen.

APRIL 19

...but when what is perfect comes, then what is partial will disappear. 1 Corinthians 13:10 GNT

I spent a great portion of my life striving for perfection—I expected it from myself and from everyone else. This kept me mired in a cycle of disappointment, frustration, and defeat. If I played a good ball game but missed a free throw, a ground ball, or served a ball into the net, I narrowed my focus onto that one mistake and berated myself over and over. If I made an A on a paper but not an A+, I reprimanded myself for my lack. When I tried to be a good friend, daughter, wife, and mom but an argument or conflict arose, I beat myself up for my shortcomings. And I was continually disappointed by others when they failed to meet my lofty (and unrealistic) expectations. It was utterly exhausting.

I'm wondering today if you can relate. We call it "being a perfectionist," and to my dismay we tend to wear the label proudly. Why do we feel the need to be perfect, my friend? We were never *meant* to do it perfectly! People are not impressed by those whose lives appear to be perfect (I say *appear*, because that's exactly what it is—a mirage!). People are drawn to others who are real, raw, honest, open, and authentic. I was *terrified* of being any of those things. I was scared to death of anyone ever discovering that my insides were a complete disaster.

I stumbled upon this verse in 1 Corinthians a few years ago. That day, as I read and absorbed the meaning and power of this one verse, my perspective began to change. The Lord graciously allowed me to see and understand that it is only in allowing my imperfections to be seen that Christ can shine His perfect light *through* my brokenness and out into a hurting world. A weight fell off my shoulders that day as I finally realized that perfection is *never* what God has called me to! He calls me to love, He calls me to be real, He calls me to encourage others on this journey. In Christ, the Perfect One, I am made complete! And so are you, Dear Friend. In His mighty and saving name, Amen.

APRIL 20

The kingdom of heaven is like a man who sowed good seed in his field. But while everyone was sleeping, his enemy came and sowed weeds among the wheat, and went away. When the wheat sprouted and formed heads, then the weeds also appeared. The owner's servants came to him and said, "Sir, didn't you sow good seed in your field? Where then did the weeds come from?" "An enemy did this," he replied. The servants asked him, "Do you want us to go and pull them up?" "No," he answered, "because while you are pulling the weeds, you may uproot the wheat with them. Let both grow together until the harvest. At that time I will tell the harvesters: First collect the weeds and tie them in bundles to be burned; then gather the wheat and bring it into my barn." Matthew 13:24b-30

This parable moves me each time I read it. I can relate to it on a global level and also on a personal level. The earth is God's field and we who are in Christ are good seed—and yet, we often find ourselves asking God why so much evil exists within our world. His answer to us is the same as that in the parable: Our enemy has planted weeds in our field. Like the land owner in the parable, our Father also exercises careful and steadfast protection of His "good seed"—the wheat amongst the weeds. And we need to be here! How can a weed know what wheat looks like if it never sees any?

How can you personally relate to Jesus' parable today? What weeds have been sown into your life by the enemy? What briers, thorns, and thistles do you wrestle to uproot from amongst your good seeds—both inwardly and outwardly? God says, "Be patient. Let them be. Allow those weeds to crowd in amongst your seeds. I am watching over your field, Child. When it is time, I will make sure that every thorn, thistle, and brier is pulled out and destroyed, leaving your precious seeds to grow and bloom in safety and security." May we entrust our fields into His capable hands. Amen.

APRIL 21

...a time to kill and a time to heal.... Ecclesiastes 3:3a

There are certain things within ourselves that need to be put to death so that we might live an abundant life in Christ. Paul specifies some of these things in Colossians 3:5: "Put to death, therefore, whatever belongs to your earthly nature: sexual immorality, impurity, lust, evil desires and greed, which is idolatry." He continues on in verses 7 and 8 with these words: "You used to walk in these ways, in the life you once lived. But now you must also rid yourselves of all such things as these: anger, rage, malice, slander, and filthy language from your lips." Note that we are specifically called to put to death whatever sins belong to *our* earthly nature. We all struggle with sin, but not all of us struggle with the same sin. What particular part of your earthly nature is an ongoing area of sin that needs to be put to death today? If none comes to mind, spend some time asking the Lord to reveal an area in you that could use some work. (We all have them!)

For me, a tremendous stronghold was the sin of self-condemnation, which is also known as pride. (I finally came to realize that thinking negative, condemning, hateful things about myself all day long still meant that I was thinking about myself all day long. Ouch.) Proverbs 12:18 (CEV) says, "Sharp words cut like a sword, but words of wisdom heal." The self-talk I struggled with was filled with sharp and reckless words of condemnation, accusation, judgment, and hate. It harmed and killed the inner parts of me; moreover, it was in direct contrast to who God says I am in Christ throughout His Word—the wisdom that could bring healing. God called me to put that sin to death and learn how to speak His truth to myself each day. Whatever your area of struggle may be, God desires for each of us to "kill" these patterns of sin in our lives so that we can continue to "heal" in His truth, the wisdom of His Word.

Father, thank You for loving me exactly as I am—and also loving me enough to challenge me to change. In Jesus' name, Amen.

APRIL 22

The God of peace will soon crush Satan under your feet. Romans 16:20a

Both of my parents were science teachers, so I grew up playing a board game called *The Food Web Game.* (Believe it or not, it is no longer available for purchase.) The premise is exactly what it sounds like: You choose a playing piece (beaver, red squirrel, spruce grouse, snowshoe hare, moose, lynx, or wolf) and you move around the board trying to collect food. I spent hours upon hours playing this game by myself and simultaneously playing for all of the characters. This meant that I found myself in the unique position of both needing to evade predators and needing to hunt prey.

The Bible is clear about our role in the spiritual food web game: Satan "prowls around like a roaring lion looking for someone to devour" (1 Pet. 5:8), and we are the sheep of God's pasture. Are you feeling like the hunted today, my friend? Are you feeling under attack? Spiritual warfare is real (see Eph. 6:12), and as the children of God we *are* being targeted! Satan cannot kill us, but he longs to deceive and discourage us enough that we live our lives in defeat, unable to embrace the freedom and calling which God has made available to us.

I have good news today: The devil may prowl around like a roaring lion, but the Good Shepherd protects His sheep from every threat. Sheep become easy prey when they wander away from their shepherd and the other members of the flock. Let's stick together and encourage one another daily as we stay close to our Shepherd.

One more thing: I went and got the food web game out today to make sure I got the animals named correctly, and here's the first thing I saw written on the inside of the box: "The winner of this game is the first animal to collect enough food to enable it to reach the beginning of all food webs—the SUN." Or, my friend, the Son—who gives and sustains all life. In His amazing name, Amen.

APRIL 23

The whole assembly responded with a loud voice: "You are right! We must do as you say. But there are many people here and it is the rainy season; so we cannot stand outside. Besides, this matter cannot be taken care of in a day or two, because we have sinned greatly in this thing." Ezra 10:12-13

There's nothing like following a sound conviction with a series of lousy excuses. I say that with much humility as one who has been there, repeatedly. Sometimes it's difficult. We can see that we are in error. We can see that we need to walk in a different way. And yet, the excuses come: There are lots of other things I really need to do. It's not the right season for this. This is a huge ordeal; I can't possibly start to sort it out right now because it will take too long. (Any of those sound uncomfortably familiar? Please know my toes are being stepped on, too!) And then, the grand finale: Yes, we're aware that "we have sinned greatly in this thing," yet we can't seem to find the internal fortitude to buckle down and do the work of turning things around. The happy news here is that verses 16 and 17 say that the people did figure out a solution to "this thing" and they had solved it in three months' time. God is so faithful to help us once we decide to act!

In what areas are you making excuses for yourself today? I've asked myself the same question. I'll share one of my answers with you: Sometimes I put off doing certain tasks because I find myself envisioning all of the things that could possibly go wrong. I then become immobile and anxious, when none of my worries are even founded in reality! When I feel the Spirit's nudging, I need to commit to taking action and following through, trusting that the Lord is able to manage any concerns I have or any obstacles that come before me. How about you? Can you identify an area in which you can commit to making one small change today? Once we commit to "taking care of the matter," God will be faithful to equip us for the task! Amen.

APRIL 24

This is what the Lord, the God of Israel, to whom you sent me to present your petition says: "If you stay in this land, I will build you up and not tear you down; I will plant you and not uproot you, for I have relented concerning the disaster I have inflicted on you. Do not be afraid of the king of Babylon, whom you now fear. Do not be afraid of him, declares the Lord, for I am with you and will save you and deliver you from his hands." [...] However, if you say, "We will not stay in this land," and so disobey the Lord your God, and if you say, "No, we will go and live in Egypt, where we will not see war or hear the trumpet or be hungry for bread," [...] then the sword you fear will overtake you there, and the famine you dread will follow you into Egypt, and there you will die. Jeremiah 42:9b-11, 13-14, 16

Sometimes one of the hardest commands to receive from the Lord is this: "Stay put." Whether it's a challenging work situation, a difficult (*not* abusive) relationship, a less than desirable location, or any place where you feel stuck and ineffective—no matter the situation, it can be difficult to stay put and wait on the Lord. In these verses God is basically saying, "I told you to remain here, where I will keep watch over you and keep you safe. If you disobey and choose to leave, the very things you fear about this place will befall you in the next." The remnant of Judah did not believe the Lord, and they left for Egypt where they were later destroyed by—you guessed it—sword and famine (see Jer. 44:12).

God clearly knows what we're thinking, and He tries His best to help us make good decisions for ourselves. Yet sometimes, Beloved, we are just not willing. In what area of your life are you finding it difficult to "stay put" right now? I invite you to take that area of concern to the Lord, and search out His directives to you. Sometimes He calls us to go, and sometimes He calls us to stay. The issue with us, as with the people of Judah, was not so much in the coming or the going, but rather in the *obedience*. Amen.

APRIL 25

David burned with anger against the man and said to Nathan, "As surely as the Lord lives, the man who did this must die! He must pay for that lamb four times over, because he did such a thing and had no pity." Then Nathan said to David, "You are the man!" 2 Samuel 12:5-7a

The extent to which we are able to hide our sin from our own eyes is troubling. We deny, rationalize, minimize, and justify—or we just don't bother to think about it at all. Yet the Lord loves us enough to send us a Nathan. He wants us to be aware of our sin, to confess it and repent of it so that we can have reconciliation with Him.

My "Nathan Moment" occurred many years ago with a friend. When she learned I was harboring intense self-hatred and making choices that harmed my body, she said: "You go to church; what do they call your body, your temple?" "Yes." "Don't put any more graffiti on your temple!" Her words pierced my heart like nothing had before. Through my friend, the Lord opened my eyes to my sin. Never had I considered, until that very moment, that my actions were hurtful and displeasing to God. It was still several years before I repented of that sin and walked away from it entirely, but her words never left me for a second.

Have you ever experienced a "Nathan Moment" in your life? A time when someone else brought you face to face with evidence of your own human weakness and sin? I've had more than one "Nathan Moment" in my life—and although painful, I thank God for those times in which He demonstrates that He loves me enough to send me someone to hold up a looking glass that reflects *His* truth, so that my own distortions are laid bare. Awareness is always the beginning of our healing; let's embrace it with thanksgiving!

Father, thank You for loving me so faithfully. Enable me to accept instruction and welcome conviction when You send it, secure in Your love for me. Amen.

APRIL 26

Look to the Lord and His strength; seek His face always. Remember the wonders He has done, His miracles, and the judgments He pronounced. Psalm 105:4-5

Whenever I find myself in a rough patch, these verses meet me there and help me redirect my focus to where it needs to be. I hope that these reminders will be timely and helpful to you today as well.

First, the reminder that we have to look *up* in order to "look to the Lord." That means we have to stop looking anxiously into the future, stop looking regretfully back to the past, stop looking despairingly around at our current circumstances, and stop looking in the mirror and thinking critical thoughts about that person staring back at us.

Second, the call to rely upon God's strength in the matter, rather than our own. We do not have to face this alone—whatever "this" is! He will help us, but we must "seek His face"—which means that we will have to be intentionally and intently focused on *Him*!

Third, the directive to remember the wonders He has done. We know who He is and all that He has done for us, but we must actively review it, rehearse it, and *remember* it. He has gifted us with memory—the *ability* to recall past trials and His faithfulness through them! We can choose to tap into that power and strength at any moment. When a time of trial arrives, when a time of despair descends, these are the three steps we can take to realign our sight and ourselves with our mighty and faithful God.

Father, I commit each area of disorder and struggle in my life to You today. When circumstances spin out of control, remind my heart to look upward, not outward. When I find my own strength lacking, remind my soul to look to You. When I feel discouraged and afraid, remind my mind to recall Your faithfulness in times past. Amen!

APRIL 27

...you are precious and honored in My sight, and [...] I love you.
Isaiah 43:4a

Every time I read this, I want to cry. I am sure that we all, at some point in our lives, have had the experience of feeling unloved. Unnoticed. Forsaken. Rejected. When is the last time you felt this way? Maybe it was twenty years ago, and the pain of that wound still throbs—or maybe it was just this morning. From whom did you most long to hear these words of love and affirmation?

If the words of our verse today are words that you longed to hear from your parents and never did, I pray that they will fall afresh on you today and stir wonder and gladness in your heart to know that the Creator of the Universe, your Heavenly Father, loves you. If these are words you longed to hear from a spouse, and instead you experienced betrayal, heartache, or divorce, I pray that today you will feel the healing balm of knowing that the Creator of All Things believes you are a precious treasure. If these are words you long to hear from your adult children, and instead you have experienced estrangement, ingratitude, or misdirected anger, I pray today that these words will comfort you in the knowledge that the Lord of All the Earth sees you, cares about your pain, and longs for you to know how valuable you are to Him.

Whoever it is that you long to hear these words from, I join you today in feeling that ache deep within your heart because of that absence. One day you may hear these words from that loved one. But if you do not, take heart, Dear One—because your Father in heaven, your Abba, thinks that you are precious. He honors you. And, perhaps most overwhelming of all, He loves you. And He is not embarrassed to say so.

Father, I thank You today for Your vast, unending, incomprehensible love for me. Thank You for loving me enough to send your Son into the world, so that I might have the gift of salvation through Him. Thank You for loving me so fully and so well every moment of my life. Amen.

APRIL 28

At least there is hope for a tree: If it is cut down, it will sprout again, and its new shoots will not fail. Its roots may grow old in the ground and its stump die in the soil, yet at the scent of water it will bud and put forth shoots like a plant. Job 14:7-9

I am intrigued by anything having to do with trees, and these verses frequently encourage me. It comforts me to know that despite the destruction a tree has suffered and a lack of any visible evidence that the tree still lives, the scent of water can bring it back to life. What kind of water, exactly? Only the Living Water can bring "dead" trees back to life. What better example of this than the one given by the prophet Isaiah?: "A shoot will come up from the stump of Jesse; from his roots a Branch will bear fruit" (11:1). What seemed dead was only dormant, my friend, patiently waiting for the Father's perfect timing.

What in your life is dead or dormant today, Beloved? What part of you has been cut down or left hanging by a ragged thread? Against what frozen tundra are your roots straining to penetrate? Under what kind of sun are your branches reaching forth? What kind of winds are swirling around you, tossing your limbs and challenging your stability? Is your trunk, your core, wounded in its heartwood? Misshapen? Bearing the effects of loss, damage, neglect, or despair? I bring good news today, my friend: When we plant ourselves next to God's Living Water, we need not fear. He will sustain us, shield us from harm, and ensure that we produce good fruit. We may have undergone a severe pruning, but the new shoots that God brings forth will not fail. Our roots will dig down deep into God's rich soil, nourished by His love, faithfulness, grace, and peace. And our fruit will serve as food, and our leaves for healing (see Jer. 17:7-8; Eze. 47:12). Our faithful Gardener will assure that we always have hope in Him.

Father, bring my broken areas to new life in You as the scent of Your Living Water reaches my soul. In Jesus' name, Amen.

APRIL 29

In fact, everyone who wants to live a godly life in Christ Jesus will be persecuted. 2 Timothy 3:12

I'm not quite sure why it still surprises us that we face trials, suffering, and painful circumstances in life. We know that God's Word tells us, in many different places and through many different voices, that trials and suffering will indeed be a fact of life for every believer. James says that trials will increase our perseverance (Jas. 1:2-4). Paul says that God can prove His power through our weakness (2 Cor. 12:9). Peter says that our faith will endure a time of testing, but we will come forth as gold (1 Pet. 1:6-7). Jesus Himself told us to expect times of trial (John 16:33). Why, then, are we still so undone and affronted when Pain comes knocking at our door?

There have been many times when I have readily identified with the words of Job: "Yet if I speak, my pain is not relieved; and if I refrain, it does not go away. Surely, God, You have worn me out" (16:6-7a). Have you ever just felt worn out by God? I've learned that God is usually "wearing me out" only to the extent that I am trying to fix the problem myself rather than taking refuge in Him. When the pain is there to stay for a while, the best option we have is to go to Him, to curl up and rest under the shadow of His wings (Ps. 91:4), and to let Him care for us. Sometimes we just have to sit with our pain. The kind of pain Job was in was one of "those kinds" of pain.

When is the last time you were in that kind of pain, Dear One? I've experienced a season like that recently, and it is tough. We feel heavy-laden and burdened by the oppressive feelings, thoughts, and emotions threatening to tug us down below the surface. When we find ourselves in that place, our work is to call to mind what we know: We know God is able (Dan. 3:17). God is faithful (1 Cor. 10:13). God is love (1 John 4:8). God can work all things for good for those who love Him (Rom. 8:28). *And He will do it* (1 Thess. 5:24)! I pray for a fresh measure of His peace to rest upon your heart, mind, and soul today. Amen.

APRIL 30

Finally, brothers and sisters, whatever is true, whatever is noble, whatever is right, whatever is pure, whatever is lovely, whatever is admirable— if anything is excellent or praiseworthy—think about such things. Philippians 4:8

The power of our thoughts and of our minds is staggering. That God gifts us with minds that possess the capability to think—and to think the complex things that we think—is amazing. Like any gift, we can choose whether to use it for good, for a lesser purpose, or even for evil.

What we believe about ourselves, about others, and about the world around us affects our attitudes. Our attitudes then affect our behaviors. When we receive the Good News of salvation freely offered to us through Jesus Christ, accept that gift for ourselves, and then continue to live our lives in defeat, something is wrong. I say that with much humility, my friend, because I lived in defeat for decades, even after accepting Christ as my Lord and Savior. I could not seem to do it differently! I couldn't seem to think differently or see myself differently or believe that I ever even had any hope of learning to do it differently. And that's where this verse from Philippians meets us today. We *can* do it differently, once we surrender our minds and thoughts to our God.

In college I had a quote (from an unknown author) that ran across my computer screen in resting mode: "Today I can cry because roses have thorns, or I can celebrate that thorns have roses." I spent many a day crying over the fact that roses have thorns, my friend. It has only been in the last few years that I have begun to learn how to see life differently—to celebrate the glorious news that *thorns* have *roses*! It's all in our perspective. It's all in how we choose to frame it. It's all in what we tell ourselves. The key to unlocking joy in our lives is gratitude, Dear One. Gratitude. When we choose to focus on our gain rather than our lack, the amazing and dynamic power of Christ is unleashed in our lives. Try it today. Focus your mind on the good. In Jesus' name, Amen.

MAY 1

And I pray that you, being rooted and established in love, may have power, together with all the Lord's holy people, to grasp how wide and long and high and deep is the love of Christ, and to know this love that surpasses knowledge—that you may be filled to the measure of all the fullness of God. Ephesians 3:17b-19

When we're starving, we'll eat anything. When we're dehydrated, we'll drink anything. When we're desperate, we'll do almost anything. Emptiness in any area of our lives begs for a filling. We often turn to whatever is closest at hand, without much regard for whether it is good and beneficial to our bodies and minds in the long run. We turn to food, beverages, and long-held coping mechanisms, most of them unhealthy and unhelpful. The instinctive need to be filled is such a driving force that we find ourselves swept along, compelled to satiate the emptiness with whatever we can find.

We are called, my friend, to be filled with the fullness of God.

What false substitutes are you filling yourself with today, Beloved? How long will it be until you are hungry again? Only Christ can be our Bread of Life (John 6:35). Only Christ can fill us so that we will never thirst again (John 4:14). Only Christ can fill our souls with hope, faith, love, and peace. Ephesians 1:23 says that Christ "fills everything in every way" (CEB). He fills the holes left by loss, divorce, and estrangement. He fills the fractures and fissures formed by chronic stress, crushing debt, loneliness, or failing health. He fills the emptiness inside of us that prompts our addictions and compulsions. He is the Living Water (John 7:38). Water moves and flows, forming itself into whatever shape or form necessary in order to fill the empty places within a vessel. His love fills us and infuses us with His mighty and holy power; it knows no bounds nor limitations. Won't you seek His filling today, Dear Friend?

Father, please fill my empty places today with the fullness of Your Son— His light, His truth, His peace, and His limitless and saving love. Amen.

MAY 2

The Israelites went out to fight the Benjamites and took up battle positions against them at Gibeah. The Benjamites came out of Gibeah and cut down twenty-two thousand Israelites on the battlefield that day. But the Israelites encouraged one another and again took up their positions where they had stationed themselves the first day. The Israelites went up and wept before the Lord until evening, and they inquired of the Lord. They said, "Shall we go up again to fight against the Benjamites, our fellow Israelites?" The Lord answered, "Go up against them." Judges 20:20-23

This passage teaches such a difficult lesson. The Israelites were torn because they were facing their own brothers, the Benjamite clan, as opponents on the battlefield. They had done everything they could to avoid such a conflict. They attempted to reason with the Benjamites and mediate a solution to the problem (vv. 12-14). When that didn't work, they sought the Lord's counsel, and were told to go to battle (v. 18). The men of the Israelite army had probably grown up hearing of the incredible victories given to Moses and Joshua as they followed God's directives to secure the land of their inheritance. Surely they must have hoped that since they had the Lord's blessing and instruction, the Benjamites would be subdued with few casualties on either side.

Instead, after the first day of battle Israel has lost 22,000 men and is in anguish. What especially touches me in these verses is that the men of Israel "encouraged one another and again took up their positions." I can just picture these warriors, shaken by the casualties of their comrades, encouraging one another on that battlefield, and slowly taking up their positions again. The worst part is that on the second day, the same thing happens: Israel loses 18,000 men (v. 25). "Then all the Israelites, the whole army, went up to Bethel, and there they sat weeping before the Lord" (v. 26a). The men fast until evening, present burnt offerings and fellowship offerings to the Lord, and then inquire of Him again: "Shall we go up again to fight against the Benjamites, our fellow

Israelites, or not?" (v. 28a). The Lord responds, "Go, for tomorrow I will give them into your hands" (v. 28b). As promised, on the third day God gives the Israelites the victory and Benjamin loses 25,100 men (v. 35). Yet it does not end there: "The people grieved for Benjamin, because the Lord had made a gap in the tribes of Israel" (21:15). For these men, "winning" the battle had come with a terrible loss as well.

Today I am reminded that God sometimes calls us to a battle in which He will not give us the immediate victory. It may be a battle that causes us considerable loss and devastation. We may return to Him at the end of each day of fighting, weary and weeping, asking if He's *sure* we need to go out and do it all again the next day. As the Israelites soon learned, the battles that cost us so much to win are the ones that are the hardest to keep fighting—especially when the opponent is your brother.

Are you fighting a battle against your own today, Beloved? Are you facing a member of your own clan on that battlefield, rather than a foreign opponent? The battles we have with those closest to us often inflict the deepest wounds, leave the worst scars, and cause the greatest grief. Our hearts are most vulnerable to those who are closest to them, and deep woundings can occur when we experience conflicts in those relationships. In what ways can you relate? Perhaps there is an area of ongoing friction in your family between certain family members. Perhaps there is estrangement, co-dependency, or abuse. Perhaps there is enabling, rationalizing, or outright denial of a problem.

Like the Israelites, we cannot stand idly by when there is a conflict. We must confront the issue at hand, and if that does not work, we may need to prepare for battle. In all circumstances, we are first called to seek the counsel of the Lord. He alone knows the entire story. He alone knows all the details. If there is a conflict in your life that needs attention, my friend, please take it to Him today. Amen.

MAY 3

And when [Peter and Jesus] climbed into the boat, the wind died down. Then those who were in the boat worshiped Him, saying, "Truly You are the Son of God." Matthew 14:32-33

I initially found it odd that here, halfway through the book of Matthew, the disciples are *just now* worshiping Jesus and saying that He truly is the Son of God. I'm not sure what part of all the other miracles didn't do it for them. They had already witnessed Him heal countless people, cast out demons, calm a furious storm, bring a dead girl back to life, and feed more than five thousand people with five loaves and two fish.

Why was *this* the moment when they worshiped Him and believed that He *"truly"* was the Son of God? Maybe because it's one thing to witness the power of Jesus in the lives of others—but when it's your own life on the line, when it's your own demon, your own physical infirmity, your own hunger, your own death? It becomes *much* more personal, doesn't it? And until you have that moment with Christ, you may not fully realize who He is and what He can do. Even when we know Christ and have witnessed His unparalleled power in our lives, we can still believe afresh—for He is a *living* Savior (1 Tim. 4:10), One who continues to work in us and through us to bring glory to the Father.

In what ways has Jesus met you in your storm and brought peace? In what ways has He brought healing from brokenness, restoration from ruin, and hope from despair? Thank Him for those times! Perhaps today you are feeling as though none of these things has yet come to pass for you. Perhaps you are still searching for Jesus, waiting for His arrival, looking for His deliverance on the horizon. Beloved, He will come—and He will walk on the waves to get to you! Continue hoping in Him.

Father, thank You for Jesus' saving work in my life. I commit and entrust those areas still in need of healing into Your mighty and capable hands. Amen.

By faith Abraham, even though he was too old to have children—and Sarah herself was not able to conceive—was enabled to become a father because he considered Him faithful who had made the promise. Hebrews 11:11

In what area of your life right now are your own limitations threatening to bring discouragement? In what area have you decided that maybe everything is a hopeless mess? Beloved, regardless of what our eyes are seeing as they look around and take everything in, *nothing* is ever hopeless for those who are in Christ—"for we live by faith, not by sight" (2 Cor. 5:7). Abraham received the blessing that was promised to him because he believed that the *One who had made the promise* was faithful! Abraham was called to *believe*. That was his task. Let this sink in: God asked Abraham to *believe* that He *could do* what He said He *would do*. And, my friend, isn't that sometimes the hardest call God places on us? What is He asking you to *believe* that He can do for you?

Abraham was too old, Sarah was barren, yet God promised them offspring more numerous than the stars (Gen. 15:5). And, my friend, *He fulfilled it*. God makes no empty promises. Even when Sarah tried to connive her way into the promise by having Abraham sleep with her maidservant (see Gen. 16:1-4), God firmly held to *His* way of doing things—and in His mercy, He did not punish Abraham and Sarah for their foolish attempts to expedite the process (see Gen. 17:15-21).

Have you ever been tempted to "help" God fulfill a promise you felt He'd made in your life? I have. Beloved, He is Lord of all creation. He does not need your assistance. Or mine. If He has promised it, it *will* come to pass! Let's be patient and hold on to the hope that we have *in Him* who has *made* the promise. You aren't meant to "fix it" or to "make it happen" on your own. You are meant to *believe*, regardless of what you see, entrusting your life and your circumstances into His capable and faithful hands. In the name of Jesus, Amen.

MAY 5

We demolish arguments and every pretension that sets itself up against the knowledge of God, and we take captive every thought to make it obedient to Christ. 2 Corinthians 10:5

Anyone who has ever tried to do this knows that it is no small task. So many thoughts flit through our brains throughout the day, sometimes even within the same moment, that it's difficult to snag each one by the scruff of the neck, examine it carefully, choose whether it's in line with God's truth or if it's a lie we're telling ourselves, and then treat it accordingly. My friend, this kind of constant vigilance feels impossible and exhaustive—because it is. The good news is that as we spend more and more time in God's Word, learning His truths and coming to know His heart, our minds will automatically respond. When an untruth tries to sneak in and lead us astray, we are immediately aware of its presence and can boot it out the door. Our minds are sacred spaces, and as such should be filled with the love and truth of our God.

Another key can be found in Colossians 3:2, where Paul writes: "Set your minds on things above, not on earthly things." We normally go through the day on "default," allowing thoughts to arrive, come in, dwell, and depart whenever they happen to do so. Some of them leave us feeling encouraged and invigorated; some leave us without much change; some leave us feeling discouraged and defeated, judged and harassed. "Setting our minds" is not something that happens by chance. It requires awareness of whether a thought is beneficial, powerful, productive, and in line with what we know is God's truth—or if it's a thought that is of this world, of our flesh, or of our enemy. Fortunately, my friend, we have the mind of Christ (1 Cor. 2:16b), and I firmly believe He expects us to use it! God blesses every moment we spend in His Word, seeking to know Him better.

Father, empower me to take Your truths into my inmost being, that I might have a discerning heart and mind. In Jesus' name, Amen.

MAY 6

From everyone who has been given much, much will be demanded; and from the one who has been entrusted with much, much more will be asked. Luke 12:48b

We often approach this verse from a standpoint of financial gifts and prosperity, which is certainly a valid perspective. Today, however, I'm wondering how it applies to our challenges—the difficulties that life has brought to us, and the struggles that we wrestle with each day. Since the fall of man in the Garden, sin and suffering have been inevitable parts of our human existence. At times we are certainly responsible for bringing about our own suffering and negative consequences, due to poor choices and failure to align our thoughts and actions with God's truth. However, some of our sufferings find us even as we go about living as best as we can in Christ, trying to walk as He would have us walk. When those kinds of trials come, we feel confused because it seems as though we are being "punished."

My friend, what if we could train ourselves to see those kinds of trials differently? If the world contains suffering, it makes sense that part of it would be entrusted to our care. How will we choose to respond to those difficulties? As in the parable of the talents (Matt. 25:14-30), will we bury them in the ground, ignoring their existence and hoping that others will never know they're there? Or will we choose to invest them, to share them, to let others see them, to allow others to see us struggle? People are not drawn to those leading problem-free lives, my friend. People respond to others who bear a few battle scars, who know about hard knocks and trying seasons. What are you doing with the difficult experiences that are part of your life? Are you keeping them hidden, or are you daring to be real with that which has been entrusted to you—allowing it to teach, to witness, and to foster hope?

Father, help me to share my struggles with others, so that we can mutually encourage one another in You. In Jesus' name, Amen.

MAY 7

...for He breaks down gates of bronze and cuts through bars of iron. Psalm 107:16

There are only two places in the Bible where this exact wording is used: here in Psalm 107, and in Isaiah 45:2. Isaiah uses these words in a prophecy concerning Cyrus, the future king of Persia (who had not even been born yet, by the way!), whose heart God would move in order to fulfill the prophecy spoken by Jeremiah (Ezra 1:1). God promises to make Cyrus's paths smooth since Cyrus will be issuing the decree to allow the Jews to return to their homeland.

The context in Psalm 107 is quite different. This psalm contains a litany of different ways in which God's children had forsaken Him and how He stepped in each time and redeemed them. This specific verse refers to God breaking the gates of bronze and bars of iron on the prison doors of those who "sat in darkness and deepest gloom, imprisoned in iron chains of misery," who had "rebelled against the words of God, scorning the counsel of the Most High" (vv. 10-11 NLT). Two totally different contexts, two totally different messages (one specific, the other a generality), and yet the very same promise: "He breaks down gates of bronze and cuts through bars of iron." Whether we're speaking of an individual or a collective group, God's abilities are the same. Whether we're trying to get in from the outside or trying to get out from the inside, God's abilities are the same. Whether we want the gates and bars to be smashed in or whether they've become our false security of self-protection, God's abilities are the same. He can, and will, break down the gates and cut through the bars.

Where are you today, Beloved? Trying to get in, to reach someone you love? Or desperate to get out of a prison that, like Joseph, you didn't deserve to inhabit? Are you in a prison dungeon of your own making, remaining there by choice? Whatever the situation, our mighty God can break down the gates and smash through the iron. He longs for our freedom! In Jesus' mighty name, Amen.

MAY 8

As a mother comforts her child, so will I comfort you. Isaiah 66:13a

When I read this verse I think about my own mom, and also the many other godly women God has graciously placed in my life through the years—women who have all invested their time, energy, prayers, and love in me. I think about the moments I have had with each of them that are the most meaningful to me, the most precious and treasured, and I hold those memories close to my heart in thanksgiving.

For some of you, Mother's Day is a day you'd rather just skip over on the calendar. Some of you had mothers who were neglectful, abusive, self-serving, or unloving. Some of you had mothers who belittled you, ignored you, or abandoned you. The pain still throbs, even years later.

For others of you, Mother's Day carries with it the acute pain of loss. It brings bittersweet memories of a mom who has gone on to be with the Lord, or it intensifies the continual ache of losing a beloved child of your own. For some of you, Mother's Day is a painful slap in the face as you battle infertility and wrestle with the desperate wish to be a mother that is still yet unfulfilled.

No matter what this day holds for you personally, Beloved, I honor whatever is in your heart. We can read this verse from Isaiah with the confident expectation that even the very best moments we have with the wonderful women in our lives, God can outdo. He will comfort us and love us to that degree and beyond. We can come to Him, climb up onto His lap, rest our heads on His chest, feel His strong arms around us, and let ourselves relax—fully trusting in His comfort, His protection, and His unfailing provision for all that we need. I invite you to seek out His comfort and presence today, and to rest in His deep, abiding love for you.

Father, I thank You that You fulfill the role of both Father and Mother in my life. When I am in need of comfort and care, help me turn to You. Amen.

MAY 9

About midnight Paul and Silas were praying and singing hymns to God, and the other prisoners were listening to them. Suddenly there was such a violent earthquake that the foundations of the prison were shaken. At once all the prison doors flew open, and everyone's chains came loose. The jailer woke up, and when he saw the prison doors open, he drew his sword and was about to kill himself because he thought the prisoners had escaped. But Paul shouted, "Don't harm yourself! We are all here!" The jailer called for lights, rushed in and fell trembling before Paul and Silas. He then brought them out and asked, "Sirs, what must I do to be saved?" They replied, "Believe in the Lord Jesus, and you will be saved—you and your household." [...] At that hour of the night the jailer took them and washed their wounds; then imme-diately he and all his household were baptized. Acts 16:25-31, 33

While Paul and Silas didn't do anything that merited being chained and locked away in the first place, God is never without purpose. Had Paul and Silas not been imprisoned, would the other prisoners or the jailer ever have received such a witness? Would the jailer and his entire household ever have been saved? Sometimes it's hard to accept a diffi-cult season in our lives, yet we can never really know how our behavior and thoughts and actions during that time of trial may be affecting oth-ers who are watching us. When we are falsely imprisoned and put through trials, we do have a choice in how we respond to them. Will we choose to curse God? Or sing?

Heavenly Father, when I go through difficult situations help me to re-member that You are never without purpose, and that You can use my difficulties to reach another beloved Child who does not yet know You. Renew my strength in You today, and enable me to persevere through my struggles. Give me the courage and the faith to sing, for my joy and my hope are in You. In Jesus' name, Amen.

MAY 10

Consequently, you are no longer foreigners and strangers, but fellow citizens with God's people and also members of His household, built on the foundation of the apostles and prophets, with Christ Jesus Himself as the chief cornerstone. In Him the whole building is joined together and rises to become a holy temple in the Lord. Ephesians 2:19-21

I am reminded today of Jenga—a game in which the goal is to pull rectangular blocks out of a tower, one by one, while trying not to be the one to make the tower collapse in a heap. As expected, the further along the game goes, the harder and harder it becomes to pull out a piece without threatening the stability of the building.

We are a Jenga-esque tower of our own as the Body of Christ. The foundation of our tower cannot be shaken, since the apostles and prophets have laid their part down in faith and Christ has laid His part down in love. However, our tower of mortal believers can sure take some beatings from the enemy, who delights in working on one piece, then another, trying to bring about the collapse of the whole thing.

It's our job to continue to build each other up as our enemy works to tear us down. We are to encourage, support, love, forgive, and strengthen one another as we journey along. As Satan tries to knock one piece off balance or push another away from the Body of Christ, it is our job as fellow believers to offer a bulwark of protection to the pieces of our Body being threatened. Jude, the brother of Jesus, writes: "But you, dear friends, must build each other up in your most holy faith [and] pray in the power of the Holy Spirit" (20 NLT). As we do our part, God does His as well: "But the Lord is faithful, and He will strengthen you and protect you from the evil one" (2 Thess. 3:3).

Father, thank You for building me into the mighty tower of believers that bears Your name. May I strengthen those around me today and continue to be in prayer for each of my fellow pieces. Amen.

MAY 11

"Bring the whole tithe into the storehouse, that there may be food in My house. Test Me in this," says the Lord Almighty, "and see if I will not throw open the floodgates of heaven and pour out so much blessing that there will not be room enough to store it."
Malachi 3:10

I sometimes think that God would like a better challenge than what we offer Him. Surely He tires of requests such as *Help me find my car keys!* and *I need a good parking spot!* and *Please don't let it rain because I just got my hair done!* Not that we can't come before the Lord with the more "trivial" things of life. As any parent of a teenager will attest, there are some seasons in which you're just thankful your child is talking to you *at all*, and the actual words uttered do not matter quite so much as the fact that the child is, hallelujah, *talking*. God welcomes all of our requests and concerns. However, I also believe that every now and then, He would appreciate a challenge that would enable Him to really show out. Sometimes, though, I think we're a little too afraid to ask.

I view this verse as an invitation: "Bring it to Me. Whatever it is. Trust Me with it first. Hand it all over to Me—every last piece of hurt, worry, concern, fear, indignation, need, or shame—because I can do something with this that you never could have even *imagined*." Please note what our part is in all of this: We have to come to Him and bring it— whatever "it" is in our lives. Whatever it is we're clinging so tightly to, in fear that if we hand over that loved one, if we hand over that long-held shame, if we hand over that wayward child, if we hand over the prognosis for that diagnosis, if we hand over our hurts or our money or our time or our wills... maybe He might require something of us that we don't think we can give. Take heart, Sons and Daughters of the King. His desire is for you to trade in your worn-out, long-held concerns so that He can respond with blessings that will be so abundant that our cups will be filled to overflowing. *That* is the amazing God we serve. Will you bring it to Him today? Amen!

MAY 12

To God belong wisdom and power; counsel and understanding are His. Job 12:13

Do you often find yourself trying to determine the reasons other people do the things they do and say the things they say? If you're like me, this habit is tempting to engage in, but always proves fruitless in the end. We have a hard enough time understanding our own motivations for our actions and words, much less inventing the reasons for someone else's! It's problematic enough in the everyday things of life, but turns into a minefield when we try to apply it to pain we suffered in the past.

For a long time I struggled with the desperate need to understand why a certain person had chosen to abuse me in my childhood; I felt I had to have this answer before I could truly move on and heal from that pain. I wanted to know *why*—the exact reasons they'd made those choices—because in my mind, I couldn't heal from what I couldn't understand. A wonderful Christian counselor was finally able to help me see that even if I had this person sitting in front of me *explaining* why they had made those choices, I *still* would not be able to understand it! Some hurts are just beyond understanding. People could tell us exactly why they did what they did and, my friend, we would STILL be baffled about it! My counselor helped me realize that no matter what this person's answer could have possibly been, the end results for me would have still been the same: I would've felt sad and hurt, and it wouldn't have erased the pain, the loss, or the brokenness I felt inside. And, if I continued to tell myself that I could only heal if this person explained the *why* of it to me, I would be limiting my own healing. Indefinitely. That was a bitter pill for me to swallow, but it released me from a snare. My healing was no longer dependent upon a variable over which I had entirely no control.

Can you relate in some way? If so, I encourage you to bring that burden before the Lord today. He can release you from the desire to know or understand that which we simply cannot. May the truth that *He* knows the answers, and will reveal them in His time, give you peace. Amen.

MAY 13

Love never fails. 1 Corinthians 13:8a

I met my husband Kevin my freshman year of college. I was initially drawn to him because he made me laugh. I find humor to be one of the most important qualities in others, because Life often challenges us with situations that are just not funny. Being friends with someone or married to someone who can still make you laugh even in spite of the life's difficulties is a keeper in my book.

I was slow to commit to the keeping, however. Remember our friend Saul, hiding amongst the baggage? That was me. (Sometimes that's still me.) Back then, that was *definitely* me. And as much as I enjoyed spending time with Kevin and as much, even, as I loved him, I still held so much of myself back because I feared hurting him or being hurt again. It's hard to fully love with only half a heart, a problem to which the nations of Israel and Judah could attest. I pushed him away with all the strength I had (which, he'd tell you, was quite formidable), but Friend, he just refused to *go*. Coming from my past background of abuse and misuse, I was so confused about relationships, about love, about intimacy, about everything. I had been mistreated in the name of love for so long that I really wanted nothing more to do with it.

One late night we were emailing back and forth, and in my frustration and despair I lobbed this one into his lap: "What is love, anyway? From all I know, it just hurts." His response came just moments later. This is what he wrote: "Love is patient, love is kind. It does not envy, it does not boast, it is not proud. It does not dishonor others, it is not self-seeking, it is not easily angered, it keeps no record of wrongs. Love does not delight in evil but rejoices with the truth. It always protects, always trusts, always hopes, always perseveres. Love never fails" (1 Cor. 13:4-8a). He was right. *That*, Dear One, is love. Love comes from God, and God's love is good and perfect in every way. May the full assurance of His vast and tender love for you wash over you today, bringing you fresh encouragement and peace. In Jesus' name, Amen.

MAY 14

But Jesus told them: You are always making yourselves look good, but God sees what is in your heart. The things that most people think are important are worthless as far as God is concerned. Luke 16:15 CEV

We live in a culture that values beauty, pleasure, wealth, and charisma. We are fascinated by celebrities and reality television. We idolize sports figures and pore over magazines providing "insider" gossip about the lives of the rich and famous. The battle against aging is a multi-billion dollar industry, and the cost of maintaining our high standards of living often exceeds our income. What is God thinking as He surveys our glittery, airbrushed lives?

Not everyone falls prey to the dazzle of bright lights and an adoring public. We can just as easily find ourselves succumbing to this trend in other ways—when we name drop at social events for work; when we spend beyond our means for lifestyles we think will impress; when we silently compare our appearance, intelligence, income, or talent with others in the room and decide we come out ahead; when we continually feel the need to let others know how "busy" and "involved" we are. Pride is insidious, my friend. It creeps in even when we think our motivations are pure. We must constantly evaluate our hearts. God looks past all the veneer and the rationalizations we tell ourselves, past the outward expressions of piety and the guises we take on to impress others. His eyes have 20/20 heart vision, my friend. And what our culture tells us is the clearest evidence of success is the surest path to spiritual poverty in the life of a believer. I don't know where this meets you today. I know I am feeling the Spirit's nudging to take an inventory of my heart, to see if I am at peace with what God is seeing in there. Will you join me?

Father, center the eyes of my heart fully on You today as I seek to live a life set apart for Your glory. In Jesus' name, Amen.

MAY 15

Whoever fears the Lord has a secure fortress, and for their children it will be a refuge. Proverbs 14:26

My heart continually overflows with gratitude for the wonderful men and women of faith whom God has placed in my life, people who have served as examples for me of what it means to live a life dedicated to serving God.

My most earnest prayer is that Kevin and I can provide a firm and sure foundation for our children, built upon the saving truth of Jesus Christ— and that that foundation will grow into a strong and secure fortress that can be their refuge during the storms and trials of life. Whenever we go through a trying season with our children, we remind ourselves of this: If we can just show them Jesus, everything else will be alright. If we can be the stepping stone to getting them into God's Word, getting them to church, teaching them how to pray and seek God's guidance... if we can do that, we've done the most important task we have as parents. We've helped show them what faith is. God is able to redeem any other mistakes we make along the way. As always, *He* is the answer to my fears. I need not fear my own inadequacies; I need only to fear the Lord—to view Him as holy and sovereign, infinitely able to work out anything in my life—or in my children's lives.

Sometimes we face the pain of children who have turned away from the faith. They may be living in open rebellion to God's Word, or they may be keeping Him at a distance, unwilling to engage in relationship. If you find yourself in that camp today, Beloved, I pray that these words from Proverbs will bring comfort as you place your faith in the One who is your firm foundation. You have planted the seeds of faith within your children. When they come to the end of themselves and the false things in which they have placed their hope come crashing down around them like a house of cards, you can be certain that the bedrock of God's love will remain, solid and sure, and that He will be standing ready to help them rebuild. Amen.

MAY 16

We work hard with our own hands. When we are cursed, we bless; when we are persecuted, we endure it; when we are slandered, we answer kindly. 1 Corinthians 4:12-13a

Recently I got a bad case of poison ivy. And to tell you the truth, it really hurt my feelings. The physical discomfort was annoying and miserable, but the idea that a plant in my very own yard could attack me with such vengeance, utterly confusing my immune system and throwing things into an uproar—Friend, that just hurt my heart.

I toughed out the spreading rash and maddening itching for about five days, and then I'd had enough. It had started on one knee and one forearm, and by the time I got to the clinic I had it on my torso, legs, arms, and neck. Even my collarbone. I kept thinking it would eventually tire of tormenting my poor body and wear itself out, but apparently it was only gaining momentum. A steroid shot and two prescriptions later, I hoped I would soon be as good as new. But not really, my friend, because now I'm a little bit afraid of my yard. And isn't that the worst part of being burned? Even when the injury heals and the scars begin to fade, we still harbor some fear of being hurt again. We never quite see things in just the same way anymore.

The hardships Paul endured while preaching the Gospel far outstrip my encounter with the unruly weed, but his sentiments have hit home for me as I've wrestled with this experience. We can't stop trusting the yard because of one bad experience with one plant—just like we can't stop trusting people as a whole because of one bad experience with one individual. When sin entered God's perfect creation, things like weeds and pride and greed came along with it. It isn't our job to take ourselves out of the world, Beloved, but to bear up under the trials we face while we are in the world, serving others and showing them the love of Christ. He's bigger than poison ivy. And anything else we might face. Be blessed in His strength today! Amen.

MAY 17

Then your light will break out like the dawn, and your recovery will speedily spring forth. Isaiah 58:8a NASB

This was the verse in my bedtime devotional book last night, and I nearly laughed out loud. Since when has anyone's recovery *speedily sprung forth*?! Obviously those whom Jesus healed personally did enjoy the experience of having their healing "speedily spring forth," but for the rest of us here, it seems like our recovery work operates on more of a long-term time frame. (This is just one instance in which it is painfully clear to me that God's time is not equal to ours [see 2 Pet. 3:8].) My healing has been akin to "slowly trudging through sludge" for the past, oh, twenty years? I don't doubt that He *can* make it "speedily spring forth," but isn't there also much purpose in the slowness and sweetness of the journey, in that time spent with Him? (You may be thinking, "Ain't no sweetness in this journey, Sister." I hear you. Sometimes we have to make it through the bitter in order to get to the sweet—kind of like that Lemonheads candy, you know?)

I will say that on my journey, there have been *moments* of "speedily springing forth." It calls to mind the driving of a tired vehicle, say a lawnmower... and you put the thing in gear and it gives one tremendous leap, but then slows to a crawl. And you wonder if perhaps it would've been much quicker to just walk behind the push mower (or to just trim it all with the scissors, perhaps). And as you sit, and it crawls along, and you despair of ever getting the yard done, suddenly it revs to life again and gives another mighty lurch—and then slows back to a crawl.... (I hope I am not the only one who can relate to this analogy.)

At any rate, I certainly know the joy of an occasional "springing" on the journey; and, my friend, I also know the weariness of the trudging. The wonderful news is that we never trudge alone. God is in the business of healing, restoration, and resurrection, and His work is ongoing and perfect. May today be a day of "springing" for you! Amen.

MAY 18

Though one may be overpowered, two can defend themselves. A cord of three strands is not quickly broken. Ecclesiastes 4:12

This verse reminds me of the schoolyard game, "Red Rover, Red Rover." You line up with a few of your friends, holding hands and making a chain of sorts. One team calls out to the other: "Red Rover, Red Rover, send [somebody's name] right over!" Then [so-and-so] lets go of his or her teammates' hands, comes charging across the gap, and tries to break through the joined hands of two players on the opposite team.

There's a lot of strategy in this game, because the team calling has to choose which opponent seems least able to break through their line, while the person who gets called out has to size up the various bonds between the members of the opposing team and run towards the one he or she deems the weakest and most likely to give way when tested. I can remember instances of friends plowing into a set of hands and doing a flip right on over the top as the bond of those two hands refused to give way. Likewise, there were times when the opposition would just let go before the person even got there, anticipating the impact and deciding to wave the white flag early.

By myself and in my own strength, I am often overwhelmed and easily overcome by the many demands of life. With a friend by my side, I gain strength, perspective, and insight—all things that help me defend myself against attack—but I still run the risk of being overtaken. With a friendship that is founded in Jesus, I become empowered, enabled, and secure. I am not easily overcome. I have one on either side of me, standing shoulder to shoulder, facing my challenges with me. The opposition can try to break through our side all they want, but with Jesus standing there with me, I will be a mighty opponent!

Ask yourself today: *Are all of my relationships founded on and rooted in Jesus, the three-stranded cord?* Amen!

MAY 19

For I have the desire to do what is good, but I cannot carry it out.
Romans 7:18b

This could be my Life Verse. I often become frustrated with myself. I try so hard to walk in love, grace, truth, mercy, kindness, and patience—and then by 7 a.m. I find myself barking orders like a drill sergeant, sighing in irritation, and muttering under my breath as my anger flares and my patience wanes. I feel like crawling back into bed and pulling the covers over my head. Yet another day of wanting to do it all *right*, and instead doing it all *wrong*. This kind of all-or-none thinking is a struggle for me, and if I'm not careful it leads me to a place of shame.

Today it occurred to me that I will *never* wake up and naturally default to the interests of Other above Self; I will *never* default to treating each person I encounter with unfailing love and grace and patience. We live in a world tainted by sin. Our default, *every day*, is to that of Self—the desire to meet our own needs, gratify our own wants, and place our interests above anyone else's. We have to *choose*, each day, to respond in ways that are in direct opposition to our natural default mechanism. What makes us followers of Christ is that we get up every day and do the very best we can *to walk in opposition* to our "default" of Self and desires of the flesh. And that alone, my friend, is cause for celebration!

If we are able to respond in patience, kindness, love, or understanding when someone else grieves us, then that is to be commended! Our Father rejoices in every step we take towards Him, which means we're simultaneously walking *away* from what the world tells us should be our focus. Instead of beating ourselves up for the few missteps we make each day, let's celebrate every instance in which we overcome the power of the flesh within us by the power of His Spirit! We will never do it perfectly, my friend, but we can surely aim to do it consistently!

Father, thank You for Your ongoing work in my life as I walk with You each day. In Jesus' name, Amen.

MAY 20

Then He said to Thomas, "Put your finger here; see My hands.
Reach out your hand and put it into My side. Stop doubting and
believe." Thomas said to Him, "My Lord and my God!" Then
Jesus told him, "Because you have seen Me, you have believed;
blessed are those who have not seen and yet have believed."
John 20:27-29

"Stop doubting and believe." I'm wondering how many of us would admit to a tendency for doubting. The good news is that we are certainly not alone. The Old Testament is filled with stories of faithful people who knew God and still wrestled with doubt (Moses and Gideon, for example), and the New Testament features many of Jesus' disciples having moments of doubt or confusion, even as they walked with Jesus in bodily form (see, for example, Matt. 16:21-23 and John 14:1-11). It is part of our human nature to doubt. The antidote to our doubting is our belief—namely, the firm belief that God is who He says He is, and He will do exactly what He says He will do, regardless of what we can see.

What doubts are you facing today, Dear One? Usually my doubting comes when I know that God *can* do something in my life, but I'm not yet witnessing any evidence of that "something" taking place. I begin to wonder if maybe I misunderstood, or if maybe that was not His plan at all. Beloved, when it comes to the Father's heart for His children, we do not have to doubt! He is not fickle and impatient. He is not waiting for us to have excellent behavior all week or earn twelve stars on our Good Deeds Chart. He is a Father who *longs* to bless us! The difficult part is that some of those gifts—such as patience, perseverance, and wisdom; inner strength, empathy, and compassion—arrive as the byproducts of trials. That's the only way we can learn them and earn them! What we perceive as a difficult season in our lives is His pathway to indescribable gifts and the blessing of a deeper relationship with Him.

Father, I believe! Help every area of my unbelief (Mark 9:24). Amen.

MAY 21

I know your deeds. See, I have placed before you an open door that no one can shut. Revelation 3:8

As someone who values hard work and determined effort, when I work hard and feel that I'm not getting anywhere, it is incredibly discouraging. It occurs to me now that perhaps, on occasion, my striving was unsuccessful because I failed to seek God's direction before staking out my course. I was probably working hard in the wrong direction, valiantly and steadfastly pulling with all my might on the door that God had labeled "Push." It comforts me to know that even if I'm pulling instead of pushing, if I'm lost in the hallway, if I've got myself facing the wrong direction, or if I can't even *see* the door, He will keep that door open for me! Whatever my purpose is, whatever your purpose is, He will see to it that it is fulfilled—provided that we are willing vessels.

That is not to say that we don't have some responsibility in the matter. Matthew 7:7-8 reminds us that we have to ask, seek, and knock before the door will be opened to us. Are you knocking today, Beloved? Or are you just sitting in the hallway staring at the floor in dejection? I've been there. Many times. Fortunately, God does not abandon us there in frustration or assign our work to another pupil who appears to be quicker on the uptake than we are. God has eternity in His hands, and He patiently waits for us to get ourselves back up, dust ourselves off, and seek His guidance and direction again.

I also think it's worth noting that there are certain plans and purposes God has for us that do not depend on our desire or effort, but upon God's mercy (Rom. 9:16). If the task is essential to the unfolding of events on God's unalterable timeline, He will step in and make sure the work is complete.

Father, I long to fulfill Your purposes for me. Please direct my steps, that I might serve you well today. In Jesus' name, Amen.

MAY 22

[Tamar] was wearing an ornate robe, for this was the kind of garment the virgin daughters of the king wore. Tamar put ashes on her head and tore the ornate robe she was wearing. She put her hands on her head and went away, weeping aloud as she went. Her brother Absalom said to her, "Has that Amnon, your brother, been with you? Be quiet now, my sister; he is your brother. Don't take this thing to heart." And Tamar lived in her brother Absalom's house, a desolate woman. When King David heard all this, he was furious. 2 Samuel 13:18b-21

God's Word speaks to every kind of trial His people face, and the rape of Tamar by her half-brother Amnon shines the spotlight on the effects of violence and dysfunction within a family. Although he advised his sister Tamar not to "take this thing to heart," Absalom himself took this thing fully to heart, as is evidenced by his calculated plan to have Amnon killed (vv. 28-29), and his later conspiracy to overthrow his father David from the throne—a mission which ended in Absalom's death. Of all the parties involved in this devastation, it is David's reaction that causes me the most pain. He is "furious," yet remains safely removed from the situation—a father who cannot or will not discipline his children or have compassion on a daughter who has been left desolate and devastated. David may have been a mighty warrior and a mighty king, but he was a lousy father. Tamar suffered the double wounding of Amnon's violent act against her, and then her father's stark impassiveness in response. Perhaps, my friend, you can relate.

How do we heal when those who should have protected us abdicated their position? We go to our heavenly Father. Like Tamar, we are sons and daughters of the King. And our heavenly Father will never fail to meet us in our time of devastation; He will never fail to surround us with His love and compassion as He holds us close. May His comfort be with you today, Beloved Child, in any area of pain you are carrying. In Jesus' name, Amen.

MAY 23

When the servant of the man of God got up and went out early the next morning, an army with horses and chariots had surrounded the city. "Oh no, my lord! What shall we do?" the servant asked. "Don't be afraid," the prophet answered. "Those who are with us are more than those who are with them." And Elisha prayed, "Open his eyes, Lord, so that he may see." Then the Lord opened the servant's eyes, and he looked and saw the hills full of horses and chariots of fire all around Elisha. 2 Kings 6:15-17

This passage always gives me goosebumps. I find it so intriguing that there are things out there in our world that are part of the unseen realm, and that God keeps our eyes veiled from seeing them. At any moment, who can say what kind of defenses God has marshalled around us to protect us from harm? This passage also brings to mind the words of Psalm 20:7: "Some trust in chariots and some in horses, but we trust in the name of the Lord our God." The enemies of the Lord trusted in those chariots and horses that they had used to surround the city. Elisha trusted in the name of the Lord his God, for he knew that God's power and might would defeat any foe, win any battle, and place a shield of protection around His chosen ones. Whatever the "chariots" and "horses" may be in our own lives, we would do well to remove our reliance on them and place it fully in the name of our mighty and omnipotent God.

Where does this meet you today? What are the chariots and horses in your life in which you tend to place your trust? Is there a situation in your life where you're feeling surrounded and trapped? Are you looking around and seeing nothing but a vast army set against you? Take Elisha's words to heart today, Beloved: "Those who are with us are more than those who are with them." God's armies are present and powerful, surrounding us with shields of His protection. I pray that you would feel their presence with you in a special way today. Amen.

MAY 24

"Don't call me Naomi," she told them. "Call me Mara, because the Almighty has made my life very bitter. I went away full, but the Lord has brought me back empty. Why call me Naomi? The Lord has afflicted me; the Almighty has brought misfortune upon me." Ruth 1:20-21

Have you ever thought about changing your name? After many tedious years of having my first name routinely misspelled, I did have some moments of feeling as though a change might be in order. Nothing, though, like Naomi. Whereas my consideration was prompted by the aggravation of repeated misspellings, Naomi desired to change her name because she wanted to rename her entire existence—going from Naomi, which means *pleasant*, to Mara, which means *bitter*. Just think about that for a moment: Can you imagine renaming yourself *Bitter*?

Naomi's sorrow and grief over the loss of her husband and sons is understandable. And yet, her sorrow consumed her entire existence. And when sorrow consumes so much of us that we lose sight of any good in our lives, that sorrow turns rancid. It becomes bitter. Bitterness moves past grief and turns the corner into resentment. Note that Naomi's focus is solely on what God has "done to her" rather than how He has blessed her. We see a similar instance in the book of Job, when Job's own wife advises him: "Curse God and die!" (2:9b). He replies, "You are talking like a foolish woman. Shall we accept good from God, and not trouble?" (2:10a). Even in our pain, God is still good.

Grief and sorrow are part of our human condition, and I am certainly not advocating that we stuff those feelings or ignore their presence. However, even in the midst of loss and pain, we do have a choice about where we allow our thoughts to rest. We can choose to keep our focus on the loss, which will lead to brokenness, or we can choose gratitude for the gift of having loved, which will lead to blessing. Let's choose wisely, my friend, and trust in Him to carry us through. Amen.

MAY 25

For physical training is of some value, but godliness has value for all things, holding promise for both the present life and the life to come. 1 Timothy 4:8

I can border on the edge of fanatic when it comes to my exercise regimen. I have a propensity to take things to excess, and my daily workout is no exception. If something comes up and I miss my morning workout, my day unfolds with me feeling out of sorts and grouchy because I have had my routine interrupted. As I read this verse from 1 Timothy, I've had to ask myself whether I take my spiritual training just as seriously. Am I out of balance in my day if I miss my morning quiet time with God and His Word? If I'm more upset about missing my workout than about missing my time with the Lord, something is not right.

I also find that at times I become preoccupied with my outward appearance—most notably during seasons in which I am trying so hard to "control" my outer self since my inner self (my thoughts, my heart) is in such disarray. It's during those times that I tend to be more compulsive about my workouts, more compulsive about what I eat, and more compulsive about how I look. This is not the answer. When the inner self is in disarray, the answer is *prayer*.

When Nathan confronted David about his sin with Bathsheba, David wrote these words: "Create in me a pure heart, O God, and renew a steadfast spirit within me" (Ps. 51:10). No amount of outward polishing is going to make our insides clean. God is the One who cleanses and purifies our hearts. God is the One who realigns our thoughts. God is the One who revitalizes our spirits. No part of us is beyond His healing power. What parts of your mind, heart, and spirit are in need of a fresh touch from the Lord today, Beloved? Please don't hesitate to bring those areas before Him.

Father, please touch my inner parts with Your mighty hands—purifying, renewing, and healing. Amen.

MAY 26

Whatever you do, work at it with all your heart. Colossians 3:23a

This verse is often interpreted to simply mean your work, your liveli-hood. In reality, everything we *do* encompasses far more than just our job. We all have many different roles within our families, churches, and society; we *do* a lot. Sometimes I think it's beneficial for us to take a step back and inventory that long list of things that we do, and evaluate whether we have a good balance in our lives. Do you "do" so much that you can only do each thing haphazardly or halfheartedly? Are you feel-ing overworked and overwhelmed? If so, that's a red flag that it's time to sit down and take an honest inventory of your time and how you are choosing to invest it.

God equips us to carry out the tasks that He has for us, but when we try to go off on our own and undertake more than what He has planned and chosen for us, we find ourselves fatigued and spent, cranky and put-upon. (These are not flattering characteristics, my friend.) Are you doing too much? Are you doing certain things for others that the Lord is calling them to do for themselves? If so, you are making yourself a stumbling block to that other person. Even if it's your spouse. Or your child. Or your very best friend. Yes, you love them! But God also has a unique calling on *their* lives that requires a certain amount of "doing" on their part as well.

Today's verse also reminds us that when we go through a season in which we aren't necessarily happy with our relationships, our work, or our circumstances, we are still called to *work at them* with all our heart. If you're struggling with your boss or a co-worker, or feel at constant odds with your spouse or another family member, take heart—any work you do out of love and obedience to God will never be in vain.

Father, equip me to discern the tasks You have prepared for me today, and enable me to work at them with all of my heart, dedicating each one to You. In Jesus' name, Amen.

MAY 27

Watch out for false prophets. They come to you in sheep's cloth-ing, but inwardly they are ferocious wolves. Matthew 7:15

My grandmother once had the decidedly unfortunate experience of finding herself confined in the small elevator at our local library with a person dressed up as SpongeBob. She was fit to be tied over the entire encounter, neither knowing who the masquerader was supposed to be ("Looked like a kitchen sponge but with pants on, and just *terrible* buck teeth!"), nor being able to understand his presence there in the first place. But what really did her in was when this costumed individual had the nerve to try to speak to her in the elevator. She was completely undone. ("I didn't even answer him back! The very idea!") Of course, *we* all found the story hysterical, and she now has a special SpongeBob notepad on her refrigerator door to commemorate the occasion—a gift from her loving grandchildren—which, of course, she refuses to use.

The lesson for us today is this: Sometimes we encounter a wolf, and it looks like a wolf. And sometimes it looks deceptively like one of us—just one more sheep in the pasture or in the pen, eating right alongside us and striking up a conversation. My grandmother knew this spongy individual next to her in the elevator was an impostor. He just looked out of place. She knew better than to trust a word he said. But how many times, my friend, are we taken in by those whose disguises are much more elaborate and finessed? How can we know when we are in the presence of a wolf who is trying to lead us astray? Jesus tells us in the very next verse: "By their fruit you will recognize them" (v. 16). The fruit reveals what's in the root. If the roots are good, the fruit will be good. This is always the best litmus test we have when it comes to dis-cerning the motives behind the words and actions of others.

Father, I ask for Your guidance and discernment as I go through my day today. Keep me in Your protection and in Your perfect peace. In Jesus' name, Amen.

MAY 28

In the desert they gave in to their craving; in the wilderness they put God to the test. Psalm 106:14

When we have those stints in the desert, destruction can come upon us quickly. It's when we feel isolated, desolate, forgotten, and despairing that we're most likely to fall back into those old, destructive habits—whatever our particular "craving" may be. When we make the choice to satisfy our cravings instead of looking to God for help, we do put Him to the test. (If you ask the Israelites, this is something that doesn't ever seem to end well.)

God allows us to experience some desert wanderings and some seasons in the wilderness because those are the times in which we come to the end of ourselves and realize our utter dependence on Him. We reach the bottom of the pit of our despair, isolation, and misery; we give in to the cravings of our flesh, the temptations that we find ourselves too weak to resist; we find ourselves in the midst of hollowness, sin, and shame. And it is in that place, Beloved, that God meets us. He does not wait until we clean ourselves up and get to church on Sunday, my friend. No, He comes to us in the desert places; He meets us in the wastelands of our shame, brokenness, defeat, and sin.

Are you in the wasteland today, Dear One? Have you come to the end of yourself? Have you given in to the craving and the desires of the flesh? Is your head bowed in shame; are you feeling the weight of despair? When I am in that desert place, I tend to want to stay there. But our God is not willing to leave us to die in the wasteland. He seeks us out and searches for us, inviting us back into fellowship with Him. No matter how long we've been there or how barren it seems, He assures us that He is "making a way in the wilderness and streams in the wasteland" (Isa. 43:19b). He will stop at nothing to get to you. He will meet you in your desert, Beloved, and He will bring the Living Water to you there. May He restore to you an oasis of hope. In Jesus' name, Amen!

MAY 29

The secret things belong to the Lord our God, but the things re-
vealed belong to us and to our children forever, that we may fol-
low all the words of this law. Deuteronomy 29:29

One thing I cherish about God is that He is vastly beyond our understanding. We could study His Word every moment of our lives and still
reach heaven not knowing some of His mysteries. He graciously shares
some of His wisdom and revelation with us—gifts He entrusts to our
care. And then there are the "secret things" that belong only to Him,
such as the hour of Christ's return (Mark 13:32).

Perhaps one of the most wondrous parts of studying God's Word is a
moment when He provides a fresh revelation, a new insight, or a word
that speaks directly to our hearts and becomes our treasure. Sometimes that revelation comes to us through the help of another's explanation, such as the Jews experienced when the Book of the Law was
read and explained to them by the Levites and Ezra the priest in Nehemiah 8:5-12. Likewise, we witness the joy of the Ethiopian eunuch who
has the words of the prophet Isaiah explained to him by Philip the apos-
tle in Acts 8:26-39.

Sometimes, however, it is God Himself who aids us. Titus 1:3 states that
at His appointed season, God brings His Word to light. This means we
can read God's Word over and over again, and each time God can provide new insight! It isn't just that we've missed the obvious during the
first three readings of a passage; it's that He brings a specific word to
light for us at just the right point in time for our lives and our circumstances—just when He knows we need it most. This phenomenon reminds me of those "Magic Eye" pictures, where you have to train your
eyes to look past the surface-level jumble and *into* the picture itself to
see the "true" image hidden within. God can equip our eyes to see
things hidden within the depths of His Word! How does this knowledge
about our God bring you renewed joy and wonder today? Amen.

MAY 30

For you have been called to live in freedom, my brothers and sisters. But don't use your freedom to satisfy your sinful nature. Instead, use your freedom to serve one another in love. Galatians 5:13 NLT

I have an anniversary of abstention from an area of addiction in my life that used to give me fits every single year when it rolled around. Although I wanted to spend the day filled with thanksgiving for God's deliverance and strength, I just couldn't seem to get there. While I was grateful to God for the freedom He had given me from my sin, I still occasionally struggled with the finality of its absence in my life. If you've ever given up a habit that you once thought you could never live without, I imagine you know exactly what I mean.

One particular year as the date neared, I was standing in the shower one night, thinking about how I could so easily go back to it again. No one but God would ever know, and He'd forgive me for my broken promise. At the very moment I had that thought, the bar of soap I'd been holding slipped out of my hand and hit the bottom of the shower, a big chunk breaking off one end. I heard God clearly saying to my heart: "That's true, Child, I would forgive you. But your promise to Me would still be broken." Later that night I sat down to read Tessa's nightly devotional with her, and this very Scripture was the one that was given. Needless to say, it hit its mark. This is exactly what I was trying to do—use my freedom and forgiveness in Christ to justify an act of calculated disobedience. This, my friend, is a steep cliff to dance upon.

Having forgiveness through Christ is not a "free pass" to indulge in sin and then play the forgiveness card. Christ suffered on the cross of Calvary for *our sin*, and I sure don't want to be glib about adding one more offense to my pile. Can you relate in any way today?

Father, thank You for the matchless gift of freedom in Christ. Please strengthen me to abide in You when I feel tempted to sin. Amen.

MAY 31

But the people refused to listen to Samuel. "No!" they said. "We want a king over us. Then we will be like all the other nations, with a king to lead us and to go out before us and fight our battles." 1 Samuel 8:19-20

When you have the Divine Warrior on your side, why on earth do you need a king to lead you? Why would you demand a flesh and blood mortal, limited by the same feelings of insecurity, fear, doubt, and temptation that plague all the rest of us? The answer can be found in Israel's demand: We want to be *like all the other nations.*

That was the problem—the motivation behind it all. God was not opposed to His people being ruled by an earthly king. Samuel, after all, would eventually be sent to anoint David as king over Israel. The problem with this particular request was the faulty reasoning behind it—Israel's desire to fit in, to assimilate, to look like all the other nations around them. It's so easy to fall into that trap, isn't it? We often look around and see what others have, and we find ourselves thinking, "I wish I had that, too." Again, the problem is not in the wishing itself; the problem is in the motivation behind the wishes.

It nearly breaks my heart to hear the people of Israel say, *We want a king to lead us and go out before us and fight our battles.* I cannot even imagine how that pierced the heart of God. He was offering them Himself—the Almighty, Omnipotent God—to be the leader of their army, to equip them in their battles, to lead them into victory (see Deut. 20:1-4)! And they turned their backs on Him, petulantly insisting that they have someone they (and others) could *see.* If we are not careful, we do the same thing still today.

Are you relying on someone else to fight your battles for you, Dear One? Or are you relying on the Lord to clear the way before you? I know which one I want as my King. We're meant to stand out and be different. We are the people of God! Amen.

JUNE 1

Praise be to the God and Father of our Lord Jesus Christ, the Father of compassion and the God of all comfort, who comforts us in all our troubles, so that we can comfort those in any trouble with the comfort we ourselves receive from God. 2 Corinthians 1:3-4

God does not "need" for us to suffer in order to teach us something. Suffering occurs in our lives because we live in a fallen world. I think we sometimes get those two things backwards in our minds. Because God is who He is, He's able to use the troubles we experience for good. In our pain, God comforts us. And in His mercy, He allows us to use that blessing of comfort to bless another Child in His name, to His glory.

What if we're finding it decidedly difficult (if not impossible, at the moment) to find this silver lining in our current time of trial? What if we find ourselves railing at God and accusing Him of not loving us? What if we can't feel His presence and we can't understand His reasons? God created us with a range of emotions and feelings that are not meant to be hidden or stuffed. He welcomes our questions, though He owes us no explanations. He welcomes our anger. He welcomes our grief, fears, and brokenness. He's stronger than whatever is hurting you, Beloved.

When you walk through a time of trial, by all means, walk that path with God. But along the way, seek out others who have gone on before you and weathered similar circumstances. And then get ready to pass it on. That's the crux of this 2 Corinthians notion—we can extend comfort and empathy to others who are suffering because we ourselves have received comfort from God in our own trials. Our pain is not always about us, Beloved. But we are oftentimes tempted to make it so. There will someday be someone who will need your example, your wisdom, and your encouragement as they navigate a trial you have already overcome—and that is His gift to us. In His hands, no pain is ever wasted; He can bring forth blessing from any area of brokenness. Amen!

JUNE 2

And you, Solomon my son, know the God of your father and serve Him with a whole heart and with a willing mind, for the Lord searches all hearts and understands every plan and thought. 1 Chronicles 28:9a ESV

I find it so interesting that David included the directive to Solomon to serve God "with a willing mind." Solomon would become widely known and revered for his wisdom, which would seem to indicate that his mind was indeed well-trained. But a *well-trained* mind isn't always synonymous with a *willing* mind. In fact, sometimes intelligence can be a hindrance—there can be too much analyzing, too much over-thinking, and too much hair-splitting. There is also the danger of placing too much stock in our own intellect, in our own ability to understand things and reason through them. Sometimes with a sharp mind we can find ourselves lacking in a willingness to be taught.

The truth of the matter is that God is the only One with perfect and infinite wisdom and understanding. We must always look to Him for guidance in every area of our lives, rather than relying on our own understanding (Prov. 3:5). A *willing* mind is a teachable mind, a mind that acknowledges God's truth as supreme over anything that man might conceive. A willing mind is humble, open to the Holy Spirit's conviction, redirection, and leading.

Is your mind willing and open to God's teaching today, my friend? Or are you sensing some resistance and rebellion that are characteristics of an unwilling mind? I imagine that, like me, you've probably experienced some of both. Today let's make a conscious effort to surrender our minds to Him, open to receiving His teaching.

Dear Father, enable me to serve You with wholehearted devotion and a willing mind, that I might have a teachable spirit and be used in a way that brings glory to Your name. Amen.

JUNE 3

What you say flows from what is in your heart. Luke 6:45b NLT

Our words have a lot to say about the state of our hearts, don't they? Ideally I would love for my speech to always be seasoned with grace, full of love, and useful for encouraging others and building them up in the body of Christ—all things that God calls us to aspire toward as we journey along together (see Col. 4:6; 1 Thess. 5:11). Unfortunately, I often find myself saying things that are decidedly *not* edifying or helpful. We all have our different areas of struggle: complaining, gossiping, using offensive language, persistent negativity, ridiculing, condescension. None of these is fitting for children of the King.

When I was younger I used to get in trouble for saying one word: *"So?"* My mother staunchly stood by the explanation that it wasn't the word so much as the *tone* that was the problem. I'm wondering if sometimes we become a little tone deaf to hearing our own speech. Are we being mindful of how we're coming across to others—in words *and* tone? As a parent myself now, I can easily identify times of trespass with my children when the issue is most certainly the tone and not the words!

We can still fall into this trap as adults: We speak harshly or impatiently; we use a tone of derision or scorn. Flattery is equally hurtful, when we mouth empty platitudes while concealing our true feelings and thoughts behind a veneer of benevolence. These are the kinds of insidious sins that creep into our habits so stealthily. We must take the time to really *listen* to what we're saying (and how we're saying it), so that we can hold ourselves accountable. I often rehearse and pray the words of Psalm 81:10b: "Open wide your mouth and I will fill it." If we seek to be a conduit of God's words, and seek to have a heart like His, our mouths will naturally begin to fall into line and profess words of edification, encouragement, affirmation, and love.

Father, help me to be mindful of my words and heart today as I interact with others. May I use my words to build others up in You. Amen.

JUNE 4

Take possession of the land and settle in it, for I have given you the land to possess. [...] But if you do not drive out the inhabitants of the land, those you allow to remain will become barbs in your eyes and thorns in your sides. They will give you trouble in the land where you will live. Numbers 33:53, 55

God had given the land to the Israelites as a gift, but they had to *take it* and go *do something* with it in order to truly receive it. They had to do some clearing out and tidying up, and they had to undertake some battles with any inhabitants who hadn't gotten the memo to flee. The thing is, they knew that when they *did act*, God would give them the victory—He'd already promised it!—but they still had to *choose* to act and to carry out the instructions that He had given them. They had to take ownership of the gift that God was giving them—and if they didn't, the gift would then attack, becoming a thorn in their side.

God certainly could have cleared out all possible threats ahead of time—but He didn't. He often gives gifts, but assigns responsibilities that come along with the gift (like a teen getting a car, or a tween being allowed increasing liberty on social media). With increased freedom comes increased responsibility—for *all* the children of God. God gave me the gift of my marriage, but I have to work at it to keep it healthy and vibrant. God gave me my children (on loan), but I have to be vigilant in their care and upbringing. God grants me opportunities to encourage and teach and work, but I have to "possess" them and "settle into" the positions He has provided for me. What examples can you think of from your own life?

It all comes down to our responsibility and obedience. He gives us wonderful gifts, yet also (like any good parent) expects us to take good care of what's been entrusted to us.

Father, enable me to settle in and possess the gifts You've given me, living in obedience to You and bringing glory to Your name. Amen!

JUNE 5

...let us throw off everything that hinders and the sin that so easily entangles. And let us run with perseverance the race marked out for us, fixing our eyes on Jesus, the pioneer and perfecter of faith. Hebrews 12:1b-2a

Anytime I do yoga or a strength training workout, the instructor will inevitably issue these words: "Find a focal point." A focal point is a fixed point in the distance that, when you train your eyes upon it, enables you to maintain your balance even when your stability is being challenged. Is it possible to achieve balance and stability without using a focal point? Yes. But it's a whole lot harder!

In fitness activities, your focal point can be anything—a spot on the floor, a picture on the wall, a tree in your yard. As Christians, the focal point of our lives, of our journeys each day, should be Jesus! When we train our eyes on Him, He enables us to remain balanced and stable amidst the swirling chaos of life that surrounds us each day. When Jesus is our focal point, it is much easier for us to "throw off everything that hinders and the sin that so easily entangles." When we find ourselves looking around at our circumstances, our eyes will always be drawn to the things that provide momentary relief rather than long-term healing. We look to the television, the refrigerator, the online shopping cart, the apps on our phone, even to other people—all things that are fine for us to enjoy in moderation, but all things that were never meant to be the focal point of our entire existence. When those things begin to receive more of our focus than Jesus, we can be sure that life will feel unstable and out of balance. Where are you sensing some instability in your life today, Friend? Recommit your focus in that area onto Jesus, and wait for your body to regain its equilibrium in Him.

Father, only You remain stable and secure amidst the storms of life. Help me center myself in You and trust in Your unfailing love and provision for me. In Jesus' name, Amen.

JUNE 6

"For I know the plans I have for you," declares the Lord, "plans to prosper you and not to harm you, plans to give you hope and a future." Jeremiah 29:11

I am always touched by the comfort and assurance of this verse, yet for some reason I had never noticed until a recent reading that it is part of a letter that God had Jeremiah send to the exiles from Jerusalem who had been carried off into Babylonian captivity. Somehow the knowledge that these words were specifically intended for those who were living in captivity—feeling frightened, confused, and perhaps even hopeless— makes it all the more tender to me. Even though God had to discipline His people for their sins, He never for one moment withdrew His love or His protection from them. He already knew the plans He had for them, the plans of restoration and hope.

The exiles may have heard this promise read to them and received it with joy; however, the present reality was that they were still in exile— and would remain there for seventy years, as God had foretold through Jeremiah (25:11-12). As a result, the exiles in Babylon found it tough to hold on to the joy of promised blessing in the midst of the pain of cap- tivity. Can you relate? I can.

God does have plans and purposes for each one of us—and those plans are all *good*. That does not mean, however, that we will never experi- ence a time of trial, chaos, confusion, or tragedy along the way. At the end of the day, we either choose to believe God or not. But before you make up your mind, let me remind you that He's got a perfect track record and is batting a thousand: "Not one of all the Lord's good prom- ises to Israel failed; every one was fulfilled" (Josh. 21:45). He knows the plans He has for you. They are good, and they will never fail. You may be in a season of pain or captivity, Beloved, but He promises you that you if you hold on to Him, He *will* bring the blessing. May this bring you encouragement and hope today. Amen.

JUNE 7

She is clothed with strength and dignity; she can laugh at the days to come. Proverbs 31:25

Today I sat down with this verse from Proverbs and considered how it applies to my life. I have a choice (we all do!) of whether I will allow myself to be clothed with strength and dignity—which are gifts from God—or if I will choose to clothe myself with the burdensome earthly vestments of anxiety, resentment, anger, or despair. I know which out-fit looks better on me, and I know which choice I would prefer, but sometimes getting there is difficult, isn't it? When you know the dark wash jeans and colorful top would look great on you, and yet you choose to pull on your ratty sweatpants and an oversized tee shirt in-stead? Oh, Dear Friend. What do you wear when your heart is hurting? My outfits tend to reflect my "in-fits." Maybe you can relate.

We still have a choice. Our Father longs to bestow strength and dignity upon us, even when we feel our weakest and most vulnerable. Praise Him that He sees us not as we see ourselves, but as we really are—as His beloved, precious children, worthy of wearing the rich garments of royalty. That's one of the perks you get when your Dad is the King. And yet we choose to pull on pauper's clothes—dirty, filthy rags of shame, guilt, condemnation, bitterness, envy, and greed.

I do understand: Things like chronic illness, unemployment, and pro-found grief do not naturally lend themselves to a "laughing at the days to come" type of sentiment. However, our God is bigger than anything or anyone on this earth that sets itself up against us. He has not lost sight of you, even if you're dressed in your worst attire or have tried to disguise yourself as someone else. His unfailing love surrounds you when you trust in Him (Ps. 32:10b). Even more, when you're in the midst of a war, He loans you His battle armor (see Isa. 59:15b-18; Eph. 6:11-17). He is not leaving you, my friend. He is always at your side. Let's accept His help in dressing ourselves well today, Dear One. We are children of the King! Amen.

JUNE 8

O Jacob, O Israel, how can you say that the Lord doesn't see your troubles and isn't being fair? Isaiah 40:27 TLB

I struggle to appreciate technology. I am not at all savvy in the ways of computers, electronics, cell phones, or other wiry gadgets. One time in college I accidentally set the default font in my email program to "Wingdings." (Think hieroglyphics—literally.) While I am certain that I could *learn* to navigate the basic ins and outs of this area, I really just don't care very much about applying myself to the task. But then when something goes wrong with the computer or my phone, I find myself thoroughly put out by my complete inability to fix it. I want to blame the device for not working rather than accepting responsibility for figuring out how to mend it. We can be unaware of our reliance on something and the importance of something until it is suddenly absent or out of commission. We become complacent, expecting things to continue working just like they always have, until the moment when we need them and discover that we have neglected our part in their upkeep and maintenance.

Let's be sure that as we go through our daily lives, we do not neglect our personal relationships *or* our faith—the care and upkeep of our relationship with the Lord. He is our Dad, and He so longs to hear from us! Sometimes, myself included, we have a season of feeling as though God isn't paying attention to our needs or is ignoring what has gone wrong in our lives. The problem isn't on God's end, my friend.

Do you check in with God as often as you check email, social media, or your phone? We should, but oftentimes we don't. Think what could happen if we did! Times of hardship can make us aware that we have neglected the upkeep of our relationship with the Lord. The good news is that God is still right there, waiting for us to seek Him, longing for us to revitalize our relationship with Him.

Father, thank You for Your love and patience with me each day. Amen.

JUNE 9

To the Jews who had believed Him, Jesus said, "If you hold to My teaching, you are really My disciples. Then you will know the truth, and the truth will set you free." John 8:31-32

I love this quotation from Aldous Huxley: "You shall know the truth, and the truth shall make you mad." Make no mistake, Beloved, God's truth will indeed set us free—but it may make us mad first. Awareness often brings along with it some unwanted friends called Conviction and Accountability.

God's Word does not simply provide us with some truth—God's Word *is* truth (John 17:17). Anything we tell ourselves that is not in alignment with His Word is a lie. When the Holy Spirit brings awareness of areas in which our thoughts, attitudes, and actions are not in alignment with the truth of God's Word, we are called to repent (turn our backs to our sin) and instead walk in a new way. God's way looks like this: "Love one another as I have loved you" (John 13:34). "Pray for those who mistreat you" (Luke 6:28). "Honor God with your body" (1 Cor. 6:20).

Sometimes being confronted with these truths can, as Aldous Huxley said, make us mad! For many years I was unwilling to repent, change direction, and do things God's way because I did not really want the freedom that comes from obedience. I was in pain but at least it was familiar. Living free in Christ seemed like a very threatening Unknown. What finally made the difference? The fear of trying to change began to be outweighed by the ongoing pain of remaining the same.

We do know the truth. We know that Christ came to earth and gave His life for us so that we could be freed from the power of sin and death (Rom. 8:2). We are chosen by God and dearly loved (Col. 3:12). And we are urged to live a life worthy of the calling we've received (Eph. 4:1). That is God's truth. It may make you mad. That's okay. Sometimes we have to get mad first. And then we can begin to submit even the toughest areas of our lives to Him, allowing Him to set us free. Amen.

JUNE 10

They dress the wound of My people as though it were not serious. "Peace, peace," they say, when there is no peace. Jeremiah 6:14

"They" refers to the priests in the land of Judah, who kept telling the people of Judah that things were going to be okay in their land. The problem was that this was a lie. The people had turned away from God and given themselves over to greed and idolatry; they were not caring for the poor and needy among them. Their hearts were no longer aligned with God's heart; they had instead become consumed by desires of the flesh. And yet, even the spiritual leaders among them were promoting their false sense of safety and security in their sin. The people's ongoing desire to live in this state of disillusionment would ultimately lead to the destruction of their temple in Jerusalem and a seventy-year exile in Babylon, where they would become captives of the culture they had worshipped.

Have you ever been told, "There, there" or "Peace, peace" when there was, in fact, no peace in your life? I have. There are two different sides to this coin: The first is when you are harboring a deep and legitimate hurt, and instead of recognizing that pain and honoring it, someone tells you to "buck up and move on." The other side is what happened to the people of Judah: Someone close to you downplays the effects or severity of a particular sin in your life. They rationalize that bad habit for you, or perhaps even encourage you to continue walking in it. See, if you decide to come clean, to get healthy, to abstain from that sin, then your "friend" will feel convicted and ashamed, and as human beings we tend to avoid those feelings at any cost.

My friend, if you find yourself in either of these situations today, please seek the Lord's heart and His wisdom in your circumstances. He longs for you to live your life in the healing light of His freedom and truth. And He deeply cares about your every hurt.

Father, I long for Your perfect and lasting peace in my life. Amen.

JUNE 11

From inside the fish Jonah prayed to the Lord his God. Jonah 2:1

I wonder what Jonah was thinking throughout his experience. I wonder if he assumed he would drown when the sailors threw him overboard. I wonder if he expected a death sentence from God for his blatant disobedience. I wonder if, even in the depths of the fish, he still didn't want to go to Nineveh. His prayer seems to indicate that he thought he was going to die in the sea, when he sank down into the depths (vv. 5-6). Then he says, "When my life was ebbing away, I remembered You, Lord, and my prayer rose to You, to Your holy temple" (v. 7). One way to interpret that would be that Jonah may well have died in the depths had he not prayed for God's deliverance. I wonder if it was at that moment in Jonah's prayer that God dispatched the great fish.

I also wonder how long Jonah was inside the fish before he prayed again to God. I find it interesting that in his prayer, he never uses the word *if*: *If* You let me live, Lord, or *if* I do not die here. Jonah seemed to know— and to *expect*, even—that God would somehow deliver him and release him from his current circumstances, dire as they were. In verse 9 Jonah concludes his prayer with a vow to sacrifice to the Lord and expresses his thanksgiving for God's mercy. Immediately following the conclusion of Jonah's prayer, this happens: "And the Lord commanded the fish, and it vomited Jonah onto dry land" (v. 10). Talk about making a lasting impression!

The good news today, my friend, is that Jonah's story teaches us that it's never too late to pray as long as we have breath within us. We can also choose to pray even when we're surrounded by unbelievably grave or challenging circumstances. Jonah had sunk down "to the roots of the mountains"(v. 6), and still his silent prayer rose to God's throne—as did the prayer he offered as he sat marinating in the gastric juices of a large fish. And not only were his prayers *heard*, Beloved—they were answered. Wherever you may find yourself today, *pray*! Amen.

JUNE 12

Israel, I will make you My wife; I will be true and faithful; I will
show you constant love and mercy and make you Mine forever.
Hosea 2:19 GNT

I don't recall much about my wedding day except that it was a very long day, my mother forgot her dress, and somehow Kevin and I didn't get any of our wedding cake. It felt like such a big and important day in my life—and it was—yet I had no idea at the time that the *wedding* was the easy part! It's the *marriage* that tests our mettle. Marriage is a union of two imperfect people walking this imperfect road of life together. We make mistakes. We get frustrated. Sometimes the walk gets mighty difficult. But living happily ever after isn't God's call on our life. *Loving others* is. Marriage is a covenant, a vow—made not only to one another *but to God*—and it entwines our souls.

Sometimes we think our marriage just isn't worth working at anymore because we're no longer *in love* with our spouse. Dear Friend, being *in love* is the biological hook, line, and sinker that perpetuates life on our planet. That's the easy part. *Loving* someone, on the other hand, means being committed to demonstrating love, care, and respect for that person regardless of how you *feel* in the moment—and whether or not they even deserve it! Remember that *while we were yet sinners,* Christ showed His love for us by dying on the cross (Rom. 5:8). As followers of Christ, we are called to do the same—to show God's love to others, even in their imperfections. For isn't that what we long to receive ourselves?

To be clear: A relationship in which one party is abusive to the other is in a different category altogether. But barring that condition, my friend, God calls us to work at our marriages with all of our hearts. Some days you're not going to "feel it." No matter. Love is not a feeling, my friend. It's a choice. It's an action. It comes from God, and when we seek it, He provides it. May He fill you with His love today! In Jesus' name, Amen.

JUNE 13

Carry each other's burdens, and in this way you will fulfill the law of Christ. Galatians 6:2

Galatians 6:5 tells us that "each one should carry their own load," which refers to our own individual responsibilities that we are called to shoulder each day. The "burdens" of Galatians 6:2 are the heavy trials that come along and all but flatten us, and we need help to carry them!

What has struck me recently is how these verses tie in to Mark 2:3-5, the story of the paralytic on the mat whose four friends cut a hole in the roof of the house where Jesus was teaching, and lowered their friend down in front of Him. Verse 5 says, "When Jesus saw their faith, He said to the paralyzed man, 'Son, your sins are forgiven.'" When Jesus saw *their* faith! This reaffirms my belief in the power and importance of intercessory prayer—and reiterates how crucial it is that we carry each other's "mats," those weighty burdens that would otherwise prove crushing were we to try and do it alone.

It also comforts me to know that although Christ is always with us and certainly carries our burdens for us (see Ps. 68:19; Matt. 11:28), that doesn't mean that our efforts to help and sustain one another in hard times are worthless, ineffective, useless, or in error. We all need to be needed! Intercessory prayer is a wonderful way to exercise that.

Who are the "mat carriers" in your life? Who are the ones who help you carry the burdens that nearly flatten you, the ones who help you find your way to Jesus when life's circumstances paralyze you? Whose mat do you help to carry? As we share the weight of our burdens, we "fulfill the law of Christ," who calls us, above all, to love.

Thank You, Father, for my "mat carriers." Thank You for their steadfast love for me and their willingness to carry my mat when I can no longer walk. Empower me to carry the mats of others as I am needed, laying their burdens before You. In Jesus' name, Amen.

JUNE 14

...whatever you do, do it all for the glory of God. 1 Corinthians 10:31b

I love to do laundry. As I empty the contents of the dryer into my laundry basket and begin to sort and fold, I am always overcome with gratitude at the realization that I have other people to do laundry *for*. I sort through Kevin's jeans (which take up half the space in the washer); Tessa's pants (which now sometimes get mistaken for mine); Blake's pants (which all have holes in the knees); and Stella's pants, tiny and small (she is our "peanut," the petite one amongst a tall set of siblings).

I look at this mixture of clothes—all the different pants and socks, the multicolored hues of shirts and shorts—and I am moved with thanksgiving every time that I have these four other people (and all of their clothes) in my life. I never really thought I would get married—not that I was opposed to the idea, but simply felt no one would ever want to marry me!—so now it just amazes me that not only am I married, *I've got three kids!* So for me, doing laundry is a daily reminder of just *one* of God's amazing, abundant blessings in my life—my family.

What "mundane" chore in your life can you approach with fresh eyes today, seeing it with renewed gratitude as God's blessing? Perhaps it's mowing the lawn of the home He has so graciously provided. Perhaps it's dusting the shelf that holds a treasured memento from a loved one. Perhaps it's washing the vehicle that allows you to travel safely wherever you need to be. Perhaps it's packing lunches or cooking dinner, a means by which you nourish and nurture your family. Perhaps it's vacuuming up dog hair from the dear companion He gave you to get you through a really difficult time. Whatever your "laundry moment" is, I invite you to embrace it with renewed thanksgiving.

Father, thank You for all of the mundane tasks I perform that are evidence of Your love and blessing in my life. In Jesus' name, Amen.

JUNE 15

But You, God, see the trouble of the afflicted; You consider their grief and take it in hand. The victims commit themselves to You; You are the helper of the fatherless. Psalm 10:14

This verse has brought me much comfort over the years. The notion that God *sees* is so important to me. Most of my younger years I functioned so well that no one else could "see" all of the hurt, pain, and wounding inside of me. It comforts me immensely to know that not one scar on my heart escaped God's notice, not one tear that fell was missed by Him. He "considered it"—thought about it carefully and completely in order to decide how best to address it in my life.

I've also noted my own part in this—I have to commit my pain to Him, trusting that He will "take it in hand" and make something good come from it. Sometimes it seems like the brokenness of my life, of my heart, and of my mind are not much for Him to work with—but then I remind myself that He created the entire universe out of considerably less. And that brings me much relief. Not only is He able to create, Beloved, He is also able to transform. When we allow Him to take our pain into His hands, He can make our broken things into blessings.

The last portion of our verse today is especially tender: "You are the helper of the fatherless." If you have experienced the absence of a father in your life, God longs to fill that empty place with His presence, His light, and His love. If you experienced a painful relationship with your earthly father, perhaps one filled with conflict, strife, or abuse, take comfort in the fact that your heavenly Father meets you in that pain, full of love, healing, grace, and compassion. If you have experienced the loss of your earthly father through death, addiction, or estrangement, God is aware of your loss, aware of your pain, and longs to bring healing and comfort. I pray that you would come and rest in Him today, trusting that He sees you clearly. Amen.

JUNE 16

He reached down from on high and took hold of me; he drew me out of deep waters. 2 Samuel 22:17

I learned to swim before I could walk. I would peacefully float on my back in the pool where I went for lessons while my mom stood beside me in the water, softly telling me stories. I was not afraid of the water then, but by age two I became terrified of it—even though I knew how to swim.

This fear persisted off and on throughout my childhood, and I can still recall one frightening time in which I was at a friend's house for a party, all of us in her family's backyard pool, and I somehow got further into the deep end than I had intended. My feet slipped on the slick bottom of the pool, plummeting me below the surface. I was terrified. *And I knew how to swim.* Yet I could not right myself; I could not get my brain to work through my panic and remember that I knew how to get myself out of this. A friend hauled me up by the arm, and I grabbed on to the pool ledge—terrified and embarrassed. What had happened? Even now, although I *can* swim, I don't really enjoy doing it.

This verse from 2 Samuel speaks to me because of that past experience, but also because at so many points in my life I have felt as though I were literally drowning in my emotions, whatever they may have been at the time: hopelessness, fear, pain, grief, loss, brokenness, abandonment. It changes from circumstance to circumstance, but I still tend to be flooded with feelings that threaten to overtake me and pull me under those black and murky waters. That is why I love this image of God stooping down, stretching out His arm, and pulling me out from under the waters that have closed over me. He is able to save us, even in our confusion. We may not know where we are, but He never loses sight of us.

Father, I thank You and praise You for every time You have drawn me out of deep waters, placing my feet back on the solid Rock. In His name, Amen.

JUNE 17

For with much wisdom comes much sorrow; the more knowledge, the more grief. Ecclesiastes 1:18

This is one of my favorite verses in the Bible, and each time I read it I am reminded of trees. I think about all the things trees witness and weather throughout the course of their lives, and how all of these experiences are recorded in their inner cores in the form of growth rings. A cross-section of a tree's trunk clearly shows the point at which any wounding has occurred—and once a ring sustains a scar, it affects future rings as well for the remainder of the tree's life.

Trees will always bear the evidence of their woundings, but they are also remarkably able to grow and thrive despite having suffered them. They can grow right up and around shrapnel embedded in their trunks, making the would-be aggressor into part of their overall beauty. They cannot hide and conceal their wounds like humans do. This hiding that we do is to our detriment. We are as resilient and beautiful as the trees, and yet we often hide our scars in shame.

Living in our fallen world, woundings are a natural part of life. The wisdom gained from the experience, however, is optional. If we choose to conceal or ignore our wounds, our internal growth rings will still bear evidence of our pain, but we will prohibit ourselves from working *through* the wounding and *to* the offering of wisdom it holds.

Where does this meet you today, Beloved? Are you willing to work through the wounding so that you can receive the gift of wisdom? Or are you hiding your wounds so that others cannot see your pain? Are you still in the midst of the wounding, without any real hope for good to come? If so, I want to encourage you today with the reminder from Romans 8:28 that our Father is able to work *all things* for our good. We may experience grief and pain, but if we persevere, Dear One, we will also know His wonderful wisdom and grace. Amen.

JUNE 18

From one human being He created all races of people and made them live throughout the whole earth. He Himself fixed beforehand the exact times and the limits of the places where they would live. He did this so that they would look for Him, and perhaps find Him as they felt around for Him. Yet God is actually not far from any one of us. Acts 17:26-27

I've often thought that perhaps I missed the call to come forth in an earlier generation. I think I may have done better back in the Pioneer days of simpler homes and life lived outside in God's creation. Or maybe the Elizabethan era would have been a better fit for me, a time in which it was considered flattering to be porcelain-skinned (i.e., pale), and long-flowing dresses helped mask the "flaws" of which we alone take note. Then again, had either of those scenarios occurred, I also would have had to face rattlesnakes and cholera; herring-bone corsets and those dreadful starched ruffs. So for all of the challenges of existing here and now, in our modern-day world—where I'm so often befuddled by technology and saddened by the loss of true leisure—I take Paul's words to heart and remind myself that God planned all of this.

Drink this one in: God *planned* your existence, and He *planned* the exact time set for you. Your existence here on planet earth is not now, nor was it ever, a "mistake." Did you also catch the fact that God planned the *exact places* where His people should live? Know that you are exactly where you are *for a purpose*! Some of us He calls to stay put, fulfilling our purpose in the familiar surroundings of our hometown; others He calls to go forth, traveling to new places to achieve His kingdom purposes there. Take comfort in the knowledge and assurance today that you are *exactly* where you are meant to be!

Father, thank You for Your perfect plan and purposes for me! May I trust in Your timing and direction for my life. In Jesus' name, Amen.

JUNE 19

Create in me a pure heart, O God, and renew a steadfast spirit within me. Psalm 51:10

How is your heart soil today, my friend? I find that mine tends to change along with the seasons. When I'm in a season of loss, despair, and pain, my heart soil is like frozen tundra, icy and hard. God has to chisel into that stony soil to get through to me. When I'm in a season of exhaustion, fatigue, and weariness, tired of carrying the same old burdens around with me like a nomad in a desert, I find that my heart soil is dry, dusty, grainy, and thin. God has to pour His Living Water into my parched and barren wilderness in order to revive me again.

When I'm in a season of growth, insight, and progress, my heart soil is soft, loamy, and nourished by God's Word, able to receive and retain His good seed planted in me. When I'm in a season of confusion, instability, and disorientation, my heart soil is scattered, tossed about in a whirl-wind of emotions, feelings, and worries. God has to calm the winds in order to center me again in Him. When I'm in a season of grief, my heart soil is soaked with my tears, saturated with my pain. God faithful-ly sends His Son and His light down into the murky bog, drawing my focus upward and back onto Him.

In what season is your heart finding itself today, Beloved? Our Father is the Master Gardener, able to skillfully work and tend the soil of our hearts, no matter the season. He takes our heart soil and adds in the perfect balance of His Sonlight, Living Water, and nourishment from His Word, cultivating hearts within us that are healthy and vibrant, open to receiving the good seed He wishes to plant there. May it take root and grow today!

Father, thank You for tending to my heart so faithfully and gently, no matter the season. Help me to seek You first in all experiences of my life, trusting Your hands to hold my heart. In Jesus' name, Amen.

JUNE 20

Despite their fear of the peoples around them, [the Israelites]
built the altar on its foundation and sacrificed burnt offerings on
it to the Lord, both the morning and evening sacrifices. [...] On
the first day of the seventh month they began to offer burnt of-
ferings to the Lord, though the foundation of the Lord's temple
had not yet been laid. Ezra 3:3, 6

Rebuilding is hard work, and it becomes even more tedious when you're being harassed by those around you as you try to work (see Ezra 4:4-5). The work on the temple in Jerusalem took years to complete, and even then it was not a smooth, linear progression.

The Israelites wisely began their work with the reconstruction of the heart of the temple—the altar. They knew that its presence would center their focus on their covenant relationship with God, despite their surrounding circumstances, and that He would empower them throughout the rebuilding process. Seventy years in Babylonian captivity had taught them the importance of obedience to Yahweh, and they surely were not about to make that same mistake again.

What are you rebuilding today, my friend? It takes a lot of time, doesn't it? Are you being harassed by naysayers in your life who would like to discourage your efforts? If so, I pray that you would find encouragement today from the children of Israel, who persevered in spite of hardship and fear. Let us also remember that we must fully commit the altars of our earthly temples—our hearts, minds, and spirits—to the Lord as we are in the process of rebuilding. As we keep Him at the center of our focus, the efforts of others to distract or hamper us will be handled by our faithful and mighty God.

Father, as I work to rebuild my areas of brokenness and seek to live more like Your Son, remind me to always begin my work at the altar, centering myself in Your will, and giving thanks to You. Amen.

JUNE 21

We will not neglect the house of our God. Nehemiah 10:39b

In context, the people of Israel are making a vow not to neglect the newly rebuilt temple of God. For believers this side of the cross, we know that the temple of God, where God's Holy Spirit dwells, is in us (1 Cor. 6:19). Thus, the New Testament application of this Old Testament vow would be, "We will not neglect ourselves." God expects us to care for ourselves—our physical temple. Not to worship the temple, mind you—for we don't worship the temple but the One who makes the temple holy—but to show care and concern in its upkeep. To nourish it, tend to it, repair it, and care for it.

How is your temple maintenance looking today, Friend? Are you free of any destructive habits that bring harm to your temple? Are you making time to rest and spending quiet time with your Creator? Are you nourishing your temple wisely, making sure it remains strong and healthy? These are all important components. Or, perhaps your focus has been too much on the outer portion of your temple, and you have neglected the inner rooms. We are called to care for our bodies, but that does not mean fixating upon our appearance—either by worshiping it *or* berating it. If your days revolve around obsessive compulsions aimed towards your outer appearance, ask God to gently refocus your attention on the inner workings of your vessel—your thoughts, your attitudes, and your heart. Most importantly, let's be mindful of not becoming so preoccupied with our temples that we neglect the One who created them. It's all about balance, my friend. We will always make time to do the things that are most important to us.

The Jews in Nehemiah's time made a commitment not to neglect the care and upkeep of the house of the Lord. They did well for a time, but then some backsliding began. The good news is that the people were able to turn things around and get back on the right track. God is always faithful to assist us when we ask. Amen!

JUNE 22

What strength do I have, that I should still hope? What prospects, that I should be patient? Do I have the strength of stone? Is my flesh bronze? Do I have any power to help myself? Job 6:11-13a

Despair and Hopelessness come calling when we get to the end of ourselves. "I can't handle this!" we think. "I'm not strong enough!" Yes, my friend. That's the whole point. Sometimes God has to allow us to come to the end of ourselves because it is only then that we peter out enough in our continual striving to stop and gain some much-needed perspective. I say this with ample humility because this is a lesson I've repeatedly learned the hard way! As time goes on, the length of time I go barreling on ahead is shortening, which is good—yet God is still working in me to help me cultivate the awareness and self-control I need to stop and hand the reins over to Him *before* I get to the place of utter frustration, despair, pain, or panic.

When we do arrive at the "Job Moment," we can bring our souls back into alignment with the Lord when we rehearse the answers to the wild questions we throw out—because Beloved, we already know the answers. So let's review them: "The Lord is my strength" (Ps. 28:7); "...those who hope in Me will not be disappointed" (Isa. 49:23b); "Be still before the Lord and wait patiently for Him" (Ps. 37:7); "'Today I have made you a fortified city, an iron pillar and a bronze wall to stand against the whole land. [...] They will fight against you but will not overcome you, for I am with you and will rescue you,' declares the Lord" (Jer. 1:18-19). See, my friend?: *He* is our strength, *He* is our hope, *He* gives us patience, *He* makes us strong, *He* will help us in our time of need. It's not about our limitations; it's about His limitless strength! Now let's step out of the way and let Him work!

Father, thank You for realigning my focus when my eyes look to my finite strength instead of Your infinite power. Amen!

JUNE 23

Light has come into the world, but people loved darkness instead of light because their deeds were evil. Everyone who does evil hates the light, and will not come into the light for fear that their deeds will be exposed. But whoever lives by the truth comes into the light, so that it may be seen plainly that what they have done has been done in the sight of God. John 3:19b-21

I lived in darkness for many years because of self-condemnation and shame. I also feared exactly what John mentions in our verses for today: Coming into the light requires that we live in truth. We do not hide and conceal parts of ourselves, nor do we engage in unrepentant sin. Choosing to stay in the darkness meant I could choose to stay in the hate, the shame, and the self-loathing, even though outwardly I probably looked okay. Coming out into the light would mean a necessary transparency and authenticity with others that I hugely feared!

Yet there is no fear in the light, Beloved, because God *is* light, and He is *in* the light (1 John 1:5b, 7). That was the part I was missing. It's okay for me to come out into the light and be real with you about my struggles and about my pain, because I know Jesus is right here with me and that my sin has been forgiven. When I show you my weaknesses and wounds and struggles, you can see them and relate to them and we can encourage one another. When we conceal ourselves in darkness, we miss out on opportunities to share the light of Christ with others. I have plenty of "dark" moments that have dotted my life, but I'm willing to bring those out into His healing light so that others can see that any good thing that I might accomplish in this life has been done by and through the grace of God, never on my own!

What darkness is threatening you right now, Friend? Entrust it to Him and allow His light to shine upon you, guiding your path into His truth, healing, and freedom. I'm cheering you on! May He empower us to live in His light, sharing His grace and mercy with our hurting world. Amen.

JUNE 24

God is working in you to make you willing and able to obey Him.
Philippians 2:13 CEV

I hate being a passenger in a car. I am certain that a large part of it stems from control issues; the other remaining piece is just fear for my life. I tend to believe that things will just go better if I manage them myself. I prefer to do things my way, which I often consider to be "the right way." Perhaps you can relate? Sometimes this works out just fine; other times there's a collision.

Occasionally I find myself not wanting to let God into the driver's seat either, and that becomes a different scenario entirely. Many of us have a desire to manage and control every last detail of everything around us because we've experienced such chaos in our lives that was completely *out* of our control. Our response to the lack of control was to become overly controlling, and it is not an endearing character trait—I say that as one who knows! Parenthood and getting older have both taught me that basically the only thing I control in my life is how the dishwasher gets loaded. And that is only because I insist upon clinging to that one last vestige of my territory (which, might I add, my toddler is now threatening). All the rest of life is up for grabs.

What area of your life have you been clutching to your chest with both hands instead of allowing God to be in control? Do you have a long-standing habit or addiction that you need to be freed from? Are you in a relationship in which you are enabling someone else's poor choices? Are you trying to micromanage every facet of another person's life? Do you wrestle with a longstanding attitude or belief that you know is not founded in the truth of God's Word? Whatever it is, I urge you to relinquish your control into God's mighty and capable hands. He is an excellent driver who will deliver you safely home!

Father, enable me to yield my will to You today in all areas of my life, trusting in Your direction and provision. In Jesus' name, Amen.

JUNE 25

The second son he named Ephraim and said, "It is because God has made me fruitful in the land of my suffering." Genesis 41:52

Joseph's statement gives me encouragement and hope. He had experienced betrayal and bondage, false imprisonment and neglect, and yet he remained faithful to God, and God remained faithful to him. Two of my favorite parts of Joseph's story are in Genesis 39, verses 3 and 23, which both say that the Lord was with Joseph and gave him success in everything he did. In the first circumstance, Joseph has been put in charge of Potiphar's entire household and entrusted with everything Potiphar owns; in the second, Joseph is in prison. Our location matters not to our mighty God. Whether we are on the mountaintop or in the valley, we are His children—He is there with us, and He can make us fruitful if we remain faithful.

Joseph knew and had experienced this personally. He was sold into slavery in Egypt, which became the "land of his suffering"—and yet God's provision and blessing were made so clear to him that he later told his brothers, "It was not you who sent me here, but God" (Gen. 45:8). He also said to them, "You intended to harm me, but God intended it for good to accomplish what is now being done, the saving of many lives" (50:20). God gifted Joseph with the blessing of perspective—of being able to see and know the *why* of it all. This is something that I pray for in my own life.

How does the knowledge that God can enable you to be fruitful even in the land of your suffering bring hope and comfort to you today, my friend? Since we will not be fully free from suffering until we die and are raised up with Christ, this means that God can and will enable us to be fruitful *right now*—in this moment, at this time, whatever it may look like—as long as we are abiding in Him and walking in obedience.

Father, thank You for Your ability and willingness to make me fruitful, even in the midst of hardship and suffering! In Jesus' name, Amen.

JUNE 26

When an impure spirit comes out of a person, it goes through arid places seeking rest and does not find it. Then it says, "I will return to the house I left." When it arrives, it finds the house un-occupied, swept clean and put in order. Then it goes and takes with it seven other spirits more wicked than itself, and they go in and live there. And the final condition of that person is worse than the first. Matthew 12:43-45a

I personally experienced this notion a few years ago when I felt a firm conviction from the Holy Spirit that my self-condemnation was a sin. I was lacerating my heart and mind with words that were not God's truth, and the damage was ongoing and painful. When I became aware of my sin, I confessed it to God and repented. I desired to walk in a new way and tried to put this into practice, but I found myself unsure of how to proceed. Speaking words of kindness, affirmation, and nurturing to myself was something I had no idea how to do, so I didn't. I just stopped hurling insults at myself all day. How did I feel? Empty. There was a quietness in my head that was almost eerie, yet it did not last because I had left my mind—my "house"—unoccupied.

I experienced discouraging defeat and shame as the condemning self-talk slowly came back; I felt like a failure for being unable to rid myself of what I now knew was sin. God finally helped me to realize that it was good for me to sweep those thoughts out. That was the right thing to do. But I had neglected the next step, which was to replace the nega-tive, condemning thoughts with affirming truths from God's Word. Once I occupied myself with the task of filling my mind with His Word and His truth, the tide of the battle in my mind finally began to turn. When those old thoughts tried to come in, they encountered a mind filled with Christ's love, hope, Spirit, peace, and truth. They are no longer welcome.

Father, enable me to fill myself with Your truth and peace today! Amen.

JUNE 27

Therefore confess your sins to each other and pray for each other so that you may be healed. The prayer of a righteous person is powerful and effective. James 5:16

I've spent some very intense time wrestling in intercessory prayer over the past several days. This morning I ended up bawling before I was done. We want so much for God to answer *in the way we want Him to answer.* We think if He doesn't provide the answer we're seeking, then He must just not be *listening* to us. This morning I thought: *What if the answer isn't what I'm hoping for, asking for, seeking so urgently and fervently?* And then the image of Jesus in the garden of Gethsemane came to mind, as He prayed to God to remove that cup from His lips (see Matt. 26:36-46). God said no. Jesus asked a second time, and then a third. God said no again. Jesus accepted God's answer, and submitted to death on the cross, willingly giving up His life for us—without which there could not have been hope for our salvation. That's when the tears came, my friend—when I understood that no matter how reasonable the petition, no matter how pure the heart requesting it, sometimes the answer is still no.

Sometimes God's answer to our prayers is not the answer we so desperately wish to receive, but that never means He's not listening or He doesn't care. We, as human beings, are limited to just this finite moment in time, our present. His vision extends into eternity; He already knows exactly what will occur in our lives. He can see how His answers will affect not only our futures, but others' lives as well. He is not in the business of granting wishes and giving us fairy tale lives, Beloved. He is in the business of winning souls for His kingdom. The "no" that Jesus' prayers received resulted in a "yes" for all of *us*, a way by which we could be saved: "For no matter how many promises God has made, they are 'Yes' in Christ" (2 Cor. 1:20a). May we continue to take our requests to Him, knowing that He hears us, trusting the pure heart and powerful plan behind His answers. Amen.

JUNE 28

As they began to sing and praise, the Lord set ambushes against the men of Ammon and Moab and Mount Seir who were invading Judah, and they were defeated. 2 Chronicles 20:22

The men appointed by Jehoshaphat to go out and sing God's praises were sent to the very front of the line (v. 21) as the army of Judah marched out to face the three armies that had come to make war against them. It doesn't specify this in the text, but I would assume that the singers were not equipped with sword and shield. Most likely they were Levites who were trained to sing and make music for the Lord (see 1 Chron. 25:1-7), and they may have had no fighting experience what-soever. Therefore, their ability to go forth against the mighty armies ahead of them *and sing* is astounding to me.

What I treasure most about this verse is that *as they began to sing... the Lord set ambushes.* As soon as God saw their faithfulness, as soon as He heard the opening words of their songs of praise, He knew that these children fully trusted in Him to do what He said He would do. And He did it! That, my friend, is faith. Interestingly, the three armies end up attacking and annihilating each other, while the army of Judah remains at a safe distance (2 Chron. 20:23-24). Their job on the battlefield that day was to sing, to express their faith in the Lord's power and deliver-ance. And they did.

In what battle is God calling you to sing today, Beloved? In what area is He calling you to lay down your weapons and lift up your voice? It may seem counterintuitive, but when the Lord calls us to sing instead of fight, that means one thing: The battle is His alone; our job is to "stand firm and see the deliverance the Lord will give to [us]" (v. 17).

Father, thank You for the deliverance in my life that can only come from Your mighty hand. May others bear witness to it and give You the glory! I will continue to sing of Your love and faithfulness. Amen!

JUNE 29

You may ask, "What will we eat in the seventh year if we do not plant or harvest our crops?" I will send you such a blessing in the sixth year that the land will yield enough for three years. While you plant during the eighth year, you will eat from the old crop and will continue to eat from it until the harvest of the ninth year comes in. Leviticus 25:20-22

I am continually moved by the promises of God's provision and the utmost thought and care He has put into providing for His people through the ages. It must have seemed unthinkable to the Israelites when they were told not to plant anything during the seventh year, but instead to let the ground rest. It must have seemed like certain death—and a painful and slow death from starvation, at that. Yet this passage reminds me that God never calls us to obedience in something without providing us with the necessary skills and tools we need to attain it. He knew exactly how much He would need to provide in that sixth year in order to satisfy the needs of His people in the seventh and eighth years; His provision in our lives is perfect!

What area are you wrestling with in terms of obedience to God right now, my friend? In what area is God calling you to trust Him for provision, rather than trusting in your own ability? Do you sense Him calling you to a change in career that may require substantial sacrifices on your part, or on the part of your family? Do you feel Him calling you to lay down a habit that has taken on too much focus in your life? Is He asking you to move to a new city or state, to follow His purposes for you there? Whatever His calling on your life is right now, rest peacefully in the assurance that our God will never assign you to a task that He will not also equip you to handle.

Father, thank You for Your gracious provision in every area of my life. Help me to trust in Your faithfulness to provide for all my needs. Amen.

JUNE 30

Those who sow in tears shall reap with shouts of joy! He who goes out weeping, bearing the seed for sowing, shall come home with shouts of joy, bringing his sheaves with him. Psalm 126:5-6 ESV

"A man reaps what he sows" (Gal. 6:7b). So how do you reap joy from tears? I've noted today that it doesn't say those who *sow tears*, but those who sow *in* tears—which must mean that *what* they are sowing is obedience, and "in tears" is *how* they're sowing it. They are going out weeping, but they are also carrying seed to sow—not just going out and wandering about aimlessly, lamenting and wailing. They are purposeful in the sowing, even in the midst of the pain—and what they're sowing is obedience to God, trusting Him even in the midst of their grief, confusion, and despair. I'm wondering if you can relate today.

When we sow obedience to God through and in our tears, we are *promised* joy. David wrote, "weeping may stay for the night, but rejoicing comes in the morning" (Ps. 30:5b). The darkness of that night of weeping may endure longer than just one literal "night"—intense grief always does. The application is more figurative than literal, simply meaning that we will not live and exist in tears and in sorrow for all time *unless* we refuse to sow. As long as we go out weeping while still carrying seed to sow—hear me on this, Dear One: *Joy WILL come.*

Our act of carrying seed to sow, even as our tears soak the ground, is evidence of our faith. Faithful people obey God and trust in His heart, even when they can't see Him. They choose to rely on what they know about God, rather than what they feel. And we know, Beloved, that our God never leaves us nor forsakes us (Heb. 13:5b). So we continue to sow faithfulness and obedience as we trust in our Father, and He responds with sheaves of joy. In whatever floodplain you find yourself today, my friend, may you keep sowing and hold on fiercely for the blessing. In Jesus' name, Amen.

JULY 1

Simon answered, "Master, we've worked hard all night and haven't caught anything. But because You say so, I will let down the nets." When they had done so, they caught such a large number of fish that their nets began to break. Luke 5:5-6

These weary fishermen had worked hard, all night, with no success, and were probably full of discouragement, exhaustion, and frustration. The suggestion to cast the nets again must have seemed preposterous, given the work they'd already put in. Yet Simon Peter agreed to do it, "because You say so." When they waited for Jesus' perfect timing, everything came together far beyond what they ever could have hoped for.

When our family was going through the twenty-month period of Kevin's unemployment, I often felt like he and I were sitting in this boat right next to Peter. We'd cast and haul in an empty net, time and time again. Six months became ten. Ten became fifteen. Fifteen became twenty. Empty nets, exhausted energy, the gnawing sense of despair. Kevin applied for anything and everything even *remotely* in his field. As a French teacher, I scoured job postings myself, thinking maybe the answer was that God wanted me to go back to work. Nothing. Finally, I received word that the principal of a new high school opening in the fall would like to interview me for the French position. My heart felt heavy, but I knew that if God's plan was for me to return to work, I had to obey. I revised and submitted my résumé, and waited to hear back about an interview. That was on a Monday. On Friday of that same week, Kevin received a call offering him a position at an engineering firm, starting in two weeks—just two days shy of our twenty-*first* month of waiting. That was Jesus, my friend, telling us to "Let down the nets, just one more time." And we did. He is so faithful.

Father, thank You for Your unfailing provision in my life. Grant me the strength, faith, and trust that I need in order to endure my time of waiting. In Jesus' name, Amen.

JULY 2

So I will always remind you of these things, even though you know them and are firmly established in the truth you now have.
2 Peter 1:12

Peter, of all people, knew what it was like to *know* something and still falter. He was the one who *knew* who Jesus was (Matt. 16:15-16), and yet he was also the one who denied knowing Him at all (Mark 14:66-72). Peter realized more than most how much our faith can waver when we are faced with frightening circumstances and confusing trials in life. Therefore, he pledged to keep reminding the believers of the promise and glory of Christ. There are times in each of our lives when we're at a point where we *know* the Word and yet cannot seem to connect with it. In those times, we must pray that God will send someone to remind us of what we know.

When was the last time Life dealt you a blow that caused you to forget what you know? I had a season a while back in which I felt so disconnected from God. I was still going to church, still going to Sunday school, still doing my Bible study, still praying, still reading God's Word—and yet I felt so detached and hollow. It was upsetting and discouraging, because I was earnestly seeking God and I knew the promises of His Word, but my heart and mind seemed to have shut down on me. It's seasons like that one, the ones that descend for no apparent reason, that I find most perplexing. It's understandable that when a crisis hits we would momentarily lose our footing or be thrown off course, but a season of distance when there is no discernable "reason"? That distresses me. During that season, I was especially appreciative of reminders from disciples like Peter and John, who wrote to us in part to simply *remind us* that we do know God and we do know His truth—and that when we emerge from the fog, we will find Him right there beside us, where He's been all along.

Father, thank You for Your faithful presence. In Jesus' name, Amen.

<u>JULY 3</u>

In addition to all this, take up the shield of faith, with which you can extinguish all the flaming arrows of the evil one. Ephesians 6:16

Although the shield of faith is freely available to us at any moment, I've noted today that we must choose to "take it up." Not only that, we can also be certain that the enemy's "flaming arrows" will be coming at us from every possible direction, so it is not enough to stand there and hold out the shield! We have to be constantly moving and on guard with it.

I also find it interesting that it is our *faith* that extinguishes the fiery darts of our enemy. Hebrews 11:1 says that faith is "confidence in what we hope for and assurance about what we do not see." When we employ our shield of faith, we are acknowledging our *certainty* of God's presence there with us in our trial and expressing our *confident expectation* that He will indeed deliver us. It is *crucial* that we believe even when we cannot see! If Satan can cause us to doubt, then we have faltered with our shield. We must choose to believe in God's deliverance, even when our foe is mighty and our strength is waning—because *we know* that our God is mightier and that He will fight for His children!

Another aspect to consider is that flaming arrows encountering a dry shield would cause it, too, to go up in flames. Our shields are able to *extinguish* flames, which means that they have to be *wet*. We must fully submerge them in the Living Water given to us by Jesus Christ. John tells us that those who believe in Christ have streams of living water flowing from within them—meaning the Holy Spirit, who dwells within those who have believed (John 7:38-39). We do believe in Him, Beloved, and those streams of Living Water flow through our bodies as we stand on the battlefield of Life. We take up our shield. We stand firm in our faith. We acknowledge the victory that is already ours in Christ. And we allow His Living Water, His Spirit, to saturate our shield, delivering us from harm. May you use your shield with renewed determination today, my friend, knowing your victory is assured in Him. Amen!

JULY 4

...if My people, who are called by My name, will humble them-selves and pray and seek My face and turn from their wicked ways, then I will hear from heaven, and I will forgive their sin and will heal their land. 2 Chronicles 7:14

The nation of Israel routinely struggled in two main areas: idolatry and pride. They succumbed to the influences of pagan cultures around them, wanting to blend in rather than be set apart as God's own people. We still experience this struggle today. The idolatry and pride of the Israelites distanced them from God and invited discipline. Our time is coming.

We inhabit one of the richest countries in the world, yet we harbor some of the poorest in spirit. In a culture that flaunts hedonism and immediate gratification, it's difficult to maintain the high moral stand-ards to which we are called as those set apart in Christ. We are often regarded as old-fashioned or intolerant on account of our views, and it can be a challenge to live our lives as we know God would have us to do. In addition, technology has made the tide of our relationships turn to-wards remarkable width but little depth. We are inclined to routinely share the attractive moments of our lives, and rarely the messy ones. This "shared superficiality" skews our perception of how life should look, and often we find ourselves harboring a spirit of insecurity, envy, discontentment, or lack. This is not in alignment with who God tells us we are in Christ, Beloved! And it's time for a change.

Would you join with me today in praying for our nation? Let's pray for our leaders in all areas of government; for our schools and universities; for our judicial system; for our economic infrastructure; for our children. Let's lift up our hearts to the Lord, seek His face, and petition Him on behalf of our country, that He may heal our land and enable us to draw others to Him through our example. May we have the courage to stand out and be different. In Jesus' name, Amen.

JULY 5

You need milk, not solid food! Anyone who lives on milk, being still an infant, is not acquainted with the teaching about righteousness. But solid food is for the mature. Hebrews 5:12b-14a

Let's talk about teeth. I guess I have teeth on my mind because Stella is cutting some molars in her lower jaw—a process that is causing all of us some fussiness and sleepless nights. It's hard and painful to cut teeth, isn't it? Just when we think we're done, six-year molars appear. Then teeth start falling *out*. And then, we think we're done again, and the twelve-year molars and wisdom teeth arrive!

The process of cutting our "spiritual teeth" is pretty much the same. As Solomon repeatedly warns in his books of Proverbs and Ecclesiastes, the pursuit and attainment of wisdom and maturity is rarely easy or painless. They are both hard-won byproducts of weathering trials and gaining closer intimacy with Christ in the process.

Back to the teeth for a moment: Some of us are early birds when it comes to cutting teeth, and some of us are late bloomers. My husband had teeth at four months. I, on the other hand, was thirteen months old before I got hair *or* teeth, which made me look like a very small (but adorable) little old man. Those of us who are slower to cut teeth manage to make do. So it is with spiritual maturity: Some of us grew up quickly into the faith, sustaining some hard knocks early on that drove us headlong into the arms of Christ. Some of us enjoyed relatively peaceful childhoods, but found ourselves walloped by life in our thirties. Some of us have walked through fires of loss and heartache in our forties or sixties. The thing about trials—and about teeth—is that we all get them eventually. The most important thing we can do is to call upon the Great Physician when we find ourselves in pain. He is faithful to bring His comfort, peace, and healing into the midst of our hurting. May we hold on for the blessing *and* the wisdom. Amen.

JULY 6

"The days are coming," declares the Sovereign Lord, "when I will send a famine through the land—not a famine of food or a thirst for water, but a famine of hearing the words of the Lord."
Amos 8:11

Have you ever felt like you were in a season of famine when it came to hearing the words of the Lord? I have. Sometimes I've sought His guidance on a matter as earnestly as I know how, and He still seems silent. I'm wondering if sometimes the silence means, "Child, I've already given you the answer." I know I do this with my kids sometimes. They ask me something and I answer, but they aren't paying attention (or it isn't the answer they wanted to hear), and so they ask me again. I don't want to answer a second time; my first answer still stands. When we feel silence coming from God, perhaps we haven't been listening, or we have chosen not to hear.

In the days of Amos, the people relied upon the prophets for any kind of communication from God. We have the wondrous privilege of having the very words of God in tangible form—in our Holy Bible. I often marvel at the fact that I am allowed to have my very own copy of the Word of God. And I can do whatever I want with it. I can read it every day, or put it on a shelf and let it gather dust. Sometimes I wonder what would happen if things in our country went terribly wrong and Christians were ordered to surrender their Bibles to be destroyed. I wonder how many of us could keep God's Word alive and going, retelling the stories and the letters and the psalms from memory. I also wonder how many parts would be lost, and how many would never even miss it.

We are so privileged, Beloved, to have the very words of God, His timeless love letter to us, in our possession at all times. Open up the pages and immerse yourself in His healing and restoring love today. May you find the answers to your questions. May He speak a fresh word to you today, and may you choose to hear Him. In Jesus' name, Amen.

JULY 7

In the first year of Cyrus king of Persia, in order to fulfill the word of the Lord spoken by Jeremiah, the Lord moved the heart of Cyrus king of Persia to make a proclamation throughout his realm. Ezra 1:1a

I love the notion of the Lord being able to "move the heart" of someone in order to accomplish His plans and purposes. I find it comforting that He can use the hearts of unbelievers, mockers, or those who do not yet know Him to achieve His kingdom purposes. Just because a person does not know God doesn't mean that God does not know him!

Is there someone in your life whose heart needs a little moving today? Maybe it's a co-worker, a neighbor, a family member, or a non-believer. This is a wonderful opportunity to engage in some intercessory prayer on this person's behalf! Or, maybe it's your own heart that needs some attention today. Maybe there's an area of sin, bitterness, or blame that needs to be uprooted. Maybe there's a hardness that needs to be softened or an area of pride that needs some humbling. God is faithful to tend to our hearts, and in these latter areas He doesn't always wait for an invitation!

Maybe, Beloved, your heart is so fragile today that you fear moving it even slightly might shatter it. I want you to know that God is able to tend to our precious hearts with the practiced hands of the One who created them in the first place. He gently holds the hurting ones and skillfully mends the broken ones. He binds up the fractured ones and collects the shards of those splintered by grief, pain, confusion, and despair. He misses nothing, overlooks nothing, forgets nothing. His heart always beats with love for you, His beloved child.

Father, I entrust my heart and the hearts of my loved ones to You today, with full confidence in the gentle and healing power of Your mighty hands. In Jesus' name, Amen.

JULY 8

How long, Lord, must I call for help, but You do not listen? Or cry out to You, "Violence!" but You do not save? Why do You make me look at injustice? Why do You tolerate wrongdoing? Destruction and violence are before me; there is strife, and conflict abounds. Therefore the law is paralyzed, and justice never prevails. The wicked hem in the righteous, so that justice is perverted. Habakkuk 1:2-4

In my teens I came across this passage and these verses leapt out at me. At that time, this is how I felt toward God and toward the difficult circumstances of my life. Like Habakkuk, I wanted answers. I wanted God to *do* something—or at least to explain Himself. I felt I was calling for help and He was refusing to listen. It seemed that He had allowed so much destruction in my life and I was well past being able to understand His reasons or purposes. It hurt to think that God could watch so much devastation occur and do nothing.

The problem is that I stopped with verse 4 and didn't keep reading to hear God's response: "Look at the nations and watch—and be utterly amazed. For I am going to do something in your days that you would not believe, even if you were told" (v. 5). This is how God responded to Habakkuk's cry of despair and grief, and this is the same answer I had to accept for my own circumstances. I had to trust that He could and would do something with it—and that whatever it is He would do, there'd be no point in His trying to tell me beforehand because I wouldn't believe it. Even though I'm still not entirely sure what the purpose is in all of the pain, I do know there *is* a purpose. And I know that God is faithful and that He can use it for good. I also know that He is continually working, even if I do not or cannot always see the evidence of it. As a teenager, that just wasn't good enough. As an adult, it's all I need to know. In what area do you need to apply God's answer today? When we cannot understand His reasons, Beloved, may we choose to trust His heart. Amen.

JULY 9

You did not choose Me, but I chose you and appointed you to go and bear fruit — fruit that will last. John 15:16a

In this passage Jesus is speaking to His disciples, preparing them for what is to come after His death. I often marvel at the differences amongst the Twelve. Peter could see Jesus for who He really was (Matt. 16:16), but he could also be impetuous and impulsive (Mark 8:32-33; John 13:9). James and John were the hot-tempered ones of the group, ready to call down fire from heaven when people dared to oppose the Lord (Luke 9:54). Matthew knew what it was like to live amongst "sinners," (Matt. 9:9-10), but abandoned this life to follow Christ—and later wrote a book about it. Andrew was the "little brother" who introduced big brother Peter to Christ (John 1:41-42). Philip is credited with bringing his friend Nathanael to Jesus (John 1:45), and Nathanael, though initially doubtful, made a quick turnaround (John 1:46-49). Thomas was cautious and meticulous (John 14:5; 20:24-25); Judas Iscariot was self-seeking and betrayed Christ (Mark 14:44-46); and not much is known about Thaddeus, James son of Alphaeus, or Simon the Zealot.

The twelve men Jesus chose to be His disciples during His earthly ministry were not the "elite" of the time but working class individuals, men who were each imperfect, sometimes misguided, and so very *human*, all with their own unique set of strengths and weaknesses. Just like the rest of us whom He continues to choose today. Jesus did not wait until the Twelve had proven themselves faithful, earned His trust, or walked in selfless compassion before He called them. He called them right where they were, in that moment of their lives, knowing that *walking with Him* is what changes us. He never expected them to follow Him perfectly; His aim was for them to follow faithfully. His call on our lives is the same, Dear Friend.

Lord Jesus, thank You for choosing me. May I bring glory to Your name as I walk this earthly journey with You. Amen.

JULY 10

Even to your old age and gray hairs I am He, I am He who will sustain you. I have made you and I will carry you; I will sustain you and I will rescue you. Isaiah 46:4

One year for my birthday, my husband and children "adopted" an elephant from the Elephant Sanctuary in Hohenwald, Tennessee, in my honor. I was delighted to receive a picture of her and a copy of her biography. Her name is Shirley.

She was born in 1948 in the wild, then captured in 1953 and brought to the United States. She performed at a circus for twenty-four years and then lived at a zoo for the next twenty-two. In her early teens she survived a fire that left multiple scars on her body; she also lost part of her right ear. When she was twenty-eight, she was attacked by another circus elephant and her back right leg was broken. It was not set and healed poorly, which led to life becoming even more difficult. Due to her injury, she lived in isolation for years at the zoo, which goes against the typical herd-like mentality of elephants. A survivor in the truest sense of the word, she weathered her trials alone for almost fifty years. She came to the Sanctuary on July 6, 1999, and she will live out the remainder of her days in a caring environment that provides nurturing, stability, security, love, and—finally—friends.

What parallels can you draw between yourself and Shirley? How long have you been "performing" for others' benefit? How long have you lived with bars around you? How many fires have you survived, and what do your scars look like? How have you survived the attacks of others? How many injuries have you sustained that were not set and healed poorly? How long have you lived in isolation?

I pray you are encouraged today by Shirley's story of resilience and hope. God has made us and will sustain us; He will rescue us and carry us—even 9,000-pound elephants—to safety in His sanctuary. He will provide for our needs as our brokenness gives way to blessing. Amen.

JULY 11

The Lord is slow to anger but great in power; the Lord will not leave the guilty unpunished. Nahum 1:3a

I think this speaks volumes about the nature of God. First, He is *slow to anger*. We, as humans, are not. There really isn't a continuum for us: "marginally angry," "lukewarm angry," "sort of angry." No, when we get angry, we are at a full 10, the red-faced heart-pounding kind of angry. Yet God is not like that. He is slow to anger. He has such great patience with us and compassion for us in our sin, struggles, and shortcomings. However, once He *does* get there, let the earth tremble. For once the "Slow One to Anger" is angry, we must also remember that He is great in power.

I think God *has* to be slow to anger *because* He is great in power. If He reacted without restraint each time His people worshipped other gods, flagrantly disobeyed Him, or complained about Him, humanity would not have survived through Genesis, much less made it to (or through) the wanderings in Exodus. Not to mention the challenges we continue to offer today. God is also slow to anger because He wants all people to come to repentance and reconciliation. He told the prophet Ezekiel, "Do I take any pleasure in the death of the wicked? Rather, am I not pleased when they turn from their ways and live?" (Eze. 18:23). Yet if they do not, the Lord will indeed dispense His righteous judgment. God's holiness demands that all unrepentant sin be punished—and He will not falter or fail.

If you are struggling with unforgiveness for someone whose actions have brought you much pain, I hope this verse will bring you comfort today. The Lord is fully aware of your hurt, Beloved, and He is fully aware of the trespass against you. Not one tear you have shed has escaped His notice. He is the Ancient of Days (Dan. 7:9), His judgments are righteous and true (Ps. 96:13), and He protects the way of His faithful ones (Prov. 2:8). "Bear in mind that our Lord's patience means salvation" (2 Pet. 3:15a). In Jesus' name, Amen.

JULY 12

Would you condemn Me to justify yourself? Job 40:8b

Our cat, Max, liked to sleep at the foot of our bed. This was not really a problem until he began the irksome habit of inching closer and closer to our heads during the night, eventually positioning himself right at the top of our pillows. If we woke up and discovered him there, he was unceremoniously relocated to the floor. One night I was lying in bed and felt, yet again, the tell-tale sign of hair brushing across my face. I reached up behind me, ready to grab our 13-pound furball, and instead I grabbed a handful of my own hair, which I had pulled up into a high ponytail before bedding down for the night. I had falsely accused the cat, my friend. I felt terrible. How much worse I feel when I falsely accuse the Lord.

Can you relate? Have you ever felt that God was being unjust, unfair, or unloving towards you? When we choose to blame God for our problems rather than approaching Him as the One who can solve them, we are in error. The Scriptures teach us plainly that God does not lie (Tit. 1:2); in Him there is no darkness at all (1 John 1:5b); and He does not change (Jas. 1:17). Our accusations of wrongdoing on His part are rooted in areas of pride, distrust, and unbelief in our own hearts.

Yes, Beloved, circumstances in life can be tragic and unspeakable. And when those tragedies befall us or others we love, it can be tempting to turn to God and say, "How could You let this happen?!" When those feelings come, Dear One, we still turn to God. Yet we must—we MUST—rehearse with Him what we know to be true about His character and His unfailing love for us (see Isa. 54:10). Satan gains precious ground when we blame God for our pain and turn away from Him. Let's not aid and abet the enemy in his work.

Father, I know that nothing I face in life is ever too difficult for You to handle. When I am struggling, help me to turn to You. Amen.

JULY 13

We want to remind you, friends, of the trouble we had in the province of Asia. The burdens laid upon us were so great and so heavy that we gave up all hope of staying alive. We felt that the death sentence had been passed on us. But this happened so that we should rely, not on ourselves, but only on God, who raises the dead. 2 Corinthians 1:8-9 GNT

Although Paul doesn't specify the trials he and Timothy had faced in Asia province, it is clear that they encountered many experiences that left them feeling certain they would not survive. When was the last time you felt certain that you would not survive the pain in your life, Beloved? Hold that thought in your mind as we glance at Paul's next words: "But this happened so that we should rely, not on ourselves, but only on God." Paul and Timothy's *"this"* was a series of experiences in which their very lives were threatened. My *"this"* was living in a dank cell of depression and self-loathing. What is your *"this"*? The list of possibilities is as endless as we who are facing them.

The paradox of pain, my friend, is that it draws us closer to the Father. Yes, we praise Him in our joy. And yet we crawl to Him in our grief, seeking Him in our pain. When *"this"* happens in our lives, we cannot rely on ourselves. We *must* rely on God. And when we do, we enjoy a sweet fellowship with Jesus that cannot be obtained in any other way. Our God can use even our *"this"* for good. The very Spirit of God who raised Jesus from the dead *lives in us* and gives us life (Rom. 8:11). *That* is how we make it through the *"this,"* Beloved. We draw close to God, who "gives life to everything" (1 Tim. 6:13)—even the parts of us we've believed long since dead.

Father, thank You for the hope offered to me through Your Word and through Your Son. May this hope become a fresh reality in my life today as I rely on Your indwelling Spirit to bring new life and carry me through my *"this."* In Jesus' name, Amen.

JULY 14

Do not be overcome by evil, but overcome evil with good.
Romans 12:21

Several years ago I quit watching the news, because every time I did, it caused my heart to hurt and my mind to incline towards despair. Life gets hard sometimes, and we can feel overcome by evil—but we are called to overcome evil with good.

We need not lead a global crusade in order to be useful to the kingdom, Beloved. We often feel like the small things we do are just that—small things with little lasting impact. This is not true. When we pray for another Child of God, when we call to check in on someone who is struggling, when we write an encouraging note, when we take the time to really *listen* to someone's story—those actions of love are *powerful*, and their effects ripple out into our hurting world. When we act in love, my friend, God pours out hope and promise among His people.

My children and I rescue earthworms. As we walk around the block, any time we see an invertebrate friend who has mistakenly made it onto the sidewalk, we stop and gently place it in the grass. I teach my children to pick the worms up gently. I teach them to introduce themselves and make polite conversation so the worms won't be afraid. I teach them to carefully set the worms down and to cover them with leaves or grass so that birds won't swoop down and get them. It's a small thing, I know. But it makes a difference to those worms. It makes a difference to my children. And in this small thing, we are learning about how to do the "big thing," the task God has set for all of us as *His* children. We are to be His hands and feet in this hurting world—that we might not be overcome by evil, but that we might overcome evil with some good.

How will you overcome for the kingdom today, Beloved? I pray for your success. Let us not become weary in doing good, Dear Friend. He is faithful to bring a harvest from our obedience (Gal. 6:9). Amen.

<u>JULY 15</u>

When I was a child, I talked like a child, I thought like a child, I reasoned like a child. When I became a man, I put the ways of childhood behind me. 1 Corinthians 13:11

For a long time I battled guilt, shame, and anger for choices I made when I was younger. I berated and condemned myself and kept thinking things like, *I should have known better! How could I have been so stupid?* I want to share something with you today; it's one of the most staggering revelations I had during many months of counseling as I worked on my healing. I finally realized that when I was a child, *I thought like a child.* When I was a teenager, *I reasoned like a teenager.* In condemning my younger self for making choices and decisions my adult self may have thought better of, I was missing the point entirely! My child self and my teenage self were only equipped with the thoughts, reasoning, and knowledge available to them *at that moment in time.* It seems so simple, but it radically changed my perspective. If this is an area of struggle for you, I hope this truth encourages you, too.

We must honor the children that we were. We must honor the teenagers that we were. We must honor the young adults that we were. And we must honor the people that we are right now. For the most part, each of us goes through life making the best choices we can, based on the information we have and resources available to us at the time. Cultivating awareness of that fact is the first step; once awareness is in place we can reach for compassion.

The Lord sees us with such love, my friend. I pray that we would learn to see ourselves with mercy and forgiveness as well. We need not continue to live our lives in shame for past choices or present mistakes. They are redeemed by the blood of our Savior, who longs to see us walking in the light of His glory. Let us learn from our mistakes, and let us also affirm the resilient spirit in the children, teenagers, and adults we were and are. In the saving name of Jesus, Amen.

JULY 16

I waited patiently for the Lord; He turned to me and heard my cry. [...] He put a new song in my mouth, a hymn of praise to our God. Many will see and fear the Lord and put their trust in Him. Psalm 40:1, 3

I am intrigued today by the notion of a "new song." I'm asking myself what kind of song I've been singing of late. Has it been a hymn of hope, or a dirge of despair? A serenade of salvation, or a ballad of bitterness? A tune of triumph, or a lament of loss? Something that continually amazes me about our God is that He doesn't just make our circumstances *look* better—he transforms them. He turns our weeping into dancing, our brokenness into blessing. He doesn't sweep our pain under the rug, gloss over it with a blessing, or pretend like He doesn't see it. When we wait upon the Lord and cry out to Him, He *moves*. He acts. He heals. And He gives us a new song.

What happens if we can no longer sing? What if life's oppression has become so burdensome that we can only groan in our affliction? In that case, my friend, *others sing for us.* Others intercede on our behalf. Others carry our mats straight to Jesus and beseech Him for our healing, waiting in expectation. "When Jesus saw their faith, He said [...], 'Son, your sins are forgiven'" (Mark 2:5). *Their* faith, my friend. If someone you love can no longer sing, would you sing on their behalf today? And if God has given you a new song, my friend, would you sing it out today, that others might hear?

Today, Father, I sing for those who have lost their voices to grief, to bitterness, to hardship, to despair. I sing for those broken by loss, addiction, and betrayal; for those paralyzed by ongoing situations and circumstances that have no foreseeable end in sight. I petition You, Father, to put a new song in their mouths—one of hope, healing, blessing, and peace. Redeem and restore, Lord, that others might witness Your unparalleled power and give glory to Your name. Amen!

JULY 17

Am I now trying to win the approval of human beings, or of God? Or am I trying to please people? If I were still trying to please people, I would not be a servant of Christ. Galatians 1:10

This is a question I have to constantly ask myself, because I tend to want to please others and sometimes I don't stop and consider if what I am doing or saying is also pleasing to God. As Peter writes, "people are slaves to whatever has mastered them" (2 Pet. 2:19b); we will always be enslaved to the person or persons from whom we most seek approval.

Seeking God's approval leads us to freedom, because He will never exploit us or lead us astray. He has no hidden agenda, no ulterior motives, and no ego that needs boosting. He is completely competent and secure in who He is, and His desire is always to lead us in the paths of righteousness. He has our best interests at heart, although He prioritizes our character over our comfort. When we place God as Master over our lives, we can rest in the assurance that He will always be acting on behalf of what is best for us in the present moment and beyond, in accordance with His perfect plan.

Seeking approval from others, however, can cause many problems—even if the other people we'd like to please are our family members, friends, teachers, pastors, bosses, co-workers, or fellow believers! Every time we approach a task or situation with the goal of pleasing another human being, it backfires. Though the immediate response may be positive, the long-term consequences are always negative. We can become addicted to having others' approval to a point where we lose our sense of self. We also set ourselves up for certain failure, because we won't always please everyone, regardless of our efforts. When we instead strive to please God, the benefits are eternal, not ephemeral.

Father, I long to please You above all else. Help my mind and heart remain in step with Your Spirit, that I might align myself with Your will. Amen.

JULY 18

Be careful not to make a treaty with those who live in the land; for when they prostitute themselves to their gods and sacrifice to them, they will invite you and you will eat their sacrifices. Exodus 34:15

I have three children, so we receive our fair share of invitations to birthday parties. Long ago I realized that we cannot physically (let alone financially) attend every party to which we are invited. During the most recent incident of a child bringing home an invitation that received a "No," my response was met with whining: "Why *can't* I go?" I replied, "We don't have to attend every party we're invited to." This morning as I considered this notion of invitations again, I realized that it applies itself well to all areas of life, whether we are children or adults!

Consider with me the fact that we do not have to attend every gossip session to which we are invited. We do not have to accept the invitation to have that second or third drink. We do not have to agree to assume financial liability for that person who has invited us to do so. We do not have to attend every social event, argument, or temptation to which we are invited. We can say no. We can respectfully decline. And many times, God *expects* us to decline.

To which events or circumstances do you find yourself continually invited? Has it occurred to you that you can respectfully send your regrets, and choose not to take part? For me, one of the biggest struggles is the continual warfare that rages in my mind; I am often plagued with insecurity and self-doubt. I considered anew today the notion that I don't have to agree to be a part of it. I can decline the invitation from the enemy to engage in self-criticism for all of my perceived shortcomings. The world continually issues invitations to us, Beloved. Will we heed the siren song of those worldly calls, or will we attune our ears to the call of our Father, who always invites us to walk in the way that leads to righteousness? The choice is ours. Let's choose wisely today. Amen.

JULY 19

He had no beauty or majesty to attract us to Him, nothing in His appearance that we should desire Him. Isaiah 53:2b

Do you know what a geode is? It's a round or oblong-shaped rock that appears very plain on the outside, but when it is cut or broken open, beautiful crystals are revealed inside. These rocks were common to find on my grandparents' farm when I was little. I would go wading down by the creek, and in the piles of rocks along the shoreline, I'd often find geodes. The best part was always taking them back to the road where I could throw them down and see the crystals inside when they broke open. I still have one of them, and every time I look at it I marvel at the unimpressive and plain exterior that conceals the remarkable beauty within.

Our verse from Isaiah today is about Christ. God is always working to help us see things as He sees them, trying to remove the scales from our eyes that obscure our vision. As He told His prophet Samuel, "The Lord does not look at the things people look at. People look at the outward appearance, but the Lord looks at the heart" (1 Sam. 16:7b). It is perfectly fitting that God would have fashioned Jesus' earthly appearance in a cloak of ordinariness. God wanted people to be drawn to Jesus because of His heart, not because of His appearance. And what a beautiful and stunning heart there was—and is—within our Savior, Beloved! As He gave His life on the cross for our sins, His broken and battered body revealed the unparalleled magnificence and brilliance within.

We, too, are like geodes. Oftentimes we require a breaking open before the true beauty within us can be unveiled. Pain and suffering draw us closer to Christ. We often fear the unveiling; we often fear the brokenness and the pain. I pray that we will be encouraged today in knowing that God is faithful to reveal His glory in us through our broken places. In Jesus' name, Amen.

JULY 20

I am the Lord, the God of all mankind. Is anything too hard for Me? Jeremiah 32:27

A few years ago during a difficult period of pain and brokenness in my life, I was out walking on an old country road when a butterfly in a thicket caught my eye. I bent down for a closer look at its yellow and black body, and my heart skipped a beat. The butterfly was wounded. Horribly disfigured. Of its four wings, two were completely torn away. And of the two remaining, the right one had holes across the top and the bottom half was torn, hanging limply underneath. I whispered, "What happened to you?" and slowly reached out my hand in the hopes that it would allow me to touch it. As my hand drew closer, it fluttered off, settling nearby.

As I watched the butterfly, I contemplated the fact that all of us are broken in some way. Some of us have physical infirmities which are outwardly visible—like my butterfly friend. Some of us have deep emotional wounds. All of us are scarred from past hurts and losses. And as I thought about this, I wondered: *How often do we allow those past hurts to be an excuse for not allowing God to use us for His glory?* This butterfly, after suffering such a horrific mauling, should have been dead. Why, then, was it still here? Maybe the thought had just never occurred to it to give up or give in.

What happened next was more than I ever could have imagined—the butterfly took flight. Yes, my friend. With its two remaining wings, it swooped and soared upward into the sun. And I felt God saying to my heart, "If the butterfly can do it, Child, *so can you.*" This creature could have chosen to let its initial wounding go ahead and kill it. But it didn't. I didn't. You didn't. We are still here. We may be wounded, but *we can still fly*, and that is to our Father's amazing glory.

Take flight today, Beloved. You can. In Jesus' name, Amen.

JULY 21

In fact, the law requires that nearly everything be cleansed with blood, and without the shedding of blood there is no forgiveness.
Hebrews 9:22

Today we're going to talk about self-injury. Although it isn't as "well-known" an addiction as alcoholism, drug abuse, eating disorders, or pornography, it's out there, and it affects many people—especially our young people. To ignore it is to do those who wrestle with it and are searching for God's truth in the matter a tremendous disservice. As with any area of sin or struggle, bringing it out of the shadows and into the healing light of God's Word and His truth is always the right answer.

This verse from Hebrews is often used by self-injurers to justify their sin. Certainly, taken out of context, it presents a rather convincing argument in favor of engaging in the behavior—even spins it with an added air of piety. It's not. It's sin. We commit another grievous sin when we pull pieces of God's Word out of context and use them to rationalize our choices and behaviors. The only way we can eradicate this dangerous habit is by wielding the Sword of the Spirit (Eph. 6:17) and slaying our distortions with the truth of God's Word. I say this not to preach at you, Dear Friend, but because I know it from painful personal experience.

The truth that relegates this verse into its proper place is found in Romans 6:14b, which says: "you are not under law, but under grace." The *law* required that everything be cleansed with blood. We are *not under the law* anymore. *We are under grace*, which was given to us as the New Covenant through Jesus Christ and the offering of *His* precious—and sinless—blood (see Heb. 7:22-28). To shed our blood in the name of sacrifice to God is to distort and misrepresent the heart of God and His Word. If you need to hear this truth today, Beloved, hear it. Let it sink down deep. If you know someone who is struggling with this area of sin, please share this with them today. May His truth bring freedom and healing. In Jesus' name, Amen.

JULY 22

Then the righteous will answer Him, "Lord, when did we see You hungry and feed You, or thirsty and give You something to drink? When did we see You a stranger and invite You in, or needing clothes and clothe you? When did we see You sick or in prison and go to visit You?" The King will reply, "Truly I tell you, whatever you did for one of the least of these brothers and sisters of mine, you did for Me." Matthew 25:37-40

I am reminded afresh today that at any given moment in our lives, we will find ourselves in at least one of the categories mentioned above. What about you today, my friend? Are you hungry? Thirsty? Alienated? In need of clothing? Sick? In prison? If at first glance you find yourself thinking, "None of these—all of my needs are met," I encourage you to probe a little more deeply. We can all be hungry for God's deliverance or thirsty for His healing water. We can all find ourselves alienated from friends or family members over a dispute or disagreement. We can all be in need of exchanging our filthy rags of sin for robes of righteousness in Christ. We can all be battling an ongoing physical infirmity or a heartsickness that knows no bounds. And finally, Dear One, we do not have to be incarcerated to be imprisoned.

So I will ask you again, now, to consider—which of these categories feels most like your area of need today? It is not a bad thing to be in need, my friend. When we are experiencing moments of hardship or seasons of difficulty, others within the body of Christ are invited to step up and minister to us—to encourage us, to pray for us, to remind us of God's heart and what we know is His truth. They help us center ourselves in the midst of our circumstances, and it is a time of mutual blessing. Each time we do this, we are fulfilling the call of Christ in our lives!

Father, enable me to share Your love with another Child in need today. In Jesus' name, Amen.

JULY 23

...being confident of this, that He who began a good work in you will carry it on to completion until the day of Christ Jesus. Philippians 1:6

Today what has struck me about Paul's heartfelt words to the congregation of believers at Philippi is that his confidence in the believers' ability to walk in the ways of the Lord was not dependent upon their efforts, their will, or their ability—but upon God.

Paul acknowledges that it was God who *began* a good work in the believers, granting them hearts that would seek Him and aspire to live in His ways; it was God who would *carry* that good work throughout the course of their lives; and it was God who would *complete* the work in them at that final moment when they were caught up into glory and received into the open arms of Jesus. God is always working, my friend!

I don't know where this thought meets you today, but for me it provides quite a bit of comfort! Although it is important that I continue to yield my heart to God and align my thoughts in accordance with the truth of His Word; although it is imperative that I love others and serve those in need; the "good work" God began in me is not a responsibility that I have to shoulder alone—which also means its fulfillment is not dependent solely upon my efforts or my performance! When we know that our mighty God is the One working in us to give us the victory (so that we might give Him the glory), the pressure to do everything perfectly falls right off our shoulders. It is our job, like the believers at Philippi, to abide in Him, to rest in Him, to remain in Him, and to accept Christ's gift of salvation in our lives. When we keep ourselves in God's love (Jude 21), He will enable and empower us to bear much fruit for His glory.

Father, thank You for the timely and blessed reassurance that You are always working in my life to carry the plans and purposes You have for me into completion. In Jesus' name, Amen.

JULY 24

Because we loved you so much, we were delighted to share with you not only the gospel of God but our lives as well. 1 Thessalonians 2:8a

God weaves our lives together like a rich tapestry, interspersing all types of fabrics in every conceivable color. Sometimes He weaves burlap into our lives, and sometimes He weaves satin. Both contribute to the overall beauty and depth of our tapestry; both are essential. Yet only some of these strands become the gold and silver threads that are woven into the very fibers of our hearts. What a twofold blessing it is indeed when God places someone in your path with whom you share a love of the Lord—and a portion of your heart and your life as well.

Whom has God woven into your life, and into your heart, in the ways that Paul describes today? With whom have you enjoyed sharing your walk with the Lord, and your very life as well—not just the superficial surface things, but the deeper things of your inner self? These friendships are a sacred gift from the Father, placed into our hands. We need the burlap and the wool and the jute and the tweed; these people smooth our rough edges and challenge us to grow. Yet we delight in the velvet, the cashmere, the silk and the satin—the ones who weave beauty, hope, laughter, and love into our hearts and our lives.

We share our love of the Gospel with billions worldwide; we share our love of the Gospel *and* our true selves with precious few. I am thanking God today for the distinct and beautiful fabrics, with their distinct and beautiful colors, that He has woven into my life through the years. I invite you to do the same. May we continue to center our friendships within the larger, all-encompassing, perfect love of Jesus Christ, whose strands of crimson, gold, purple, and white weave their way through all of our lives, through all the millennia, binding us all together in Him. Amen.

JULY 25

Because Your faithful love is right in front of me—I walk in Your truth! Psalm 26:3 CEB

I noted today that David didn't write, "Your *law* is right in front of me." He wrote, "Your *love* is right in front of me." I often get so caught up in following the checklist of what I think I "should" be doing that I end up placing unrealistic expectations on myself. And then when I inevitably fall short of them, I become frustrated with myself and tend to slink off towards that dark, airless dungeon of "Not Good Enough." This is not what God has in mind for His children.

David rightly honed in on the *love* of God, the *heart* of God. I need to realign my focus likewise. When our eyes are focused on God's love as the beacon shining forth ahead of us, providing the light to guide our footsteps along the path, we will find ourselves naturally walking in His truth and willingly following His commands. We will trust His heart to lead us in paths of righteousness for His name's sake (Ps. 23:3). And we will know that even if we find ourselves on rocky terrain or in a dense jungle; even if we are teetering on a narrow precipice or paddling through dark and murky waters, His love is ever before us, illuminating the way forward and securing our steps.

A life lived focusing on God's *law* instead of God's *love* is what the Pharisees did. They carefully obeyed every letter of the law and yet fell short in the end because they missed out on the loving—which is what lives devoted to God are all about. As Paul writes, "Love does no harm to a neighbor. Therefore love is the fulfillment of the law" (Rom. 13:10). When we are in tune with God's love for us, our natural response is the desire to live our lives in a manner that shares that love with others.

Father, I long to live my life in a way that brings You glory. As I remind myself of Your unfailing love for me, guide my steps and enable me to walk in Your truth. In Jesus' name, Amen.

JULY 26

Circumcise your hearts, therefore, and do not be stiff-necked any longer. Deuteronomy 10:16

A few years ago I went through a period of time where I routinely suffered from debilitating neck pain. It would come on suddenly and acutely, without any warning or reason. It would take days to abate, leaving me in agony and confusion. Often this verse would come to my mind during those times, since I was literally experiencing the sensation of being "stiff-necked." I wondered if God was trying to tell me to stop being stubborn and disobedient in some area of my life. I pondered what being "stiff-necked" actually meant. What it meant for me was that I could not turn my head well in any direction, and looking *up* or *down* was excruciating. All I could do was focus on what was immediately in front of me.

When we look to God for help and guidance, typically we look upwards to heaven. And when we pray to Him for clarity and direction, we typically bow our heads. In my "stiff-necked" state, I could do neither. That season taught me, repeatedly, that I *do not* want to be stiff-necked in my relationship with the Lord! In what areas of your life are you feeling a bit of neck stiffening coming on, Beloved? I encourage you to bring those areas before Him today, and ask for His direction and clarity.

Secondly, what does it mean for us to circumcise our hearts? It seems to imply cutting off the flow of blood to the diseased parts of our hearts that cause confusion and sin, and letting the healthy part of the heart take over. This task seems daunting to me, if not impossible. Then, I discovered this: "The Lord your God will circumcise your hearts [...] so that you may love Him with all your heart and with all your soul, and live" (Deut. 30:6). How gracious and merciful is our Father, that He is willing to step in and do for us what we cannot do for ourselves? Entrust your heart to Him today, Dear One. He is able to fill it with light and love. Amen.

JULY 27

So my heart began to despair over all my toilsome labor under the sun. For a person may labor with wisdom, knowledge and skill, and then they must leave all they own to another who has not toiled for it. This too is meaningless and a great misfortune.
Ecclesiastes 2:20-21

As I read this I cannot help but think (with horror) of what the repercussions would have been for us if Jesus had undertaken this viewpoint as the end of His life drew near. Obviously Jesus' wisdom, knowledge, and skill were unsurpassed. And did God *really* expect Him to leave His work in the hands of the bumbling Eleven who squabbled over who got the best seats in heaven and which one of them was the greatest on earth (see Mark 10:35-41; Luke 9:46-48)?

Fortunately for all of us, Jesus did not see it that way at all. He knew the time and love He had invested in His chosen ones. He knew that their hearts were committed to Him and that they would be filled with the Spirit and accomplish great things for the kingdom after His death. In fact, He told them outright: "It is for your good that I am going away. Unless I go away, the Advocate will not come to you; but if I go, I will send Him to you" (John 16:7b). He knew that the time He had devoted to them had been worthwhile. They were ready.

We are all in this together. Older believers are continually teaching and preparing younger ones for a time in which they will have to step up. Those of us in the trenches of parenting young children are showing them how to pray, reading the Bible with them, talking about Jesus and His wondrous love for us. One day we will all find ourselves in the sunset years of our lives, getting ready to pass the baton to the next ones in line. I pray that we can make the hand-off with full assurance that we have run our leg of the race well and that our confidence is well-placed in the next runners in the relay of Life. I can't wait for the celebration that awaits us all in heaven. Be encouraged in your walk today. Amen!

JULY 28

Though you search for your enemies, you will not find them.
Those who wage war against you will be as nothing at all. For I
am the Lord your God who takes hold of your right hand and
says to you, Do not fear; I will help you. Isaiah 41:12-13

It occurred to me as I read this that if God is holding on to our right hands, that most likely means that He is holding on to us with His left hand. Perhaps there are a few different reasons for that.

First, His power and might depart from His right hand; it's the source of His deliverance (see Ex. 15:6; Ps. 44:3)—so He would need that hand free to do His work. You may be interested to know that He also "spread out the heavens" with His right hand (Isa. 48:13) and planted Christ, the Root of the vine of Israel (Ps. 80:14-15) with that self-same hand. And not only that, God's right hand also upholds us (Ps. 63:8), sustains us (Ps. 18:35), and saves us (Ps. 17:7)! Second, we know that Jesus sits at the right hand of God (Mark 16:19; Rom. 8:34), which means that spot is already (and indefinitely) taken! The last possibility is that God is taking firm hold of our right hand in order to squelch any feeble attempts we might be making to accomplish something by our own "power." (See His response to this specific issue in Job 40:6-14.) It's as if He's saying, "Listen, Child, your right hand is just not going to the get the job done here. Let Me hang on to that for you, and now you just watch and I'll show you how it's done." And there's Jesus, sitting next to that powerful right hand, looking over at His Father and smiling.

Which of these truths brings you the greatest comfort today, Beloved? In what situation do you currently need the right hand of God to deliver you, sustain you, or save you? Hear His words to you today: "Do not fear, Child; I will help you."

Father, I echo the words of David today in the fullest assurance of their truth: "I keep my eyes always on the Lord. With Him at my right hand, I will not be shaken." (Ps. 16:8). In the mighty name of Jesus, Amen.

JULY 29

I have come into the world as a light, so that no one who believes in Me should stay in darkness. John 12:46

For a long time, I believed in God but I lived in darkness. I knew that God was calling me to come out of that darkness and into His light, but I could not do it. I *would* not do it. I wrestled with deep levels of self-hatred and saw myself as unworthy of God's notice, much less something as staggering as Christ's torturous death on a cross *for me.* I believed that God really should not have been so gracious to me, and I desperately wanted to atone for my own sins. Finally I realized that in my misguided desire to pay for my own sin, I was basically throwing Christ's blood back in His face and saying, "No thanks. Not good enough. I'd rather earn it on my own."

When confronted with the galling pride within myself, I felt such shame. God has been so faithful to walk with me through that place of confusion and distortion, patiently guiding me with His truth and His light. He calls each one of us out of our darkness, Beloved, but it's up to us whether we choose to come out or stay there.

I don't know where this meets you personally today, my friend, but I do know that some of you know exactly what I'm talking about. Today I want to say to you that God loves you so much. He longs for you to trust Him, to trust His heart, and to trust that He sent His Son to die for you—and Jesus accepted the assignment—because they love you so! They longed to provide that gift to you. Will you choose to accept it, and hold out your hands to receive the gifts of love, grace, mercy, truth, forgiveness, and dignity that they long to bestow upon you? You may think, "I'm not worth it!" The gift does not choose its own worth, my friend. The Buyer gets to decide how much He is willing to pay. Jesus chose you and paid for your life in full—with His very own. I pray that we would accept His gift of love, light, and sacrifice today with renewed thanksgiving and praise. Amen.

JULY 30

The Lord turned to [Gideon] and said, "Go in the strength you have and save Israel out of Midian's hand. Am I not sending you?" "Pardon me, my Lord," Gideon replied, "but how can I save Israel? My clan is the weakest in Manasseh, and I am the least in my family." The Lord answered, "I will be with you." Judges 6:14-16a

This is one of my favorite exchanges between God and man in the Bible. I can relate to Gideon's fear, anxiety, and doubt. And it is understandable that he would feel that way, since his people had been harshly oppressed by the Midianites for seven long years. After that long in captivity, existing under the constant threat of harm, Gideon had reasonable grounds for anxiety. Yet, it is precisely those who *can't* win the battle in their own strength whom God calls. This dialogue is beautiful: God says, "Go in the strength you have," and then we have Gideon's bewildered response: "How can I do this? My clan is the weakest, and I am the least." Notice that all of Gideon's focus is on his own limitations: "I can't do this. I am the weakest and the least." When our focus is limited to our own shortcomings and weaknesses, we make excuse after excuse about why we can't do what God is calling us to do. God has to gently refocus Gideon's eyes on the one truth that makes all of this possible: "I will be with you!" It isn't our "I can't" that matters, my friend; it's His "*I can!*" In God's skillful hands, our weaknesses are turned to strength (Heb. 11:34b).

In what area of your life right now do you need for God to turn your weakness to strength? Whatever answer comes to mind, He can do it! It is precisely in our human weakness that God shows Himself strongest (2 Cor. 12:9). The only requirement is our willingness to allow *His* strength to fill us, ceasing to strive on our own. Maybe, like Gideon, God is calling you to do something you *know* you cannot do. It's time to stop making those excuses, my friend. Once He calls you to it, He'll equip you to do it. He *never* sets us up to fail. Amen!

JULY 31

I the Lord do not change. So you, the descendants of Jacob, are not destroyed. Malachi 3:6

God does not wear masks, my friend. He doesn't disguise His true feelings, saying one thing and meaning another. He's not in the business of promising something and not following through. He doesn't conceal Himself behind a curtain, manipulating us like marionettes on strings. He is alive, He is present, He is eternal. And He does not change. His emotions don't get the best of Him. His feelings don't run away with Him. His patience doesn't give out even when we whine, pout, sulk, and accuse Him of not listening to us and not loving us. He doesn't lose His temper. He may get *angry*, Beloved, but He is always in full control of Himself, even in His righteous anger. I need to know that He does not hold on to resentment, harbor unforgiveness, or operate out of passive-aggressive insecurity. Nor will He ever. He will always be light, love, goodness, grace, peace, mercy, and hope because that's who He *is*—not what He *does*.

The second part of this verse makes me smile. God is reminding us that *because* He is not subject to the limitations of our human condition, His constancy and His binding covenant with His children (no matter what their behavior or backsliding) will never be destroyed. The hope that we have in Him is secure, because He will never forsake us or break His oath to us. He does not change.

What part of God's unchanging character means the most to you today? Maybe it's His grace. Maybe it's His ability to deliver you from despair. Maybe it's His light that shines in the darkness. Maybe it's the hope we have through His Son. Maybe it's His power to resurrect what has been thought long dead. Maybe it's His willingness to reach out and touch a leper. Maybe it's the fact that He knows every last thing about you and loves you infinitely all the same. Whatever it is, would you take some time to thank Him and praise Him today? Amen.

AUGUST 1

Yet some gleanings will remain, as when an olive tree is beaten, leaving two or three olives on the topmost branches, four or five on the fruitful boughs. Isaiah 17:6a

It had never occurred to me before today that in order to harvest its fruit, an olive tree has to be beaten. A quick search revealed that on occasion, olives are picked one by one—but for the most part, harvesting is done by placing nets around the trees and shaking them. Obviously, bearing fruit can be a painful process at times! Just because we've done the job well and have borne a bountiful harvest doesn't mean we won't occasionally suffer a beating from life. However, our faithful Gardener will assure that all the hard knocks that come our way will serve to remove the good fruit so we will be ready to bear another crop. (If you're thinking that you'd prefer to forgo the beating and keep your fruit, remember: Fruit is meant to be harvested and shared, not left to rot on the tree!)

As for the point of this verse within the chapter, the focus is not on the beating the olive tree suffers, but rather on the "gleanings" that remain—in other words, the "remnant." The Old Testament often refers to a "remnant" of God's people, the ones who remain faithful even when the larger population has turned away. God promises again and again that He will save and restore this remnant (see, for example, Isa. 37:31-32). Remnants are not just a thing of the past. Paul speaks of them in the book of Romans, saying: "So too, at the present time there is a remnant chosen by grace" (11:5). In the very same chapter he goes on to compare us, the Gentile believers, to a wild olive shoot that has been grafted into the Lord's cultivated olive tree of Israel (vv. 17, 24). We are all one body, one tree, rooted in Christ Jesus; "we share in His sufferings in order that we may also share in His glory" (Rom. 8:17).

Father, thank You for grafting me into the Tree of Life and helping me bear fruit for Your glory. In Jesus' name, Amen.

AUGUST 2

I have listened attentively, but they do not say what is right. None of them repent of their wickedness, saying, "What have I done?" Each pursues their own course like a horse charging into battle. [...] Are they ashamed of their detestable conduct? No, they have no shame at all; they do not even know how to blush. So they will fall among the fallen; they will be brought down when they are punished, says the Lord. Jeremiah 8:6, 12

We live in a culture where blushing is becoming a rarity. A constant onslaught from media sources inundates us with images, messages, and information that, if we are not careful to guard ourselves, can desensitize us and lead us astray. Yet we cannot blame others for our lack of self-control. While the media continues to churn out graphic images, shocking shows, and explicit language, we are the ones buying into their products. The people of Judah tried the blame game too, my friend, and it earned them seventy years of exile in Babylon. God loved His children far more than He loved the city that bore His name. He can easily restore a city. It's a wayward child who proves more difficult—because He will not violate our free will.

The people of Judah gave no thought to their detestable ways, each one pursuing his own desires "like a horse charging into battle." Although war horses *would* charge bravely into the battle scene, they didn't normally charge without the sound of a trumpet or the command of a rider urging them on. Who's the rider on your horse today, Beloved? Are you being urged to charge ahead into a danger zone where sin waits to entrap you? Or perhaps you're disregarding the voice of your rider and charging ahead in your own recklessness. We must seek the counsel of our supreme commander, the Lord of Heaven's Armies, to give us the orders of when to charge and when to retreat. Let's hand the reins over to Him, my friend. He will always direct our paths to safety and lasting security in Him. Amen.

AUGUST 3

[God] knows the secrets of the heart. Psalm 44:21b

Today and tomorrow, we're going to talk about secrets. Why do we keep secrets, my friend? What is it that we are so afraid for others to know about us? What things do we resolve to keep so deeply hidden that they may never see the light of day? The trouble with keeping things in the dark, away from the light, away from the Son, is that they mutate. They multiply. They rot and spread dankness and disease throughout their host. We are the hosts, my friend, so let me ask you: What's eating you alive inside today?

This topic really hits home for me, because I spent many years hiding the "real" me, afraid that if others could see the brokenness and wreckage within, they would avert their eyes in disgust. I kept myself functioning well on the outside, but inside I was battling self-hatred, shame, anger, and confusion. I was trying so hard to heal myself and rely on God to bring healing, but I seemed to be getting nowhere and was so ashamed of my mess. Letting others "see" it was anathema to me.

I eventually realized that we cannot truly help one another and encourage one another if we keep hiding our pain and our struggles. Christ's light can only shine out into the world through *broken* vessels, my friend—not perfect ones. I finally realized that He was calling me to face down my fear and to open up, to be authentic, to be real, and to share my heart and my struggles with others. We are all, for the most part, doing the best we can each day. We need affirmation, encouragement, love, and support from one another—not masks, façades, and judgment.

Where does this meet you today, Beloved? Do you find it easy to be open with others, or is it a challenge? How do you typically receive the openness of others? Even though transparency can be hard, Jesus calls us to have the courage to do it anyway. May we rise to the occasion today, my friend, empowered by His strength and grace. Amen.

AUGUST 4

Rather, we have renounced secret and shameful ways; we do not use deception, nor do we distort the Word of God. On the contrary, by setting forth the truth plainly we commend ourselves to everyone's conscience in the sight of God. 2 Corinthians 4:2

Hebrews 4:13a says, "Nothing in all creation is hidden from God's sight." To some of us, that may be cause for anxiety; for others, it may bring a blessed sense of relief. There are two types of secrets: "past secrets" that we keep out of shame or guilt, fearing that if other people knew *that* truth about us, they might judge us or decide not to like us. There are also "present secrets" that we keep, usually from a desire to conceal areas of ongoing sin. Those are the ones I want to talk about today.

Jesus said, "Everyone who does evil hates the light, and will not come into the light for fear that their deeds will be exposed" (John 3:20). And we know that "God is light; in Him there is no darkness at all" (1 John 1:5b). Thus, when we are "walking in the light," we are walking in openness and truth, without hiding and concealing anything. Yet, as we find in the book of Job, "There are those who rebel against the light, who do not know its ways or stay in its paths" (24:13). Even when we rebel, Beloved, guess what: "Our secret sins [are] in the light of [God's] presence" (Ps. 90:8). We cannot hide ourselves from God, my friend. And we cannot heal in the dark.

Are you walking in any areas of darkness today? Whatever the secrets may be that you are harboring, the solution is to bring them out into the healing and restorative light of God. Not all of our "stuff" is meant to be shared with everyone, but all of our "stuff" *must* be shared with God! Paul writes, "For you are all children of light, children of the day" (1 Thess. 5:5a ESV). We are children of the *light*, Dear One. Not of the darkness. You have been chosen by God, "that you may declare the praises of Him who called you out of darkness into His wonderful light" (1 Pet. 2:9b). May He give you the strength and the courage to walk in His light today, surrendering any areas of darkness to Him. Amen.

AUGUST 5

For the kind of sorrow God wants us to experience leads us away from sin and results in salvation. There's no regret for that kind of sorrow. But worldly sorrow, which lacks repentance, results in spiritual death. 2 Corinthians 7:10 NLT

After talking about the importance of turning from our "secret sins" (Ps. 90:8) yesterday and bringing them before God, I felt as though I could not leave it at that and move on to an uplifting text from Leviticus. Conviction is always welcome in the life of a believer; yet when we just don't know what to do *next*, we can end up feeling confused, discouraged, and twice as ornery as we were to begin with.

Today's verse does a wonderful job of explaining *why* it is so important for us to turn from sin and run into God's open arms. Unfortunately, if you generally use the NIV version (as I do), that translation of this particular verse can cause some questions to form. Consider the wording in the NIV: "Godly sorrow brings repentance that leads to salvation and leaves no regret, but worldly sorrow brings death." I don't mind telling you that I spent *years* grappling with this verse because I truly felt sorry for my sins, I really thought I had repented and was walking in God's light, and I was certain of my salvation—but I still felt such *regret!* The problem was that I hadn't forgotten the mistakes I had made, and no amount of repenting made me feel as though those choices had been okay. I still regretted that I'd not chosen differently. Therefore, I spent (again) *years* thinking that I had not done the "godly sorrow" thing the *right way*, because here I still had regret! Oh, Dear Friend. Different translations can be lifesavers. Literally!

The New Living Translation helped me gain the perspective I needed in order to understand Paul's intent behind these words. Pain is inevitable in this life, but how we choose to receive it and direct it can make all the difference. Pain that leads us headlong into the arms of God is *never wasted*, and we never have to regret it! It has brought us *blessing*, because it has brought us *Christ!* Yet if our pain leads us away from Christ and into worldly means of relief—such as blaming, numbing, or engaging in addictive behaviors—*that* kind of pain will cause untold regret for us. Note the key words in our verse: worldly sorrow *lacks repentance.* We've allowed the pain to turn us *away* from God and into the false comforts of this world—which means that we are walking in darkness, away from the light of the Lord. The good news, Beloved, is that not even darkness is dark to God (Ps. 139:12). Even if you've made a terrible mess of things, He still sees you, He still loves you, and He is *always* eager for you to come running (or even limping) back to Him.

Remember the story of the prodigal son in Luke 15? When the father sees his son, whom he had feared forever lost, walking down that dusty road with his head hanging down, what does this father do? He gathers up his robe, takes off running to meet his son, throws his arms around him, and kisses him (v. 20). And then he throws a huge party to celebrate (vv. 23-24). Beloved, *that* is how God responds when His children come back home. *That* is the kind of lavish, forgiving, demonstrative love that He has for each and every one of us! You never have to worry that once you get back to the house, He'll pretend like He hasn't seen you from the window and hasn't heard your knock. No, Dear One. Our Father is watching for us, waiting to see our tired and weary frame appearing on the horizon. As soon as we start towards Him, He takes off running to meet us, scooping us up and twirling us around in sheer delight. *He loves you so!*

As Jesus said, "there will be more rejoicing in heaven over one sinner who repents than over ninety-nine righteous persons who do not need to repent" (Luke 15:7b). If you are experiencing pain and sorrow today, my friend, I pray that you will choose to let it propel you towards God, rather than away from Him and into the false comforts of this world. He is always waiting and hoping for His wayward children to come back home. In the saving name of Jesus, Amen.

AUGUST 6

But you, keep your head in all situations. 2 Timothy 4:5a

Sometimes we just have a misfire, don't we? I recently experienced one as I was trying to finish up a Bible study assignment for the day and mis-read the verse I was to close with. What I *thought* I saw was Hebrews 13:4, which says: "Marriage should be honored by all, and the marriage bed kept pure, for God will judge the adulterer and all the sexually im-moral." Alas, my friend, it was supposed to have been Hebrews 13:14, which reads: "For here we do not have an enduring city, but we are looking for the city that is to come." My eyebrows had shot up to my hairline as I stared down at the stern warnings to keep my marriage bed undefiled (all good reminders, mind you!), and then come to find out I was supposed to have been sweetly basking in the gentle truth of God's promised city of the New Jerusalem for those of us who are in Christ. God's Word resonates with truth, yet at times we can strike some inter-esting chords!

Where does this reminder from Paul meet you today, my friend? In what situation are you currently feeling inclined to "lose your head," as well as perhaps your temper, your patience, or your mind? Or maybe it's a situation that's causing despair rather than anger. Do you feel as though you are clinging to the last remaining vestiges of your strength, hope, or even faith?

I bring good news today, Beloved: Jesus promises us that He is with us until the very end: "And surely I am with you always, to the very end of the age" (Matt. 28:20b). We don't have to handle the situation perfect-ly before He chooses to meet us there and congratulate us on our aplomb. Far more often, we find Jesus rolling up His sleeves and jump-ing into the conflict, the grief, the pain, or the fear right alongside us, comforting us with the assurance of His presence. *That* is what enables us to "keep our heads" in all situations, no matter the complexity or the conflict. He enables us to do *all things* through His strength (Phil. 4:13)! May that reassurance bring hope to your heart today. Amen.

AUGUST 7

When the Lord saw that Leah was not loved, He enabled her to conceive. [...] Leah became pregnant and gave birth to a son. She named him Reuben, for she said, "It is because the Lord has seen my misery. Surely my husband will love me now." She conceived again, and when she gave birth to a son she said, "Because the Lord heard that I am not loved, He gave me this one too." So she named him Simeon. Again she conceived, and when she gave birth to a son she said, "Now at last my husband will become attached to me, because I have borne him three sons." So he was named Levi. She conceived again, and when she gave birth to a son she said, "This time I will praise the Lord." So she named him Judah. Then she stopped having children. Genesis 29:31a, 32-35

Leah's husband Jacob was tricked into marrying her by her father (vv. 22-27), and Jacob was in love with her younger sister, Rachel. It's interesting to see Leah's transition in thinking with each child she bore to Jacob: "Surely my husband will love me now." "The Lord heard that I am not loved, so He gave me this one too." "At last my husband will become attached to me." And then, "This time I will praise the Lord." Finally, after four children, Leah realizes the truth: Nothing I do can make another person love me. God sees me, hears me, and loves me, so I will praise the Lord.

For some of us, it takes harder lessons and greater devastation than the birth of four children to realize that we can't make someone else love us. Graciously, God blessed Leah with the lesson *and* the gift of her sons. Can you relate? Are you trying to "earn" someone else's love today? More painful still, have you given up on the love and begun hoping for just an attachment? Most importantly, have you learned the lesson that Leah learned? Circumstances may not always be as we would wish, but in *any* circumstance, even if our hearts are hurting, we can still choose to praise the Lord. He loves us always. Amen.

AUGUST 8

Moses reported this [the Lord's promise of deliverance and freedom] to the Israelites, but they did not listen to him because of their discouragement and harsh labor. Exodus 6:9

When is the last time you've felt like the Israelites did—in a season of discouragement and imprisonment that appeared to have no end in sight? Maybe you're there right now. I know I've been there. When we're in that place of despair and doubt, seeking the Lord but having trouble finding Him, it can be hard to pull ourselves out of it—and it can be difficult to believe His promises of freedom when we look around and see the four walls of a jail cell. I pray that you would find encouragement today in the reminder that "we live by faith, not by sight" (2 Cor. 5:7). I often cling to this verse when what I *see* is not looking so great. I have to remind myself that everything I can *see* is only temporary! We are in a constant state of flux, evolving and adapting to ever-changing conditions in our environments and within ourselves.

Sometimes despair comes when we feel that things *aren't* changing. We feel stuck and discouraged, whether in relationships or in circumstances. We know that God *can* bring deliverance and freedom, but in our darkest moments it all feels so hopeless. Take heart, Dear Friend: "We have put our hope in the living God, who is the Savior of all people, and especially of those who believe" (1 Tim. 4:10b). The same deliverance and freedom that God promised His children in Egypt applies to you today as well, in your own land of captivity. You may be struggling with the ability to claim His promises for yourself and your life. Fortunately, His follow-through does not depend on our fortitude! Whether we can conceive of it or not, we can still choose to believe Him—for our hope is not in ourselves but in Him.

Father, strengthen me to continue moving forward in faith, setting my heart at rest in You. May I take comfort in the assurance that You are working on my behalf in each area of my life that I have committed to You. In Jesus' name, Amen!

AUGUST 9

[A shepherd's] sheep follow him because they know his voice. But they will never follow a stranger; in fact, they will run away from him because they do not recognize a stranger's voice. John 10:4b-5

Our voices are so distinctive, aren't they? They are a trait that no two people share—like fingerprints, but even more sacred. Only our magnificent Creator could fashion different voices for each of His children, over the course of millennia. It just boggles my mind! We know and recognize the distinct voices of our loved ones. Do you know and recognize the distinct voice of your Good Shepherd?

Mimics have honed the skill of impersonating someone else's voice. Sometimes the enemy is successful in leading us astray by confusing us in this way—what we think is the voice of our Good Shepherd is really the enemy trying to mimic Him. For that very reason, Dear One, we must train our ears to recognize the one and only true voice of Jesus.

Earlier in the passage from today, Jesus says that the sheep listen to the shepherd's voice as he calls them by name and leads them out into pasture (v. 3). How can we be certain that we are following the Good Shepherd, and not an impostor? Again, the answer is in the action: "The thief comes only to steal and kill and destroy; I have come that they may have life, and have it to the full" (v. 10). The voice of our Good Shepherd calls us by name. It will always bring specific direction, conviction, guidance, and help. We may not always like the boundaries it sets for us, but the goal of our Shepherd is the safety of His sheep—and He lays down His life for us. Worldly voices that are trying to lead us astray will abandon us when trouble comes and may even celebrate our downfall. Are there any false shepherds in your life, my friend, mimicking our Shepherd's voice?

Father, please equip me today with a heightened ability to hear Your distinct voice. I long to follow You! In Jesus' name, Amen.

AUGUST 10

Nothing outside of a person can enter and contaminate a person in God's sight; rather, the things that come out of a person contaminate the person. Mark 7:15 CEB

This verse is a portion of Jesus' response to a question from the Pharisees about His disciples eating food with hands that were unwashed (and therefore "unclean" [vv. 1-2]). His point is that unwashed hands don't make food unclean, and food itself cannot make *us* unclean. We are not made sinful by what goes into us, but rather by the actions and words that come forth from our sinful hearts.

I'd like to take a slightly different approach today to this idea of being "contaminated" in God's sight. Jesus' words here resonate deeply with me; I spent many years feeling "unclean" because of the sexual abuse I experienced as a child. Survivors of abuse often feel that they are permanently tainted, damaged, or marred because of what has been done to them. If you can relate, I pray Jesus' words will bring you comfort today. We *must* remember that the actions of others against us cannot make us unclean. Nothing done to us by someone else makes us tarnished in the sight of God! Indeed, whoever touches us touches the apple of His eye (Zech. 2:8). If your body, your holy vessel, was hurt, harmed, or misused by someone else, God takes that abuse *very* seriously. My friend, He sees you with love, compassion, care, and dignity. You are precious to Him, and your pain *matters*.

If abuse has left you feeling as though you are damaged and broken, I understand. If you feel as though no one else will ever want you because you have been contaminated by another's sin, I understand. I also want to meet you in that painful place today, Beloved, and share with you the wonderful news that God loves you, cherishes you, and longs to bring healing to those broken places—and, Beloved, *He can*. No matter how others may see you or how you see yourself, God sees you clearly and loves you beyond all human understanding. Will you allow your heart to be set at rest in His love for you today? Amen.

AUGUST 11

The king's edict granted the Jews in every city the right to assemble and protect themselves. Esther 8:11a

Recently I was walking outside on an overcast day when suddenly the clouds broke apart and blinding sunlight streamed through. Not only was I caught without my sunglasses, which caused me to squint and shield my eyes, I was also caught without my sunscreen. I try to remember to slather it on every morning, yet sometimes I become lax in this habit—especially if the day is rainy or overcast. What I realized that day as the sun blazed down on my unprotected face was that my sunscreen doesn't do me a bit of good unless I apply it. *Every day.*

God's Word is like sunscreen. We have to apply it daily in order to receive the benefits and protection that it affords us—and if life's rays are especially intense for you right now, you may need multiple applications a day! God's Word is your SPF 1,000 against the schemes of Satan (SPF=Satan Protection Factor) and nothing else will do. Ephesians 6:17 says that we are given one offensive weapon to wield against the enemy, and that's the Sword of the Spirit—the Word of God. We can't wield it if we're not wearing it, Beloved. We have to clothe ourselves with God's truth every single day, rain or shine. Like the Jews in Esther's time, we have a God-given right to protect ourselves from the schemes of the devil—but unless we agree to take up our sword and fight, our weapon does us no good. Spiritual warfare is real, and we have to deliberately and mindfully equip ourselves with the protection God has provided—*every single day*. How do we apply it? We apply God's Word by jumping in and immersing ourselves in it—and it is never a moment too late to start.

Father, stir in my heart an insatiable desire for Your Word, that I might seek it out and apply it each day as I take my stand against the enemy. I know that my victory is assured through Your Son and through the strength of Your unfailing Word. Amen!

AUGUST 12

I lift up my eyes to the mountains—where does my help come from? My help comes from the Lord, the Maker of heaven and earth. He will not let your foot slip—He who watches over you will not slumber. [...] The Lord will watch over your coming and going both now and forevermore. Psalm 121:1-3, 8

This is my grandmother's favorite Psalm. She doesn't just know it intellectually; she has lived it. She was widowed at age 60 when my grandfather died suddenly of a heart attack. He was buried on her birthday, two days later. Life handed her a tragedy she'd never anticipated or bargained for. Such is the nature of adversity in our lives. When tragedy comes, we do have a choice: We can curl up and shut the world out, or we can go on living. This Psalm was read at my grandfather's funeral, and it was probably also the life preserver that carried my grandmother through those first dark, pain-filled months and years as she grappled with loss—not only the loss of her beloved husband, but the loss of the dreams she had had for their future, of what she had hoped life would hold for them together.

My grandmother is 88 now. We see her several times a week, and going to G.G.'s is one of my kids' favorite activities. When they're there, she watches television with them, fixes lunch for them (healthy fare such as hotdogs, chips, and her famous milkshakes), and plays games with them. She reads books to them. They go get the mail together. She prays for them. Her presence in their lives is such a gift. I'm so thankful she didn't decide to let tragedy cripple her heart, that she didn't close herself off to love after it must have felt like love had been wrenched away from her in one fell swoop. She has chosen to *live*, my friend. She has chosen joy *in spite of* plans and dreams that had to be diverted. I challenge you today, Dear One... whatever your area of tragedy, may you know that your help comes from the Lord, that He will not allow you to fall, and that He *will* deliver you from all harm. In the saving name of Jesus, Amen.

AUGUST 13

Uzziel son of Harhaiah, one of the goldsmiths, repaired the next section; and Hananiah, one of the perfume-makers, made repairs next to that. They restored Jerusalem as far as the Broad Wall. [...] The repairs next to [Meremoth] were made by the priests from the surrounding region. [...] And between the room above the corner and the Sheep Gate the goldsmiths and merchants made repairs. Nehemiah 3:8, 22, 32

I treasure the mental image of these returned exiles taking up their positions along the wall, shoulder to shoulder, as the work of rebuilding took place. What I especially love about these verses is that it's clear that those working so hard to rebuild the wall weren't necessarily the ones most skilled to do it. Next to goldsmiths you have perfume-makers and merchants and priests. What did any of these people really know about rebuilding a wall? Yet there they were, voluntarily working on sections of the massive wall, helping to restore the protection around their beloved city of Jerusalem. Once again I am reminded of the fact that if God sets a task before you, He'll provide you with the skills you need to complete it!

Likewise, Ephesians 4:16 tells us that in Christ, the whole body of believers "grows and builds itself up in love, as each part does its work." We are all members of the same body, with Christ as our Head. We share a common purpose, a common goal, and a common destination that drives us forward. We are called to take up the positions designated to us by God in our own lives, committing ourselves to the work that He calls us to do—not only within the larger world, but in building one another up as well. He infuses our efforts with His love and power, enabling us to meet the demands of each task set before us while bringing glory and honor to His name. May we take up our positions today and work shoulder to shoulder. Amen!

AUGUST 14

For we wanted to come to you—certainly I, Paul, did, again and again—but Satan blocked our way. [...] So when we could stand it no longer, we thought it best to be left by ourselves in Athens. We sent Timothy, who is our brother and co-worker in God's service in spreading the gospel of Christ, to strengthen and encourage you in your faith, so that no one would be unsettled by these trials. For you know quite well that we are destined for them.
1 Thessalonians 2:18, 3:1-3

Is there someone in your life whom you desperately want to get to and can't right now? Maybe it's a wayward teenager. Maybe it's a straying spouse. Maybe it's an adult child—or their spouse—with whom you walk on eggshells. Maybe it's a friend who seems to have put some distance between the two of you or a co-worker who seems suddenly withdrawn. Paul, Silas, and Timothy were eager to visit the believers at Thessalonica, but Satan himself stepped in and thwarted their efforts. Like these three, we too must not be deterred! If we cannot go to someone in person, we still have other options. They agreed that if they couldn't all go together, at least one of them needed to make the trip—so they sent Timothy to strengthen and encourage the believers. That wasn't all they did, however; they also prayed continually: "Night and day we pray most earnestly that we may see you again and supply what is lacking in your faith. Now may our God and Father Himself and our Lord Jesus clear the way for us to come to you" (3:10-11). And while they waited, Paul was writing.

What options are available to you today in the relationship you thought of earlier? Can you breach the distance yourself, or somehow send encouragement? Have you thought of writing that person a note, sharing your thoughts and feelings? Are you praying for God to open the way forward for you? I encourage you to choose one or more of those options and commit to taking that step forward today. May He grant you success! Amen.

AUGUST 15

Furthermore, tell the people, "This is what the Lord says: See, I am setting before you the way of life and the way of death. Whoever stays in this city will die by the sword, famine or plague. But whoever goes out and surrenders to the Babylonians who are besieging you will live; they will escape with their lives."
Jeremiah 21:8-9

It's when God gives directions that seem almost counterintuitive to our sense of self-preservation that I find it hardest to trust Him. I can see where the people of Judah would have thought it foolishness to walk out of the walled, fortified, "safe" city and into the hands of the enemy who had surrounded and besieged it. However, had they thought things through, it may also have occurred to them that they were slowly starving to death *in* the city itself. What had once been a means of protection had become the means of starvation. Nothing could get in through those walls. Their only hope of deliverance was to walk out of them, into what appeared to be the waiting arms of their enemy.

God continually sets before His children the choice of life or death. God desires for all of His children to have life—and to have abundant life in Him (see John 10:10)—but the choice is ours, and the choice boils down to obedience. For me, the hardest times to obey are when I fear that my obedience may result in God taking something or someone away from me. The people of Judah did not want to walk willingly into Babylonian captivity, yet God was plainly telling them that their obedience to this command would be the only way they would survive the siege.

Are you finding yourself slowly starving to death within the "safety" of your walled city? I have been there! God called me to walk out of my walled fortress and into the light of His healing and restoration. For years, I did not want to. Finally, I realized that if I continued to disobey I would die in that walled-off city. Walking in obedience is how we receive Life, my friend. May we courageously trust Him today. Amen.

AUGUST 16

Let us not become weary in doing good, for at the proper time we will reap a harvest if we do not give up. Galatians 6:9

This is my go-to verse in parenting. When the sibling squabbles and lackluster attitudes make each minute last three hours; when the backtalk and complaints sap the energy right out of me; when the door slams rattle the window panes and the dinner I worked so hard to prepare goes untouched by all three kids, I call this verse to mind. I remind myself that the short-term investment will be more than worth the long-term gain. Some of you have older children and bigger issues at stake. Whatever the current area of challenge may be for your family, it still falls under this umbrella of promise. We have set a firm foundation for our children. (And if we haven't, it is never too late to start. God will bless our efforts!) They may wander from it or oppose it outright. However, that foundation will stand—not because we built it, but because we built it upon the Rock of Jesus Christ (see 1 Cor. 3:10-11).

I'm wondering today what makes you weary. For me, this verse lends itself well to parenting. For you, it may be better applied to a stressful work environment, the final two semesters of graduate school, a difficult relationship with a loved one, or a chronic health condition that is burdensome. Whatever your struggle, my friend, keep sowing. Keep going. Keep living. Keep loving. Moment by moment, day by day, walking forward with the Lord at your side. If it becomes too much, take heart: The Lord will pick you up and carry you (Isa. 46:4) any time your legs give way. The harvest of righteousness, sown from obedience to the Lord, awaits you.

Father, please strengthen me in my areas of struggle and enable me to keep doing what is good. I know that You are faithful to honor each one of Your promises, and I am confident that You will magnify and bless every effort I make in Your name. Amen.

AUGUST 17

The gatekeepers had been assigned to their positions of trust by David and Samuel the seer. They and their descendants were in charge of guarding the gates of the house of the Lord—the house called the tent of meeting. [...] The four principal gatekeepers, who were Levites, were entrusted with the responsibility for the rooms and treasuries in the house of God. They would spend the night stationed around the house of God, because they had to guard it; and they had charge of the key for opening it each morning. 1 Chronicles 9:22b-23, 26-27

It occurred to me as I was reading this that as believers under the New Covenant, we are the gatekeepers of our own "tents"—our earthly bodies (see 1 Cor. 6:19-20). As it was with the Levites, this is a position of immense responsibility and trust. We are called to be watchful and alert about the things and people we allow to come in close proximity to the outside of our tent. Likewise, we must be vigilant about what types of things we allow to come inside our tent, being certain that we are choosing things that will glorify and edify the Lord, rather than those that will bring Him dishonor or grief. We are also responsible for the general upkeep, care, and maintenance of our tent—both outside and inside—including all of those "rooms and treasuries" within. It's no wonder that this solitary task kept the Levites occupied all day long!

How is your gatekeeping looking today? Are you fastidious and methodical about evaluating which things and people you allow to come near your tent? Or have you become lax and careless, not paying much attention to what's surrounding you? How about your inner rooms and treasuries? Have you been faithfully tending to them and clearing out clutter and cobwebs, or are things piled about in disarray, concealing trash that needs to be thrown out and things that have begun to decay? Our distinctive tent has been specifically entrusted to us by God. Let's make the commitment to guard it well, my friend. Amen.

AUGUST 18

If we are thrown into the blazing furnace, the God we serve is able to deliver us from it, and He will deliver us from Your Majesty's hand. But even if He does not, we want you to know, Your Majesty, that we will not serve your gods or worship the image of gold you have set up. Daniel 3:17-18

This is one of my favorite Bible stories—the faith of Shadrach, Meshach, and Abednego. They knew with all certainty that if and when calamity befell them, their God was able to save them. They also realized with equal certainty that just because God was *able* to save them did not mean that He *would*. That, my friend, is formidable faith.

Two things I want us to rehearse today about the character of God: First, He is able. Second Peter 2:9a says that the Lord knows how to rescue godly people from trials. This gives me such comfort. He does not need my assistance in solving the problem. He does not need any help or suggestions. He *knows* how to rescue us from our trials! Second, He may or may not choose to deliver us in the way that we would expect or even desire. Jesus intentionally waited until after Lazarus had died before he traveled to Bethany. God heard Jesus' prayers in the garden of Gethsemane and His answer was still "No." Sometimes illness *does* end in death. Sometimes loved ones are not saved from affliction. What then?

When we face that kind of loss, Dear Friend, we recall truths like these about our God: "...in all things God works for the good of those who love Him, who have been called according to His purpose" (Rom. 8:28). "As the heavens are higher than the earth, so are My ways higher than your ways and My thoughts than your thoughts" (Isa. 55:9). In those times of pain, Beloved, we either trust Him or we don't. But make no mistake—death is never the end of the story for those who are in Christ. It is but a doorway into the next glorious adventure with Him, and our final triumph over the enemy (see Rev. 1:17b-18). Amen.

AUGUST 19

Love does not delight in evil but rejoices with the truth.
1 Corinthians 13:6

When I was about six years old, everyone in my Sunday school class got a little wooden statue of a pink bear with a fabric bow tied around its neck. Across the bottom of the base of wood were painted these words: "Love bears all things. 1 Cor. 13:7." For the longest time, I was so confused by this. I loved *all* animals and was so undone that the Bible was apparently telling me to love bears *more* than all things. (At least that's how I had interpreted it in my mind, you see.) I faithfully loved panda bears and koalas, but felt mighty guilty for my secret affinity for dinosaurs, cats, hermit crabs, fish, and turtles. I have no idea how many more years passed before it finally dawned on me that "bears" was not a noun, as I had thought, but rather a *verb*. See, my friend, love is always an *action*.

Today's verse tells us that love does not delight in evil but rejoices with the truth. I'm wondering if you're struggling with any area today in which you feel as muddled about things as I did as a six-year-old staring at that command to love bears as it sat on my nightstand. I spent years feeling guilty for not following a word from God that was *not at all* a word from God! Is there an area in which you have misunderstood God's heart? Is there an area in which you are struggling or condemning yourself that He longs to bring His healing and grace into? "God is love" (1 John 4:8b). Therefore, as our verse for today says, He does not delight in evil but rejoices with the truth.

If there is an area of sin that has you in a headlock of bondage today, He longs for you to confess it so that the truth can set you free! He is not sitting on the edge of His throne waiting to condemn us, Beloved—He is earnestly waiting for the moment in which we confess so that He can *forgive*! He is love, and He is able to bear all of our "things." Will you entrust Him with yours today? Amen.

AUGUST 20

Then Jesus told them, "This very night you will all fall away on account of Me, for it is written: 'I will strike the Shepherd, and the sheep of the flock will be scattered.' But after I have risen, I will go ahead of you into Galilee." Peter replied, "Even if all fall away on account of You, I never will. [...] Even if I have to die with You, I will never disown You." And all the other disciples said the same. Matthew 26:31-33, 35

Loyalty can be a challenge. My dad was a steadfast Detroit Tigers fan throughout my childhood, despite the fact that they rarely enjoyed a successful season—and, in fact, had some of the worst seasons in the history of baseball. As a child, I never understood why he didn't root for a team that was... you know... *winning*. But then, that's not the definition of loyalty, is it? That's popularity, and those of us who have survived high school and beyond know that that's a different notion entirely. Popularity is a fickle, tenuous position that can rise and fall many times throughout the course of a single day. Loyalty is a steadfastness that remains *in spite of*, rather than existing *because of*. Loyalty perseveres even when the going gets tough.

Jesus' disciples all pledged their loyalty to Him as He warned them of impending betrayal and His imminent death. Perhaps their minds could not conceive of the series of events that was about to unfold, or perhaps in some place within them they did not believe Christ's death would truly come to pass. Whatever their reasons, their pledges of loyalty dissolved once Jesus was betrayed: "all the disciples deserted Him and fled" (26:56b).

It tenders my heart to know that Jesus fully knew in advance that His chosen ones would desert Him—and yet *He still chose them*. He still washed their feet. He still prayed for their protection. He still loved them. Even when our loyalty falters, Beloved, He remains loyal to the end. All praise and glory to His amazing name. Amen.

AUGUST 21

His divine power has given us everything we need for a godly life through our knowledge of Him who called us by His own glory and goodness. 2 Peter 1:3

When Tessa was in kindergarten her class "adopted" and incubated some eggs that eventually hatched into chicks. One day she brought home a picture of a chick with its body parts labeled, and I was curious to see something called an "egg tooth." I asked Tessa what this was, and she explained to me that it's what the chick uses to break through its air sac so that it has enough air to breathe during the hatching process. The egg tooth is also used to break through the egg's shell, granting the chick its freedom. "Does it keep its egg tooth after it hatches?" I asked, wondering how I'd never known about this before. "No, it loses it after a few days." This just amazes me. Who but our God could create creatures that are perfectly equipped *from birth* to manage every challenge that faces them?

We are the same. If God equips chicks with an egg tooth so they can break free and gain life; if God equips caterpillars to enter into dark cocoons and emerge as butterflies, we can be certain that He also equips us with the specific skills, strengths, instincts, and tools we need in order to become what we were designed by Him to be.

What is especially touching is that many of God's creatures cannot break free and come forth if humans try to intervene and assist them. They are uniquely and perfectly designed to manage the process on their own. It may require immense struggle and weariness, but it is through the struggle that they are able to gain the strength that they'll need in order to survive once they are free. If you are struggling today, Dear One, take comfort in the knowledge that He has already given you everything you need to come forth and become the beautiful creation within. In Jesus' name, Amen!

AUGUST 22

A friend loves at all times, and a brother is born for a time of adversity. Proverbs 17:17

One of my favorite movies as a child was *The Parent Trap*, where Hayley Mills played the role of the twins, Sharon and Susan. One of my most desperate wishes during the years of my childhood abuse was that I'd had a twin. In my mind, things would have been different if I had had someone else there with me. A twin would have been ideal, but I would've been glad to have had *any* sibling. Just *someone. Anyone.* It seemed to me that if I'd had another witness, another person to share the confusion and the pain with, that it would have somehow been more bearable.

As I reflect on that, I am reminded yet again of how very alone we can be—and feel—during some of the most difficult seasons of our lives. I'm wondering what example you could share from your own life today. The loss of a spouse. The loss of a child. A bitter divorce. Abuse. Neglect. Prison. Deployment. Single parenthood. At times we may be surrounded by other people and still feel deeply isolated and alone—as though the world is continuing on around us, completely unaware of the suffering we are holding in our scarred and shaking hands.

I've been in that place in different seasons of my life, and it's a brutal weight to bear. Fortunately, my friend, we never truly carry it alone. Jesus, our Savior, comes to us in the vortex of our pain. He helps us defend ourselves from the onslaught of grief, depression, and despair. He stands at our side, giving us strength (2 Tim. 4:17). Jesus will meet you in the darkness, bringing light; He will meet you in the bitterness, bringing sweet hope; He will meet you in the destruction, bringing restoration and healing. You have a loyal Friend (John 15:13-15) and Brother in the Lord who will never leave your side.

Father, enable me to feel Jesus' presence in my life today in a uniquely special way. In His name I pray, Amen.

AUGUST 23

Now if I do what I do not want to do, it is no longer I who do it, but it is sin living in me that does it. Romans 7:20

This section of chapter 7 always gets me so confused with all of its do's and do not's in rapid-fire succession. Today, the light bulb went on for me, and I think I finally grasped Paul's point. Once we accept Jesus as Savior, we become aware of the Law—aware of our sin and trespass— and we have the inner desire to do things differently (for we now have the mind of Christ [1 Cor. 2:16]). However, we still have the fallen body of Adam (or Eve), which then places us in a continual struggle of flesh versus spirit. We *want* to do what is right. Sometimes we do—all glory to God! But when we find ourselves not doing the good that we want to do as we try to follow Christ, *that* is sin. Our flesh at work. Since self-control is fruit *of the Spirit* (Gal. 5:22-23), its *absence* in our lives in any way indicates that we are acting in the flesh—and, therefore, sinning.

I don't know about you, but to me this feels like both good news and bad. The good news is that I have blessed clarity in the matter! The bad news is that I'm sinning a whole lot more than I thought! I generally think of sin as the Ten Commandments, and thus I usually think I'm do- ing a pretty good job of toeing the line. But no. When I worry, it's sin, because I'm not choosing the Spirit's peace. When I'm harsh with my children, it's sin, because I'm not choosing the Spirit's patience and gen- tleness. When I'm critical of myself or others, it's sin, because I'm not choosing the Spirit's kindness. It is sin. Not a "bad habit." Not "just the way I am." Sin. Letting the flesh win, stifling the Spirit's self-control.

Wow, my friend. I need Jesus more than ever! But here's the good news: Being aware of our sin is *never* meant to bring us condemnation. Rather, it is a means by which to bring gratitude and thanksgiving for His matchless grace—for "where sin increased, grace increased all the more" (Rom. 5:20b). In other words, you can't out-sin God's love for you. He always loves you more. Be blessed today, Dear One! Amen.

AUGUST 24

When Israel was a child, I loved him as a son and brought him out of Egypt. But the more I called to him, the more he rebelled.
Hosea 11:1-2a TLB

If you are still in the trenches of parenting a toddler, this verse hits home doesn't it? If your children are older or grown, you may need a quick refresher course. The mystery of memory is that we tend to look back on past seasons in our lives wearing rose-tinted glasses, imagining that those times were ever so much easier, more idyllic, and peaceful—not because they truly *were*, but because that time is not *this* time, and because the Lord has graciously erased all of the daily grit and strain from our minds, leaving behind the soft-focused picture of a time when all was good.

Please allow me to bring into sharper focus what life is like with a toddler: They whine—loudly and frequently. They know all of three words: "No," "Mine," and "Uh-Oh." They routinely empty out whatever you have just put away. They refuse to nap and fuss because they're tired. They climb stairs like mountain goats and then get stuck and cannot get down. You buy them toys and instead they play in the toilet. They throw your lovingly prepared dinner in the floor but eat small rocks and grass. They want to be picked up and carried but when you need to carry them they want to be put down. You put them down and they wander off. You call for them, and they run in the opposite direction. I could go on. The point is, children are challenging. They are also wonderful and fascinating and inspiring.

We are God's children. Some of us are still toddlers. Some of us are whining. Some of us have wandered off. Some of us need a nap in the worst way. Wherever we are, our Father sees us with such love and affection. He never stops calling us and never stops loving us, even when our relationship goes through difficult seasons. He's in it for life. May that bring peace to you today, Precious Child of the King. Amen.

AUGUST 25

Our God, will You not judge them? For we have no power to face this vast army that is attacking us. We do not know what to do, but our eyes are on You. [...] This is what the Lord says to you: "Do not be afraid or discouraged because of this vast army. For the battle is not yours, but God's." 2 Chronicles 20:12, 15b

The Israelites had the right response in this situation: They acknowledged their own inability to overpower a vast army that was attacking them; they also trained their eyes upon the Lord. He is the One who gives us the strength to overcome our adversaries; He is the One who arms us for battle when it is our turn to fight. And sometimes, as we are learning along with the Israelites today, *it's not our battle*. We have no trouble sensing when we are under attack, do we? We can feel it—in our hearts, in our minds, in our spirits, and in our "gut"—right? But sometimes, the battle isn't ours to fight. It's God's. He knows when we are outmatched, overwhelmed, and unequipped for the task at hand. And that's precisely the point: It's in our darkest hour, Beloved, that His light shines brightest.

What example comes to your mind today as you consider an area in which you need for God to do the fighting? Maybe it's cancer or another chronic illness. Maybe it's an addiction that impacts your life or the life of a loved one. Whatever it is that speaks to you, it is most likely something that you are completely unable to overcome in your own power and strength. Are you weary of trying to fight it? The Lord may be speaking to you today, saying, "Step aside, Child, and allow your Daddy to fight on your behalf." He is the Lord of all creation, and He *does not fail!* The end result may not look like what you thought it would—or even wished it would—but His ways are higher than our ways (Isa. 55:9), and His purposes will prevail (Prov. 19:21)!

Father, I praise You for Your willingness to step in and do what I cannot. May Your name be glorified in my life. Amen.

AUGUST 26

You provide a broad path for my feet, so that my ankles do not give way. 2 Samuel 22:37

I smile every time I read this verse. I once had some of the weakest ankles on the planet, and several pieces of equipment (high-top shoes, ankle braces, a "boot," and a pair of my very own crutches) to attest to this fact. It wasn't until I began a daily exercise regimen in my twenties that my ankles began to strengthen—a result of the repeated demands I was placing on them to support and carry me as I moved. However, it took a while for this to happen. And when I first started running, it was my ankles that ached above all else! They have grown stronger and sturdier over time, now more able to bear my weight—and my mis-steps—without faltering and breaking down. The higher expectations and continual testing that I've placed on them have strengthened them.

We often shy away from tests and trials in our lives, and yet it is precise-ly the work undertaken in these challenging circumstances that increas-es our strength, stability, and flexibility. Without use, joints and muscles atrophy. The same is true of our spiritual muscles. When they aren't being consistently challenged to grow, we risk watching them decline. In what areas of your being is God challenging your growth right now?

I find it interesting that David's ankle strength did not come from being "on the run" all the time (which he was!)—but from God's willingness to broaden the path beneath him so that he had a flatter, firmer, surer footing on which to run. Maybe we need both: ankles strengthened by repeated conditioning and weight-bearing, and a path beneath us broad enough to travel upon. We can motivate ourselves to run, but only God can broaden our path.

Father, please broaden my path today as I run the good race You have marked out for me (Heb. 12:1), that I may serve You well and fully with my whole being. In Jesus' name, Amen.

AUGUST 27

Once you were alienated from God and were enemies in your minds because of your evil behavior. But now He has reconciled you by Christ's physical body through death to present you holy in His sight, without blemish and free from accusation. Colossians 1:21-22

We could probably spend all day commiserating about how nice it will be to finally appear "without blemish" for all eternity, but I'd like to focus on the deeper issue of being found "free from accusation." Whether you've been falsely accused by another or legitimately held accountable; whether you've stood trial before a jury or find yourself continually on the witness stand within your own mind, the good news for us today is that Christ's sacrifice for us leaves us "free from accusation." Not because we aren't guilty, Beloved, but because Christ has stepped in and paid for our sins in full.

Whom has Christ vanquished with His sacrifice for us? Satan himself, who has served as the Accuser of the children of God since the times of Job (see Job 1:6-12). Revelation 12:10 promises that when the kingdom of God appears on earth, Satan, the Accuser, will be hurled down. Satan knows his time is short, my friend, and like any caged animal, he tends to attack more furiously when cornered. When you feel under attack and the condemning lies of the Accuser resound in your head, refute his attacks with the truth of God's Word, choosing to believe what He says about you rather than the lies the enemy is whispering in your ear. The words of Isaiah 43 are always a good place to start: "Fear not, for I have redeemed you; I have summoned you by name; you are Mine. [...] you are precious and honored in My sight [...] and I love you" (vv. 1b, 4a). The Accuser gets no say in our value or worth—not now, not ever.

Father, thank You for the reconciliation offered to me through Jesus; thank You for the ongoing work of Your Spirit within me as I seek to live a life devoted to You. In Jesus' name, Amen.

AUGUST 28

The Lord will vindicate His people and relent concerning His servants when He sees their strength is gone and no one is left, slave or free. He will say: "Now where are their gods, the rock they took refuge in, the gods who ate the fat of their sacrifices and drank the wine of their drink offerings? Let them rise up to help you! Let them give you shelter! See now that I Myself am He! There is no god besides Me." Deuteronomy 32:36-39a

When we turn to other gods for help, comfort, and deliverance in our lives, it grieves the Father's heart. He knows we are settling for cheap counterfeits and unworthy knockoffs while rejecting Him—the One and only true God who is able and willing to deliver us from harm.

Obedience is key in our lives, Dear One, because at the end of the day we cannot be saved, rescued, healed, or unequivocally loved and under-stood by anyone but God—the One who created us, knit us together, and infinitely understands how we think, how we feel, how we react, and how we interpret our world, our struggles, and our pain. Only someone with that kind of knowledge is truly able to help us and heal us. Have you been running to other gods for fulfillment and safety? For security and reassurance? That ground will soon crumble under your feet, because God cares so much more about our character than our comfort—and He *will* shake that ground beneath your feet until all that remains is the bedrock of His love for you.

Our God can save us from any person or circumstance that sets itself up against us in this world—but nothing in this world can ever save us from the right judgment and discipline of our God. What are you clinging to today, Beloved? Things and people of this world, or the unchanging God who created them? This is something I struggle with too. The good news is that we can always choose to return to God; He delights in see-ing His wayward children making their way back home. Amen.

AUGUST 29

Therefore, in order to keep me from becoming conceited, I was given a thorn in my flesh, a messenger of Satan, to torment me. Three times I pleaded with the Lord to take it away from me. But He said to me, "My grace is sufficient for you, for My power is made perfect in weakness." 2 Corinthians 12:7b-9a

Oh, how I wish we could sit down together over a cup of coffee or tea today and discuss our thorns. Thorns are one of those things that I find so intriguing in our lives. Each of us has different thorns, but we all have thorns! What are they? Are they physical infirmities? Are they trying relationships? Are they emotional difficulties? Are they handicaps we battle due to past circumstances?

The interesting thing about thorns, my friend, is that no matter how much we weed the garden of our lives, trimming and pruning, we always seem to have at least one thorn! I think this is God's way of reminding us (as He reminded Paul) that He alone is sufficient to meet our every need. When we're going along without any difficulty, pride has a perfect opportunity to take root and begin to grow. It's the thorns, those weeds in our gardens, which humble us and keep us at the attentive task of tending and weeding.

I wonder where this meets you today. What areas of difficulty in your life would you classify as your thorns? I pray it brings comfort to you today to know that God promises His sufficiency in that specific area of struggle or strife. He is the Master Gardener, the One who is able to reach into our lives, into our hearts, and pull out those thorns and briers unscathed. It's our job to continue to sow good seed and allow Him to bring strength in our weakness as evidence of His unparalleled power.

Father, thank You for the mixture of beautiful flowers and occasional thorns that You weave into my life. May I nurture the good seeds You have given me, that I may bear fruit for Your glory; may I abide in Your love and provision as I wrestle with my thorns. In Jesus' name, Amen.

AUGUST 30

For the Word of God is alive and active. Sharper than any double-edged sword, it penetrates even to dividing soul and spirit, joints and marrow; it judges the thoughts and attitudes of the heart. Hebrews 4:12

Second Timothy 3:16 tells us that "all Scripture is God-breathed," so it should come as no surprise to us that God's Word continues to be alive and active, equipping us, preparing us, teaching us, and correcting us so that we will be "thoroughly equipped for every good work" (2 Tim. 3:17). The sword of God's Word cuts off the branches within us that do not bear fruit and prunes our remaining branches to make them more fruitful (John 15:2). When God sends His Word out amongst His people, it brings healing (Ps. 107:20). And it never comes back to Him empty, but accomplishes the purpose for which He sent it (Isa. 55:11).

In what area of your life do you need a fresh word from God today, Beloved? Do you need for His Word to cut through your confusion and doubt, bringing clarity and direction? Do you need for His Word to carve a swath of discernment for you on the path ahead, or lay waste to an enemy threatening to overtake you from behind? Do you need for His Word to slay the giants of Fear, Guilt, or Anxiety within you? Do you need for His Word to chisel through the layers of numbness or pain, so that you can begin the process of healing in Him?

The fact that God's Holy Word is *alive* means that it is always speaking to us and is always able to meet us in our every circumstance and need. There's just one main requirement: As with any weapon, we have to *use* it. We cannot just let the Bible sit on our nightstand and expect amazing things to happen! Open up the Book today, Beloved, and seek His presence on the pages within. He will meet you there!

Father, send Your Word to me afresh today, that I might discern Your will for my life and Your direction for my path. May Your Word be my delight and my strength as I journey with You today. Amen.

AUGUST 31

It is for freedom that Christ has set us free. Stand firm, then, and do not let yourselves be burdened again by a yoke of slavery.
Galatians 5:1

I spent many years finding the notion of freedom very frightening. I had spent so long limping along in the darkness of my pain and skewed thinking that it seemed impossible that I would ever walk without the limp or make it into the light. Broken bones that are poorly set can remain deformed for life; broken hearts and broken minds that are poorly set can carry their own marks of deformity. Yet this is not always a bad thing, as long as we are surrendering our areas of brokenness to Christ. After all, we are not meant to be cookie-cutter copies of one another.

You are the only person on planet earth with your unique life story and life experiences. You are the only person equipped with your distinct set of skills, talents, and hard-earned wisdom. You are the only person with your unique sphere of influence. There is only one you, and Jesus intends for you to use your life to bring glory to His Father's kingdom! We may always have a limp, Beloved. The important thing is that we are still walking, moving forward in faith, knowing that Christ is with us on each step of the journey.

Are you struggling to move forward today, my friend? If so, what is holding you back? Paul reminds us that Christ died so that we could be set free. Free from what? Free from the law of sin and death (Rom. 8:2). Our just punishment for sin is death—yet Christ has interceded on our behalf to become our ransom, the atoning sacrifice for our sins (1 John 2:2). He gave His life for us so that we can dedicate our lives to Him, being His hands and feet in our current spheres of influence. Our hands and feet may bear scars, Beloved. His do, too—because He believed we were worth it.

Father, help me to walk and serve in the freedom Christ has given me, that I may be a witness to others of Your grace, mercy, and love. Amen!

SEPTEMBER 1

The eye is the lamp of the body. If your eyes are healthy, your whole body will be full of light. But if your eyes are unhealthy, your whole body will be full of darkness. If then the light within you is darkness, how great is that darkness! Matthew 6:22-23

How's your vision today, my friend? There are two components to our vision that merit our consideration today: what we look at, and how we see things. On what are your eyes focusing? Things of this world—your to-do list, your work stress, your problems, your bank statement—or things of eternity? If the eye is the lamp of the body, then what we allow our gaze to rest upon affects whether we bring light or darkness into our souls. Do you often find yourself gazing at your appearance, your social calendar, or the positive feedback you receive on social media? Do you find yourself habitually focused on your problems, your worries, and your fears? Do you allow your eyes to be routinely assaulted with violent or pornographic images? Are your eyes looking to a habit or a person to soothe or mask your anxieties? Or are they focused upon the timeless promises of your God, found in His holy Word?

Secondly, how do you typically see things? Do you choose to see the positive side of a person or situation, or the negative? Can you see each person you meet through the lens of God's love, as evidence of His wondrous creation? Or do you tend to look at others through cataracts of distrust, envy, judgment, or superiority? We can choose to limit our vision to the outward appearance or we can train ourselves to look upon the heart. I long to bring light into my body and my soul, rather than darkness. I long to see others through the merciful eyes of the Father and the compassionate eyes of Jesus, rather than with my own skewed vision. The good news is that our God is an expert at restoring the sight of those who are earnestly seeking His healing.

Father, open my eyes to the things of light today. In Jesus' name, Amen.

SEPTEMBER 2

"The glory of this present house will be greater than the glory of the former house," says the Lord Almighty. "And in this place I will grant peace." Haggai 2:9a

Haggai prophesied to the exiles who returned to Jerusalem to rebuild the temple of the Lord. After becoming lax in the work and drifting off to tend to their own affairs, the people found themselves struggling to make ends meet. God sent Haggai to give them the message that prosperity would not be forthcoming until they finished the work of rebuilding the Lord's house *first*. Happily, the people received the message *and obeyed*, and God faithfully sent words of encouragement to them through Haggai as they worked. Our verse for today is just one example of many found within this small but powerful Old Testament book.

I'm wondering what you're working on rebuilding today, Beloved. Is it a broken relationship? Battered self-esteem? Better health after an illness or injury? Maybe you're trying to build a bridge of reconciliation, restore a ruined reputation, or reconstruct your life after a devastating loss. Maybe you're working on recovery, the rebuilding of your very self from the inside out—a process that is particularly slow and tedious, and one that can often be discouraging.

In any rebuilding process, much pain has to surface and be dealt with before it can be resolved. We often find ourselves in the same position as the returned exiles, tripping over rubble and wondering if the end result of our work will really be worth the struggle. Beloved, it will. I want to assure you that God's help and guidance guarantees that what we *will* become, through Him, will be even greater and will bring Him even more glory, than the "former house." And here's the important part: In this new place, *He will grant peace.* As much as we strive to find peace, seek peace, and cultivate peace, our efforts are always futile. God *grants* peace. He *gives* it. As we continue our work in His name, Dear One, He blesses our dwellings with His peace. Amen!

SEPTEMBER 3

In that day the Lord Almighty will be a glorious crown, a beautiful wreath for the remnant of His people. He will be a spirit of justice to the one who sits in judgment, a source of strength to those who turn back the battle at the gate. Isaiah 28:5-6

Are you sitting in judgment today, my friend? Are you feeling judged by others, or perhaps by yourself? For me, it's almost always the latter, and my inner judge is harsh, critical, exacting, and unforgiving. It can be pretty painful. I am strengthened and encouraged today by this word from Isaiah, that God will be "a spirit of justice to the one who sits in judgment." God's judgment, you see, is based on truth (Rom. 2:2)—and ours, my friend, is not! No matter how well we *think* we know the specifics of the situation, the motivations of the people involved, and the complete explanation of the matter—we don't. God is wise, gracious, all-knowing, and just. He is the kind of judge I would gladly relinquish my duties to, allowing Him to work in the situation and administer His wisdom and justice as He deems most effective. What about you? Are you willing to hand over that robe and gavel to Him today and allow Him to pronounce your sentence? I can already tell you what He'll say: "If you've confessed it and repented of it, Child, then it's already forgiven. Paid for in full by My Son. Go in peace." (If you haven't yet confessed and repented, please read 1 John 1:9 for inspiration!)

God is also "a source of strength to those who turn back the battle at the gate." My friend, I certainly waited until the battle was at the gate, and maybe even halfway over it, before I decided to turn it around and fight for my right to live in God's truth, peace, love, abundance, and security. I am still working on it. It is an ongoing journey, with Him at my side. But what a vast difference that makes, Beloved, when we are not fighting or journeying alone. Will you journey with Him today?

Father, I fully trust Your righteous judgment in all things. Thank You for being my strength as I turn back the battle at the gate. Amen.

SEPTEMBER 4

However, the Lord your God would not listen to Balaam but turned the curse into a blessing for you, because the Lord your God loves you. Deuteronomy 23:5

A few winters ago, the temperatures plummeted so low here in middle Tennessee that schools were closed for "cold." (I know you Northerners are laughing, but with highs hovering at zero degrees, things got pretty serious down here.) For one rare window of time, it was possible for us Southern folk to do a little science experiment: You take boiling water outside, throw it up into the air, and watch as it *poofs* into harmless snow dust on its way back down. I worked up the nerve to try it, having only *heard* about its success prior to this moment in time.

The kids and I tromped outside into the icy air, ready to see the show. Being the one with an adult's logic and reasoning, I was admittedly a little wary. I mean, here I was, about to throw *boiling water* into the air above my head (I made my kids stand outside the potential circle of boiling rain) *trusting* that it would not come right back down *boiling hot*. I'm pleased to report that God faithfully turned what could have been a curse into a blessing before my very eyes. My children were delighted, and I was relieved.

What has He turned from a curse into a blessing in your life, Dear One? For many of you, it's something much more serious than a science experiment for Southerners. In my life I've seen God bring blessings out of my parents' divorce, my intense struggle with self-condemnation, and my abuse. He's also been faithful to bring blessings from difficult trials like unemployment, miscarriage, and loss. In this verse I can substitute "Balaam" with "Satan," and it rings all the more true. How about you? What the enemy intends to use for our harm, my friend, God can use for our good—and hopefully, in some way, for the good of others as well. When we share the ways in which God has been faithful to deliver us from trials, we bring edification and encouragement to the body of believers and glory to His mighty name. Let's do some sharing today. Amen!

SEPTEMBER 5

Whoever belongs to God hears what God says. John 8:47a

The day I came upon this verse and really took in what it was saying, I felt like I'd just walked face-first into a plate glass door (which I've actually done before). I knew I belonged to God, but I was not listening to what He was saying. Oh, I was *hearing* Him just fine, but I was not *listening* and obeying. I still wanted to do things my own way. In other words, I was listening to myself over God—which is always a bad idea.

I was reminded yet again of 2 Corinthians 10:5, which has so often been a thorn in my strong-willed mind: "We demolish arguments and every pretension that sets itself up against the knowledge of God, and we take captive every thought to make it obedient to Christ." I *knew* this Scripture; I'd *heard* it, but I was having a great deal of difficulty *listening* and *doing*, because to be honest with you it truly felt impossible to me. I tend not to have much quiet space in my head. I'm constantly thinking about something, and if I don't take control of my thoughts, they are prone to wander towards the unproductive zones of Anxiety, Doubt, or Condemnation. The problem is that there are just so *many* of them to contend with! However, this verse from John gave me a sobering mental shake and helped me see that getting my thought life in order had to become my top priority.

The thing about it is, Dear One, we cannot serve both God and Self, because they are constantly and irrevocably at odds. We operate within the mortal realm, occupied with things of the flesh; He is of the spiritual realm, concerned with things of lasting importance that we cannot see. He had been patiently allowing me to straddle the chasm between my own beliefs and His truths, but no more. I felt He was giving me the same ultimatum the Israelites had received: "Choose this day whom you will serve" (Josh. 24:15). I took a page from Joshua and said, "I will serve the Lord."

Father, I belong to You. Enable me to listen to what Your Word says, and to follow through in obedience! In Jesus' name, Amen.

SEPTEMBER 6

Violence and destruction resound in her; her sickness and wounds are ever before Me. Jeremiah 6:7b

Over the years this has been how I believed God saw me when He looked at me. Maybe you can relate. For some reason I assumed that all He could see was the bad—the violence, the destruction, the sickness, the wounds. And naturally, I believed that He would be repulsed by that. I knew I was.

Whenever I would come across verses that talked about being pure and blameless in God's sight because of Christ's sacrifice for me, my mind literally could not wrap itself around the notion. Looking in the mirror, all I saw was ugliness, desolation, and wounds. It's not that He doesn't see my flaws, my hurts, and my sin—it's more about the fact that He can also see *past* that into my heart and mind. He could see that I so desperately wanted to please Him, but just couldn't seem to get there. As I spent more time reading and studying His Word, I realized that His vision penetrates past outward appearance (1 Sam. 16:7), and that He calls things that are not as though they were (Rom. 4:17b). That means that He sees us as we *will be*, Dear One, not just as we *are*. And, praise to Him unending, He never sees us as we see ourselves.

I don't know where this verse meets you today. If the Lord has freed you from a past entanglement of sin and destruction, from a pit of misery and despair, I join with you today in praising His almighty name! If you are still experiencing life as a weary soldier on the battlefield, facing those same old foes again, I join with you today in asking for God's mercy and deliverance from darkness into His healing light. If your battle is more in your own mind; if you project an outward façade of competency and contentment while secretly harboring shame and condemnation, I join with you today in feeling the relief and wonder of knowing that God sees you as the worthy, beloved child that you *are*—not as you are seeing yourself. May we come before Him with renewed thanksgiving today. In Jesus' name, Amen.

SEPTEMBER 7

They do not cry out to Me from their hearts but wail on their beds. Hosea 7:14a

At first it would seem that there isn't much difference between crying out and wailing, but there is. Crying out comes from a place of desperation within our heart; we're well aware that we cannot fix whatever is wrong and we cannot continue with things as they are. In other words, the burden has become too heavy. Crying out is our soul's way of seeking help, of making our pain known. We know we've come to the end of ourselves, and we are urgently and actively petitioning God for help.

Wailing, on the other hand, is a more passive (and heathen) expression of grief in this context. The unrepentant Israelites were not crying out to God in the streets while covered in sackcloth and ashes—evidence of a repentant heart. They were wailing upon their beds. Rather than getting up, going out, and publicly petitioning God for His swift and speedy deliverance and aid, they were simply bemoaning the situation on their beds. When things get desperate for us, my friend, it is not the time for wailing. It is the time to go before the Lord and cry out.

With my own children, I'm still trying to explain the difference between whining and calling for help. Whining means they'd like for their circumstances to be different, but they are taking no ownership in helping to find a solution, nor are they approaching me in a way that makes me feel inclined to offer assistance. Calling for help, on the other hand, means they've realized a situation is dire, they are in over their heads, and they need help immediately. They call out for it, and their tone immediately alerts me to come running. I think a fair comparison could be drawn between the wailing and whining and the crying out and calling out. How is your voice sounding as you petition the Lord today?

Father, I come before You with a repentant heart, willing to do things Your way. In my areas of need, I cry out to You from my heart, confident in the knowledge that You will respond. In Jesus' name, Amen.

SEPTEMBER 8

You were running a good race. Who cut in on you to keep you from obeying the truth? That kind of persuasion does not come from the One who calls you. Galatians 5:7-8

A few weeks ago I went through a period of intense struggle. I found it difficult to maintain my positive attitude, I was easily irritated, and I felt generally weepy and numb. Not one bit of it was pleasant, and despite my best efforts and lots of praying, I just wasn't able to shake it—which in turn brought more frustration, shame, and confusion. I was trying to describe what this heavy discouragement felt like to Kevin, and I said: "It's like I'm running a race, going as fast as I can, working as hard as I can, doing the best that I can... and my shoe keeps coming untied! I get my momentum back going and then I have to stop and re-tie it again. It's exhausting and so frustrating!"

I'm wondering if you can relate today, Dear One. Is there an area of struggle in your life where Satan keeps untying your shoes or is tying your laces together in knots? Like it or not, we're going to have some roadblocks on our race route. Sometimes the reason for a rough patch is clear, and sometimes it seems to come upon us for no good reason at all. When I have those inevitable times, these verses from Galatians always come to mind. The portion I kept focusing on and pondering in my most recent time of struggle is that "this kind of persuasion" (the darkness, heaviness, temptation, or despair we feel) does not come from the One who calls us. So that means it's coming from the enemy, who is trying to thwart our efforts to remain steadfast in obedience to God as we run this race. I don't know about you, my friend, but I am just not going to stand for that!

My solution during this most recent time of struggle was to write out a prayer to Jesus, asking Him to give me the victory over my enemy through His power. As I claimed *His* power in my life, I felt renewed. Why? Because the One who *does* call us is faithful, and when we cry out to Him, He will indeed deliver us! Amen.

SEPTEMBER 9

When Pharaoh let the people go, God did not lead them on the road through the Philistine country, though that was shorter. For God said, "If they face war, they might change their minds and return to Egypt." So God led the people around by the desert road toward the Red Sea. Exodus 13:17-18a

Have you ever felt that God was leading you along the most illogical, circuitous route possible between point A and point B in your life? I certainly have. When the Hebrew people left Egypt, God deliberately did not take them in the direction that would have been the quickest to reach their destination. He instead chose to take them along the safest route, knowing that a people still shell-shocked from years of slavery would be unable to face another battle successfully so soon.

As God delivers us from our own Egypts, we at times find ourselves perplexed by the meandering routes He takes us on, confident that we could have been to the Promised Land much more quickly had He just done *that* instead. Yet *that* may have been the very circumstance that would have caused us to run right back into the comforts of our captivity—when we realized ourselves not yet a match for the battle, not yet strong enough to fight.

Your journey may involve some wandering, my friend. It may involve some discontent. But it will also involve some manna being provided to you each day, in accordance with what you need. And it may even involve a Red Sea being parted that you never could have imagined, and never would have seen, had you chosen to remain behind in your captivity. No matter how puzzling it seems, agree to trust His timing. He may not "arrive" when you think He ought to be there, but He is *always* on time and is never lacking in purpose for your life.

Father, sometimes I feel frustrated and confused about how long it seems to be taking me to reach my goal. During those times, enable me to rest faithfully in You as I agree to trust in Your timing. Amen.

SEPTEMBER 10

Who shall separate us from the love of Christ? Shall trouble or hardship or persecution or famine or nakedness or danger or sword? [...] No, in all these things we are more than conquerors through Him who loved us. Romans 8:35, 37

Few things cause us to come to a screeching halt in our busy everyday lives. Heavy traffic or construction? We detour around, even if we go forty-five minutes (or miles) out of the way. Red light? We jockey for a spot in the lane with fewer cars so that the green light sends us forth six seconds sooner. Long line at the grocery store? We use the self-checkout and hurry on our way. We are a people, and a culture, that abhors waiting. When we're faced with a problem, we want to solve it immediately—and preferably with our own talent and skill.

But then there *are* the things that turn our lives inside out: a call from your doctor with devastating news. A spouse walking out on you. A family member lost in an accident. A pink slip from your boss at work. A call from a teacher or counselor at your child's school. An officer knocking on your door. These are the times in which our knees buckle and life, Time itself, seems to stop—suspending its onward march as we struggle to process the information. What's the last thing that has happened in your life that caused this kind of impact?

In these kinds of circumstances, detours are not an option—these challenges have to be dealt with and faced head-on. And most of the time, we will find ourselves woefully unequipped to solve the problem alone. Where, then, do we go when life comes crashing down on us? We go to God. We choose, as Paul wrote, to fix our eyes not on what is seen (our circumstances), but on what is unseen (our mighty God), because we know that what we can see is only temporary, whereas our God is eternal (2 Cor. 4:18). Whatever the challenge you are facing, Beloved, "He will keep you strong to the end" (1 Cor. 1:8a NLT)—for we are *more than conquerors* through Christ Jesus. Amen.

SEPTEMBER 11

On the evening of that first day of the week, when the disciples were together, with the doors locked for fear of the Jewish leaders, Jesus came and stood among them and said, "Peace be with you!" After He said this, He showed them His hands and side. The disciples were overjoyed when they saw the Lord.
John 20:19-20

Today I'm pondering why we have scars. I'm contemplating why God chose to craft our bodies in such a way that some injuries leave "remainder marks" on us. He certainly could have chosen to make our skin able to withstand more than a cut from a piece of paper, or chosen to make it miraculously regenerate itself without blemish when it was injured, but He didn't. Since God is never haphazard in His work, there has to be a reason—maybe several.

Perhaps one reason is that scars remind us of the battles we have endured. The car accident we recovered from. The surgery that saved our life. The trials we have weathered. The labor we've done as our life's work. Not only do our scars remind *us* of what we've walked through, they also serve as silent witnesses to others that we have *lived*, that we've known suffering, that we've felt pain. Airbrushed versions of ourselves would not spread the Gospel of Christ as effectively. People relate and respond to healers who have first been wounded themselves—for if we have not experienced pain, suffering, and loss, how can we help guide those who are coming behind us, looking to us for encouragement and hope?

Jesus came back after the resurrection and appeared to His fearful disciples, speaking peace to them and showing them His scars. His scars proved that He wasn't some apparition, a ghostly wisp of His former self. He was real, He was alive, and He had conquered death. Your scars speak to what you have conquered, through Him. May each one serve as a witness to others—and as a reminder to you—of His healing power in our lives. Amen!

SEPTEMBER 12

Woe to me because of my injury! My wound is incurable! Yet I said to myself, "This is my sickness, and I must endure it."
Jeremiah 10:19

I spent many discouraging years in the same camp as Jeremiah, believing that my wound was incurable and my brokenness was just something I was going to have to live with for the rest of my life. I'm wondering if there's a similar area in your life, one in which you've also reached that place of dejected acceptance of a situation that feels unchanging and irreparable. Maybe it's a broken relationship. Maybe it's a difficult marriage. Maybe it's past baggage that refuses to leave, or a present struggle that has no end in sight. No matter what the circumstance and how long you've been in it, guess what, Beloved: There is still hope. *Nothing* is beyond the healing power and redemption of God. *Nothing* is beyond His reach or beyond His sight.

Lazarus was irreparably dead until Jesus called him to come forth. The woman in Luke 8 had irreparable bleeding until she touched the hem of Jesus' cloak. Abraham and Sarah were irreparably childless until God gave them Isaac. Moses and the Israelites were irreparably trapped until God parted the Red Sea. Job's losses were irreparably gone until God restored them. Daniel and Jonah were irreparably dinner, and the three in the fiery furnace were irreparably ashes—until God intervened. Your situation can seem irreparable, Beloved. And yet you can still hope that God will salvage it. As the three in the fiery furnace said: We know that God can save us. But even if He chooses not to, we still believe He *can* (Dan. 3:17-18). That's how I feel about my own areas of persistent brokenness. There are simply parts of me that I can't fix, nor am I supposed to. I believe that God can make me whole again. How He does it is a mystery known only unto Him.

Whatever your areas of brokenness are today, Beloved, they never mean you can't still hope for His healing. May we remind ourselves today that nothing in all creation is impossible for the Creator, the One who is before all things. In Jesus' name, Amen.

SEPTEMBER 13

You have wearied the Lord with your words. Malachi 2:17a

This verse always makes me smile. If anyone can weary the Lord with words, I should be near the top of the list. In this particular context, the people of God have wearied Him with their words because they are complaining about a perceived lack of justice from God towards those who are doing wrong. (It's unfortunate that we often fail to realize that if God complied with our requests for swift judgment and no mercy, we'd routinely find *ourselves* being disciplined as well!) Complaining certainly wearies the Lord. Nagging, blaming, and making excuses for ourselves are offensive approaches as well. In addition, when we're all talk and no follow-through, we weary the Lord with empty words.

This verse also reminds me of my tendency to be a bit long-winded in my prayers at times. I think about Mary's method of asking for Jesus' help in John 2:3: "When the wine was gone, Jesus' mother said to Him, 'They have no more wine.'" No suggestions as to how He might best solve that problem. Just state the issue and move on.

Another example is the centurion in Matthew 8:6, who just states his problem as well: "My servant lies at home paralyzed, suffering terribly." Jesus replies, "Shall I come and heal him?" (v. 7) and the centurion responds, "Lord, I do not deserve to have You come under my roof. But just say the word, and my servant will be healed" (v. 8). And he was.

I continually marvel at these instances of people who placed their faith and trust in Jesus' ability to meet their needs rather than in their own ability to explain the problem with adequate urgency and detail! My friend, may we be reminded today that "the Lord knows how to rescue the godly from trials" (2 Pet. 2:9a). Whatever concerns are upon your heart, Dear Friend, He is well equipped to provide a solution.

Father, help me simply to state the problem, fully trusting in Your ability to respond to my needs and Your faithfulness to deliver me. Amen.

SEPTEMBER 14

...and these three men, firmly tied, fell into the blazing furnace. Then King Nebuchadnezzar leaped to his feet in amazement and asked his advisers, "Weren't there three men that we tied up and threw into the fire?" They replied, "Certainly, Your Majesty." He said, "Look! I see four men walking around in the fire, unbound and unharmed, and the fourth looks like a son of the gods."
Daniel 3:23-25

What I most treasure about these verses is this: The three men were *firmly tied* when they *fell* into the furnace. Yet moments later they were *walking around* in the fire, *unbound and unharmed*. Satan can use other people and circumstances to bind us. In our own power we are helpless, and at times even face certain (earthly) destruction. Yet, when we give the situation over to God, trusting in His sovereignty, we are set free. Even *in the midst* of the fire of tribulation, we will walk around, unbound and unharmed, when we are abiding in the power of God to work in our circumstances.

In what fiery furnace do you find yourself today, Beloved? Were you thrown in or pushed? Did you fall in accidentally? Did you jump in of your own accord? Are you still tied up and bound as you sit amongst the flames? Or have you petitioned God to free you to walk about within the blaze? Are you allowing Him to walk with you, to be your "fourth man" in the fire? Or have you been trying to put out the flames with a watering can? Here's the most amazing thing that can happen when you invite God into the fire with you: When the three men came out of the furnace, the king's officials "saw that the fire had not harmed their bodies, nor was a hair of their heads singed; their robes were not scorched, and there was no smell of fire on them" (v. 27b).

When He's in the fire with you, Beloved, you come out of the furnace of affliction not even smelling like smoke. Instead, you are permeated by the sweet scent of His mercy and saving grace. Won't you seek His presence with you in your trial today? Amen.

SEPTEMBER 15

They will have no fear of bad news; their hearts are steadfast, trusting in the Lord. Psalm 112:7

Several years ago I came upon this verse and wrote it down in order to memorize it. I routinely struggled with the tendency to worry, and decided it would be a good one for me to commit to mind. I personalized it when I wrote it down: "I will have no fear of bad news; my heart is steadfast, trusting in the Lord." When I first started repeating it to myself, I understood it to mean this: "Nothing bad will happen, because I trust in the Lord."

A few months later, an acquaintance of mine had a newborn baby that almost died. I was shaken and upset to hear this, and as I was praying for them I suddenly realized that this verse does not mean that because we trust God, we'll never have bad things happen to us! It means exactly what it says: When bad news *does* come, we will not *fear* it—because our hope and trust are in our God, and we know that the *Good* News of Jesus Christ trumps any "bad news" Satan tries to throw into our path!

This revelation hit me like a ton of bricks. Here I'd been speaking and praying this verse for months, and never in the sense of what it truly meant! I felt like the people of Nehemiah's day, who "went away [...] to celebrate with great joy, because they now understood the words that had been made known to them" (Neh. 8:12). I am so thankful God is faithful to bring clarity!

We will all get bad news. That's part of living. Bad things and painful things happen to all of us, and to those we love. Yet we do not have to fear the trial, Beloved, because we know that our God is *for us* and that He will be *with us* through every moment of the storm.

Father, I know that no amount of bad news will ever overcome the Good News of my salvation and victory in Christ Jesus. Thank You for this truth today! In Jesus' name, Amen.

SEPTEMBER 16

So [the prophets of Baal] shouted louder and slashed themselves with swords and spears, as was their custom, until their blood flowed. [...] But there was no response, no one answered, no one paid attention. 1 Kings 18:28, 29b

Every time I read these verses, my heart hurts. I picture these prophets of Baal—cutting and slashing themselves, hoping that their god would take notice of them if they spilled their blood—and yet "there was no response, no one answered, no one paid attention."

During my years of struggle with self-destructive behaviors, I often faced this same feeling of forlorn devastation. I was a wreck inside, and yet no one seemed able to see it. There were a few people who did notice and care, who did try to help, but none of us had the answers, and I remained mired in the pit of self-loathing for years. What I never realized was that God never missed a single moment of my self-inflicted harm. He paid attention, and He was deeply grieved to see me in that much pain. He didn't intervene because I didn't ask or allow Him to. But He has not missed one second of my struggle, Friend—or yours.

Have you ever attempted to attract someone else's attention to your brokenness and pain in ways that were unhealthy or harmful? During that time of rebellion or self-destruction in your life, did you feel as though no one cared or was even aware of your pain—including God? I pray that you have come through that painful time and into a closer relationship with Him, knowing without a doubt that He is always by your side. If you haven't, please know that He is there, He does see you, and He is waiting for your invitation.

We do not have to harm ourselves to attract the attention of our God. He has given us a far better way to make our pain, grief, and needs known to Him. It's called prayer. When you pray to Him, Beloved, He hears you (Job 22:27). And He is faithful to answer, every single time. Be encouraged today, in Him. Amen.

SEPTEMBER 17

God is not unjust; He will not forget your work and the love you have shown Him as you have helped His people and continue to help them. Hebrews 6:10

It's interesting to me the kinds of things God never forgets, and the kinds of things He chooses not to remember. His Word tells us that He does not forget His covenant (Deut. 4:31), His children (Ps. 137:5; Isa. 44:21; 49:15), or, as our verse for today says, the love that we have shown Him as we have loved others. In contrast, what kinds of things does He choose to "remember no more"? Our wickedness, our transgressions, and our sin (Isa. 43:25; Jer. 31:34).

Memory is a curious thing. Some of us still feel pained when we recall past sins or poor choices we made, even if we have confessed and repented and have not fallen back into them since. At best, we may experience fleeting regret when they come to mind; at worst, we career down the path towards guilt, shame, and condemnation. Yet the One who sits on heaven's throne—and the *only* One with the authority to judge us for our sins—instead chooses to "remember them no more" once we have confessed them, repented, and asked for forgiveness. My mind can barely wrap itself around the notion.

What, then, is God calling to mind when He looks at us? What is it that helps Him remember which Child we are amongst the masses? He knows us by our *good* deeds, my friend. By all the times we did it *right*. When we heeded the call, followed through in obedience, and were His hands and feet amongst the lost and hurting of this world. The times when we *loved*.

The next time you feel yourself bogged down in the remembrance of regret, call to mind the fact that Your Father is not focusing on the shots you missed; He's celebrating that you're on the court and wearing His name on your jersey. Give it all you've got out there today, my friend! I am praying for your success. Amen.

SEPTEMBER 18

Beware of turning to evil, which you seem to prefer to affliction.
Job 36:21

What habits are you tempted to turn to when you're feeling the pain of affliction? I tend to want to eat—and not carrot sticks either, my friend. I crave junky stuff that doesn't nourish my physical body and fills my thought compartment with guilt. Then I go off the deep end in the other direction, running several extra miles to try and compensate for whatever it was I consumed in order to comfort myself. It's an ugly and embarrassing cycle, one that I have confessed before the Lord as sin, and I am currently working towards overcoming it in the strength of His power and grace.

What about you? (I hope *something* has come to your mind during my time of confession, and that I am not the only one who does this!) Food may not be your false comfort in affliction. Maybe you lose yourself in video games or social media. Maybe you watch endless amounts of television. Maybe you go shopping and spend more than you make. Or you've become a workaholic because you don't want to deal with the problems at home. Maybe you engage in sexual sin. Maybe you abuse alcohol or drugs. Maybe you become physically or verbally abusive. Or maybe you live in the otherworld of Denial, refusing to acknowledge there's even a problem in the first place. Our list could go on. The point is, whatever behavior or habit we're choosing to cling to when times are tough is going to prove unproductive, unhelpful, and undoing when we choose that false comfort over God.

Seasons of affliction are hard. Yet God wants us to come to *Him* when we are hurting, not run to other flimsy and temporary comforts of this world. When we fill ourselves with mindless or sinful habits in an attempt to run from affliction, we end up miring ourselves in the muck even more deeply. The good news is that we can stop right where we are, call to Him for help, and He will pull us out of the mire and place our feet back on the solid rock of Christ (Ps. 40:2). Amen!

SEPTEMBER 19

Be kind and compassionate to one another, forgiving each other, just as in Christ God forgave you. Ephesians 4:32

Sometimes it's much harder for us to forgive ourselves than it is to forgive others. For a long time I struggled with believing that my childhood abuse was my fault and that I deserved it. I thought I must have somehow caused it—because even when I finally got out of that abusive situation, I seemed to fall right back into similar patterns with different people in my teens. I had deep levels of self-hatred and shame, and struggled constantly with a desire to hurt myself in whatever ways I could, trying desperately to "atone" for all of my shortcomings.

Feeling like we deserve to be mistreated is the diseased fruit borne of a toxic root of shame. It is not God's truth, but when we're stuck in that dark place, it's a root that is maddeningly difficult to yank out of the soil of our hearts. Clarity in this matter finally came to me in my late teens. A friend of mine said to me over the phone: "Do you think that I would deserve that, Allyson?" "No, of course not." "Okay. Well from here on out, whatever the issue is, if it's something that you think I would deserve, then it's a good thing. If it's something you think I wouldn't deserve, it's a bad thing." This sounds so incredibly simple, my friend, but it had a *huge* impact on my life. I saw myself through such distorted lenses that I truly had no hope, apart from the saving power of Jesus, to ever see myself any differently. Through my friend, the Lord was able to plant those *good* seeds in my heart soil, relying on my ability to have love and compassion for others, even when I had none at all for myself. I used this standard over and over again for many years whenever I needed to evaluate objectively if something was good for me or not. The Lord has been faithful to mature this part of me through the years, but I had to start somewhere—and this was it for me.

Father, may I forgive others and myself as freely as You forgive each one of us. Fill my heart with Your truth and love in exchange for my hurts, grievances, and distortions. In Jesus' name, Amen.

SEPTEMBER 20

In those days Hezekiah became ill and was at the point of death. The prophet Isaiah son of Amoz went to him and said, "This is what the Lord says: Put your house in order, because you are going to die; you will not recover." Hezekiah turned his face to the wall and prayed to the Lord, "Remember, Lord, how I have walked before you faithfully and with wholehearted devotion and have done what is good in your eyes." And Hezekiah wept bitterly. Before Isaiah had left the middle court, the word of the Lord came to him: "Go back and tell Hezekiah, the ruler of My people, 'This is what the Lord, the God of your father David, says: I have heard your prayer and seen your tears; I will heal you.'" 2 Kings 20:1-5b

When we are in despair, we can bring our feelings before God. Hezekiah did not accuse the Lord of unfairness; he simply expressed his feelings of grief and anguish to God. And God can be swayed by our prayers. By this I mean that He honors His relationship with us as Father. If fathers are rigid and unwilling to hear and respond to the cries of their children, we say that they are cold, unloving, aloof, or controlling. God is none of those things. Therefore, it makes perfect sense that He would welcome us to share our thoughts and feelings with Him. When a father receives good reason from a child to reconsider a decision, he has every right to change his mind. God does as well.

I believe that in some things, eternal kingdom plans and purposes are set and cannot be changed. Yet in others, I think God allows us to have some space to come to Him and request His reconsideration. What I love about God's response in this passage is that it is immediate: "Before Isaiah had left the middle court," God had sent him right back to Hezekiah. I wonder how often Isaiah heard, "Hold on, I changed My mind." Probably not too often. Isn't it comforting to know that our prayers *matter* to God, that He hears and *listens* to them, that they *affect* Him? That's our Father, Beloved. Won't you praise Him and thank Him today? Amen.

SEPTEMBER 21

Dear children, keep away from anything that might take God's place in your hearts. 1 John 5:21 NLT

My daughter Tessa loves to read. And when I say loves to read, I mean *loves* to read. When she gets off the bus in the afternoon, she's reading. Walks to the door, reading. Comes in, sits down on the couch, still reading. I love that she loves to read. I love to read, too. However, there's a problem. Several evenings we've had clashes at bedtime over the "Just let me finish this chapter!" plea. Sometimes she's late to dinner because she's so wrapped up in her book that she doesn't hear us call her. The past two years in school, her teachers have said that the only problem they ever have with her is that she reads while they are teaching—which means that sooner or later, she's going to find herself confused, behind, and completely lost.

So it is with idols, my friend. I like the New Living Translation's version of this verse because it includes the word *might*. We are to keep ourselves away from anything that even has a *chance* of taking first place in our hearts. If the Teacher is teaching and we're too busy reading, cooking, golfing, singing, painting, gardening, building, crafting, fishing, playing, writing, or watching television to *hear Him speaking to us*, then we have an enormous problem, just like my daughter did. One of her teachers had previously taught an upper grade, and she did not hesitate to let Tessa know that if she kept on with this habit, she'd quickly find herself behind—which I appreciated! (Sometimes the children take the warning and rebuke ever so much better if it does not come from the *parent*, right?!) So I'm asking you to join me today in taking an inventory of your hobbies, the leisure activities in which you spend your time, and evaluate whether or not you can still hear the Teacher teaching. If not, my friend, it's time we put the book down and listen.

Father, help me keep You first in my heart always! In Jesus' name, Amen.

SEPTEMBER 22

"The pride of your heart has deceived you, you who live in the clefts of the rocks and make your home on the heights, you who say to yourself, 'Who can bring me down to the ground?' Though you soar like the eagle and make your nest among the stars, from there I will bring you down," declares the Lord. Obadiah 3-4

No matter how high we climb in this life, my friend, we are still under God's feet. The builders of the Tower of Babel learned this firsthand, when their attempt to build a city with a tower that reached to the heavens (Gen. 11:4) was met with swift discipline from the Lord. Verse 5 begins, "But the Lord came down." Oh, me. Can you recall ever receiving a rebuke along the lines of, "Don't *make* me come down there!"? Woe to these foolish builders, who had incited the Lord to *come down* to see the city and the tower they were building. The Lord was not pleased.

The city itself was not the issue, nor was the tower. God knew good and well that these mortals could build until they perished by an untimely death from exhaustion at the age of 523 and *still* not be one millimeter closer to reaching Him in heaven. No, my friend, the Lord's anger had been aroused because of the *pride* of these people. His response was to confuse their language and then scatter them all over the earth— whenceforth, as you might imagine, "they stopped building the city" (v. 8). We can choose to humble ourselves, Beloved, or God will gladly step in and do it for us when we become afflicted with pride.

May I invite you to do a little "Pride Check" along with me today? We're not always building towers to heaven. Pride sometimes sneaks in so subtly that we overlook it. Just recently I found myself feeling pleased because I was the first to locate a rather slim book of the Bible during my Bible class. Guess which one. Yep—Obadiah, my friend, where it turns out the Lord had a timely word for me.

Father, keep humbling my heart that I may live first for You! Amen.

SEPTEMBER 23

Surely it was for my benefit that I suffered such anguish. In Your love You kept me from the pit of destruction; You have put all my sins behind Your back. For the grave cannot praise You, death cannot sing Your praise; those who go down to the pit cannot hope for Your faithfulness. The living, the living—they praise You, as I am doing today; parents tell their children about Your faithfulness. Isaiah 38:17-19

Have you ever wondered why God kept you alive through a particular season of your life that ought to have killed you? I went through a long and painful period in which each day was a monumental struggle, and I could not even begin to conceive of any future benefit coming from my past trials or my present pain. Yet God, in His mercy, did not allow me to self-destruct. His hand was on my life, bestowing protection and guidance—although I did not see it at the time, nor did I even want it. Can you relate in some way? It is my prayer that we will all reach a point when we can see and know the blessings that God has faithfully brought forth from our brokenness. Had we not known the depths of the pain and the despair, we never would have been able to see or experience the joys of the restoration.

As we journey through our pain, we can give Him praise and glory for His steadfastness within the gale. As we eventually reach the other side of it, we can share our testimony of what the Lord has done for us; we can tell others about His faithfulness. God is in the business of redemption, Beloved, and He does not intend for one ounce of our pain to go to waste. If we are willing, He can use it in a mighty way to bring encouragement and hope to others. The gift we receive is the deeper relationship we gain with Him in walking along the path of healing together, witnessing His faithfulness and love firsthand. Remember, God's peace is not found in the *absence* of trials, but rather in the midst of them.

Father, thank You for keeping me from the pit of destruction; may I continue to sing praises to Your name! Amen.

SEPTEMBER 24

Who is a God like You, who pardons sin and forgives the transgression of the remnant of His inheritance? You do not stay angry forever but delight to show mercy. You will again have compassion on us; You will tread our sins underfoot and hurl all our iniquities into the depths of the sea. Micah 7:18-19

I can almost hear the wonder in Micah's voice as he said these words: *Who is like You? Who else pardons sin and forgives like You do? Who else delights to show mercy?* I think we can sometimes get tangled up in humanizing God too much. When we sin, we expect God to react as any other person with a moral conscience would. We expect disgust, rejection, and withdrawal of love. That's what makes sense to us.

But we're not dealing with another mortal here, my friend; we're dealing with the Almighty God. He sees beyond the sin and into the heart of the sinner. He understands exactly why we did what we did infinitely better than we ever will! His ability to understand us does not lead Him to excuse us or abide our sin without consequence; however, it does mean that He is able to judge rightly, to judge fairly, to grant leniency, to acquit us when we have come to Him in true confession and earnest repentance.

Our God does not want us to *fail*, Beloved; He is eager for us to *succeed*! He wants us to live, to love, to encourage, to share, to build up, to help, to give, to inspire, to bring Him honor and glory, for He is our Father! As soon as we come to Him with a spirit of true contrition, He treads our sins underfoot and *hurls* all of our iniquities into the depths of the sea! He will obliterate our sin from His eyes, not just casting it but *hurling* it away from Him so that we can be cleansed and made new. Who loves like that but our God? If you are stuck in a place of feeling "beyond His reach" today, Beloved, I pray that Micah's words will bring you fresh hope. Our sin does not define us; our Savior gets the final say. Praise His wondrous name. Amen!

SEPTEMBER 25

When I am afraid, I will put my trust in You. Psalm 56:3 NASB

I appreciate David's transparency here. Oftentimes we're told that fear on our part is evidence of a lack of faith. I disagree. It's evidence of the fact that we are human! From Genesis to Revelation, we see mighty men and women of God express their fear and own it. God's steadfast response of "Do not be afraid" is not an angry rebuke, but rather a loving reminder to His children that He is there and He is able to deliver them. The important thing is not that we are never afraid. The important thing is that *when* we are afraid, we know where to go. David wrote in Psalm 34:4, "I sought the Lord, and He answered me; He delivered me from all my fears."

What fears are you facing today, Beloved? Are they fears based in current circumstances and trials? If so, bring those fears before the Lord and let Him know what is on your heart. Like David, you can remind yourself of your aim: "When I am afraid, I will put my trust in You." And then you can follow through on it.

Sometimes, however, our fears are not in the present, but are based more on the anticipation of a future loss. These are unrealistic and unproductive fears, which are rooted in anxiety, doubt, and worry. This is harboring a fear of the dark when it's still daylight, a fear of drowning in the ocean while you're still on the shore. When you're in the dark, when you're in the depths, by all means: call on God. *Immediately.* But if it's a "what if" anxiety, lasso that thought and hand it over to Christ. Banish it from your mind, and recommit yourself to a steadfast trust in God. When we earnestly seek His peace, He is faithful to provide it.

Almighty Father, thank You for understanding my human nature to be afraid sometimes. Thank You for Your willingness to calm my fears and strengthen my frame. I bring my fears to You today, Lord, exchanging them for the trust I have in You, in Your almighty name, and in the saving power of Your Son, Jesus Christ, in whose name I pray. Amen!

SEPTEMBER 26

To the one who is victorious, I will give some of the hidden manna. I will also give that person a white stone with a new name written on it, known only to the one who receives it. Revelation 2:17b

Our names are so intriguing, aren't they? Our parents give us our birth names, our sweethearts give us our pet names, and our grandchildren give us the sweetest names imaginable. Throughout our lives, others give us nicknames. Some we like better than others, and some are just hurtful or embarrassing (one coach called me "Rambo" due to my rather, ah, competitive nature on the ball field). What someone calls us says a lot about our relationship with them and the level of intimacy we enjoy together. What name do you tend to use when you're talking to God? When I talk to God, I usually call Him "Abba," since I view Him as my Dad. Whatever name we choose to call Him, He loves to hear our voices praying to Him, praising Him, and talking over our concerns with Him—and we can be certain He knows our names as well (see Isa. 43:1).

I find it interesting that Christ will give those who are victorious a white stone with a new name on it. I read through some different theories of what the name might be, and the crux of it is that we still don't know! (I love this about God.) The majority of Bible scholars seem to agree that the "new name" is not our own personal new name, but rather a new name of Christ or of God Himself (see Rev. 3:12; 19:12) that will be revealed only to those who receive the white stone. (The stone itself likely symbolizes the absolution of guilt through Christ and the acceptance into the family of God.) I love that no matter how much we study God's Word, seek to know Him, and are in relationship with Him, we still can't know everything about Him. He reserves the right to keep some things a mystery until we see Him face to face.

Father, thank You for the hidden blessings in my life yet to be revealed. In Jesus' name, Amen.

SEPTEMBER 27

If one part suffers, every part suffers with it; if one part is honored, every part rejoices with it. Now you are the body of Christ, and each one of you is a part of it. 1 Corinthians 12:26-27

Members within the Body of Christ can sometimes squabble over differences of opinion with such fervent conviction of their singular "rightness" that the entire Body suffers. We sometimes lose sight of the fact that we all share one common belief, which is the gift of God's salvation given to us through Jesus, who Himself reminded us that a house divided against itself cannot stand (Mark 3:25).

My Thursday morning Bible study group contains some of the most phenomenal women I've ever met, and amongst our set are ladies from all different denominations and backgrounds. We enrich one another's lives, and I love how the Body of Christ is edified every week as we come together as one to read and study God's Word, to encourage and lift one another up, and to pray with one another and for one another as we share our lives. We have traveled through many trials and triumphs together. We are real with each other. And these are most likely women I never would have even met had I cloistered myself up only within my own denomination. My friend, I would have missed out on such an exquisite blessing.

How about you? Are you blessed and enriched by the presence of others in your life whose faith in Jesus roots you in the same soil, and yet whose differences of denomination or interpretation allow you to be a pleasing grove of different trees? There's nothing wrong with enjoying some time with your like-fruited trees, but our lives open up in new and unimaginable ways when we welcome other cultivars into our midst.

Father, thank You for all of the beautiful trees in my grove. Help me to rejoice in what others in the Body are doing to bring glory and honor to You, remembering that we are all one in Your Son, Jesus Christ! Amen.

SEPTEMBER 28

So then, those who suffer according to God's will should commit themselves to their faithful Creator and continue to do good.
1 Peter 4:19

This is easy to read and agree with—when you're *not* in the midst of a trial! When we are in a time of intense struggle, it can be so difficult to commit ourselves to God and "continue to do good." Typically we want to question God, blame Him, or pull away from Him in our pain, feeling as though He has deserted us.

Committing ourselves to Him and to His will in the midst of our heartache is so very difficult. It can be like trying to run a marathon on a broken ankle, sing the Hallelujah Chorus with laryngitis, or make a crucial presentation at work with the stomach flu, a broken ankle, *and* laryngitis. Physical pain affects and limits our physical performance, just as emotional pain affects and limits our emotional equilibrium. Likewise, our spiritual struggles impact our spiritual life, crippling us when we're trying to walk with God through the pain and continue to "do good."

I'm wondering in what area you're feeling most handicapped today, Beloved. Are you battling chronic illness or addiction? Are you struggling with a psychological condition or heavy-hitting emotions like grief, blame, anger, or shame? Are you wrestling with God right now over a circumstance in your life that is causing such pain that your eyes feel blinded to being able to see His hand in all of it?

Peter sets the course of action before us: We must commit ourselves to our faithful Creator. In other words, we *choose* to trust Him. We place our circumstances and our pain in God's hands, and we continue to walk forward. God "is able to keep you from stumbling and to present you before His glorious presence without fault and with great joy" (Jude 24). He's not left you, Beloved. He is right there, walking with you, carrying you, keeping you from falling. Even in your weakness, you are made strong in Him. In Jesus' name, Amen.

SEPTEMBER 29

Acquitting the guilty and condemning the innocent—the Lord detests them both. Proverbs 17:15

Have you ever acquitted someone of guilt and labeled it forgiveness? Consider Jesus' words today: "If your brother or sister sins against you, rebuke them; and if they repent, forgive them" (Luke 17:3). Forgiveness is an essential part of our well-being and there are many situations in which we must exercise it. However, Jesus first directs us to hold the person accountable. And then He says, "if they repent, forgive them." Let's be sure that we are correctly distinguishing between true forgiveness, and what the Bible refers to as "acquitting the guilty."

"Acquitting the guilty" is synonymous with rationalizing, justifying, minimizing, or excusing harmful behavior and poor choices. In other words, it's enabling someone to continue in sin without the open love of a godly rebuke. Are you making excuses for someone today, Beloved? Are you acquitting their guilt because it's easier than speaking the truth in love? Are you afraid of their reaction or response? Take heart. We are called to hold one another accountable, to correct, rebuke, and encourage; and to speak the truth in love (2 Tim. 4:2; Eph. 4:15)—even when speaking the truth may be a hard word to speak.

We can also find ourselves "condemning the innocent." For years I struggled with my past history of abuse; I often made excuses for those who hurt me and blamed myself instead. Perhaps it gave me a false sense of control in the situation, or made me feel as though I were being kind and forgiving. Either way, it displeased the Lord. I was heaping false guilt and shame upon myself, and "acquitting the guilty" in the matter by choosing not to place the responsibility for the damage at the feet of those who had perpetrated it. It wasn't that I needed to see anyone punished for an offense—it was that I needed to stop punishing myself for what was not my fault. Can you relate in some way today? I pray that God would grant us His wisdom and discernment as we seek to judge rightly in all things. He can provide the clarity we seek. Amen!

SEPTEMBER 30

Return to your fortress, you prisoners of hope; even now I an-nounce that I will restore twice as much to you. Zechariah 9:12

God is our fortress, Beloved. When we take shelter in Him, He offers us protection and promises to restore what has been lost—even twice that. If I am going to be a prisoner, I would rather be a prisoner of hope than of despair. If we hope, we can hope for restoration and transfor-mation. If we despair, we sentence ourselves to desolation.

In Jeremiah 30:17, God promises His children that He will restore them to health and heal their wounds. It's important for us to acknowledge that *God* restores us and *God* brings healing. His Word does not say, "When you have worked hard enough and I think you finally deserve it, you will have earned the right to your healing and restoration." No, Beloved. Our healing and restoration are not dependent upon our ef-fort, our work, or our timeframe. They're dependent upon our *hope*. When we hope in the Lord, we are agreeing to place our trust in His sovereign plan, His timeframe, and His heart that beats with unfathom-able love for each one of us.

Where does this meet you today, Dear One? What enemy are you fac-ing on the battlefield right now, the one that is wearing you down and wearing you out? Or maybe the enemy isn't on the battlefield standing against you; it's the person staring back at you in the mirror. The wars that rage within us can sometimes surpass the ones around us in terms of exhaustion, casualties, and despair. Wherever you find yourself fighting today, my friend, find sanctuary in your Fortress. Return to your God, the One who loves you and gives you "eternal encourage-ment and good hope" (2 Thess. 2:16).

Father, I confess that sometimes it is hard to rest and remain in You. Quiet my fears, calm my heart, still my mind, and grant me Your peace. In Jesus' name, Amen.

OCTOBER 1

Then the word of the Lord came to Jonah a second time: "Go to the great city of Nineveh and proclaim to it the message I give you." Jonah 3:1-2

Jonah has had quite an ordeal, hasn't he? So far he's been tossed overboard, nearly drowned, and swallowed by the big fish; he prayed for deliverance and was vomited back out onto dry land. Now that Jonah is safely back on land and has his wits about him, God is ready to give the instructions a second time. And I absolutely love that God tells Jonah the *very same thing* He did the first time (see 1:2).

This speaks a mighty lesson to us about obedience. When God tells us to do something, we can do it the first time—*or*, we can run the other way, flee the assignment we didn't want, cause a mighty calamity to come upon others, be thrown into raging waters, swallowed by sea creatures, vomited onto land, and *then* we can receive the same command a second time and go do what God has asked us to do. Can you relate today, my friend? In what areas are you resisting God's call or running in the opposite direction?

Could God have given up on Jonah and used a different prophet to bring His warning to Nineveh? Certainly. It wasn't that the Ninevites specifically needed Jonah; it was that Jonah specifically needed to learn *obedience*. However, here is the good news that Jonah's story brings to us today, Beloved: The Lord did speak to him *a second time*. Even when we take our instructions and run the opposite way with them, ignore them, or bungle the mission entirely, God still graciously speaks to us a second time. Jonah 3:3 says that Jonah obeyed the word of the Lord and went to Nineveh. He still wasn't happy about it, mind you, and God had plenty more to teach him in that regard. But He does not give up on us, even when our hearts are hard and our pride is overweening. He teaches us, corrects us, and sets us on the right path again.

Father, I praise You for Your faithfulness. Amen!

OCTOBER 2

Now to Him who is able to do immeasurably more than all we ask or imagine, according to His power that is at work within us, to Him be glory in the church and in Christ Jesus throughout all generations, for ever and ever! Amen. Ephesians 3:20-21

I would love to sit down with you today and hear about the Ephesians 3:20 moments of your life. The times when God answered prayers you hadn't even thought of offering yet. The times He provided answers to prayers you'd long since thought had received a "no." The times when He worked out complicated details and sequences of timing and events that would boggle the human mind. The times He brought someone new into your life and only later did you realize that that person would turn out to be one of your dearest friends—or your spouse. His boundless ability to work in our lives is simply beyond our comprehension.

Sometimes an Ephesians 3:20 moment occurs when God sends you a sign that means something infinitely special only *to you.* One of those moments for me came several years ago, when I was going through a difficult season of wanting to fall back into old, unhealthy habits. I went to pick up my race packet for a 5K I was running the following week, and when I received it I stared down at my bib number in shock: 1023. My firstborn's birthday. The very reason (and the *only* reason) I had committed to ending my cycle of self-destructive behavior in the first place. I felt God saying to my heart, "Remember, Child? *This* is why you are choosing obedience. I love you." Oh, Beloved. I pray that He will bring countless more Ephesians 3:20 moments to your life and mine as well. Sweet moments like these always prompt me to cry over the love that God has for us. He is our fortress, mighty to save—and yet He also has such thoughtfulness and gentleness in Him. Even more amazing still, He is not afraid to show it or to lavish it upon us.

Father, I praise You and thank You for Your ability to do far more than all I could ever ask or imagine. In Jesus' name, Amen!

OCTOBER 3

Although most of the many people who came from Ephraim, Manasseh, Issachar and Zebulun had not purified themselves, yet they ate the Passover, contrary to what was written. But Hezekiah prayed for them, saying, "May the Lord, who is good, pardon everyone who sets their heart on seeking God—the Lord, the God of their ancestors—even if they are not clean according to the rules of the sanctuary." And the Lord heard Hezekiah and healed the people. 2 Chronicles 30:18-20

This, my friend, is a *huge* deal, something that had never before happened in the history of the Israelites. They are a month late celebrating the Passover because not enough of the priests had consecrated themselves at the proper time, and the people had not assembled at the proper time (v. 3). The Levites had to kill the Passover lambs for all those who were unclean and therefore could not consecrate their offerings to the Lord themselves (v. 17). It is noted that "the priests and Levites were ashamed" of this catastrophe (v. 15).

God's holiness demanded respect and reverence for every letter of the Law, and any action that deviated from that dishonored Him and was immediately punishable by death—even if it was entirely accidental. (Such as when Uzzah was put to death for reaching out to steady the Ark of the Covenant when the oxen stumbled [see 2 Sam. 6:6-7].) The very idea of the Israelites gathering together to eat the Passover meal at the wrong time and while still in a state of uncleanness was *unthinkable*. Therefore, this particular instance speaks mightily to the merciful heart of our God.

After a succession of bad kings who led the people astray, only recently had Hezekiah come to power and tried to make things right again and lead the people back to God. His prayer of intercession for the people was heard and answered by God. And, true to form, God did not simply accept the prayer, nor did He simply accept the people's offerings even though the people were not ceremonially clean. Instead, God Himself "healed the people." In effect, He voided the need for them to follow the proper channels of action in order to consecrate themselves, and instead touched them directly. So moved was He to see His children trying to walk in obedience that He withheld His wrath at their faltering, stumbling steps and blessed their muddled efforts. This whole account is amazing!

God hasn't slowed His game since. Under the New Covenant, He continues to forgo the requirements of the Law and touch His children directly in order to bring forgiveness, atonement, and cleansing. He does this through the saving grace of His Son, Jesus Christ. Back in the days of the Israelites, atonement could only be made by going through the proper channels of sacrificial offerings and purification rituals. For New Testament believers, we see Solomon's words come to pass through the sacrifice of Jesus Christ: "Through love and faithfulness sin is atoned for" (Prov. 16:6a). That doesn't mean our *own* love and faithfulness can atone for our sin; that means that *Christ's* love for us and His faithfulness to lay down His life on the cross for us had the same effect as God reaching His hand down and "healing the people" who were doing the best they could to walk in obedience. God's love for us is so exquisite that we can barely even begin to comprehend it!

Is there an area of your life today that is a total mess, Beloved? Are you trying to get yourself together so you can come to God in a half-presentable state and beg His forgiveness or mercy? If so, I earnestly pray that this story of the Israelites, and of Hezekiah's faith in the loving heart of our God, will encourage you to run straight into Jesus' arms at this very moment and find the peace you are so frantically seeking.

Father, thank You for loving me even when I make a mess of things. I am so grateful that Your love and faithfulness are constant, and never dependent upon my performance. In Jesus' name, Amen!

OCTOBER 4

And the God of all grace, who called you to His eternal glory in Christ, after you have suffered a little while, will Himself restore you and make you strong, firm and steadfast. 1 Peter 5:10

I treasure this promise that God *Himself* will restore us after we have suffered. It's hard to comprehend how intimately acquainted He is with each one of us; He knows the precise moment when our "little while" has become "long enough," and when that time comes, He hastens to restore us and make us strong.

But what if we haven't yet experienced that restoration, that assurance of having weathered the trial and emerged victorious? What if we're still in the trial, suffering for "a little while" longer? If we're still there, Beloved, there's a reason we're still there. And while we abide in Christ through the storm, we remind ourselves of God's Truth.

First, even in our weakness we are strong, because the Word of God, the Spirit of Christ, lives *in us*, and through Christ, we have already overcome the evil one (1 John 2:14b). We are *assured* this victory because the One who is in us is infinitely greater than the one who is in the world (1 John 4:4b)! Secondly, God promises us that He will surely deliver us "for a good purpose" (Jer. 15:11a). If we require delivering, you can be sure it won't be from something good. God will deliver us *from* the trial and *to* something infinitely better that He has in store for us! Third, God means business. He takes careful note of Satan's schemes in our lives, because "whoever touches you touches the apple of His eye" (Zech. 2:8b). Don't think He doesn't notice it. Oh He sees us, Beloved. And He knows just how hot to let that furnace of affliction become (Isa. 48:10) so that the dross can be burned away, leaving us purer and more refined, more closely resembling His perfect Son, than we were when we started.

Life is a series of refining moments, Beloved. Let's be willing to submit to them and "come forth as gold" (Job 23:10b). Amen.

OCTOBER 5

Your love, dear brother, has brought me great joy and much encouragement! You have cheered the hearts of all of God's people. Philemon 7 GNT

In my Bible study group one time, a discussion arose about whether we would consider ourselves a "puppy" or a "porcupine." The canine friends were described as those who are generally open and friendly to just about anyone, eager to interact, talk, and share with others. The porcupine contingency were those who are a bit slower to warm up, the ones who keep themselves safely guarded with their quills—and they have to learn how to relax those sharp points before others can sidle up close enough to give them a squeeze. Of the entire group of twenty or so, there were about eighteen professed puppies, and two quiet, solitary porcupines. (As you may have guessed, I was—and still am—a porcupine.)

Which group suits you better, Beloved? Do you find it easy to be open and engaging with others, sharing your joys and sorrows alike? Or do you tend to keep things to yourself, rarely talking in a large group, doing a lot more listening to the thoughts of others? We need the puppies *and* the porcupines, my friend, just like we need the introverts and the extroverts! Being one or the other is not bad or wrong—we're all just wonderfully different!

We also have many things to learn from one another. Puppies help the porcupines to s-l-o-w-l-y lower those quills and allow others to get close. Porcupines teach (by example) the value of not sharing every single thought that pops into your mind. Puppies energize and invigorate a group, spreading infectious joy and laughter. Porcupines, when they do finally speak, invite contemplation and introspection with their observations and insights. Wherever you find yourself on the puppy/porcupine spectrum, take heart in knowing that God gifted you with the unique blend of qualities that you possess—and others are blessed by you! In the mighty name of Jesus, Amen.

OCTOBER 6

He will judge between the nations and will settle disputes for many peoples. They will beat their swords into plowshares and their spears into pruning hooks. Nation will not take up sword against nation, nor will they train for war anymore. Isaiah 2:4

This notion of beating swords into plowshares and spears into pruning hooks occurs twice in the Bible: once in Isaiah and once in Micah (4:3). They both offer nearly parallel prophecies to the people of Israel about how God would bring peace in the last days ("the last days" meaning when Christ returns to earth). The flipside of this passage is found in the book of Joel, in which Joel prophesies that the nations that have *oppressed* Israel will be judged by God and must prepare for battle. Thus, these nations are being called to "beat [their] plowshares into swords and [their] pruning hooks into spears" (3:10a). Whereas swords and spears were objects of war and conflict, plowshares and pruning hooks were used for peaceful sowing and harvesting. The scarcity of metal in those days often forced people to choose whether to mold their share of it into a tool of peace or a weapon of warfare.

What are you molding your metal into today, Beloved? Are you in a time of peaceful plowing, turning up the earth in order to allow the Lord to plant some new seeds? Or are you crafting a sword or spear to use in preparation for a battle? Some of us like to keep our metal in sword and spear form just in case we might find ourselves under attack. That can sure make our work of sowing and reaping a whole lot harder.

Remember that God calls us to use the weapons *He* has provided for us (see 2 Cor. 10:4), namely, the Sword of the Spirit which is the Word of God (Eph. 6:17). Remember that His Word is sharper than any iron on earth (Heb. 4:12), guaranteed to give us the victory. Let's mold our share of metal into plowshares, Beloved, and sow some good seed today. May we bring honor, glory, and praise to our Father's name. In Jesus' name, Amen!

OCTOBER 7

[God] gives life to the dead and speaks of the nonexistent things that [He has foretold and promised] as if they [already] existed.
Romans 4:17b AMPC

Which parts of yourself have you assumed long since lost, dead, broken, or beyond resurrection? Is it a portion of your heart, seared into numbness by an ongoing conflict or a betrayal by someone you thought you knew? Is it a portion of your mind, held hostage by a long-held set of false beliefs you've harbored about yourself or another person? Is it a part of your spirit, resting dormant after weathering a season of loss, pain, or ongoing trial that has left you wondering if God is even aware of your existence, much less of your pain? I want to reassure you today my friend that He is absolutely aware of your pain, and He is absolutely affected by it. Because He loves you, your pain *matters* to Him.

God "speaks of nonexistent things as if they already existed." Not only does He know our stories, not only does He meet us in our present circumstances, whatever they may be—He is also fully aware of our futures, of what we *will* become. Paul says that we were created by God to do good works which He prepared in advance for us to do (Eph. 2:10). We can trust God's calling on our lives without having to wonder if we will be up to the task or able to successfully complete the mission. He *already knows* that we will be successful in our calling, because He sees us not just as we are—but as the people He knows we will become! He has created you, my friend, fully equipped to meet the unique challenges and tasks that await you on the journey ahead.

So what about those areas of deadness within you that seem as though they will never heal? God's specialty happens to be bringing dead things back to life. When He speaks things into being, Beloved, they obey. Today I invite you to offer up any areas of deadness within you to the Healer who longs to bring life, hope, and resurrection. He can, indeed, breathe life into anything, and it *will* live again (see Eze. 37:3-6; John 11:25-26). Amen.

OCTOBER 8

Come near to God and He will come near to you. James 4:8a

A few months ago I was standing at my kitchen sink when I noticed a moth flitting past me. I attempted to gently catch it in my hands and release it back outside into the fresh air. This proved far easier in theory than in practice.

I patiently waited for the moth to alight, so that I could scoop it up gently into my hands without hurting its wings. But the moth clearly had other things in mind, such as banging into the window pane and blinds in its efforts to free itself. The longer I stood and waited, the more frantic the moth became, fluttering more and more wildly as I tried to help. I began to feel the stirrings of irritation, thinking: *What is the matter with this thing?! I am trying to help it to freedom!* It was clearly lost, clearly disoriented, and clearly in need of my help! However, this moth was not willing. And as I stood there, I felt God saying to my heart, "Child, you do this, too!" Ah, yes. I do.

God is always near to us, closer even than breath, so this verse from James speaks more to the gift of free will that He gives to us. He allows us to draw near to Him and rest in His presence, and He also allows us to pull away from Him (or flutter around frantically in our disoriented chaos, trying desperately to free ourselves). When we choose to come near to God, it isn't as though we and God are each taking ten paces toward each other. It means that we are choosing to receive and accept the closeness that He always desires with us and provides for us.

Are you that moth today, my friend? I often am. Resting in God and trusting Him completely can sometimes be a challenge, but often it isn't until we come to the end of our own strength and agree to rest in Him that we enable Him to do the freeing work in us that He so longs to do.

Father, help me draw near to You today, trusting in Your heart and Your plan. In Jesus' name, Amen.

OCTOBER 9

Knowing their thoughts, Jesus said, "Why do you entertain evil thoughts in your hearts? Which is easier: to say, 'Your sins are forgiven,' or to say, 'Get up and walk'? But I want you to know that the Son of Man has authority on earth to forgive sins." So He said to the paralyzed man, "Get up, take your mat and go home." Matthew 9:4-6

Jesus' words here bring me comfort. Yes, it's easier to heal the physical infirmity—the symptom—rather than expend the energy and love needed to address the underlying cause. Yet He can, and does, do both. Not only can He forgive us of our sins, He can also heal all of the other symptoms that have come about as a result. Today I am spending some time pondering my "causes" and my "symptoms." Knowing that Jesus is able to heal both gives me great comfort; at the same time, I also feel as though it's important for me to have a solid grasp of what exactly I need to petition Him to heal.

In our lives, the "causes," the bad roots, produce many different "symptoms," the rotten fruit. Sometimes we just want Jesus to give us new fruit without tackling that nasty underground root. I've experienced this in my own life. My root of self-condemnation (also known as pride—remember, thinking awful things about yourself all day still means you're thinking about yourself all day) spawned all kinds of rotten fruit. Just when I'd get one variety cleared off my tree, another crop popped up. I was discouraged and confused, not understanding why my efforts to control my behavior were still not curing my problem. It's because I was not attending to the *cause*, my friend, the *root* of the problem. When I sought Jesus' healing and restoration from my sin of self-condemnation, I began to see other symptoms resolving themselves on their own. Once we ask Jesus to kill it at the root, Beloved, the poisonous vine ceases to be. How can you apply this knowledge in your own life today?

Father, I praise Your willingness to heal causes *and* symptoms. Amen!

OCTOBER 10

Even though I was once a blasphemer and a persecutor and a violent man, I was shown mercy because I acted in ignorance and unbelief. The grace of our Lord was poured out on me abundantly, along with the faith and love that are in Christ Jesus. 1 Timothy 1:13-14

I invite you to personalize Paul's statements here by mentally rewriting the first sentence with examples of your own sin. Like Paul, we sometimes commit grievous sins while truly believing that we are in the right. Although this never excuses our sin, God has compassion on us in our misguided state and begins the process of conviction in our lives through His Spirit. The problem comes when we choose not to hear the Spirit's warning and see the error of our ways. Jesus spoke about spiritual blindness in John 9:41, saying: "If you were blind, you would not be guilty of sin; but now that you claim you can see, your guilt remains."

When we accept Christ as our Savior, we agree to accept God's truth (His Word [John 17:17]) as sovereign in our lives. When we know His truth in a matter and still choose to walk in a way contrary to that truth, that is what John refers to as "walk[ing] in darkness" (1 John 1:6). That doesn't mean we're confused about things and do not realize we are in error. That means we have been shown the truth and have chosen to reject it in favor of a life of habitual, unrepentant sin.

If you are currently struggling in an area of ongoing sin, Jesus is willing and able to forgive you! As Paul writes, "Christ Jesus came into the world to save sinners" (1 Tim. 1:15b). That was His reason for coming to earth, dying on a cross, and being raised again. He came, Beloved, so that we might have life, and have it "to the full" (John 10:10b). If anything is holding you back from claiming your birthright to abundant life in Christ, please bring it before Him today. He longs to bring healing and restoration. If you have already experienced His freedom and forgiveness in your life, praise Him today! Amen.

OCTOBER 11

But the Lord said to Samuel, "Do not consider his appearance or his height, for I have rejected him. The Lord does not look at the things people look at. People look at the outward appearance, but the Lord looks at the heart." 1 Samuel 16:7

Every Saturday morning, Kevin gets up and makes banana nut pancakes from scratch. What I've learned over the course of many Saturdays of pancake consumption is that the most delectable pancakes Kevin makes occur when he uses the worst-looking bananas you can imagine. Why? Because their added life experience—the extra bruises and knocks they've taken throughout the week, coupled with the simple fact that they've seen more and endured more—makes them sweeter, softer, and better suited for this particular purpose.

Samuel gazed at the row of Jesse's sons and his eyes zeroed in on Eliab, the most handsome of the bunch. Instead, God directed Samuel to choose David, the son whose heart would be wrenched, challenged, broken, and mended, yet would always remain faithful to the Lord. *He* was the specific one needed to fill this place in God's recipe.

Different bananas are needed for different recipes. Breads and desserts require the ripest, worst-looking ones we can find in order to turn out well. For cereal or as a stand-alone snack, often the more attractive ones are a better choice. It just depends on the task and the need.

God knows His needs and tasks. If you're feeling like the solitary, unwanted banana left at the end of the shelf today, take heart my friend— at any moment God's hand will reach for you, needing your specific blend of wisdom, maturity, and experience to make His recipe turn out to perfection. His eyes look past our outward appearance and search for the unmarred fruit that is inside—that's your precious heart that He is seeing, Beloved. And He can use it for something amazing. Be encouraged today. Amen!

OCTOBER 12

My people consult a wooden idol, and a diviner's rod speaks to them. Hosea 4:12a

When we look to the world for guidance, we will always find it lacking. Things of this world are limited by their own mortal and natural boundaries. When we bring our concerns before the Living God, He knows no limitation. His answers will not prove false. He takes the smallest detail into consideration, and already knows how our singular choices and actions will affect ourselves and others in the process.

Perhaps you haven't been consulting a wooden idol, but we consult many a false god in our attempts to make sense of life. We often seek counsel from our friends, our pastors, our counselor, or myriad self-help books. There is nothing wrong with any of these avenues, provided the people in question are godly individuals who are willing to be honest with us—even if the truth will be difficult to hear.

The problem arises when we allow those individuals or avenues to take the place of consulting God in our lives, and we find that we have come to rely on human wisdom and guidance rather than the Lord's truth and provision. No matter how well another person knows you, Beloved, that person will *never* know you as well as your God knows you. His fingers knit you together in your mother's womb; He knows your thoughts, wishes, dreams, hopes, and fears. He knows what makes you tick. He understands the motives of your heart. He knows what you need better than anyone else ever has or ever will—including yourself!

I have been prompted today to take a personal inventory of what or whom I consult when I need guidance in my life. I invite you to do the same. Are we are running to those people or things first over God? If so, that is a sign to us that we need to recalibrate our focus. (More on how to do that tomorrow!) I am praying for you today. Amen.

OCTOBER 13

Take words with you and return to the Lord. Hosea 14:2a

So what's the game plan if we've found ourselves consulting sticks of wood? What if we've done an honest inventory and realized that we tend to run and call our girlfriends, our golfing buddies, our mothers, our pastor, or our counselor whenever Life throws a curveball at us? If we've come to the realization that we tend to call others before we put in a call to God, then that's still cause for celebration—because that means we've gained insight and awareness, which means we can begin the work of changing that pattern. So what do we do next? We take words with us, and return to the Lord.

When we find that we've gotten off track, our return to the Lord will always require some sort of verbal communication on our part. Not because He needs an explanation, but because we need to hear ourselves speak. We need to hear our confession of disobedience, our confession of our hardened hearts, our words of apology and repentance as we lay our sin and iniquity before Him. We need to hear ourselves own our sin and acknowledge that without Him at the center of our lives, we are utterly lost. If we return without words, my friend, we haven't really returned at all.

When you do your consulting today, Beloved, make sure that you are coming to God first with whatever is weighing on your heart. He will be faithful to bring clarity, discernment, and His inerrant truth to any matter. Remember that He alone knows everything about you—and He knows you infinitely better than you know yourself. He is able to work out all things for your good (Rom. 8:28), and He always longs to hear from you. You are His beloved child, and He loves you so much!

Father, please keep me close to You today, bringing insight and encouragement as I earnestly seek Your counsel. When I am tempted to call on others before I call on You, send Your Spirit to gently remind me to redirect my focus back onto You, the center of my life and heart. Amen.

OCTOBER 14

*...**with God all things are possible.*** Matthew 19:26b

Sometimes I find myself disbelieving Jesus' words here to His disciples. It's an insidious kind of disbelief, one that requires me to carefully examine what I'm saying to myself—and, in turn, what I'm saying about God. Consider this example: "I will never be fully free from the lingering effects of past abuse on my life. I will always be crippled in some way." Although I often *feel* this way, when I tell myself these kinds of untruths I am also, in effect, telling myself that God's Word is untrue.

God's Word promises me that with God, *all things* are possible. Am I the one and only exception to the rule? Do I have the only problem that God is unable to solve? Has He finally been stumped by my circumstances, my situation, my failures, my lack? I dare not think so, Dear One. I'm not the one exception to His ability to work out all things, nor are you—or your circumstances.

What untruths are you telling yourself today that are, in turn, leading you down a path of telling untruths about God? Perhaps your untruths resemble mine. Perhaps there's an area of struggle in your life that you feel is beyond His power to heal or restore. Even more oblique statements that we tell ourselves can fall under this umbrella, such as "I'm too old for that" or "I'm no good at that" or "I could never do that." Pause and read our verse for today again.

With God, *all things* are possible. If you continue to believe the lies you are telling yourself, you are limiting yourself and limiting God. He *can* work amazing things in your life and He *can do* the impossible! However, there's an ingredient called *faith* that He expects to be in the mix before He does His mighty thing. The next time you catch yourself saying something that is in opposition to this promise from the mouth of Jesus, stop yourself right there, name the wayward thought, and replace it with this unfailing truth: With God, *all things are possible.* He will not be outdone, Beloved! May you feel His power anew today. Amen.

OCTOBER 15

I know your deeds, your hard work and your perseverance. [...]
You have persevered and have endured hardships for My name,
and have not grown weary. Revelation 2:2a, 3

These words are spoken by Christ to the Church in Ephesus, though I take much comfort from them for myself as well. I often place unrealistic expectations on myself, and when I inevitably fall short of them I feel shame and frustration. I'm learning that God *does see* all of my efforts, the hard work and the struggle and the perseverance. He hasn't missed a moment of it. However, God does not need for me to run myself into the ground striving so, especially when it routinely causes me discouragement, false guilt, and a sense of being inept! He just wants my heart. He just wants your heart. When we relinquish our hearts to Him, Beloved, when we simply walk with Jesus, then our behaviors and thoughts and actions will follow suit. The change doesn't come in all the *doing*, but rather in the *being*—the being *with Him*.

I recently sought the Lord's guidance and counsel in this specific matter—the constant desire I have to work hard and change myself and be "better." This is what I felt Him saying to my heart in return: "Stop striving so, Child, and just rest in Me. The time you spend with Me is what helps you to change your heart. I'm proud of you for your willingness to change. I'm proud of your efforts at renewing your mind with My truths. I'm proud of the time you spend reading and studying My Word. All those things are *good things*, Child, but I'm proud of you simply because *you are Mine.*"

It was a fresh revelation for me, to consider that God loves us simply because we're His children. The problem with our busyness and frantic need to *do* more, *be* more, and *achieve* more is that it places our focus right back on Self rather than God. When we look to Him first, He will faithfully equip us with all the skill, energy, innovation, and resources we need to complete the tasks He's given us. In Jesus' name, Amen.

OCTOBER 16

No one has ever seen God; but if we love one another, God lives in us and His love is made complete in us. 1 John 4:12

My husband Kevin is a talented woodworker. Back when we were engaged, I was away at school and he had a tiny apartment near his place of work. When he asked me what I wanted for my birthday, I mentioned that I really needed a bookcase. Never in a million years would I have imagined what he came up with and created for me: a six foot tall bookcase—that also happens to be a perfect replica of Snoopy's doghouse from *Peanuts*. How he managed to build it in the tiny living room of a tiny apartment is beyond me, but I'll tell you one thing: That spoke love to me. And I'm loved by many others whose unique qualities help me know and experience what love is.

Isn't it amazing how we all love one another so differently? As I consider John's teaching on this, it makes perfect sense that we would all love differently—because our distinct efforts at loving one another altogether encompass the many different ways in which God loves us.

How do you know that some else loves you, Beloved? Maybe they say it or write it, and you never tire of seeing and hearing the words. Maybe they spend time with you, doing an activity you both enjoy—or just simply sitting and talking over a cup of coffee. Maybe they enjoy doing kind and helpful things for you, and you are touched by their thoughtfulness. Maybe they never show up empty-handed—they've always found a book that you'd like to read or tickets to an event they know you'd love to see—and you appreciate the tangible reminders of their love for you. Or maybe you know you are loved by the hugs received from friends, the kisses from your children, and the intimacy you enjoy with your spouse. All of these are wonderful ways of expressing love, and the best part is that we never run out of options when it comes to showing our love for others. That's because God *is* love, Beloved, and He is without limit! Let's lavish His love upon others today. Amen.

OCTOBER 17

I am the vine; you are the branches. If you remain in Me and I in you, you will bear much fruit; apart from Me you can do nothing.
John 15:5

Today I was considering the concept of abiding. It seems like it ought to be the easiest thing in the world to do, but it's really not. Why? Maybe because abiding requires us to *rest* in the will of God. We don't typically rest very well, do we? We so often want to run off in our own direction, pursuing our own goals. Or, if the storm swirling around us is intense, our human inclination is to flee—not simply to abide, to "stay put," to remain, to "sit there and do nothing" (or at least that's how we perceive it, oftentimes). We forget that God is always working. And if He's having to "tend" to us as we wander off or forge ahead or send out off-shoots of our own will and plans, it takes time away from what He is trying to do, if we'd only be still and let Him.

Note the conditional clause here: *If* you *remain* in Me… you *will bear* much fruit. A conditional clause means that the second thing can only occur if the first requirement is met. In order to bear fruit, we must remain in the Vine. Are you remaining today, my friend, or are you finding yourself forging your own path ahead? If it feels decidedly difficult (if not downright impossible) simply to abide in the Father today, what is behind those feelings? Plumb your heart and mind and search out the reasons. Is it fear? Is it anxiety or worry? Is it distrust or unbelief? Is it a root of rebelliousness?

Whatever is hampering your ability to rest and abide in Him today, I encourage you to talk it over with Him. He is always delighted to hear from His children, even when we are feeling angry, anxious, hurt, or distrustful. Give Him the chance to speak His truth in your situation to your heart today. Give Him the chance to reassure you of His love for you and His personal faithfulness to you. As you remain in Him, He *will* enable you to bear much fruit! In Jesus' name, Amen.

OCTOBER 18

The heart is deceitful above all things and beyond cure. Who can understand it? Jeremiah 17:9

All too often I get bogged down in my feelings about something. Our feelings are God-given, and are not inherently "good" or "bad." However, when we begin to confuse a feeling with a permanent, undeniable *truth,* the distortion begins to affect our attitudes, beliefs, and behaviors. And then, my friend, we have a problem—because our *feelings* are not *truth.* God's *Word* is truth (John 17:17). Anything else is just perspective and conjecture.

As many wise teachers have pointed out, feelings are not facts. When we treat them as factual information, our skewed thinking can get us into all sorts of binds. For me this comes into play with negative self-talk and all of its nasty repercussions. I feel inept or impatient or inferior, and then the next thing I know, my brain is telling me I *am* all those things. God's Word (the *truth*!) tells me otherwise (see Phil. 4:13; Isa. 26:3; Rom. 8:33-34). How about you? In what areas do your feelings tend to hijack your firm grasp of God's inerrant truth in your life?

The good news that God's Word brings to us today, Beloved, is that God fully understands the intricacies of our deceitful hearts—even if we do not. Even better, He longs to give us a new heart and enable us to walk in His ways (see Eze. 36:26-27). One of the biggest obstacles for me in my healing was that I just didn't feel it. I didn't feel I was worth the effort. I didn't feel like I could make it a reality, even if I tried. And yet, here is God's truth in this matter: If we look to Him and seek His face; if we build our hopes and lives on the Rock of Jesus Christ and believe, *by faith,* that He *can* transform our hearts (and our lives), then He *will*—whether we are "feeling it" yet or not! Are you willing to believe His truth instead of your feelings today?

Father, I long to abide in Your truth and not be tossed about by my feelings in each moment. May this become a reality in my life! Amen.

OCTOBER 19

And let us consider how we may spur one another on toward love and good deeds, not giving up meeting together, as some are in the habit of doing, but encouraging one another—and all the more as you see the Day approaching. Hebrews 10:24-25

Are you a loner, my friend? Do you pride yourself on not needing anyone else for anything? I've been there, and I have a word for you today: We all need each other. We are called to be the Body of Christ. If you are an ear, and I am an eye, and someone else is the foot, we are going to have a hard time serving others in this hurting world if we never work together. I can see those in need of help, but you can hear their specific pleas. Neither of us is able to go and do anything to help, however, if the feet are unwilling to step out and come with us.

We need every single part of the Body in order to serve. And not just the big parts that we think of, but all the tiny parts, the inner parts, the muscles and ligaments and tendons that hold the parts together and help them move as one. Sometimes we may not even realize a certain part is essential until something goes awry and it suddenly isn't there or is in great pain, crippling the rest of the Body. Let's not allow things to degenerate to that point, my friend!

What keeps you from engaging in fellowship with others? Is it anxiety or insecurity, a fear of being judged and found wanting? We are all equal in the Body of Christ! Is it a distrust of others or a fear that you'll have to reveal too much of yourself? You are free to share only what you feel comfortable sharing! Is it a sense of being too busy, that you just don't have enough time? Make time, Friend. Nothing is more important than being in fellowship—with God and with fellow believers. You are an integral part of the Body of Christ, and the rest of the Body cannot function at optimal capacity without you!

Father, kindle the desire for fellowship within me, that I may be a blessing to others and be blessed in return. In Jesus' name, Amen.

OCTOBER 20

He heals the brokenhearted and binds up their wounds. Psalm 147:3

What wounds are you nursing today, Beloved? What is causing you pain, getting you down, or threatening your outlook on life? Have you offered that painful wound up to Lord, inviting Him to clean and bandage it for you and begin the process of healing it? Sometimes we come to find that we rather enjoy looking at our wounds. They become crosses we are keen for others to see us bearing. So instead of seeking God's healing, we just keep picking off the scabs, inviting gangrene to set in. Sometimes we refuse to heal because we're afraid of the Unknown on the other side of it, and sometimes we refuse to heal because we think we deserve to stay in perpetual pain. We begin to take a perverse comfort in our wounds. My friend, none of these scenarios is God's will for us as His beloved children.

Jesus Christ laid down His life for us so that we might have abundant life in Him (John 10:10)—not stagnation. Some of us don't harbor physical wounds but are nursing age-old emotional pain. What happens when we continue to "stuff" all of the feelings we're having, refusing to express them in healthy, productive ways? We become septic, my friend. Things continue to pile up inside of us until we are filled with toxic thoughts, poisonous pride, and stagnating spirits. We need one another, remember? If you've been carrying the full weight of your burdens alone, it's time to seek out some fellow shoulders in the Lord and begin to share the load.

Above all, seek the Lord Himself. He heals the brokenhearted and binds up their wounds—the inner ones and the outer ones; even the ones you've inflicted on yourself. Offer them over to Him, Beloved. Be courageous enough to accept His help and His healing. The freedom on the other side is glorious, because of the time spent in sweet fellowship with Jesus on the journey. I believe in you. You can do it! In His name, Amen.

OCTOBER 21

But you will not leave in haste or go in flight; for the Lord will go before you, the God of Israel will be your rear guard. Isaiah 52:12

Our God does not fight His battles haphazardly or in a disorganized fashion. When we advance at His command, we can be certain that He goes before us to clear the way ahead *and* He takes up His position as our rear guard, protecting us from attacks and ambushes from behind.

One of the greatest pieces of French literature is a medieval text called *La Chanson de Roland*, "The Song of Roland." Roland is the head of the *arrière-garde*, the "rear guard" of Charlemagne's army. At the end of the tale, Roland's section of the army is ambushed, incurring heavy losses, but Roland refuses to sound his *olifant*, the horn that calls for help. By the time he decides to sound it, it is too late. My friend, God does not ever fail to sound the warning in time. Whether we heed it or not is up to us.

Isaiah 58:8b says, "the glory of the Lord will be your rear guard." First, I'm struck by the fact that only God could guard us solely with His *glory*! Secondly, I've often needed God as my rear guard specifically because of my tendency to keep looking backward at a path strewn with devastation, destruction, personal failures, and past mistakes. The minute God takes up His position as my "rear guard," when I look back I can only see His glorious power to redeem and transform.

Is there an area of intense battle in your life today, Friend? I pray that today's verse will bring you much encouragement as it reminds you of the fact that God is already before you, carving a path ahead for you on your journey, just as He did for the Hebrew children leaving Egypt. And because He is omnipresent, He is not only before you, but with you in every moment, and behind you as well, guarding you with His glory.

Father, thank You for Your ongoing and perfect provision in all areas of my life, no matter the season or circumstance. Amen!

OCTOBER 22

Stop and consider God's wonders. Job 37:14b

As I was driving my kids to school last week, I realized yet again that stop signs are for *our benefit.* This thought occurred to me right after watching someone blaze through one, not slowing down a bit, endangering the rest of us who were also at the intersection. When God puts up a metaphorical stop sign in our lives, we would do well to heed it. It may not be an octagonal red beacon, but when He needs for us to receive the message, Beloved, He'll make sure it comes through loud and clear. If we fail to heed the warning, we're endangering not only ourselves and our passengers, but others at the intersection as well.

Let's take a quick tour of some stop signs the Lord gave His people: "Stop bringing meaningless offerings!" (Isa. 1:13a); "Stop trusting in mere humans, who have but a breath in their nostrils" (Isa. 2:22a); "Stop turning My Father's house into a marketplace!" (John 2:16b NLT); "Stop sinning or something worse may happen to you" (John 5:14b); "Stop grumbling among yourselves" (John 6:43a); "Stop judging by mere appearances, but instead judge correctly" (John 7:24); "Stop doubting and believe" (John 20:27b). Whew! Which of these "stop statements" is most relevant to you today? I think every single one of them applies to my life in one area or another!

When we're feeling adrift or out of sorts, it's always a good thing to stop and search out the right direction that the Lord would have us to go. God says, "Stand at the crossroads and look; ask for the ancient paths, ask where the good way is, and walk in it, and you will find rest for your souls" (Jer. 6:16b). The "ancient paths" were the original guidelines God gave His people, the rules they should follow so all would go well with them (see Deut. 30:11-20). God also assures us that He will never stop doing good to us (Jer. 32:40b).

As you stop and consider God's wonders today, I pray that you would be reminded anew of His abundant love for you. Amen!

OCTOBER 23

Now you, brothers and sisters, [...] are children of promise. Galatians 4:28

A couple of years ago, my older daughter Tessa played basketball in a local recreational league. Her team didn't win a single game. In fact, I don't think they ever scored more than six points in *any* of their games. Some games they lost by six or eight points; others they lost by sixteen or twenty. As a player, it was discouraging. As a parent, it was brutal. We watched as our girls cried and wrestled with frustration, week after week. They practiced hard and played hard, but something just wasn't coming together for them. Their coach was wonderfully positive and encouraging throughout the entire season. As difficult as it was for the girls, they taught us—the adults—a thing or two about perseverance, endurance, and having a good attitude. In their last game, one of Tessa's friends from school was on the opposing team. On the way out to the car afterward (after another dismal loss), Tessa said, "I'm sad we lost again but I'm happy for my friend's team!" Kevin and I glanced at each other, equally surprised and touched.

It's fun when you're having a winning season, and it's easy to say "Good game!" afterwards if you won. It's a whole lot harder to say "Good game" when you got creamed, when you haven't won a game all season, and when you haven't even made a basket. But our girls did that, and we could not possibly have been prouder of them. I think God views it this way, too. Sometimes we're having a winning season, and He celebrates along with us. But when we're having a losing season, Beloved, He is all the more proud of us as we keep going, as we continue to love, as we continue to cheer others on, and as we continue to hope. Those kinds of seasons build character in ways no winning season ever could. We are not loved by God based upon our performance. He loves us just as much during a losing season as a winning season. The fact that we're still getting out there and giving it our best is what matters most to Him. Amen.

OCTOBER 24

But Moses said, "No, Lord, don't send me. I have never been a good speaker, and I haven't become one since You began to speak to me. I am a poor speaker, slow and hesitant." The Lord said to him, "Who gives man his mouth? Who makes him deaf or dumb? Who gives him sight or makes him blind? It is I, the Lord. Now, go! I will help you to speak, and I will tell you what to say." But Moses answered, "No, Lord, please send someone else." Exodus 4:10-13 GNT

Have you ever had the "Moses Moment"? A time when you felt God calling you to do something, but it was way out of your comfort zone so you found yourself begging Him to please choose someone else? God promises Moses that He will attend to all of his fears—in fact, He basically says, "I'm bigger than your stuttering problem, Moses." Moses seemed uncertain because his speech had not miraculously improved after God had called him. Sometimes we think that once God calls us to do something, all of our insecurities will suddenly vanish. Nope. God calls us *because* of those areas of insecurity, knowing full well that we'll have to rely all the more on *Him*. Moses's insecurity was his speech. What did God call him to do? Speak.

Likewise, we see the same type of situation play out with Gideon in Judges 6:14-16: "The Lord turned to [Gideon] and said, 'Go in the strength you have and save Israel out of Midian's hand. Am I not sending you?' 'Pardon me, my Lord,' Gideon replied, 'but how can I save Israel? My clan is the weakest in Manasseh, and I am the least in my family.' The Lord answered, 'I will be with you, and you will strike down all the Midianites, leaving none alive.'" What was Gideon's insecurity? His lack of strength. What did God call him to do? "Go in the strength you have and save Israel." Gideon knew he didn't *have* any strength—at least, not on his own. But that was the whole point. God reminded him, "I will be with you." And when He is with us, Beloved, our victory is assured—insecurities notwithstanding. In His mighty name, Amen.

OCTOBER 25

My eyes will flow unceasingly, without relief, until the Lord looks down from heaven and sees. Lamentations 3:49-50

For a long time I believed that God didn't really *see* all of the pain I carried, the brokenness I felt, and the hopelessness that engulfed me. Have you ever felt that way? He does see us, my friend. He sees everything about us and around us. And He's seen every bit of it, all along the way. Sometimes, however, it seems to us as though God isn't seeing us or isn't near to us in our time of pain and need. In our verses for today, we see Jeremiah experiencing that same struggle himself.

At first he speaks of his pain and of the feelings of distance he is experiencing between himself and God. A few verses later, we see the resolution: "You came near when I called You, and You said, 'Do not fear.' You, Lord, took up my case; You redeemed my life. Lord, You have seen the wrong done to me." (vv. 57-59a). Jeremiah remembered to call. And when we call, Beloved, God hears. He answers. How do we call Him? We pray. When Jeremiah called, God responded. He spoke to His prophet and told him, "Do not fear." Jeremiah realized that God had indeed *seen* everything and that He would be faithful to uphold him!

Jeremiah wasn't the only one to have this type of experience. Isaiah wrote, "How gracious He will be when you cry for help! As soon as He hears, He will answer you" (30:19b). Daniel experienced this firsthand: While he was still praying, the angel Gabriel came to him in swift flight saying, "God thinks highly of you, and at the very moment you started praying, I was sent to give you the answer" (Dan. 9:23a CEV). God didn't even need to carefully listen to each portion of Daniel's request and petition! *As soon as Daniel began to pray*, God was already sending the answer!

Oh, He *sees* us, Beloved. He sees everything—things we can't even see ourselves! When we call to Him and pray, He meets us in our pain, He strengthens us, and He delivers us. Amen!

OCTOBER 26

The Lord's name is a strong tower; the righteous run to it and find refuge. Proverbs 18:10 CEB

Oftentimes there is mad dashing around my house with much loud shrieking and frenzied giggling until suddenly there is a thump and a wail, and one child cries out: "Moooooom! S/he won't stop chasing meeeeee!" See, my friend, the game is all fun when you have a willing runner and a willing chaser. But when one party decides that they're done for the day, the other finds itself at a loss.

Sometimes we find ourselves in a chaotic game of chase with our ene-my, the devil. He pursues us and we run; he corners us and we flee; he entraps us and we start wailing. What would happen, Beloved, if we just refused to run? Kevin and I often find ourselves saying this very thing to our children: "S/he can't chase you if you don't run." In order to be chased, we have to *give* chase. We have to run. Often in life, we do run. We run from pain. We run from loss. We run from hardship and betrayal and confusion. Any direction would be better than *that* direction. Guess what always happens in the end, my friend. We get caught.

So I ask you again to consider: Instead of running *from* it—the pain, the anger, the loss, the grief, the fear, the confusion—what would happen if we just decided to stop right where we are and lean into it instead? To accept that times of trial and suffering will come, yet we can take heart in knowing that we are in Christ, and that Christ has already overcome the world (John 16:33)? God is on *our side*, my friend, any time Satan is chasing us. If we choose to run at all, let it be into God's open arms, where we will find protection, refuge, and deliverance from our enemy.

Father, please give me the courage to stop running and to face my fear and pain, knowing that You will be beside me in every moment. In Je-sus' name, Amen.

OCTOBER 27

With such nagging [Delilah] prodded [Samson] day after day until he was sick to death of it. So he told her everything. [...] "If my head were shaved, my strength would leave me, and I would become as weak as any other man." Judges 16:16-17

As a child I was fascinated by the story of Samson and his incredible strength—which all seemed to come from his hair! Only later did I come to realize that his strength had not one bit to do with his hair, but rather his heart. His hair was simply the outward evidence of his being set apart for God. When Samson chose to treat his inestimable gift from the Lord with contempt, the gift was removed—both the outward sign and the inner power. Samson was physically strong, but lacked inner strength and resolve, allowing the nagging of a woman to wear him down to the degree that he threw away his gift.

Jesus spoke to this very concept in Matthew 7:6, saying: "Do not give dogs what is sacred; do not throw your pearls to pigs. If you do, they may trample them under their feet, and turn and tear you to pieces." In context Jesus is speaking about the sharing of the Gospel with those who have contempt for it, yet we would do well to apply it on a personal level as well. Our holy vessels, and certainly our God-given gifts, are not meant to be squandered, misused, or arbitrarily bandied about.

Another example of one who experienced a withdrawal of God's gift and favor in his life is Solomon, renowned for his unparalleled wisdom. His undoing, incidentally, also came about because of the persuasion of a woman—or, to be precise, *many* women—his foreign wives, who turned his heart to other gods (see 1 Kings 11:1-11). Both the wisest and strongest men to ever live forsook their unparalleled gifts from God in favor of temporary gratifications from this world. I know that I don't want to fall into the same pattern. Whatever our gifts and blessings, Beloved, let us continually dedicate them (and ourselves as well) to God for His chosen purposes. Amen.

OCTOBER 28

For it has been granted to you on behalf of Christ not only to believe in Him, but also to suffer for Him. Philippians 1:29

According to Paul's words here, it would seem as though both our belief in Christ and our sufferings for Christ are *gifts*. I wonder how that truth meets you today. I think all Christians would readily agree that our ability to believe in Christ, to accept Him into our hearts as our personal Savior, and to receive salvation through Him is certainly a wondrous and blessed gift. But how many of us have held fast to the belief that our sufferings for Him are also a gift? And yet, this idea is not a new one! In fact, the same sentiment can be found in several places throughout God's Word. Here are two examples:

"Not only so, but we also glory in our sufferings, because we know that suffering produces perseverance; perseverance, character; and character, hope" (Rom. 5:3-4).

"In all this you greatly rejoice, though now for a little while you may have had to suffer grief in all kinds of trials. These have come so that the proven genuineness of your faith—of greater worth than gold, which perishes even though refined by fire—may result in praise, glory and honor when Jesus Christ is revealed" (1 Pet. 1:6-7).

I wonder if you would be willing today to choose to view your present trials, whatever they may be, as specific burdens that the Lord has *entrusted* to you as a gift—knowing in advance that you would be able to carry them in such a way that others might see Him in you. I don't know about you, but this shift in perspective feels like a radical and fresh new outlook to me—both positive and encouraging. I pray that it will be for you, too.

Father, thank You for entrusting me with the burdens You have allowed me to carry. Equip me to carry them well, that I might bring honor and glory to Your name. Amen.

OCTOBER 29

Though the fig tree does not bud and there are no grapes on the vines, though the olive crop fails and the fields produce no food, though there are no sheep in the pen and no cattle in the stalls, yet I will rejoice in the Lord, I will be joyful in God my Savior.
Habakkuk 3:17-18

The prophet Habakkuk witnessed the ongoing injustice in Judah, and his heart was broken. The Lord had promised to do something, but then gave no indication of when He would actually *do* it (see 1:5). Oftentimes we, like Habakkuk, find ourselves caught in a painful period of waiting. We trust God, we believe Him and His Word, we know that He is faithful and that He will act. But *when*? Habakkuk's response to this circumstance is one we would do well to emulate in our own lives.

First, he simply states what he sees with his physical eyes, laying it all out before the Lord: This is my reality right now. Then, he reminds himself of who God is, and of the miraculous wonders that God can do, and he *chooses* to place his trust in God. And Beloved, when we choose to trust God *even in* the painful waiting, we free our hearts, minds, and spirits to also choose joy.

I'm wondering today what your "though" and "and" are. I spent some time writing my "though" and "and" statements down, and then concluded with Habakkuk's words. I invite you to try it. Fill in the blanks below according to your own personal walk today:

Almighty Father,

Though _____ and _____, though _____ and _____, though _____ and _____, yet I will rejoice in You, Father; I will be joyful in You, my God and my Savior.

In Jesus' name, Amen!

OCTOBER 30

The Spirit has given each of us a special way of serving others.
1 Corinthians 12:7 CEV

I've been thinking a lot lately about gifts. Not presents. Not things we buy for one another, but the spiritual gifts that God pours out amongst His children so that we can bless one another. That's the part of it that has just come into focus for me.

For a long time, I believed that God doled out the spiritual gifts, some received more gifts than others, and the rest of us ambled along, trying to find some way in which to be useful during our tenure here on earth. I'm wondering if you can relate. But that's not how it works. *Each* of us has a gift! Those who have the gift of song, sing. We are blessed by the beauty of their voices, the moving themes of their music. Those who have the gift of medicine, heal. We are blessed by their skilled hands performing intricate surgeries, their vast knowledge culled from years of study, practice, and experience. Those who have the gift of teaching, teach. We are enriched by their lessons, enlightened by their wisdom, blessed by the fruits of their research, study, and passion for their subjects. Those who have the gift of encouraging, encourage. We are blessed by their words, bolstered by their exhortations, comforted by their faith. And I could go on!

Have you caught it yet? That important word? Not gift. *Blessed.* See, my friend, we all have gifts—but when we use those gifts, it is *others* who can be *blessed* by them. You were created by the Almighty God, and you were blessed with gifts from Him so that you can in turn be a blessing! A friend of mine says I have the "gift of font," because I have nice handwriting. I'll admit that seems like not much to run with, but I use my gift when I write down Scriptures and mail them to people I'm praying for, or when I send notes of encouragement and love.

I dare you to use your gift today, Beloved, so that another Child can be blessed. In Jesus' name, Amen!

OCTOBER 31

Woe to you, teachers of the law and Pharisees, you hypocrites! You are like whitewashed tombs, which look beautiful on the outside but on the inside are full of the bones of the dead and everything unclean. In the same way, on the outside you appear to people as righteous but on the inside you are full of hypocrisy and wickedness. Matthew 23:27-28

This is one of those statements from Jesus that just steps all over my toes. I spent many years carefully concealing all of my inner pain, turmoil, confusion, and shame under a lovely veneer of competency, confidence, and control. I was a whitewashed tomb, my friend—appearing immaculate on the outside, and slowly rotting to death within. My mask concealed all of my insecurities and fears, all of my failures and inadequacies, and yet I routinely compromised myself because others saw the mask and believed it was real. I then struggled with when, or even *how*, I could possibly remove the mask and reveal the scarred face underneath to those who'd become accustomed to seeing the beauty of the mask. Wouldn't the stark contrast of the disfigurement be even more shocking and repulsive? I was terrified of others' rejection.

I finally began to understand, through God's infinitely great patience and compassion, that people don't need perfection from me. They need authenticity. They need transparency. They need for me to have the courage to say, "I have struggled with this, and Jesus has been so faithful to help me gain the victory in this fight." The Pharisees emphasized outward appearance over inner depth, and Jesus made it clear to them that they had chosen wrong. I'm more in favor of depth, Beloved. The deeper we dig, the more messy things can get—but in sifting through the depths, we find the treasures He's hidden for us there.

We only get one shot at this, my friend. Let's pull off the masks and allow Christ's healing light to dance upon our faces. In Him, we are made flawless and whole. Amen.

NOVEMBER 1

What the locust swarm has left the great locusts have eaten; what the great locusts have left the young locusts have eaten; what the young locusts have left other locusts have eaten. [...] Before them the land is like the garden of Eden, behind them, a desert waste—nothing escapes them. Joel 1:4, 2:3b

Several years ago, the cicadas came. The noise was deafening and the destruction far reaching as the females burrowed deeply into tender limbs of trees to lay their eggs. Almost every tree in our yard still bears the scars. I am reminded of that today as I consider these verses from Joel. Have you gone through a time in your life when it felt as though not one area seemed immune from attack? I spent many years there, unable to even conceive of a time when things would be made right, when I would be made whole.

During that season I discovered this promise, also from the book of Joel: "I will repay you for the years the locusts have eaten—the great locust and the young locust, the other locusts and the locust swarm—My great army that I sent among you" (2:25). Not only will He repay you for the years the locusts have eaten, Beloved—He will repay you for the *specific things* each swarm took away and devoured. He knows our losses and our devastation, and He can bring redemption and restoration. How? Look at Nahum 3:17: "Your guards are like locusts, your officials like swarms of locusts that settle in the walls on a cold day—but when the sun appears they fly away, and no one knows where." *When the Son appears* the locusts fly away, my friend, because "when what is perfect comes, then what is partial will disappear" (1 Cor. 13:10 GNT). It is Jesus' *presence* in your life that begins that process of restoration.

Almighty Father, Your Word assures me that every promise You have made has been fulfilled and not one has failed (Josh. 23:15). Today I assert my claim to Your healing and restoration in my life, and I place my trust in Your perfect plan for me. In Jesus' name, Amen.

NOVEMBER 2

When neither sun nor stars appeared for many days and the storm continued raging, we finally gave up all hope of being saved. Acts 27:20

Have you ever been in this place, sitting alongside Paul and his companions in a boat out on the open sea, in the midst of a terrible storm? Your eyes search for hope on the horizon in the form of the rising sun or a twinkling star, and instead they are met with dense blackness, heavy winds, torrential rain, and a ship being threatened with capsizing. Have you, as Paul writes, ever given up all hope of being saved? Not saved in the sense of your eternal salvation with the Lord, but saved in the sense of being delivered from this nightmare of pain while walking out your time here on earth?

We have the benefit of knowing that Paul and all of the crew on board the boat arrived safely to their destination, although the ship was destroyed and the cargo had to be tossed overboard (vv. 27-44). Have you ever had to toss your cargo overboard in order to save your vessel? Have you experienced being shipwrecked on top of that? The good news, Beloved, is that God had a plan for your safe deliverance to the shore even before the storm began to swell. You are not going down with the ship. He calms the wind and the waves. He brings peace in the midst of our storms. Just because we cannot see the sun or the stars does not mean they aren't there, or that they've ceased to exist.

Remember that our hope is not in what we can see, but in what we *cannot* see (2 Cor. 5:7). We cannot see love, hope, kindness, or faith, but we can see the effects of them in our lives and in the lives of others. When the stars and the sun are blocked by the clouds and the storm, they are still there, Beloved, shining brightly, waiting for God to give them the cue to burst forth in their radiant glory again, dispelling the darkness and despair. Until then, Dear One, He is keeping them—and you—safe in His mighty arms. Amen.

NOVEMBER 3

This is a trustworthy saying that deserves full acceptance. That is why we labor and strive, because we have put our hope in the living God, who is the Savior of all people, and especially of those who believe. 1 Timothy 4:9-10

I am blessed to have some marvelously wonderful, godly older women in my life who have provided me with invaluable guidance and wisdom along my journey. One in particular has walked with me through many a trial and storm. When I was a teenager and railing against God for things I could not understand, she held fast in the gale and continued to remind me of God's truth and His presence in my life—whether I felt it or not, whether I even welcomed it or not. No matter how hopeless I felt, she was always full of hope for me and my future. When I see passages in the Bible that talk about hope, I always think of her. Now that I have the gift of some distance from those difficult teenage years, and have gained some perspective on my life, I too have come to have an unshakable hope in the Lord—even in times of immense trial and pain.

In what are you placing your hope today, Dear One? Is it in other people—your spouse, friends, or children? Is it in your wealth? Your career? Your importance? Your church activities and leadership? Your own strength? I have a word for you today, Beloved: Unless we are putting our hope in the Lord Jesus Christ, we will find ourselves disappointed, disillusioned, and despairing. All other worldly things will inevitably fail us. We were not created to be God. We were created to *seek* God, to be in relationship with Him, to love Him and to serve Him, to go and make disciples for Him—but we cannot be God to one another. Our job is to encourage each other and to remind one another of God's love, faithfulness, and truth when we falter.

Father, thank You for the precious ones You've placed in my life who provide wisdom, insight, guidance, and hope. May I in turn share Your hope with others when they are in need. In Jesus' mighty name, Amen.

NOVEMBER 4

By the rivers of Babylon we sat and wept when we remembered Zion. [...] How can we sing the songs of the Lord while in a foreign land? Psalm 137:1, 4

Yesterday we talked about having hope even in the midst of pain. Our verses for today come from some of the exiles of Judah who were finding it decidedly difficult to sing the songs of the Lord in the land of their captivity. They question if such a feat is even possible. Yes, it is. We can *always* sing the songs of the Lord while in a foreign land—even if it's a land of uncertainty, exile, or captivity. God hasn't changed. God hasn't moved. Our location and surroundings may be different, but the good news is that "Jesus Christ is the same yesterday and today and forever" (Heb. 13:8). Where is the hope in exile, in discipline, even in death? The hope is in the One who never forsakes us, even in the midst of it. He is with us, Beloved. The trial will not last forever, but the God whom we serve *will*. He is "from everlasting to everlasting" (Neh. 9:5). His presence and His love in our lives are not determined by how well we're doing and how successful we are. His presence is guaranteed—in *every moment*!—because He loves us and we are His children.

God was with Joseph and blessed him—both in the palace and in the dungeon. God was with Elijah and provided for him—both in his triumph and in his fear. God was with David and never forsook him—both in his sin and in his obedience. God was with Jonah and delivered him—both in his rebellion and in his submission. God was with Mary and comforted her—both in the birth of her Son and at His death on the cross. God was with Paul and Silas, keeping them from harm—both while they were preaching and while they were in prison. God was with His children—both in their homeland and in their land of captivity.

What's your "both/and" statement to add to our list today, Beloved? I invite you to name it here and spend some time thanking God for His unfailing presence in your life. Wherever you are, dare to sing. Amen.

NOVEMBER 5

This is how we know that we belong to the truth and how we set our hearts at rest in His presence: If our hearts condemn us, we know that God is greater than our hearts, and He knows everything. 1 John 3:19-20

Do you need a heart set at rest today, Dear Friend? Do you need to exchange a heart that condemns for a heart like His? I do. I battled ongoing, relentless self-condemnation for years. It was miserable, discouraging, and painful. I had the "head knowledge" that God loved me and saw me with acceptance, grace, forgiveness, and love, but I just kept getting tangled up in the jumble of lies my brain continued spewing out. It was like having my own personal accuser in my head who never seemed to tire. I understood that I needed to get control of my thought life, but the attacks were so overwhelming and so constant that I had no idea *how*. I tried, but was never successful.

One morning as I was seeking God's help (again!) in this matter, I felt that He was calling me to read the book of 1 John. *Great*, I thought, *all of that stuff about love*. I opened my Bible and began to read, and when I got to today's verses I just stared at them, stunned. I can set my heart *at rest* in God's presence whenever my heart condemns me, because *God is greater than my heart* and *He knows everything*! This was revolutionary for me.

For some of us, the idea that He knows *everything* might make us feel decidedly uneasy, especially when it comes to things we really wish nobody else knew we thought, felt, said, or did. However, this verse brought me immense comfort, because there's no hiding! He already knows! Anything I feel ashamed of, anything I worry about disappointing Him with, He already knows. Which means that now when that condemning voice starts up, I can silence it with this truth from God's Word: He already knows. And He still loves me. I will rest in Him. Amen!

NOVEMBER 6

I planted the seed, Apollos watered it, but God has been making it grow. So neither the one who plants nor the one who waters is anything, but only God, who makes things grow. 1 Corinthians 3:6-7

Paul's words here bring me much comfort. Oftentimes we can find ourselves trying just a little too hard to "help" someone else find the right path, lay down that bad habit, change for the better, seek a deeper relationship with God, or think differently about a certain matter. Our efforts, even if carried out with good intentions and a sincere heart, are missing the mark, my friend. Only God makes things grow. Is there a situation in your life this speaks to today?

This is not to say that we don't have responsibilities to others and a God-given purpose as sowers and waterers. Paul clearly states that we *do* have these opportunities to share and sow God's Word, and to come along behind other sowers and water the seeds that have been planted. And yet, when we have done our part, we are then called to take a step back and watch and see what God will do. Some plants germinate quickly, and others languish so long under the soil that we begin to anxiously despair of the little seed ever beginning to sprout. Did we not plant it deeply enough? Did we not wait until all threat of frost was gone? Did we water it too much? We need not worry or fear, Dear Friend—for God is watching, waiting, and always working. He knows when to make things grow.

Let it be noted that God, our Master Gardener, is also an expert in composting. Not one effort we make in His name, with a sincere heart, will ever fall on barren soil. He takes the apple cores, egg shells, melon rinds, and coffee grounds—the parts and scraps we have no idea what to do with—and turns them into a rich, loamy, fertile soil that is able to support and nurture a little seed as it waits for its time to grow. May we sow and water with confidence today, knowing He is working. Amen!

NOVEMBER 7

Always be prepared to give an answer to everyone who asks you to give the reason for the hope that you have. 1 Peter 3:15b

Sometimes we receive the kind of news that knocks us flat to our faces on the floor. I'm wondering what experience from your own life comes to your mind as you read that, or if maybe you are living it right now. One of the most moving things to witness and experience as a follower of Christ is a moment in which the Spirit enables us to receive that kind of news and respond with hope and strength in the Lord rather than falling apart. These are the moments in which any normal person *would* fall apart—and no one would dispute their right to do so! And yet, something keeps us anchored even in the midst of a raging, furious storm. What anchors us in the face of betrayal, divorce, loss, illness, and grief? Hope, Beloved. Hope is what holds us fast to the delivering and sustaining power of God, even in the midst of the pain.

I experienced this personally when I went back in for a follow-up ultra-sound with our third pregnancy. The initial ultrasound had indicated some possible problems, and Kevin and I knew there was a chance that things might not turn out as we'd hoped. We had braced ourselves for the worst and had handed it over to God. The precious ultrasound technician stared at the screen for several moments before saying, "I'm not seeing any heartbeat." She paused and then said, softly: "These are the days I hate my job." My OB peered at me rather curiously a short time later, saying, "You really seem to be okay." I nodded. "I am." I was—and yet it had not one iota to do *with me*. It was God holding us fast, keeping our feet on the Rock, even as Life hurled debris.

Losing our sweet baby was devastating. My heart shook and splintered, and it will always bear that scar. This isn't about being unaffected by tragedy; it's about our choice to hold on to our God even in the rawest kind of pain. He has conquered death and anything else that can set itself up against us. Our confidence is in Him, the One who is unseen and eternal. That's why we can still hope, Friend, even in the pain. May you *know* today that He holds your precious heart in His hands. Amen.

NOVEMBER 8

I know whom I have believed, and am convinced that He is able to guard what I have entrusted to Him until that day. 2 Timothy 1:12b

Some versions translate that last portion of Paul's sentence as "He is able to guard what I have entrusted to Him," whereas others translate it as "He is able to guard what has been entrusted to me" (ESV). Apparently the Greek connotes the reciprocity of the entrusting, since the Amplified Bible, Classic Edition, translates the phrase as "He is able to guard *and* keep that which has been entrusted to me *and* which I have committed [to Him] until that day."

God has certainly entrusted all of us with things that require guarding and keeping. Every time I read this verse, my first thought is immediately of my children, whom God has entrusted to me and whom I must always entrust back to Him. Other examples could be our work, our finances, our churches, our responsibilities, our discipleship, and even our sufferings. All of these things have been specifically entrusted to us by God, and we are called to entrust them into His care in return, fully believing that He is "always at work for the good of everyone who loves Him" (Rom. 8:28 CEV).

Are you entrusting back into His capable hands all that He has entrusted into yours, Beloved? Or are there things that you find yourself holding back? Maybe it's your children. Maybe it's your finances. Maybe it's a difficult relationship or an area of struggle that you keep trying to fix by yourself. Problems arise when we fail to entrust ourselves and all within our care back into God's gentle, powerful, and saving hands.

Father, I know and believe that You are always working to bring about good in my life. Yet I confess that there are areas in which I am clutching things tightly to my chest, afraid to let them go. I pray for the strength to release them into Your care today. Replace my illusion of control with the certainty of Your perfect provision. Amen.

317

NOVEMBER 9

When the people had eaten their fill, [Jesus] said to His disciples, "Gather the leftovers so nothing is wasted." They went to work and filled twelve large baskets with leftovers from the five barley loaves. John 6:12-13 MSG

I cherish the knowledge that Jesus is not ashamed to gather up leftovers and that God wastes *nothing* in our lives. I'm reminded of two Old Testament examples—the Israelites and their manna, where God provided exactly enough for the people *each day* so that nothing would be wasted (see Ex. 16:11-30); and His command to allow some gleanings in the fields and vineyards to remain during the harvest so that the alien and the poor would have food (Lev. 19:9-10). The Creator of the universe could easily just create more, and yet we see both God and Jesus demonstrating intentionality about not letting anything go to waste. I am so very thankful that includes us!

Even though we are inherently flawed, self-serving, and weak, God still redeems us from our failings and forgives our sins and shortcomings. Furthermore, Jesus died for us while we were still sinners (Rom. 5:8). Although God could easily create "extra" people to replace those who have turned away from Him, He doesn't. He pursues each one of us diligently, passionately, and relentlessly. He loves each and every one of His children, and He will stop at nothing to draw us back to Himself.

I am also grateful that God wastes none of our hurt or pain. He can take all of the pieces, fragments, and broken shards, fitting them together to form something beautiful and whole. In what area of your life are you finding yourself with some leftovers today, my friend? Perhaps you're housing a broken heart. Perhaps a close relationship has splintered. Perhaps your security—whether financial, emotional, or physical—has been shattered. Will you entrust the pieces to the One who is willing *and able* to use every last scrap to create beauty from your brokenness? I pray you would hear His invitation to you today: *Bring it to Me, Child. I'll take care of it for you.* Know this for sure, Dear One: Nothing we place in God's hands is *ever* wasted. In Jesus' name, Amen.

NOVEMBER 10

Take My yoke upon you and learn from Me, for I am gentle and humble in heart, and you will find rest for your souls. For My yoke is easy and My burden is light. Matthew 11:29-30

Jesus says that in sharing His yoke, we will find rest. This makes sense. Our own yokes are often laden down with burdensome things such as grief, fear, anxiety, doubt, frustration, pain, bitterness, and loneliness. Jesus carries around things like love, peace, forgiveness, mercy, hope, and grace. Is it any wonder that when we choose to take on His yoke, we find *rest*?

Yokes were designed to be worn by teams of animals, to help share the workload. Jesus is telling us that when we become overtaxed in our lives, we would do well to come to Him and allow Him to walk beside us, sharing our load (which is burdensome) while He shares His load with us (which is light). We find rest in this transfer, because we are no longer staggering around under a weight too heavy for one person to bear. When we team up, we balance the weight.

In what areas of your life today do you need to come to the Lord and seek His rest? He is always available, yet it is our job to seek Him out and take His yoke of blessing upon ourselves, exchanging ours in return. He does not force us. It moves me to think that we have a Savior who is willing to yoke Himself to us, to help us do our work and help us shoulder the loads that have become too heavy for us. As we journey along with Jesus at our side, consider the kinds of lessons He will teach us and the qualities about Him that we will learn to imitate. Consider the joy of watching Him laugh, or seeing His heart tendered by our pain. We share in His sufferings, Beloved, and the relationship is reciprocal: He also shares in ours. His Spirit is within us, walking with us each day, helping us navigate the seasons of life.

Father, thank You for sending Your Son to me, who helps me shoulder my burdens and walk uprightly. In His name I pray, Amen.

NOVEMBER 11

"Honor your father and mother"—which is the first command-ment with a promise—"so that it may go well with you and that you may enjoy long life on the earth." Fathers, do not exasperate your children; instead, bring them up in the training and instruc-tion of the Lord. Ephesians 6:2-4

I realize this can be a minefield. I want you to know at the outset today that it certainly is for me. This is a passage I've struggled with for a long time. As I've mentioned before, my dad and I are estranged. And I've struggled with how to honor him and fulfill God's commandment when some things about our falling out were not honorable things. I think the key is that this commandment is a two-way street. Note that Paul fol-lows up the reminder with a word of caution to the fathers: "Do not exasperate your children." A parallel can be found in Colossians 3:20-21: "Children, obey your parents in everything, for this pleases the Lord. Fathers, do not embitter your children, or they will become dis-couraged."

How, then, is a father supposed to love his children? Paul writes, "For you know that we dealt with each of you as a father deals with his own children, encouraging, comforting and urging you to live lives worthy of God, who calls you into His kingdom and glory" (1 Thess. 2:11-12). What, then, if this has not been our experience? I once asked a pastor friend of mine about this issue. Her response was this: "Allyson, you do not have to honor what was not honorable." Those words are still seared into my heart.

Even with the worst earthly parent, surely there was at least one action or one good moment that we can honor. All of the other moments— the painful ones, the neglectful ones, the abusive ones, the intolerant ones, the hurtful ones? We do not have to honor that which is not hon-orable. Above all, we honor God—our heavenly Father—who demon-strates His perfect love in our lives from beginning to end. Amen.

NOVEMBER 12

Better a dry crust with peace and quiet than a house full of feasting, with strife. Proverbs 17:1

I had to chuckle as I read this verse today, thinking of how dinnertime goes at our house on occasion. It's hard to sit and enjoy one's food if there is fighting, sulking, or criticizing going along with it—and that's just from the kids. Throw in the adult-sized weights of stony silences, dagger-filled glares, or outright provocation and you've got a recipe for disaster at your family table.

The holiday season can be tough. The calendar tells us we're supposed to be happy, joyful, and giddy from mid-November until January first. When we just aren't feeling it, then we're doubly walloped by shame and despair. "Special occasions" are often harder than everyday life simply because we put such pressure on ourselves to feel a certain way, do a certain thing, or attend events we'd just rather not. I've been struggling with this myself this week—I'm just not feeling the joy I usually have over Thanksgiving—and it's hard to say exactly why. Part of it is fatigue. Part of it is how commercialism is slowly seeping in, changing our Day of Thanks to a jump-start for Christmas shopping. My heart is also heavy for the families who will face an empty chair at their Thanksgiving table this year. I grieve over the wrenching holes that death, loss, and estrangement tear in the fabric of our hearts.

What lifts my heart and spirit today is the knowledge and assurance that our God is able to work out everything in conformity with His will (Eph. 1:11), and nothing escapes His notice. He sees our inner struggles; He knows our deepest hopes and darkest fears. He knows exactly what we need at every moment. And no matter what our earthly family dynamics may be, we are always welcome at our Father's table. May this bring you fresh encouragement today, Beloved, as you rest securely in Him and in His unfailing and limitless love for you. In Jesus' mighty name, Amen.

NOVEMBER 13

When times are good, be happy; but when times are bad, consid-er this: God has made the one as well as the other. Ecclesiastes 7:14a

I love this verse, and I cannot count the number of times it pops into my mind on days when I am feeling grouchy, self-righteous, impatient, or out of sorts. It always gives me a firm mental shake and gets my thoughts recalibrating. Its parallel is found in Job 2:10b when Job asks his wife, "Shall we accept good from God, and not trouble?" When things have gone wrong in my life, I often ask myself Job's question. Am I only a fair-weather believer? Do I only love, trust, and praise God when He is pouring out good things and blessings into my life? When bad things come along, times of trial or sickness or death, do I turn my back on Him in petulant disgust for His inability to just get it right and bless me? (Whew, that can sure hit close to home, can't it?!)

When I was little, my mom taught a lesson in my Sunday school class that related feelings to colors. I know that the whole rainbow was rep-resented, but the only one that has stuck with me over all these years has been "Pouty Purple"—probably because my mom would often tease me by calling me a "Pouty Purple" whenever I was having a sulky moment. Even today I find myself saying it to my kids!

It is so *human* of us to pout, to sulk, to go off in a huff when things do not unfold as we wish they had. It's okay that we feel disappointment—we are, again, *human*! However, we must exercise caution in not allow-ing the disappointment to take root and begin to sow its toxic seeds of resentment, bitterness, and envy. There is a Yiddish proverb I absolute-ly love that perfectly sums up this whole notion: "God gives burdens. Also shoulders." Use those shoulders well today, Beloved.

Father, thank You for the blessings in my life, as well as the times of trial. I know that You use all situations to refine my faith so that I might become more like Your Son. In His name I pray, Amen!

NOVEMBER 14

Do you not know that you are God's temple and that God's Spirit dwells in you? If anyone destroys God's temple, God will destroy him. For God's temple is holy, and you are that temple. 1 Corinthians 3:16-17 ESV

Back in January I shared with you that these verses, along with Paul's statements in 1 Corinthians 6:19-20, were the catalyst in a major turning point in my life. Prior to reading these words, I had never considered the fact that my body was not my own but God's, and that as such I was expected to honor my body and not inflict harm upon it. My personal offense to my temple was a desire to deface it with evidence of the self-condemnation I felt, although the placement of "graffiti" on our temples can take many different forms. And sometimes, we don't do the defacing—someone else does.

Our verses today indicate that "if anyone destroys God's temple, God will destroy him." God takes the misuse and abuse of our temples very seriously, Beloved, whether the damage is inflicted by someone else or is done by our own hand. If you find yourself in the former camp today, I pray that you would spend some time letting your mind and heart dwell upon the notion that whoever harms your temple is harming something sacred and precious to the Lord of all creation. He hasn't missed it. If someone has harmed you, God is faithful and just and will see to it that that person answers for their sin.

If you find yourself in the latter camp, what external behaviors or internal thinking patterns in your life are putting graffiti on your temple? What choices do you make that cause harm to your physical body? What thoughts or beliefs do you harbor that cause toxic feelings to saturate your mind? Most importantly, how does the knowledge that God sees *you* as His holy temple and that He cares about the way your temple is being treated affect the way you want to live your life? I encourage you to spend some time talking it over with Him today. Amen.

NOVEMBER 15

For the eyes of the Lord range throughout the earth to strengthen those whose hearts are fully committed to Him. 2 Chronicles 16:9a

This is one of my favorite verses. It gives me such peace and comfort to know that our God is always awake, always alert, always watching, and is earnestly seeking someone to strengthen who is striving to do His will. He longs to provide us with strength, perseverance, endurance, and hope in all of the battles we face. In what area of your life are you in need of some strengthening today, Beloved?

Perhaps you are weary from fighting an age-old foe—just as your head breaks free of the waters and you draw in a shuddering breath, something beneath the surface drags you back down again. Perhaps you're suffering from a chronic health condition or struggling through a grueling recovery process. Perhaps you're mired in the middle of an ongoing family conflict. Perhaps you have a wayward child whose choices and decisions keep you lying awake at night. Perhaps you've experienced loss or betrayal, and you find yourself feeling alone and uncertain of what the future holds for you.

Or maybe you are finding yourself in the midst of a new trial today, one that has come upon you suddenly and left you reeling from the shock. Perhaps sudden changes in your workplace or job description are creating turmoil in your life. Perhaps a financial catastrophe has just befallen you or your family. Or maybe you've just received word of a distressing diagnosis for yourself or for someone you love. All of these struggles are difficult, and all of them tax our energy reserves and challenge our mental and physical stamina. What a blessing it is to know that God is constantly on the lookout for children in need of strengthening.

Father, I long for Your strength to infuse my being as I go out to do Your work today. In every area where I am feeling weak and uncertain, I recommit myself to trusting in Your plan and provision for me. Amen.

NOVEMBER 16

Overhearing what they said, Jesus told him, "Don't be afraid; just believe." Mark 5:36

The year Blake was in kindergarten, his teacher invited all of the parents to meet in the classroom a few minutes prior to the Thanksgiving lunch so that the students could share a surprise with us. As twenty kindergartners each stood up and read a list of things for which they were thankful (ranging widely on the scale from Spiderman to donuts to one's Grammy), the parents smiled indulgently and applauded each child's contribution. As Blake stood to read his paper to the group, I was curious to see what he would say. This is what he read: "I am thankful for Mommy because she is fun. I love my mommy because she gives me cuddles and she's cool. I am thankful for Dad because he tucks me in."

Hearing him read those words aloud, my heart nearly stopped—and probably not for the reasons you would think. See, my sweet boy had specifically named my two biggest areas of insecurity as a parent—the two areas in which I have the most fear of being so deficient that I will somehow stunt my children for life. I'm really not very "fun." I don't "play" well, and I'm especially terrible at "pretending." I can do games, puzzles, sports, or coloring, but in terms of being "fun," I'm really just not. I often worry that my children just see me as a tall, fussy drill sergeant. As for the cuddles, I cannot even begin to aptly put words to this part of it. Because of my past abuse, I struggle with being physically close to others. Being affectionate doesn't come naturally to me; I have to really make a concerted effort at it. And what did my boy express his thanks for? My "being fun" and my "giving cuddles." My two main areas of perceived lack, and my son honed in on them, giving me praise, encouragement, and *hope*. An unspeakable blessing. I cried and cried.

That, Beloved, is the Father's redeeming love, poured out into our lives. In His hands, the splintered shards of our broken vessels are restored. We need not be afraid of our limitations, Dear One. We need only to believe in His infinite ability to heal, to redeem, and to transform. Be blessed in Him today, *knowing* that He is working in your life. Amen!

NOVEMBER 17

And this is love: that we walk in obedience to His commands. As you have heard from the beginning, His command is that you walk in love. 2 John 6

It's hard, sometimes, to walk in love. Some days I feel inclined to walk in busyness, frustration, or impatience. Sometimes I walk in defeat, resentment, or insecurity. Walking in love takes a concerted effort to carry out. We have to keep our focus on God, rather than on ourselves or our circumstances, in order to do it.

It's also hard to walk in love with a desensitized heart. Sometimes we cauterize our hearts because we're so weary of wrestling with the same old feelings of pain, hurt, grief, and despair. We choose to sever those ties and tell ourselves that we're tough, we don't need anyone, and we can make it on our own. Sometimes our hearts become hardened out of self-defense and fear; sometimes we close them off out of pain and frustration. I spent a long season living with a deadened heart, and it was a scary place to be. I didn't feel much pain anymore, but I also didn't feel much joy—or sadness, or compassion, or anything else. I tried to be stoic because I was so tired of being hurt. I ended up with a heart that had turned to stone. And with a stony heart, it's nearly impossible to walk in love.

Life is in the loving, my friend. If we aren't loving, we aren't really living. Loving others challenges us and even wounds us sometimes, but we are called to love anyway. I remind myself of that often. Our hearts are fickle; they are "deceitful above all things and beyond cure" (Jer. 17:9). Purity of heart is gained from abiding in the Lord, yielding our hearts to Him that He might mold them into vessels that will shine His light, love, truth, and peace out into this hurting world—through those broken places within us. When we walk in His light, we are walking in His love—and following His highest command. May we choose to live in obedience to Him today, sharing His love with others. Amen.

NOVEMBER 18

When I fed them, they were satisfied; when they were satisfied, they became proud; then they forgot Me. Hosea 13:6

Today I am pondering how we go from being fed and satisfied to forgetting the Lord. God warned the Israelites about this even before He brought them into the Promised Land: "...when you eat and are satisfied, be careful that you do not forget the Lord, who brought you out of Egypt, out of the land of slavery" (Deut. 6:11b-12). And yet that is exactly what they did! We do the same today. We are fed and satisfied; when we are satisfied, we become proud. And when we become proud, we forget God. How do we break this cycle?

The opportunity comes in that finite window of time between experiencing satisfaction and allowing pride to take root. When pride takes root, we've missed it. We fancy ourselves self-sufficient and capable; we forget that it was God who fed us. God gives us the ability to work and provide for ourselves. When we begin to take credit for our wealth and good fortune, our righteous God will discipline us. Why? Because He loves us. The Lord knows that nothing becomes a stumbling block between us and His love like our false notions of self-sufficiency. When we believe we can manage everything ourselves, we invite the unmanageable as He reminds us of our misconceptions.

The surest and strongest weapon we have against pride is gratitude. Giving thanks—acknowledging that every single good thing we have or do in our lives comes from God—is the *only* way we are able to avoid the same cycle that ensnared the Israelites and still threatens to pull us in today. As Paul said, we are called to "give thanks in all circumstances; for this is God's will for you in Christ Jesus" (1 Thess. 5:18).

Father, help me to continually pursue a mindset of gratitude, and a heart filled with thanksgiving. In Jesus' name, Amen!

NOVEMBER 19

So then, just as you received Christ Jesus as Lord, continue to live your lives in Him, rooted and built up in Him, strengthened in the faith as you were taught, and overflowing with thankfulness.
Colossians 2:6-7

I continually need Paul's reminder here to root myself in Christ's love as I weather the seasons of life. In what do you typically tend to root yourself when adversity comes your way? Legalism? Relationships? Busyness? Anxiety? Beloved, when we face seasons of hardship and discipline, times of trial and painful circumstances, we *must* root ourselves *in Christ*—and not in anything or anyone else of this world. It is important to understand that we do not suffer trials because God is angry with us or because He "needs" for us to learn something. Simply put, we suffer because we live in a broken world. Our faithful and loving God is able to *use* those trials for good. He loves us and longs to foster new growth and deeper maturity within us; our trials, then, are the crucible that He uses to purify us (Isa. 48:10). Enduring them enables us to come forth with wisdom and insight that will in turn allow us to minister to others enduring similar circumstances—and we become more like Christ.

Times of testing are never without purpose or value—*if* we are willing to submit. In exercise physiology, it's called "resistance training"—our bodies have to work harder when there's something exerting more force on us, and through that work we increase in both strength and endurance. As the winds of Life whip our branches and toss our leaves about, God calls us to dig our roots down deeper into the nutrient-dense soil of Christ's love for us, which helps us remain steadfast in the storm. Without a firm rooting, we lack flexibility and risk being broken or snapped by the fierce winds of Life. And if we refuse to root ourselves in Christ's love, we lack stability and risk being uprooted entirely. Times of trial *will* come, yet we can weather them successfully as we abide in the power of God. May we commit ourselves to His faithful care, rooting ourselves in Christ's love today. Amen.

As iron sharpens iron, so one person sharpens another. Proverbs 27:17

I'll be honest with you; I am not a fan of conflict. I dislike arguments, confrontations, and criticism. I dread offering up a viewpoint in direct contrast to someone else's, preferring to just "keep the peace." However, Jesus said, "Blessed are the peacemakers" (Matt. 5:9a)—not the peace *keepers*. On occasion, we do have to be willing to clash with others; it's the clash of iron on iron that sharpens us, although at times sparks may fly. I recently found myself in this exact type of situation—and although I worked myself up into a little knot of frayed nerves over the inevitable clash, God was so faithful to be with me in every moment, and it went well. Mind you—it isn't always going to go well, and He's just as much with us in those encounters, too!

My friend, iron cannot sharpen itself. In order to sharpen one another, we have to be in relationship with each other. We are instructed to speak the truth *in love* to one another (Eph. 4:15). This calls for a degree of "conflict willingness" in such situations, even if they may be difficult. To be clear: Conflict does not mean disrespect, disparagement, or judgment—that's not conflict; that's abuse.

We can also be sharpened in a less abrasive way through the sloughing off, the chipping away, the gradual transformation that occurs in the course of everyday life. I am currently finding myself in this kind of situation as well, and it has not been pleasant! Yet I've been reminded over and over again that when I am in need of some "ironing," God does not hesitate to get to work!

Almighty Father, help me allow others to sharpen me through my interactions and relationships each day. I know that Your desire is to continue to shape and form me into a clearer image of Your Son. Help me remember that some friction is necessary in order to combat stagnation and enable me to grow. In Jesus' name, Amen.

NOVEMBER 21

Though my father and mother forsake me, the Lord will receive me. Psalm 27:10

Most of us have experienced the sting of rejection at some point or other in our lives. Some of us have also undergone the pain of abandonment. Rejection and abandonment from friends can be painful; rejection and abandonment from one's parents, siblings, spouse, or children can be brutal. God's Word brings us hope and encouragement today in this particular area of struggle. For even if we are forsaken and rejected by loved ones in our lives, our God will *always* receive us.

Our Lord Jesus is well acquainted with the pain of rejection. Isaiah foretold of the rejection Jesus would experience hundreds of years before His birth: "He was despised and rejected by mankind, a man of suffering, and familiar with pain" (53:3a). Jesus' familiarity with sorrow and suffering, rejection and betrayal, is what makes Him so able to relate to us in our own pain. He told His disciples that He would be rejected by the elders, chief priests, and teachers of the law (Luke 9:22) before being killed and raised to life again. Peter describes Jesus as "the living Stone—rejected by humans but chosen by God and precious to Him" (1 Pet. 2:4).

We, too, have been chosen by God (1 Pet. 2:9), in spite of the rejection we may have suffered at the hands of others. God's plan and purposes will prevail in our lives, just as they did in the life of His Son. Psalm 118:22-23 states, "The stone the builders rejected has become the cornerstone; the Lord has done this, and it is marvelous in our eyes." Although we may experience rejection from earthly loved ones, the limitless and all-encompassing love of our Almighty Father will never fail us; He will *never* leave us or forsake us (Deut. 31:8).

Father, in moments when I feel forsaken and rejected, help me to recall Your words of love and faithfulness to me, holding me fast and secure— knowing that I am always welcome at Your table. In Jesus' name, Amen.

NOVEMBER 22

Every good and perfect gift is from above, coming down from the Father of the heavenly lights, who does not change like shifting shadows. James 1:17

Thanksgiving is my favorite holiday. I love that we have a day set aside to give thanks for all of our blessings, without the need for additional gift-giving or commercialism. As we enter into this season of giving thanks, I thought it would be helpful and uplifting for us to consider that some of the most precious commodities we have in our lives are gifts from our God, unattainable by our own efforts or merit. Consider that God gives us the following:

Ability to Work (Deut. 8:18) * Comfort (1 Cor. 1:3) * Encouragement (2 Thess. 2:16) * Endurance (Rom. 15:5) * Grace (Jas. 4:6) * Happiness (Ecc. 2:26) * Hope (2 Thess. 2:16) * Joy (1 Thess. 1:6) * Knowledge (Ecc. 2:26) * Life (Job 33:4) * Light to Our Eyes (Ezra 9:8) * Peace (2 Thess. 3:16) * Power (Ps. 68:35) * Rest (Ex. 33:14) * The Spirit (John 3:34) * Strength (Ps. 29:11) * The Victory through Jesus Christ (1 Cor. 15:57) * Wisdom (Prov. 2:6).

Which of these gifts from God means the most to you today? Which one do you find yourself most in need of today? Remember that God longs for us to come to Him and ask for whatever we need, and He faithfully bestows good gifts to His children in direct proportion to their need (Matt. 7:7-8, 11)!

On a separate note, I also find it encouraging that James says in our verse for today that our Father in heaven "does not change like shifting shadows." We've all experienced the illusion of things not being as they seemed. God never appears to be one thing and then reveals something else to the contrary. He is trustworthy and true, faithful and merciful in all He does, abounding in love and grace. We can trust that His heart beats with love for us in every moment of our lives. Amen!

NOVEMBER 23

I have made you, you are My servant; Israel, I will not forget you. I have swept away your offenses like a cloud, your sins like the morning mist. Return to Me, for I have redeemed you. Isaiah 44:21b-22

I enjoy waking up to a dense fog, because it always brings these verses to mind. A few years ago I ran in a four-mile race on Thanksgiving Day, and we ran that entire race in a dense fog. It was eerie yet exhilarating. We couldn't see more than twenty feet in front of us, so we had to trust that we were going in the right direction and were still on the race course! The other runners in front of us served as a guide of sorts, leading the way, but if you happened to find yourself a singleton separated from the pack, it was disorienting!

Fog is a perfect parallel for seasons of our lives in which we cannot see the way ahead. We cannot see what's around us or above us. We have to live fully in the present moment, in our present space, trusting as we walk that what lies ahead of us on the path will be made clear as we haltingly advance. Sometimes a figurative fog descends on us in a time of immense trial, when we find ourselves unable to see beyond the present moment and the present pain. Other times a fog can descend on us when we find ourselves caught in a sin that has ensnared us. What I treasure about these verses from Isaiah is God's promise to His children that He can sweep away our offenses like a cloud, our sins like the morning mist. In other words, Beloved, *effortlessly.*

The most intriguing thing about fog is that it can be so dense that we cannot see the way forward at all, and yet when we aren't looking, the sun breaks forth and the fog is dispelled. God's ability to shine His (Son)light through our darkness, through our sin, is like that as well.

The next time you wake up to fog, I encourage you to remember these verses and thank Him for His mighty and effortless provision in your life. Amen!

NOVEMBER 24

There remains, then, a Sabbath-rest for the people of God; for anyone who enters God's rest also rests from their works, just as God did from His. Let us, therefore, make every effort to enter that rest, so that no one will perish by following [the Israelites'] example of disobedience. Hebrews 4:9-11

I am confident that someone is going to collapse in relief today to see that God calls us to *rest*. If you've been wearing yourself out doing all of the cooking for Thanksgiving dinner, take a page from the Israelites and gather the manna God has already prepared for you. If you've been careening along trying to manage ten different things all at once, take a page from the young boy who gave his five loaves and two fish to the Lord, trusting that in the capable hands of Jesus, anything we give will become sufficient.

We are not meant to run ourselves into the ground in the name of service and sacrifice. Nor are we meant to constantly and ceaselessly strive towards doing more and being more, while wearing ourselves out in the process. Nor does our Father wish for us to go through each day expending untold amounts of energy to make it *look like* everything is fine and okay to the rest of the outside world. Our sweetest blessing in this life is knowing and being known by the Almighty God and by His Son. He invites you to come and rest in His presence today, Beloved. Will you?

Lay down your worries, fears, burdens, and anxieties. Lay down the thoughts you've been chasing around like rabbits and the what-ifs that have been causing you to lie awake at night. Come to Him and rest today. Allow His presence to heal all of those microscopic tears that Life inflicts upon you throughout your day. Allow His healing to deeply penetrate the larger wounds that you spend your waking moments trying to hide or distance yourself from. He longs to provide you with His healing, restorative rest. Will you come today, Beloved? Amen.

NOVEMBER 25

A woman giving birth to a child has pain because her time has come; but when her baby is born she forgets the anguish because of her joy that a child is born into the world. So with you: Now is your time of grief, but I will see you again and you will rejoice, and no one will take away your joy. John 16:21-22

My third child, Stella, arrived a month early, surprising all of us. As I lay on the hospital bed at 4:15 a.m., waiting for the doctor to arrive, I knew what to expect. The process would be painful, but so very worth it. Still, my mind knew what my body was in for, and I could not stop myself from shaking so much that my teeth rattled. Women who have had children can attest to the fact that in spite of the pain of delivery, God really does enable us to essentially "forget" the pain in favor of the joy that our children's arrival and presence brings. We know that the birthing of this "new thing"—be it infant, career, or stage in life—will give way to blessing, and yet it's hard to remember that fact when we're in the midst of the painful birthing process itself.

Jesus compares the pain of being in the throes of childbirth to the pain the disciples would soon experience upon His impending death. It brings me immense comfort to know that even when it is our time of grief, we *will* come through that grief and again know rejoicing—and furthermore, *no one will take away our joy.* No one will *ever* take away the joy of our salvation that is in Christ Jesus, and the promise of eternal life with Him!

So, may I ask you: What are you "birthing" today, Beloved? What pain is racking your heart and mind? What is keeping you awake at night? As with all birthing processes, once we begin, we will have to reach a place of completion. The nature of life is that of constant change and renewal, yet sometimes we feel afraid because things will look "different." Beloved, "different" need not mean "*worse.*" In fact, what if "different" ends up meaning "even better"? Let's hold on for the blessings that God has in store for us. Amen!

NOVEMBER 26

When Your words came, I ate them; they were my joy and my heart's delight, for I bear Your name, Lord God Almighty. Jeremiah 15:16

It comforts me to read my Bible, the timeless story of God's enduring, resolute love for His children and His faithful pursuance and deliverance of His chosen ones. This is essentially the theme of the entire Bible, interwoven throughout all sixty-six books. No matter which book you read, there will surely be some edifying, sustaining, sweet words to comfort your soul. There will also undoubtedly be some passages that leave us feeling like we choked on the words as they went down. For me, those choking moments can provide some of the best lessons, as God pounds me on the back and performs the Heimlich as I gasp for breath and cough my way through His Word. I'll share a few of my cough-inducing verses with you today—words from God that were difficult to swallow, but have nourished me in the long run:

"Better to live on a corner of the roof than share a house with a quarrelsome wife" (Prov. 21:9).

"If I have a faith that can move mountains, but do not have love, I am nothing" (1 Cor. 13:2b).

"Don't have anything to do with foolish and stupid arguments, because you know they produce quarrels. And the Lord's servant must not be quarrelsome but must be kind to everyone, able to teach, not resentful" (2 Tim. 2:23-24).

Sometimes God's Word goes down like honey, and sometimes it's like dry cotton. Sometimes it leaves us feeling full and satisfied, and sometimes it causes heartburn. No matter how it tastes going down, we can be certain it will always bring nourishment and vitality to our souls.

Father, thank You for Your Holy Word, which fortifies and sustains me each day. Amen.

NOVEMBER 27

Barak said to her, "If you go with me, I will go; but if you don't go with me, I won't go." "Certainly I will go with you," Deborah said. [...] Then Deborah said to Barak, "Go! This is the day the Lord has given Sisera into your hands. Has not the Lord gone ahead of you?" So Barak went down Mount Tabor, with ten thousand men following him. At Barak's advance, the Lord routed Sisera and all his chariots and army by the sword. Judges 4:8-9a, 14-15a

After such a feeble start, I have to admit I was a tad nervous that when Deborah commanded Barak to "Go!" that instead of going, he'd again say, "I won't go unless you go with me." Thank goodness he went, since the Lord's routing of the army depended on Barak's advance! I wonder how often God's actions in our lives depend upon our willingness to advance—to take that first step out on faith, choosing to believe that He will guide our steps along the path.

In what area of your life is God calling you to "Go!"? Are you marching forward with confidence, assured that God will bring you the victory? If so, I commend you! Are you wringing your hands in anxiety, uncertain as to whether or not that was "really the Lord" telling you to go? If so, I can relate. I especially tend to take this approach if the "Go!" command seems to be in reference to something I find intimidating or out of my comfort zone. He will bless us when we obey and go, my friend. May He give you the strength and courage today to do it! Or, perhaps you have turned your back on that command to "Go!" and are actually walking in the opposite direction. I have been there, too. (So has Jonah.) I encourage you today to stop where you are and spend some time talking to God about your fears, anxieties, and unwillingness to do what He is asking. Know that He will never call you to go to a place where He will not be there to meet you!

Father, when You call me to go, may I go with a willing heart! Amen.

NOVEMBER 28

Moreover, when God gives someone wealth and possessions, and the ability to enjoy them, to accept their lot and be happy in their toil—this is a gift of God. Ecclesiastes 5:19

One of the greatest gifts God bestows upon us is the gift of contentment. Contentment is not to be confused with the flighty notion of happiness, which tends to come about because something which we deem "good" has happened to us. Gifts like contentment and joy are those in which we feel peace not *because of*, but rather *in spite of*. We can be in terrible life circumstances and still find joy. We can be in painful seasons and still find contentment.

The gift of contentment comes from knowing that God is with us, present in every moment, and that our lives are infused with meaning and significance that He has fashioned for each one of us. We are never wandering without purpose. He is never at a loss for what to do with us. Nothing escapes His notice, and He is able to use any difficult circumstance to mold our characters to be more like that of His Son.

Paul writes that "godliness with contentment is great gain. For we brought nothing into the world, and we can take nothing out of it" (1 Tim. 6:6-7). He also notes that in spite of severe trials and hardships, he had "learned to be content whatever the circumstances" (Phil. 4:11). What was Paul's secret to contentment in any circumstance? *Jesus*, who gave him the strength he needed in any task (Phil. 4:12-13). The writer of Hebrews states, "be content with what you have, because God has said, 'Never will I leave you; never will I forsake you'" (13:5b).

Our contentment comes from knowing that this life is not the end of our journey. We are simply passing through, travelers on our way to meeting Jesus face to face. We will have hardships and challenges on the journey, Beloved, but the destination that we know is awaiting us and the power of God's Spirit dwelling within us are enough to give us strength to weather them with His grace. Amen.

NOVEMBER 29

They will be called oaks of righteousness, a planting of the Lord for the display of His splendor. Isaiah 61:3b

My favorite tree is a majestic oak about a mile from my house; I pass by it regularly on my running route. From one side, the tree looks completely normal—hale and hearty, healthy and full. From the other side, you see a different story. It bears a cavernous hole in its trunk where a huge limb was once wrenched away. For years I have felt like this tree and I were kindred spirits—one side looking just fine, and the other evidencing the devastation within. Like humans, trees can compartmentalize the damage their wounds inflict, and they go right on living. However, they can't hide their scars—as we are prone to do.

Had this tree not suffered the loss that it did, I would never have known the extent of its strength or seen evidence of its extraordinary resilience. And because it cannot conceal its wounds, I have the privilege of repeatedly marveling at its ability to heal and thrive in spite of its wounding. For the most part, humans have an elective vulnerability— we can choose to share the stories of our unseen wounds with others, or we can keep them hidden. Whether our wounds remain physically visible or not, we still carry them (and the lasting evidence of their presence) in our hearts, minds, souls, and bodies.

What would happen if we chose visibility, my friend? If we chose transparency? If we allowed others to see our wounds, and then see that we are still here living? What if we were open about our struggles instead of concealing them and hiding the wounds that helped to shape us into who we are? What if we allowed others to see that our Creator created us with unique and specific strengths and skills that enabled us to survive the woundings Life would inflict upon us? Think of how our witness could inspire others and bring glory to God! We too could become oaks of righteousness, a planting of the Lord for the display of His splendor. What's holding you back today, my friend? I encourage you to place it at His feet, trusting that He can equip you for the task. Amen!

NOVEMBER 30

He wore cursing as his garment; it entered into his body like water, into his bones like oil. May it be like a cloak wrapped about him, like a belt tied forever around him. Psalm 109:18-19

As I read these verses today, I was prompted to ask myself: *What am I wearing?* It was a sobering question to contemplate. I know what I'd *like* be wearing, but I realized that this week I have not been wearing it. This week I've been wearing despair as my garment. It had indeed entered into my body like water, slowly seeping into my mind, thoughts, feelings, and heart. It had become like a heavy cloak that was slowly and steadily suffocating the life, joy, and hope out of me.

What we "wear" *does* soak into our inner being, doesn't it? We absorb it into our hearts, minds, and marrow. I've walked around all week in a shroud of despair, feeling powerless to affect change in my life. This is not God's truth. While I can't change other people or circumstances, I can certainly change my outfit! As I peacefully wait on God to work things out and provide clarity, I need not weigh myself down in cloaks of despair and chains of fear or anxiety. I can choose to array myself in something more fitting for a daughter of the King. So I decided to try this on for size: "She wore hope, trust, and faith as her garment; they entered into her body like water, bathing her heart, mind, spirit, and soul in truth and in light. They were a fine linen robe wrapped around her, the belt at her waist secured by the Father's perfect love."

Whew! I'm feeling worlds better after that shift in perspective today, my friend. I invite you to do a little wardrobe adjusting of your own if there are any pesky garments dragging you down rather than lifting you up in the Lord. Any time we cast off the garments of Self and put on the Hope of Jesus Christ, our lives will improve immensely—even if our circumstances haven't changed a bit.

Father, enable me to take off the things which hinder and to put on the hope that empowers—each and every day. In Jesus' name, Amen.

DECEMBER 1

Now the Jordan is at flood stage all during harvest. Yet as soon as the priests who carried the ark reached the Jordan and their feet touched the water's edge, the water from upstream stopped flowing. It piled up in a heap a great distance away [...]. The priests who carried the ark of the covenant of the Lord stopped in the middle of the Jordan and stood on dry ground, while all Israel passed by until the whole nation had completed the crossing on dry ground. Joshua 3:15-16a, 17

The Red Sea wasn't the only body of water God held back for His children. How about this lesser-known story from Joshua, where around 40,000 fighting men (Josh. 4:13) (plus women, children, and Levites!) crossed the Jordan into the Promised Land, while the waters of the Jordan stood "piled up in a heap"? Can you even imagine? And when God parted the waters, His children weren't even left to trudge across a swampy, mucky, slippery riverbed. They walked across on *dry ground*, my friend. In chapter 4 God continues to hold the waters back while the Israelites attend to another task He sets for them: Twelve men chosen by Joshua are sent back into the middle of the Jordan to take up twelve stones, which are to be carried back across to the new land and made into a memorial there (vv. 1-9). Joshua says to the people, "In the future, when your children ask you, 'What do these stones mean?' tell them that the flow of the Jordan was cut off before the ark of the covenant of the Lord" (vv. 6b-7a).

Sometimes we need some stones—a visible reminder of God's power and past faithfulness in our lives, which we are so humanly prone to forgetting during a time of testing and trial. God counted upon the curiosity of children, as they looked at the pile of river stones, to ask questions that would help the people remember where they had come from and the God who had delivered them across dry ground into the Promised Land. What blessing or deliverance in your life are you reminded to thank Him for again today? Amen!

DECEMBER 2

I will send the hornet ahead of you to drive the Hivites, Canaan-ites and Hittites out of your way. But I will not drive them out in a single year, because the land would become desolate and the wild animals too numerous for you. Little by little I will drive them out before you, until you have increased enough to take possession of the land. Exodus 23:28-30

When Blake was three weeks old, he was hospitalized with an infection of which it took some time to determine the cause. While Kevin and I sat on the hospital bed with the minutes ticking by, we turned on the television for a distraction.

The Winter Olympics were on, and the only event that ever seemed to be airing was curling. It was the first time I'd ever seen this sport, and I was intrigued. We watched as teams took turns sliding a huge granite stone down an icy stretch; the goal was for the stone to come to rest as close as possible to the center circle of its "home." Even more interest-ing was watching the "sweepers"—two people with brooms who stayed right in front of the stone as it traveled, intently focused on changing the state of the ice in front of the stone's path.

This is how God works in our lives, clearing the way ahead of us as we move forward. Bit by bit, little by little, He moves debris out of our way and makes the path smooth for us to travel upon. So often we are im-patient, wanting Him to clear the way ahead of us all at once, immedi-ately opening up the route to our destination. Yet in His wisdom He clears our path one bit at a time, protecting us from our own inclination to charge blindly ahead—as well as from enemies we may face along the way. He knows exactly what we are able to manage at any given point along our journey.

Father, thank You for preparing the way ahead of me. Enable me to trust in Your ongoing provision for my path. In Jesus' name, Amen.

DECEMBER 3

Do not gloat over me, my enemy! Though I have fallen, I will rise. Though I sit in darkness, the Lord will be my light. Micah 7:8

There are many references in the Bible to God as light. Please note that Micah doesn't say that God will just "provide" some light—he says that God will *be* his light! God Himself *is* light, and in Him there is no darkness (1 John 1:5b). This means that His presence in our lives illuminates the path forward—and since He *is* light, the brightness of His light will never flicker, fade, or burn out.

We can dispel darkness with light or weaken its territory, but only God can turn darkness *into* light (2 Sam. 22:29b). Even when we think in darkness, feel in darkness, and despair of ever getting out of the darkness, take heart Beloved: He is there, and not even darkness is dark to Him (Ps. 139:12). When you are walking in darkness, confusion, pain, or limitless grief, remember that *He can still see*. You need only ask Him to shine the light of His presence onto your path. He longs to bring you out of that darkness into His wonderful and glorious light—yet oftentimes He patiently waits for us to seek Him and ask.

What areas in your life need some fresh illumination today? What uncertainties have your stomach in knots and your thoughts in a tangled heap? What decisions are you facing that seem as though no clear line of action is being made known to you? Take these things to Him today. Right now. Seek His presence; seek His light.

Father God, thank You for *being* my light! I long to live my life walking in Your presence. Shine Your light and truth into the dark areas of my life; make me aware of any thoughts, behaviors, attitudes, or beliefs that keep me in the shadows. Bring those to mind now, Lord, so that I can confess them and be freed from them. Illuminate my way forward and turn my darkness into light, that I might give You all the glory and bring honor to Your name. Amen.

DECEMBER 4

Because of the Lord's great love we are not consumed, for His compassions never fail. Lamentations 3:22

I recently sat down with a friend of mine to catch up on life. A short time later, after we had said our goodbyes and I was alone, I sat there feeling completely overwhelmed by all of the difficult things she had on her plate at the moment: family issues, friend issues, health issues, and major life transitions. I was overwhelmed, and it wasn't even my life! I love her dearly, and her concerns always make it onto my prayer list. Yet I had to sit and question myself about why I was feeling such despair over things that did not even directly affect me!

Sometimes, we take things on just a bit too much. We are called to love, support, and encourage one another, to carry each other's burdens (Gal. 6:2)—and yet at times I find myself not just *concerned* about the burden of another, but *consumed* by it. That's a red warning flag for me that something in me is out of balance. Maybe you can relate with me here when I say that God has given me a deeply sensitive heart. Other people's pain sincerely and profoundly affects me, and sometimes I have trouble separating myself from it. This is where I was finding myself after spending that time with my friend that day: heavyhearted, overwhelmed, consumed.

The good news, my friend, is that God is never consumed by the depth of our pain or our need. While I need to do some work in my own life to balance out that propensity, He is always in perfect alignment. He has compassion on us, yet His love and concern for us do not propel Him down a path of being consumed or overwhelmed by it.

If there is an area in your life that is consuming you today—whether it's a personal concern or the burden of a loved one, consider handing it over to Him. He will trade yokes with you—your heavy one for His (Matt. 11:28-30)—and He will give you rest. In Jesus' name, Amen.

DECEMBER 5

But knowledge puffs up while love builds up. Those who think they know something do not yet know as they ought to know. But whoever loves God is known by God. 1 Corinthians 8:1b-3

Knowledge "puffs up," filling us with air. I think of popcorn. Balloons. Beach balls. All of those things, when confronted with hot water, severe pressure, or sharp conflicts, will go flat and become useless and lifeless. Love, on the other hand, builds up. It creates more. It sets a firm and strong foundation in Christ (see 1 Cor. 3:10-15) and can serve as a source of strengthening, edification, and support.

In our culture we esteem knowledge and place a lot of emphasis on all the wrong kinds of love. It's easy to become caught up in "what we know." Knowledge is not a bad thing, but it is better to love God and be known by God than to have knowledge, for even "the wisdom of this world is foolishness in God's sight" (1 Cor. 3:19a). Love is the bedrock of our faith. Filled with knowledge, we focus on self—how much we know—and veer towards pride. A heart filled with love naturally seeks a source to pour that love into—and in so doing, we bless others and are blessed in return. Knowledge invites division as we compare what we know to what others know, or vie to see who is "right." Love seeks to include, to invite, to multiply, to share. It always seeks the greater and common good.

Are you feeling puffed up or built up today, my friend? Over and over in the Word of God, we are told that love is the foundation to everything. Love is the key. Love is the evidence of our obedience to the call of Christ; without it, we are nothing. Knowledge is not bad, but it's the kind of knowledge we have that matters. To know God is to know grace, mercy, truth, hope, healing, peace, salvation, and love. Those are the things worth knowing. And He is the One worth loving, with everything you've got. In Jesus' name, Amen.

DECEMBER 6

Trust in the Lord with all your heart and lean not on your own understanding. Proverbs 3:5

This is a verse that we can readily apply to virtually any situation or circumstance in life. Today I want to speak specifically to the notion of trusting God in the midst of our struggle for healing.

Many of us grew up relying on our own determination, resilience, strength, and intellect to survive the difficult and painful situations in which we found ourselves. We have now become adults who still operate out of this perceived necessity to be in control of all things at all times, lest something get the better of us again like it did when we were children. We try to manipulate circumstances, events, and even other people in order to make things play out in the way we would prefer. We do not like change, and we loathe surprises.

The key to wholeness and healing in our lives is choosing to accept God's truth over our own. How *we* see things is simply that: our *perception* of our world. *God* sees things as they actually *are*. It is not enough (nor is it wise) to rely upon our own perceptions and "understanding" as we try to navigate the trials of life.

Which would you rather have: a compass you've rigged out of a magnifying glass, a needle, and some aluminum foil, or an exquisite map hand-drawn for you by the Creator of every star and grain of sand? God's truth can provide the understanding we are so earnestly seeking, but we must first lay down our own "need" to be in control. Our Father is loving and true, and He longs for us to live in peace and wholeness in Him. It's not about our effort, Dear One. It's about His mercy, His willingness, and His *ability* to make us whole. He is asking you to trust Him—with your life, your healing, and your heart. It is safe. You don't have to be able to see where you're going when you know and trust the One who is leading you. In Jesus' name, Amen.

DECEMBER 7

Everything is clean to the clean-minded; nothing is clean to dirty-minded unbelievers. They leave their dirty fingerprints on every thought and act. They say they know God, but their actions speak louder than their words. Titus 1:15-16a MSG

I have three children, so you can imagine how every surface in our house teems with fingerprints: sticky ones and grimy ones; helpful ones and huffy ones; and, yes, permanent ones. I am intrigued by the notion of our thoughts and actions also leaving fingerprints behind. I'm wondering if my "thought-prints" and "act-prints" are helpful, edifying, and leave lasting encouragement with the recipient, or if they are hurtful, stinging imprints left upon a mind or heart. I cringe at the thought of the latter, although I know there are times I have said and done things that left wounds upon another's heart.

Not only can we "imprint" on one another, Beloved, we can also be imprinted upon. What kinds of prints cover your mind and heart today? Are you basking in the warm and lingering glow of soft words of kindness or affirmation from a beloved friend or family member? Are you encouraged and nurtured by the kind "act-prints" of a stranger whom you encountered this week? Or are your mind and heart plagued with painful, searing prints left behind by sharp words of criticism, a cutting remark from someone you love, or prints still left from past abuse? It's certainly something to think about, isn't it?

Each person's fingerprints are unique—which means that the invisible prints we leave on one another each day through our words and actions are also unique—for good or for bad. I am certainly feeling called to be more mindful today of what kind of prints I'm leaving on others as I go through my day. The good news is that we are each lovingly created by the Father, meaning that *His* fingerprints of love, hope, joy, and salvation will never vanish from our frame. To our faithful God be all the glory and praise, forever and ever. Amen!

DECEMBER 8

Jesus said to the centurion, "Go; it will be done for you just as you have believed." And his servant was healed that very moment.
Matthew 8:13 CEB

For some, the anticipation of Christmas sparks gleeful, child-like excitement. For others, the Christmas season can be a challenge. There are not many things more difficult than trying your best to be happy and joyful because the calendar tells you that you should be. If anything, it sets us up for failure and disappointment, thinking that something must be wrong with us because we're just hoping all of the frivolity will soon be over and we can get back to life as normal. As you prepare to embark on the whirlwind of the Christmas season, remember that your anchor in the storm of family conflicts, office parties, children's wish lists, and jam-packed schedules is a baby in a manger who came *for you*.

The centurion's faith led him to say to Jesus, "Just say the word, and my servant will be healed" (v. 8). The centurion's faith was distinctive because He was *convinced* that Jesus could do anything, just by saying the word. Notice Jesus' response: "It will be done for you just as you have believed." This can be a help *or* a hindrance to us, because what we tell ourselves about our circumstances and our ability (or inability) to manage them can affect their outcome. Consider these two examples: "We got behind on the bills again this month, just as I believed we would"—or—"We managed to make ends meet this month, just as I believed we would!" Our attitudes have a lot of influence on how we act—whether we're even aware of it or not!

As you face the oncoming days of Christmas, consider which camp you'd prefer to join: the ones plagued by doubt? Or the ones who believe good things will happen simply because God is fully able to do "immeasurably more than all we ask or imagine" (Eph. 3:20)? My friend, choose wisely—and then *believe*! In Jesus' name, Amen.

DECEMBER 9

Once when Jacob was cooking some stew, Esau came in from the open country, famished. He said to Jacob, "Quick, let me have some of that red stew! I'm famished!" [...] Jacob replied, "First sell me your birthright." "Look, I am about to die," Esau said. "What good is the birthright to me?" Genesis 25:29-32

I've often felt a slight sense of scorn for Esau, so quickly giving up his birthright for a meal. It seems so foolish. And yet, as I consider Esau's story anew today, I realize that we all have the same capacity to despise our birthright. His argument, after all, held a kernel of valuable truth: "Look, I am about to die. What good is the birthright to me?" Have you ever been there, my friend? I know I have.

When we're in that place of feeling like we won't make it through the day, much less the year, then it becomes easier to forsake the birthright for the short-term gratification. Whether it's hunger pangs or withdrawal symptoms; a broken heart or a diseased thought life, we cannot see past the moment—and in that desperate moment of needing to be filled, we despise our birthright as Sons and Daughters of the King in favor of the short-term filling.

I've asked myself today: *What is my bowl of stew?* The truth is that Christ's sacrifice for us meets every need we have in any moment; it gives us the power to forsake the temporary and hollow filling of our bowl of stew and instead look to Him to be filled in our deepest and most wounded places. But we have to dig down deep to hold on to it, Beloved—when we're in starvation mode, we default to our false comforts in a flash. Like Esau, we will soon be hungry again. Soon be famished again. Soon be in need of filling again.

God reminds us that we are His. We share in His inheritance. There is nothing in our lives that He is unable to redeem or unwilling to buy back. To reject His filling in our time of desperation is to despise our birthright. May we rely upon His strength and hold on for the blessing. Amen.

DECEMBER 10

And as for you, brothers and sisters, never tire of doing what is good. 2 Thessalonians 3:13

I enjoy the satisfaction of a freshly vacuumed rug—which, I confess to you, does not happen frequently at my house. Vacuuming has found itself near the very bottom of my to-do list, namely because I dislike the noise and because it seems as though the only time my rugs are free enough of clutter for me to wield the vacuum are the times when it would be insanely foolish to do so—namely naptime and bedtime. So it's a rare thing for me to be able to enjoy the look of a freshly vacuumed rug. That being said, most of the time I think my rugs look fine. Yes, I can see a speck of something here and there, but they still look *clean...* right? And then, my friend, when I do vacuum and go to empty the canister of the vacuum cleaner, I am *appalled* to see all that was lurking on my floors of which I was totally unaware.

Our lives also require regular maintenance and care to keep them humming along at optimal efficiency. We need to routinely run the metaphorical vacuum over ourselves in every area of our lives, picking up the microscopic debris that can, when left unattended, begin to make us sick. When we neglect the systematic care of our physical, mental, emotional, and spiritual needs, our bodies respond by breaking down in ways that draw our attention back to what we need.

A much more beneficial solution is a proactive stance in which we regularly take inventory and see what areas are in need of a deep cleaning—or, at the very least, a surface scrub to remove the grit and grime that daily life can affix to us. Will you do some vacuuming with me today, my friend? When we stop making excuses for why now isn't a good time and just go ahead and do it, we will be amazed at what comes to light that we didn't even know was there.

Father, equip me with the awareness and compassion I need in order to be fully committed to my own self-care. In Jesus' name, Amen.

DECEMBER 11

As you do not know the path of the wind, or how the body is formed in a mother's womb, so you cannot understand the work of God, the Maker of all things. Ecclesiastes 11:5

Sometimes I need this reminder that I'm never going to be able to understand everything in life or get it all figured out—and there is a blessed kind of peace that comes from accepting that I will not know and that I'm not *supposed* to know. God reserves His sovereign right to keep some things hidden and veiled from our eyes, while allowing us insight and revelation into others. At the end of the day, we can either accept His omnipotence and His plan with trust and assurance that He is present and alive, working and faithful, or we can choose to default to a place of fear and doubt. I would certainly like to come down on the side of trust and assurance far more often than the side of fear and doubt. How about you, my friend?

Modern science has given us great insight into the enormously intricate process of how the human body forms within a mother's womb. Yet God still tells us plainly here that we cannot and will not ever truly understand the miraculous weaving together of human life, the union of flesh and spirit, that He carries out within the "depths of the earth" (Ps. 139:15). Even if we think we understand, even if we have detailed explanations with accompanying photographs for each infinitesimal stage of development, we're still cobbling it together, not really comprehending the intricacies of God's workmanship. This brings me comfort.

I need to know that the God in whom I believe and trust, the God whom I long to honor and serve with every part of my being, is vastly beyond any human knowledge or comprehension. I need to know that He is mightier than anything else in existence—and that certainly includes both my daily cares and weightier burdens.

Father, in some things You reserve the right to retain Your mystery. In the not knowing, help me to have peace. Amen.

DECEMBER 12

For we live by faith, not by sight. 2 Corinthians 5:7

Stella likes to ride in her trusty red wagon. I don't mind pulling her around the block in it, except for the fact that she has a habit of lying down in the wagon as I'm pulling it along—which makes it appear to anyone who may be observing us as we pass by that I am some crazy lady pulling an empty wagon around and around the block. Worse still is the fact that I'm apparently *struggling* to pull the "empty" wagon around the block, because there's a thirty-pound "invisible" weight in it!

What about you, my friend? What are you pulling around in your wagon? Oftentimes we pull around a lot of extra weight that is burdensome to us and yet unnoticeable to others. I vividly remember feeling this way when we were in the process of going through our miscarriage. I would interact with people as though everything were just fine, all the while thinking: *My heart is broken. Doesn't it show, somehow?* The scariest thing for me to realize during that time—and in subsequent times as I've watched others weather trials while giving no outward sign of their pain—is that we are horrifically capable of hiding our pain. Why do we do this? We pull invisible weights around with us, encumbering our walk and crippling our frame, while telling everyone we're fine! When will we be brave enough to say, "I have a thirty-pound weight in here that I'm pulling around, and I need some help!"? It takes fierce courage to be real, my friend.

The lesson I've taken away from Stella's "vanishing act" is that I can always be more mindful of what may be in someone else's wagon. When I see someone and say, "How are you?" I can take the time to search their eyes as they respond. Better yet, I can ask: "How can I pray for you today?" We are called to help carry one another's burdens (Gal. 6:2)—whether we can see them or not.

Father, give me Your eyes today. Make me aware of others in need of a smile, a word of comfort, a hug, or a prayer—and may I provide it, in Your name. Amen.

DECEMBER 13

Blessed are those who fear the Lord, who find great delight in His commands. Their children will be mighty in the land; the generation of the upright will be blessed. Psalm 112:1b-2

God will never forsake us (Deut. 31:8), and He will supply all of our needs through the riches found in Jesus Christ (Phil. 4:19). The children of God will be blessed! Are you feeling blessed today, my friend? We can struggle with this notion at times because we tend to equate "blessed" with "unburdened." The problem with that kind of faulty logic is that when we inevitably find ourselves burdened, we can have a tendency to experience that as being "not blessed." Blessed does not mean a lack of painful circumstances in our lives. Blessed does not mean never experiencing loss or pain. Blessed does not mean a conflict-free, hurt-free existence. Those things aren't blessings, Beloved—they're breeding grounds for pride, narcissism, and a lack of empathy.

Our culture yearns to convince us that only those who are affluent, popular, or glamorous are truly "blessed." That's a lie, Beloved, and we can dismiss it in the full assurance that God's Word is sovereign: If He promises that His children will be blessed, then blessed we will be! "Blessed" simply means we are never without the full assurance that we know God, and that Jesus Christ lives in us and walks with us each moment of our lives. "Blessed" means we know and own the complete certainty that Life will indeed wallop us on occasion, and yet we also know God is bigger than anything we will ever face!

David wrote, "God arms me with strength, and He makes my way perfect" (Ps. 18:32 NLT). *Perfect*, my friend—not painless. God's idea of perfection is that we walk our road as Christ walked His road. There will be difficulties. There will be struggles. There will be pain. There will also be One who walks right alongside us, carrying us when we falter, encouraging us when we despair. I'll take His "perfect" way any day over the "painless" road of walking by myself. How about you? Amen.

DECEMBER 14

...if keeping the law could make us right with God, then there was no need for Christ to die. [...] How foolish can you be? After starting your new lives in the Spirit, why are you now trying to become perfect by your own human effort? Galatians 2:21b, 3:3

I can almost *hear* Paul saying this in my mind as I read it. The level of incredulity in his voice would have been sky-high; I envision him red-faced and fuming, indignant and exasperated. The people were completely missing the point! We still miss the point today. I often need this reminder that it is just not possible that we could ever be "good enough" on our own to merit the love and favor of God, nor the salvation offered to us through the sacrifice of Jesus Christ. I often feel the need to "*do*" something in order to be useful or to earn approval or respect or love, so it is sometimes hard to accept that *nothing* I could ever do would be enough to make myself blameless in the sight of God. Yet it stirs thanksgiving within me for His plan, and for Jesus' willing sacrifice, so that I can be made right with God.

How about you? Do you struggle with the need to "earn" God's love or salvation? It can be difficult for us to remember that God's love and salvation are both *gifts* that He *gives* us in our lives. The only "doing" on our part is the action of accepting that gift with open hands and thankful hearts.

Consider how you would feel if you had spent a lot of time and thought picking out just the right gift for someone you love in your life. Think about your giddy anticipation of giving that gift to them. Then, to your dismay, what if they refused the gift? What if they told you that you really shouldn't have gone to such trouble, or they felt they were unworthy of it? What if they said they'd only accept it after they had done something huge and grand in your honor? Wouldn't you be thinking, "You are completely missing the point! I just want to give you this gift!" Let's not miss the point today, my friend. Let's accept God's lavish love for us and receive it with hearts full of thanksgiving. In Jesus' name, Amen.

DECEMBER 15

Be still, and know that I am God. Psalm 46:10a

Sometimes being still is the hardest part, isn't it? When I am hurting, I tend to want to run—both literally and figuratively. Often I find that it is precisely when I am hurting the most inside that I feel the most driven to run miles and miles *outside* in an attempt to outrun whatever it is that is chasing me, hounding me, plaguing me, or pursuing me. I never do. Why? Because we can't outrun pain. The only way we can truly work through pain is to turn around and face it head-on, letting the tidal wave wash over us and carry us back to shore.

Sometimes, my friend, going through the motions is the best we can do. In the days and weeks following a loss, a diagnosis, or the onset of a time of trial, getting through each moment of the day is an achievement. In our paralyzed state it can be difficult, if not impossible, to mentally engage ourselves in the task of seeking God and reminding ourselves of His promises and faithfulness. Sometimes we find that we can't even pray. We need not be ashamed, Beloved. God, in His infinite wisdom and mercy, has already provided what we need: "We do not know what we ought to pray for, but the Spirit Himself intercedes for us through wordless groans" (Rom. 8:26b).

As the Spirit intercedes for you with the Father, lean into Him. You are His beloved child. "The Lord will fight for you; you need only to be still" (Ex. 14:14). When you are still and quiet in His presence, *He moves.* Even if you are curled up in a ball of pain, He carries out His mighty work on your behalf. Even if you have no strength to go on, He becomes your strength and carries you through. Even if you feel like you may never get any better than being numb for the rest of your life, He has plans and purposes for you that *will not fail.*

The next time Life happens and Pain breaks down your door, invite it in, Beloved, and turn and lean into your mighty God, trusting and knowing that *He is God* and He *will* deliver you. In the name of Jesus, Amen!

DECEMBER 16

You study the Scriptures diligently because you think that in them you have eternal life. These are the very Scriptures that testify about Me, yet you refuse to come to Me to have life.
John 5:39-40

The Pharisees spent so much time studying and executing a life fully in tune with each word of the Law that they missed the very Word made flesh, dwelling among them. What they kept missing was the fact that a life without Jesus at the center of it is like fool's gold: It may look good on the outside, but it's empty and worthless in the long run. They were willing to settle for the outward sparkle and shine, thinking that others esteemed them for it. In the end, they came up empty.

What's the secret to living a life that's worth more than pure gold? Having Jesus in your heart. When we stop keeping Him at arm's length and instead invite Him into our messy and unkempt hearts, He gladly makes His home there and starts about His work of tidying us up from the inside out. We so often go about it in the opposite way, trying to clean up the outside and then hoping the inside will look pretty good too. I haven't had much luck with that. How about you?

For me, what ignited the fire in my heart for Jesus was the realization that He loved me exactly as I was—a complete and total wreck, mired in self-hate, which manifested itself outwardly in many ways. He met me there, forgave my sin, and loved me. Like the woman in Luke 7:36-50, I loved much because I had been forgiven much. I realized how far I'd fallen and that He had chosen to die on the cross for me anyway.

The Pharisees thought themselves so good and righteous that they erroneously believed they didn't *need* a Savior to cleanse them of their sin. Nothing could be more frightening. There's only one way to have true and abundant life that's worth more than anything else in the world, Beloved. And His name is Jesus. Amen!

DECEMBER 17

...you have a very special place in my heart. Philippians 1:7b TLB

I often marvel at all the many things our hearts can hold: joy next to grief; elation next to despair; contentment next to restlessness; love next to pain. In addition to all of the feelings we hold in our hearts, there are also all of the *people* we hold in our hearts! It never ceases to amaze me that as life unfolds, our hearts just keep increasing to welcome more and more people within. Since God created man in His image, it makes sense that we would have hearts that are flexible, pliable, welcoming, and expansive. We have a heart like His.

The people who are in my heart are lodged there forever—no matter the season or circumstance; no matter the loss or distance. I feel comforted to know that all of my loved ones have ample space within my heart. It doesn't reach some kind of maximum storage capacity and then require that I delete some files to make more room. God perfectly fashioned our malleable hearts to keep growing and to keep loving. I feel secure knowing that I have my own space in others' hearts, too. We are not in a competition with each other, Beloved. We all have a place in the hearts of those who love us, just as they all have a place in ours. And some have "a very special place."

Perhaps the sweetest blessing today comes from knowing that we each have our own special place within the Father's heart—a place no other Child can fill. Where does that beautiful truth meet you today, my friend? I feel a decided sense of wonder and awe.

Father, thank You for Your wondrous and perfect crafting of our incomprehensible hearts. Thank You that Your love within us never ceases to multiply, enabling us to welcome more and more new people into our circles of fellowship. Enable me to love freely, wholly, abundantly, and sacrificially, as Jesus loved me first. And thank You, Lord, for all of those who have "a very special place" in my heart. Amen.

DECEMBER 18

...turn from these worthless things to the living God, who made the heavens and the earth and the sea and everything in them.
Acts 14:15b

Today I am asking myself what kinds of "worthless things" keep drawing my attention away from God and His truth and provision in my life. My main answers are fear, worry, and anxiety. If I'm being honest with myself, I have to admit that I spend a lot of energy in those places. I may not be bowing down to a carved wooden idol, but the amount of space and time I allocate to these things in my mind and in my heart is essentially the same thing—which is troubling!

Fortunately, God never brings about conviction in our lives without a means by which we can learn to do things differently. We serve the *living* God, Beloved. He is bigger than anything we will ever face, even death itself. I long to stop wasting time and energy in fear and anxiety, because those two things assume catastrophic circumstances I think I can't survive. That kind of thinking indicates that I have forgotten that God will be with me and will carry me through whatever I may face. For that very reason, God is making it clear to me that persistent fear, anxiety, or worry is a form of unbelief. (Ouch.)

What "worthless things" are distracting you from the living God today, Beloved? Maybe you are finding that, like me, your main culprits are places to which your mind wanders when you forget that God is able to accompany us to the uttermost depths and outermost places. Maybe you are discovering that your "worthless things" are flighty pursuits like popularity, status, or wealth. Perhaps you're dealing with darker distractions like depression or crippling anxiety. Or perhaps there is a longstanding habit or addiction that is drawing your focus away from God's presence and provision. Whatever it is, my friend, we are called to lay it down and refocus our gaze on the One who formed the heavens, the earth, and each one of us—whom He dearly loves. Amen.

DECEMBER 19

Here I am! I stand at the door and knock. If anyone hears My voice and opens the door, I will come in and eat with that person, and they with Me. Revelation 3:20

When my sister was young, she had some difficulty grasping the concept of idiomatic expressions. Upon her declaration that she could never pursue a career in medicine because she had "weak ankles," it took some time for us to discover that her concern was not being on her feet all day, but rather the fact that she could not stand the sight of needles. "You mean you have a weak *stomach*?" "Oh. Yeah, I guess."

Another such instance occurred when Kevin and I got married. My mom cautioned my sister (who was about twelve at the time) about not being over at our home too often because we would need our space. "Yeah," she confided to me later, "Mom said I can't be over here all the time. I don't want to stand on the doormat." "Um. Do you mean, *wear out your welcome*?" "Oh. Yeah, I guess." Our family still makes jokes about our "weak ankles" and our fear of "standing on the doormat."

Our verse today finds Jesus literally "standing on the doormat," knocking. Two things have to happen in order for Him to come in: First we have to hear His voice, and then we have to open the door. The thing about it is, He calls out to us repeatedly, every day! Yet all too often our ears are so attuned to all of the white noise of the world around us that we miss His voice. How do we remedy that? We train ourselves to listen for Him. And once we hear His voice, we again have a choice: We can open the door to Him; we can ignore His call; or we can even be like Rhoda in Acts 12:13-16, who heard Peter knocking and recognized his voice—but then became so excited she left him standing there outside!

Let's listen for Jesus today, my friend, and let's invite Him in—into our homes, into our lives, into our hearts—so that we may enjoy sweet fellowship with Him. In His precious name, Amen.

DECEMBER 20

But may all who love You be like the sun when it rises in its strength. Judges 5:31b

As I read this verse today, I found myself thinking—rather ruefully—*I'm more often like the feebler late-fall, early-winter sun than the robust summer sun.* Then it occurred to me that the sun itself is always equally strong. It's our distance from it that makes it *seem* weaker.

As fall draws to a close and winter is upon us, I lament the shorter days and plummeting temperatures. Winter often seems bleak because there is so little daylight and even the bit we receive seems sterile and standoffish, lacking in warmth. But again, it's not the *sun* that has weakened or forsaken us at all—it's our distance from it that is altering our perception. We aren't alone. Trees and animals are affected. Constellations shift in the sky. Nature responds to its lengthened distance from Earth's heat source by hunkering down, hibernating, and waiting.

Enter the parallel of Jesus, the Son. Sometimes I feel His presence with me as a comforting, gentle warmth. Sometimes His presence kindles a blazing fire of conviction, or a searing burst of gratitude within me. And sometimes He feels distant. I know He's still there, but things feel detached, sterile, and cold. The Son has not moved, Beloved. I have. It's *my* position that's influencing my perception. As I go through various "seasons" in my life, the blazing warmth of His presence ebbs and flows—in my human experience. The divine truth, however, is that the sun—the Son—never changes. It holds its position, sends forth its warmth and light, and encourages all things in creation to reach towards it—towards Him—and grow.

Father, I praise You that You are constant and unchanging, from everlasting to everlasting. When life feels distant and cold, help me seek the warmth You long to provide for me. In Jesus' name, Amen.

DECEMBER 21

...I will allure her [Israel] and bring her into the wilderness, and I will speak tenderly [and] to her heart. There I will give her her vineyards and make the Valley of Achor [troubling] to be for her a door of hope and expectation. And she shall sing there and respond as in the days of her youth and as at the time when she came up out of the land of Egypt. Hosea 2:14b-15 AMPC

The second chapter of Hosea contains an allegory about the nation of Israel, whom God compares to an adulterous wife. Although Israel has betrayed God by lusting after pagan gods, He still pursues her—not in wrath, but in love. He draws her away from her temptation, her sin, and her shame in order to speak tenderly to her. God doesn't bring us into the wilderness as a means of punishment, but as a means of love.

When we find ourselves in the desert, God has almost certainly drawn us there so that we can re-learn that He is the One who meets our every need. We are not self-sufficient, as we may have come to believe. We are not self-reliant, as we may have hoped. Apart from God, we can do nothing. Sometimes we lose sight of that. In the desert, away from all other distractions, we can be refreshed, refocused, and renewed in His presence, reminded of the fact that He alone is sufficient for our needs.

I find it especially touching that God makes our Valleys of Achor—which means *Trouble*—into doors of hope and expectation. There is no desolation in your life that God cannot turn into a door of hope. There will never be a desert without an oasis of His love and provision. And there will never be a journey to a promised land without a desert! Life itself brings times of joy and times of trial. God promises us that He is just as present, and just as faithful, in both. That's why we can sing, Beloved, even in the Valley of Trouble. Because we know we're walking through that valley with Him, and that we're journeying on toward Zion.

Father, help me to embrace my desert seasons, knowing that it is always Your desire that I seek and find all my fulfillment in You. Amen.

DECEMBER 22

The Lord Himself goes before you and will be with you; He will never leave you nor forsake you. Do not be afraid; do not be discouraged. Deuteronomy 31:8

This is part of Moses's farewell speech to the Israelites as they prepared to cross over into the Promised Land under the new leadership of Joshua. This is one of my favorite verses because it speaks to all of the fears I have: Fear of the unknown ahead of me? God is already there. Fear of abandonment? God will never leave me or forsake me. Fear of failure? God is with me; I need not be afraid or discouraged.

The Israelites had finally arrived at their destination and could see the Promised Land just across the Jordan River. God had delivered them from a land of slavery to bring them into this new land, in which He promised that He would prosper them and build them up. I imagine they stood there gazing across the Jordan feeling the exact same things we would be feeling: Uncertainty. Anxiety. Fatigue. Hope. What would the new land be like? Would it be worth all the years spent in nomadic wandering? Would they be safe there? Would Joshua be a good leader? Would God bless them as He had said He would? What if they didn't like it there? I love that God has anticipated each of these questions beforehand and has directed Moses to specifically address these fears.

My prayer is that these promises fall afresh on you today, my friend, wherever you are in your own journey. Perhaps you have just now left your Egypt. Perhaps you are standing on the banks of the Jordan, looking at the Promised Land. Perhaps you have already made it across. Wherever you are, may Moses's words encourage your heart today in the knowledge that God goes before you and is always with you. He will never leave you or forsake you. And in any circumstance that sets itself up against you, you need not be afraid or discouraged. For the Lord Almighty walks ahead of you to prepare your way. Amen!

DECEMBER 23

When the builders laid the foundation of the temple of the Lord, [...] all the people gave a great shout of praise to the Lord, because the foundation of the house of the Lord was laid. But many of the older priests and Levites and family heads, who had seen the former temple, wept aloud when they saw the foundation of this temple being laid, while many others shouted for joy. No one could distinguish the sound of the shouts of joy from the sound of weeping, because the people made so much noise. Ezra 3:10a, 11b-13a

Change, even for the better, can often cause both joy and weeping. Even though I know that what God has in store for me is just as wonderful or even better than what I have in the present moment, there is still a fear of letting go of the familiar. It won't look the same anymore. Whatever new thing He builds won't look exactly like what I once loved. Yet the very essence of life is that it is always changing and evolving— we are never truly the same person in two different moments of our lives. Circumstances are constantly changing, and people are also in flux—growing, learning, and evolving. We can either yield ourselves to the rushing, tumbling streams of change in our lives, or we can choose to plant ourselves in the riverbed like a boulder, demanding that Life go around us on its course.

If we choose the former, we are continually renewed and refreshed as we encounter beautiful and challenging new experiences on our journey. If we choose the latter, we spend our days becoming gradually worn down by the relentlessly moving waters around us, being slowly eroded and ultimately forced to give way to the inevitable changes we had so resisted. I think I'd rather be part of the rippling, bubbling water than a stodgy boulder (although my tendency to resist change often places me alarmingly close to boulder-like status!). I'm mindful of that fact today as I ask God to help me be more like the Living Water, flowing freely where He beckons and directs. Amen!

DECEMBER 24

The Lord said [to Elijah], "Go out and stand on the mountain in the presence of the Lord, for the Lord is about to pass by." Then a great and powerful wind tore the mountains apart and shattered the rocks before the Lord, but the Lord was not in the wind. After the wind there was an earthquake, but the Lord was not in the earthquake. After the earthquake came a fire, but the Lord was not in the fire. And after the fire came a gentle whisper. 1 Kings 19:11-12

God is able to speak through anything He chooses, be it man, beast, or natural phenomena. He could certainly have been in the wind, the earthquake, or the fire had He so desired. And yet, He chose something else. When He wanted to reassure his weary and heavy-hearted prophet of His presence, He chose to do it through a whisper. No one but our God can both harness and disperse power through the softest of sounds. Moreover, the same voice that spoke the world into being still speaks to our churning minds and broken hearts today.

I am likewise reminded of a later instance in which God once again spoke, this time through just one Word: "In the beginning was the Word, and the Word was with God, and the Word was God. [...] The Word became flesh and made His dwelling among us. We have seen His glory, the glory of the One and Only Son, who came from the Father, full of grace and truth" (John 1:1, 14). When God wanted to send a Savior for His people, a Messiah who would triumph over death and demolish the power of sin in our lives, He sent a baby.

What does this say about the heart of our God? That He need not win us over with might. He need not command our respect through fear. He need not gain our approval by doing something outlandishly showy. He can whisper. He can send a baby. He still speaks. May we listen attentively for His voice, a gentle whisper amidst the clamoring voices of this world. May we remember why we have reason to rejoice. Amen.

DECEMBER 25

"The virgin will conceive and give birth to a son, and they will call Him Immanuel" (which means "God with us"). Matthew 1:23

God with us. These three words are more than I can wrap my mind around. I've been pondering them for a while now, just trying to comprehend God's plan and purpose, His vast knowledge even before the creation of the world, even before "Let there be light" ever passed His lips. Even then, He knew of this moment. Even then, Jesus had agreed to go when the Father said, "It is time." Even then, Jesus knew what would be required of Him on earth—including that really hard part at the end—the loss, the pain, and the suffering. *He was still willing.*

Before God even began creating, He had a firm plan in place for our redemption. Before there was a Genesis, there was already a glorious Revelation. Before there was a Good Friday, there was already an Easter. He is never haphazard. He is never caught off guard. He is never at a loss for how to save and rescue His children. All of the in-between time, the millennia that we have seen come and go on planet earth, were foreknown by Him, planned by Him, down to the smallest detail. It gives me great peace and comfort to know that this is my God. This is your God. He is mighty to save, able to redeem, abounding in love, faithful in all He does. He creates and sustains, sends forth and calls home. He is trustworthy and true. He will never leave us or forsake us. For He is Immanuel—God *with* us.

If Christmas is your favorite season, breathe it in: *God with us.* If Christmas is a painful time of brokenness and lack, breathe it in: *God with us.* If Christmas brings joy in giving and joy in receiving, breathe it in: *God with us.* If Christmas is a special time of being with family and friends, loving one another, breathe it in: *God with us.* If Christmas starkly highlights an empty chair at your table this year, one missing from your midst, breathe it in: *God with us.* No matter what, Beloved, He is with us. Merry Christmas, Precious Child of God. Amen.

DECEMBER 26

Don't destroy yourself by getting drunk, but let the Spirit fill your life. Ephesians 5:18 CEV

Paul's message here is about false comforts in our lives, and he chose to make his point by using the example of drinking wine. Please note that Paul is specifically talking about habits that are fine *when enjoyed in moderation.* (Sin is *never* okay, even in "moderation"!) Any habit can be substituted for Paul's warning above, because what destroys us is not the habit itself but our propensity to take it to excess. Our habits may fill our physical vessels for a fleeting period of time, but they will always leave us empty in the long run.

What is your habit? It might be drinking. Maybe it's shopping or gambling. Maybe it's eating or exercising. Maybe it's escapism with television, video games, or social media. Maybe it's gaining approval. Or perhaps it's a person. Whatever it is, I challenge you to own it today and fill in Paul's verse with your own specific habit. (I am doing it, too!)

The issue at hand is not about the specific habits we employ in an effort to find comfort or diversion—it's about the fact that we choose those habits over Christ. We try to fill ourselves with food, with wine, with things, or other people. None of these will ever produce lasting fulfillment in our bodies, our minds, or our hearts, because we are not filling ourselves with the *Spirit.* I love how The Message translates the first part of verse 19: "Sing hymns instead of drinking songs!"

What habit are you "singing to" today, Beloved? What distraction are you employing in a futile effort to cope with your stress or your pain? We all long to be filled, but I can guarantee you that things of this world will never truly satisfy us; we will always be left feeling empty. Jesus calls us to drink in draughts of His Living Water, which will quench our deepest longings and needs. Christ is the answer—not whatever habit you've been harboring. When you are feeling empty, come to Him. Trust that He will fill you with His light and His love. Amen!

DECEMBER 27

Don't let your hearts be troubled. Trust in God, and trust also in Me. John 14:1 NLT

Jesus speaks these words to His disciples just after explaining to them that He will soon be betrayed and will only be with them a little while longer. The disciples are understandably confused. Thomas honestly confesses: "Lord, we don't know where You are going, so how can we know the way?" (v. 5). The disciples, I think, were often as muddled and confused about things as we can often find ourselves these days.

I'm wondering if you ever have great difficulty with the task of "not letting your heart be troubled." My heart is one of the more difficult members of my body to control. It's as though Jesus were saying, "Do not let your intestines be troubled." Well, how often do we experience circumstances in life that lead to evidence that our intestines are, indeed, troubled—despite our best efforts to keep them content? Our hearts can be just as challenging. We often fall prey to our feelings—and the problem there is that feelings, my friend, are not *facts*.

I don't believe Jesus is saying that we are never to allow painful feelings or difficult emotions to affect us. The trouble comes when those feelings and emotions hijack our entire being and we begin to experience things such as crushing anxiety, persistent worry, numbing hopelessness, or deep despair. Those kinds of emotions indicate that we have allowed the feelings to carry us too far.

How, then, do we not "allow" our hearts to be troubled? Jesus provides the answer Himself: Trust. "Trust in God, and trust also in Me." God has promised us that He will never leave us or forsake us (Heb. 13:5); He will meet every need that we have (Phil. 4:19); and that He can work in any circumstance to bring about good (Rom. 8:28). When we choose to trust God and believe Him, our troubled hearts can begin to find rest. Do you need a heart set at rest today, my friend? I do. May we seek His presence in each area of our lives today. Amen.

DECEMBER 28

Hezekiah received the letter from the messengers and read it. Then he went up to the temple of the Lord and spread it out before the Lord. And Hezekiah prayed to the Lord: "Lord, the God of Israel, enthroned between the cherubim, You alone are God over all the kingdoms of the earth. You have made heaven and earth. Give ear, Lord, and hear; open Your eyes, Lord, and see; listen to the words Sennacherib has sent to ridicule the living God." 2 Kings 19:14-16

This passage intrigues me. The letter that Hezekiah received was sent from Sennacherib, the king of Assyria, who instructed Hezekiah to "not let the god you depend on deceive you when he says, 'Jerusalem will not be given into the hands of the king of Assyria'" (v. 10). Hezekiah received the letter and read it, and here's where it gets interesting: He went up to the temple and "spread it out before the Lord." Why?

Maybe because he needed to see the full extent of what he was facing, the full extent of what was causing him fear. And I think he wanted God to see it, too. In times past I've thrown away letters that have caused me fear, hurt, anxiety, or pain; I've deleted emails or texts for the same reason. Our natural inclination is to thrust the offending message as far away from us as possible. Instead, Hezekiah did the opposite. He took the letter, spread it out before the Lord, prayed for God's help, and faced down his fear.

What do you need to spread out before the Lord today, Beloved? It may be an actual letter, email, or text, or it may be a challenging situation like the one Hezekiah was facing. I encourage you to take a moment to write it down on a piece of paper and set it before the Lord. I do this frequently myself, and it always helps to know that He sees it.

Father, I pray for the courage to "spread it all out" before You today. I know that You are able to work in all of my circumstances and in every area of struggle I am facing. In Jesus' name, Amen.

DECEMBER 29

A horse is a vain hope for deliverance; despite all its great strength it cannot save. But the eyes of the Lord are on those who fear Him, on those whose hope is in His unfailing love, to deliver them from death and keep them alive in famine. Psalm 33:17-19

The truth of verse 19 has hit me afresh today: God delivers us from death and keeps us alive in famine. We know that first part pretty well: When life deals its final, fatal blow, God redeems and transforms it into deliverance into His kingdom—our finest and most glorious hour! But did you catch that last part? God keeps us alive in famine.

What part of your life is in a time of famine today, my friend? In what area are you finding yourself in a season of lack? We all experience seasons of isolation or desolation, periods of confusion and conflict. Famine times are hard times, lean times—and often helpless times. Yet who is *keeping us alive* during those most challenging of seasons, Beloved? God is. And whom do we often feel has "forsaken" us when we find ourselves in a famine time? God!

This feels so significant to me today—the notion that God sustains us *in* our times of famine. Whether it's a physical famine of food or finances, or an emotional famine of love or security, He is there. He is carrying us through, providing enough to sustain us in every moment—*if* we are choosing to place our hope in Him. Are you? Or are you hoping in something else? Who or what are your "horses"—the things or people you're looking to for rescue, fortification, or deliverance? Our horses can't carry us through a famine, my friend, because they starve to death too. They fall prey to the same conditions as we do. Only God keeps us alive even in the famine, until He finally calls us home.

If you are finding yourself in a famine time today, rest in the assurance that He is aware of your need and is already setting things in place to provide for it. This knowledge fills me with thanksgiving and joy anew today. All praise to His mighty and saving name. Amen!

DECEMBER 30

You will surely forget your trouble, recalling it only as waters gone by. Life will be brighter than noonday, and darkness will become like morning. Job 11:16-17

The everyday aggravations of life do tend to fade with time; we forget the minor struggles of past seasons. Other troubles, however, tend to leave behind some residual pain. Things like loss and grief permanently etch their marks on our hearts, although time and God's love usually help take the sting out of it. Some wounds may always ache a bit, and that's okay. Forgetting our trouble isn't the goal—moving forward is.

After many years of grappling with the work of recovery, my life is brighter these days than it's been in a while. There has finally been a peaceful arrival at a sense of having laid it all out, wrestled it to the mat, and lived to tell of the fight. I will not forget it, but it no longer over-shadows me. Some of the sweetest and most meaningful moments I've ever experienced with the Lord have come on this long (and at times very painful) journey. Even with others in my life, this journey has been one that I've mostly walked with the Lord alone. Those kinds of walks are the ones that have the most to teach us, Beloved, because we are journeying along in the unmatched presence of the Teacher Himself.

I still have areas of challenge and struggle; there are still periods of doubt and even despair, when something I thought long since dealt with rears its head up again. Such is the cyclical nature of our lives and of our work as we heal. God will be just as faithful to help us slay the gi-ants to come as He was to help us slay the ones that now lay behind. Our God does not just change things; He transforms things. Our painful areas and broken places can be restored by the light and life of His Son.

As Jesus says in John 16:22, "Now is your time of grief, but I will see you again and you will rejoice, and no one will take away your joy." Our days upon this earth will pass in the blink of an eye, Dear Friend. Let's live well and press on for the joy of heaven. Amen!

DECEMBER 31

He who was seated on the throne said, "I am making everything new!" Then He said, "Write this down, for these words are trustworthy and true." Revelation 21:5

What a journey this year has been, my friend. I'm taking some time today to think back on all of the highs and lows, the peaks and valleys, of our past year together. We have loved, laughed, and shared one another's joys. We have grieved, experienced loss, and weathered some challenging trials. Life is fierce, Beloved. You are far fiercer. You are made strong because the Word of God *lives in you* (1 John 2:14b). No matter the test, God empowers us to withstand it and come forth victoriously, bringing honor and glory to His almighty name.

As we prepare to look ahead to a new year, let's take some time to affirm our successes and recommit ourselves in areas of struggle. God is faithful to equip us for every challenge we face. We may at times feel lonely, but we are never truly alone. It has been my joy and privilege to walk with you through this year. We in the Body of Christ are a mighty band of believers, sent to encourage and exhort one another, to build one another up and share in life's joys and trials. God is constantly working in us to renew us and refine us. No matter how challenging life gets, isn't it comforting to know that He never reaches a point of feeling like He needs to scrap the whole process and start over again? Even in the eternal glory that awaits us, we will still retain some vestiges of Self—the exquisitely unique things that make us who we are. God does not make all new things, Beloved. He makes all things new.

I wish you a blessed New Year. May you continue to walk with Him each day of your precious and beautiful journey. He loves you more than anything in all the world.

Father, You give us grace upon grace. Help us to go forth and share Your love and light with the rest of the world. May we live each day to Your glory. In Jesus' mighty name, Amen.

Made in the USA
Lexington, KY
12 June 2016